Praise for *The Fine Guide to Making the Right Investment Decisions*

'Despite being an investment manager for 30 years, there are explanations, concepts and material in this book that teach me things I didn't know (and some of the things I should know). It clarifies things that are often difficult to grasp and provides a fresh perspective on key investment concepts. Highly recommended.'

Adrian Frost, Artemis

'This is an excellent, down-to-earth book about investing that focuses on the fundamentals of business success. It manages to put into context issues such as the role of management, use of debt and fundamental investment analysis without resorting to the kind of confusing jargon that often plagues other financial authors.'

Brian Taylorson, Finance Director, Elementis

'Michael Cahill's invaluable experience as an analyst and ability to explain complex concepts in simple, straightforward terms means this book is an invaluable tool to novice and professional investors alike. It provides an invaluable understanding of how the stock market actually works in practice and not just in theory.'

Russ Mould, Editor, Shares Magazine

The Financial Times Guide to Making the Right Investment Decisions

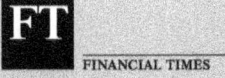

In an increasingly competitive world, we believe it's quality of thinking that will give you the edge – an idea that opens new doors, a technique that solves a problem, or an insight that simply makes sense of it all. The more you know, the smarter and faster you can go.

That's why we work with the best minds in business and finance to bring cutting-edge thinking and best learning practice to a global market.

Under a range of leading imprints, including *Financial Times*, we create world-class print publications and electronic products bringing our readers knowledge, skills and understanding, which can be applied whether studying or at work.

To find out more about Pearson Education publications, or tell us about the books you'd like to find, you can visit us at
www.pearsoned.co.uk

The Financial Times Guide to Making the Right Investment Decisions

How to analyse companies and value shares

Michael Cahill

Second Edition

Financial Times
is an imprint of

Harlow, England • London • New York • Boston • San Francisco • Toronto • Sydney • Singapore • Hong Kong
Tokyo • Seoul • Taipei • New Delhi • Cape Town • Madrid • Mexico City • Amsterdam • Munich • Paris • Milan

PEARSON EDUCATION LIMITED

Edinburgh Gate
Harlow CM20 2JE
Tel: +44 (0)1279 623623
Fax: +44 (0)1279 431059
Website: www.pearsoned.co.uk

The Financial Times Guide to Making the Right Investment Decisions was previously published as *Investor's Guide to Analyzing Companies and Valuing Shares*.

First published in Great Britain in 2003
Second edition published 2010

© Michael Cahill 2003, 2010

The right of Michael Cahill to be identified as author of this work has been asserted by him in accordance with the Copyright, Designs and Patents Act 1988.

Pearson Education is not responsible for the content of third party internet sites.

ISBN: 978-0-273-72984-6

British Library Cataloguing in Publication Data
A catalogue record for this book is available from the British Library

Library of Congress Cataloging-in-Publication Data
Cahill, Michael, 1962-
  The Financial times guide to making the right investment decisions : how to analyse companies and value shares / Michael Cahill. --2nd ed.
    p. cm.
  Includes index.
  ISBN 978-0-273-72984-6 (pbk.)
  1. Investment analysis. 2. Corporations--Valulation. I. Title. II. Title: Guide to making the right investment decisions.
  HG4529.C34 2010
  332.63'2--dc22
                                2010000014

All rights reserved. No part of this publication may be reproduced, stored in a retrieval system, or transmitted in any form or by any means, electronic, mechanical, photocopying, recording, or otherwise, without either the prior written permission of the publisher or a licence permitting restricted copying in the United Kingdom issued by the Copyright Licensing Agency Ltd, Saffron House, 6–10 Kirby Street, London EC1N 8TS. This book may not be lent, resold, hired out or otherwise disposed of by way of trade in any form of binding or cover other than that in which it is published, without the prior consent of the publishers.

Typeset in 9pt Stone Serif by 30

To My Dad

Peter Joseph Cahill
1925–84

With Love

Contents

Acknowledgements / xi
Introduction / xiii

1 The Valuation Villa / 1

2 Sector and market background / 33

3 Management and strategy / 60

4 Performance and returns / 113

5 Financial position / 164

6 The outlook / 204

7 Absolute valuation – discounted cash flow (DCF) / 227

8 Relative valuation / 249

9 The investment decision – buy or sell? / 295

Glossary / 323
Index / 341

Acknowledgements

This second edition reflects the incredible benefit of having spent six years presenting courses to a wide collection of people. Their interest, questions and desire to learn stimulated my own development and helped me reflect on how the information can be made even more accessible. The 'Valuation Villa' and structure of this book is the result. It has made this complex subject much easier for audiences to access, and is a great framework for organising and understanding the information that underpins valuation.

The opportunity to present these courses was helped considerably by Miranda Lane at Finance Talking. Her faith in my skills and capabilities as a trainer is much appreciated and I learned much from her ability to simplify things and make material accessible.

My own passion to become an ever better trainer and coach has given me the opportunity to learn some wonderful techniques from some wonderful people. This has led to my being a far more effective trainer and coach and, consciously and unconsciously, informed my approach to the writing of the book. As well as being a much better book, it was also a lot more fun to write. Getting it done easily and in a focused way owes much to the great input from my 'thinking partners', Anne Murch and Gaby Porter.

As I reflect on the financial crisis, the excellent grounding I received working with high-quality professional people is something I am even more grateful for. Over the years, many people have provided valuable input and advice in the development of my analytical skills.

Particular mention must go to the building team at Warburg's, past and present. This provided a very high-quality environment to learn about analysis. In particular, thanks are due to Phil Raper for having faith in recruiting me, and to Mark Stockdale from whom I learned a great deal. Andrew Rodgers has been extremely important in terms of his confidence in my ideas for both the training business and the book. Importantly, he also provided lots of excellent ideas (albeit not all of them used) and kept me up to date with market developments. I am also grateful to Keith Robinson and Alex Cobbold for lending a fund management perspective and very useful input on sectors and valuations.

Excellent technical input was provided by Mike Monkton. His faith in the idea, patience in going through early drafts and always useful suggestions are very much appreciated.

Special thanks are due to Martyn Ralph for his constant support and his constructive comments on major parts of the book. His thoughts on companies, sectors and valuation methodology have helped considerably in improving the finished product. His review of the glossary was also very welcome.

Clearly all of this input was vital in ensuring the quality and technical credibility of the book. Any errors or misinterpretations are very much my responsibility.

I am also grateful to Richard Stagg at Pearson for having faith in the original idea, and for his enthusiasm for a second edition.

The first edition was a great foundation to build on and Cheryl Stroud's considerable patience and wonderful practical support were vital to that edition. These foundations were strengthened considerably by the insight and wisdom of Patricia Bishop. Our work together helped me appreciate the importance of relationships and gave me real insight into what drives value in the long term.

Last but not least, I would like to thank Katie Oakley for her wonderful way of being, her faith in me and her support. I appreciate these qualities enormously and much else besides.

Publisher's acknowledgements

We are grateful to the following for permission to reproduce copyright material:

Figures
Figures 2.1–2.7 courtesy of Thomson Reuters DataStream; Figure 2.8 reprinted by permission of *Harvard Business Review*. From 'How competitive forces shape strategy' by Porter, M., March/April. Copyright © 1979 by the Harvard Business School Publishing Corporation, all rights reserved.

Text
A selection of quotes in Chapters 3 and 6 from *Good to Great*. Copyright © 2001 by Jim Collins. Reprinted with permission from Jim Collins.

In some instances we have been unable to trace the owners of copyright material, and we would appreciate any information that would enable us to do so.

Introduction

This book provides you with a comprehensive and accessible framework for appreciating and understanding the factors that drive long-term wealth creation and the valuation of a business.

The commonsense of investing is often mystified by jargon. Throughout the book, my aim is to explain the importance of the underlying concept, how it works and how it affects your investment decision. Increased familiarity with the key factors influencing a company's value and how they fit together will help you be better informed and feel more confident about your investment decisions.

The demise of many household names and the various crises that have characterised the past 18 months have put share prices and company finance firmly in the spotlight. If we are to make a better job of appreciating what factors enable companies to create wealth on a more sustainable basis we really need to learn the lessons from what has happened. Having a more holistic and grounded view of how we can sensibly invest for the long term is more important now than ever.

In terms of where we are now, a combination of an aggressive focus on growth, the role of dominant CEOs and the 'cult of debt' to fund that growth has formed a wealth equivalent of the Bermuda triangle. The corporate scandals of the early part of the decade – the Enrons, Parmalats, Worldcoms and Global Crossings – provided ample early warning signs of the dangers and yet were ignored. Markets are driven by 'fear and greed' and it would seem that management teams have also become infected by these emotional drivers that so distort the decision-making process. However, while the market exists to facilitate day-to-day minute-to-minute decisions, companies in theory are taking decisions on building their competitive position on a much longer-term basis.

The financial scandals highlighted, among other things:

- the wealth-destroying impact of pursuing growth for growth's sake
- how mergers and acquisitions create companies that destroy wealth and cannot be managed rather than companies that can grow
- that if you reward management on hitting earnings targets then accounting trickery, if not fraud, may take over if the business slows
- how focusing on earnings targets distorts decision making
- that companies with dominant CEOs whose ambitions are unchecked tend to destroy value sooner rather than later
- that funding business with debt causes serious issues in a downturn
- when the focus of activity is to manage the share price *not* the business, the business will often implode.

Yet the same mistakes were being repeated less than five years later. Hopefully we can learn a lot more from the current crisis about what contributes to long-term wealth creation and importantly the management of risk. We also need to be able to predict the characteristics of companies and management teams that are likely to destroy wealth.

Growth and risk

Taking these issues into account we can immediately see how risks increase dramatically when management is focused solely on (earnings) growth and using debt to achieve that. A focus on growth often leads to acquisitions which rarely add value but do add a considerable amount of risk (especially if funded with debt). And risk is one of the elements that appears to have been ignored over the decade – and if not ignored it was pretended that it could be adequately captured by some mathematical equation. This is curious when one considers that the fundamental tenet of investing in shares is risk/reward yet all these efforts to grow the business were done in a way that incurred significant risks. Furthermore risks were taken in the business – for example, lending to people on the basis of five times their salary for an over-valued asset or indeed allowing people to self-certify their income. The growth in sub-prime lending is an excellent example of growing while incurring significant risk.

Risk comprises business and financial risk. While there has been a tendency to use mathematical notions of risk this does not capture the real-world events that tend to undermine businesses and their profitability.

As the current financial environment has made abundantly clear, the level of debt in a company is a key element of risk. One of the key lessons from the credit crunch is that while debt is fine when the economy/business is doing well, when the economy slows down then it can be disastrous for many sectors. Financing businesses with debt became widespread during the boom years of 2004–07 – debt was cheap and easily available. Indeed the advantages of using debt were seen to be so obvious that the debt-backed private equity sector grew considerably, while the company sector, often under pressure from private equity or shareholders wanting more 'efficient balance sheets', engaged in massive share buy-backs. Many investors, including the banks, also geared up to invest in mortgage-backed securities and other 'securitised' products. This debt seemed to be an appropriate funding mode for all companies and all investments. Private equity bought Chrysler, for example. Yet combining high debt with a company sensitive to economic forces and high fixed costs is a recipe for disaster – as well illustrated by the plight of the automotive and airlines sectors as well as the banks, housebuilders and construction companies. When put together, a strategy that combines high financial risk with high business risk – where the economics of the business are far from certain – results in an inevitable outcome.

In the current environment – and this is likely to feature for some time – management's ability to identify and manage risk more effectively will be vital. Shareholder value is a combination of returns and risk and yet the focus has been very much on the returns side of the equation.

Growth and quality

The other element that got lost when the cult of growth took hold is that earnings *quality* is as important as earnings *growth*. This will be explored in more detail but in essence there are four key signals of earning quality:

- the sustainability and visibility of the company's earnings
- earnings are coming from the company's core business
- earnings convert into cash efficiently
- the company adopts conservative accounting policies, which ensures that the earnings number is a true reflection of how the business is really performing.

Growth and returns

The irony of the focus on growth is that it was often delivered at the expense of returns or the quality of earnings. The other key element of returns is of course shareholder value – it may be that the company is generating growth but the risks incurred are very high. As we will see, it is very easy to grow earnings while using debt. This debt may be used to fund an acquisition, for example, so we may see an expansion of earnings – but at considerable risk.

All the statistical evidence suggests, however, that the key driver of share price performance over time is return on capital employed – not growth. In the current environment companies that generate cash are in a significantly stronger position – they will be less dependent on a fragile financial system. Reflecting the importance of this cash generation, many investors prefer to look at 'cash flow return on capital'. Importantly, the higher the return on capital the more cash the company will be generating. This cash allows the company to fund its strategy and remain very competitive. It also finances rising dividends – another key driver of share price appreciation. The high returns give us confidence that the company can reinvest its strong cash flows to grow and create sustained long-term returns.

The 'Valuation Villa' – a framework for your investment decisions

Growth provides a very partial view of corporate success and tends to ignore the impact of risk and returns – the fundamental basis of investment. To provide a more comprehensive view of a company's performance and prospects the 'Valuation Villa'™ has been developed as an organising framework to bring clarity and simplicity to the process of deciding what drives value. It helps us take a view as to whether or not a company is able to create long-term wealth. This will then help determine whether a share is cheap or expensive. You will meet the Valuation Villa in Chapter 1 and revisit it on your journey through the book.

We have identified growth, risk and quality as being the key ingredients to assess the potential for wealth creation by a company. Having a focus on all three prevents getting caught up in any one measure. These are then further reinforced by drilling down into the management and strategy of the business, its financial position, the returns it generates and its outlook. This will equip you with all the aspects that drive the fundamentals of valuation and prevent the one-dimensional focus on growth that has characterised the past decade.

Investing is buying a share in the long-term competitive position of the business. This means management must have a clear and compelling strategy to develop the capabilities to build and sustain a competitive position. In the long run that competitiveness will deliver

- high and consistent returns on capital
- strong cash generation and
- value-added growth.

This combination will drive the share price higher. These measures of health demonstrate that you have bought into a business with real competitive advantage. Importantly, they are also the key drivers of long-term wealth creation and successful investing.

Using the Valuation Villa will help you better understand the competitive position of any company, and thus be better placed to take a decision as to whether to invest or not, and decide whether the risks are worth taking. The process and skills developed will enable you to take much better informed investment decisions and identify the characteristics of companies that will make you money. It is also an invaluable tool for business owners, to understand how their business would be valued in event of a sale, and how to better manage and prepare the business for a profitable and valuable sale for all parties concerned.

1

The Valuation Villa

What topics are covered in this chapter?

- Why the Valuation Villa is effective – a comprehensive view of what drives value
- Growth, risk and quality – generating sustainable returns
- Growth
- Risk
- Quality
- Shareholder value – the current debate
- Shareholder value – an intuitive guide
- Cost of debt
- Cost of equity
- Beta
- Liquidity
- Calculating the cost of equity
- Other measures
- Increasing shareholder value – the key drivers
- Summary
- Checklist

Why the Valuation Villa is effective – a comprehensive view of what drives value

The Valuation Villa has been developed as an organising framework to bring clarity and simplicity to the task of deciding what drives share prices and whether a share is cheap or expensive. By examining the seven aspects that make up the Valuation Villa (see Figure 1.1) you will have a more comprehensive view of a company, the key issues affecting it and the potential it has for making money. This has proved a remarkably effective way of thinking about valuation; seeing the factors at work and how they interconnect. Having considered these aspects of the company's competitive position you are then in a much better position to take an informed decision.

We start with the three key drivers of value for any equity:

- growth
- risk and
- quality.

The triangle formed by these three factors provides a more comprehensive way of thinking about a company, its prospects and its share price. This means we are in a stronger position to identify a wider pool of potential issues that will shape the performance of the business and its share price. It also takes us away from a one-dimensional view of company performance, such as **earnings per share (EPS)** growth, which has tended to dominate thinking over the past ten years. Yet, as we shall see, this is often an irrelevant measure of a company's performance and the risks achieved to incur the growth can literally be critical.

Having an effective overview of the growth, risk and quality characteristics of a company we then look at the 'rooms in the house':

- Management and strategy (Chapter 3)
- Performance and returns (Chapter 4)
- Financial position (Chapter 5)
- Outlook (Chapter 6).

These are the key areas to investigate as part of the valuation process – how money can be made or lost will be driven by these factors.

We have structured the book into these specific chapters to provide clarity on what the important issues are for each component. Having a grasp of the issues influencing the four rooms of the villa – and considering the

Why the Valuation Villa is effective 3

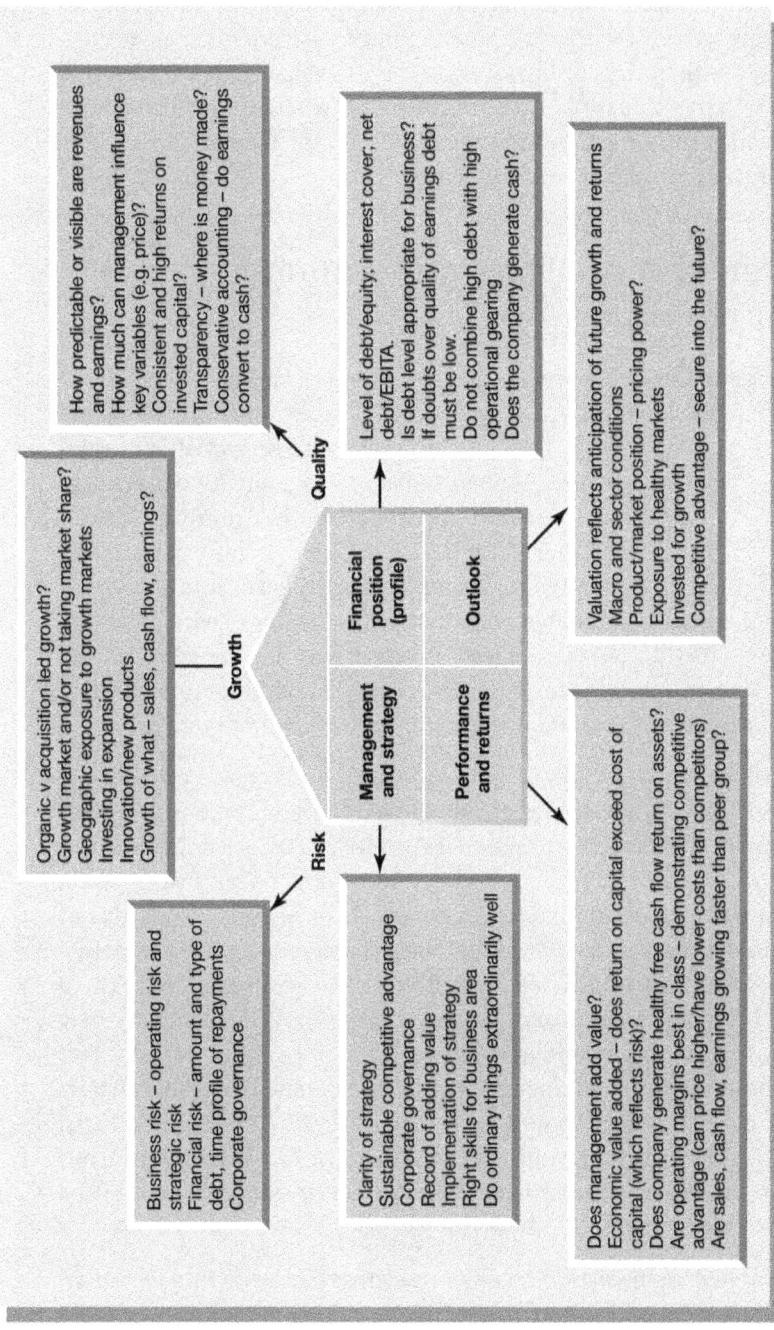

Figure 1.1 The Valuation Villa

outlook – we then explore how they impact on valuation. Here we will look at how these factors influence the company's cash flow and risk profile, and how we can use that to value the business ('absolute valuation' – Chapter 7). We then turn to how we can use the Valuation Villa to appreciate how 'relative valuation' (Chapter 8) works: where we are comparing two companies and how they are valued. While they may be superficially similar they may be valued very differently.

Growth, risk and quality – generating sustainable returns

Considering the incredible events experienced in the past few years, one of the key elements has been the way in which there has been a complete preoccupation with growth. The inherent risks of these growth strategies as well as their impact on the quality of **earnings** are now only too apparent. The resulting lack of balance – not paying enough attention to risk and quality – is a real lesson for us all. It is also a crucial reminder that sustainable returns from a business with a strong competitive position that manages risk effectively are the key route to long-term wealth creation. Importantly, from an investment perspective avoiding disasters is as important as picking winners (if not more so).

the resulting lack of balance is a real lesson for us all

The key risk incurred during the growth phase was of course funding the growth with debt. When things are going well funding the business with debt has many advantages. As Figure 5.1 (p. 166) shows, earnings per share (EPS), **return on equity** and shareholder value can all be boosted by using debt rather than equity to fund the business. This was done irrespective of whether the business/sector concerned was capable of carrying this debt – the business may have been very sensitive to the economic cycle, there may have been high **operational gearing** (see p. 7), or the company may have been in a very competitive sector with little pricing power. In effect high business risk and high financial risk were combined. All these characteristics suggest that debt should be at modest levels. Yet house builders, car manufacturers (private equity bought Chrysler, funding it with debt!) and banks, among others, carried substantial levels of debt which raised risk profiles considerably.

Growth also had an impact on quality of earnings – moving into areas that were far more difficult to project or where returns were far more variable and dependent on the economic cycle. How sustainable were the earnings from securitisation and selling loans to people who had little chance of paying them back?

Mergers and acquisitions (M&As) – often funded by debt – were a big element of this growth, with the RBS bid for ABN Amro (in competition with Barclays) being the exemplar. History tells us that deals rarely work for the acquiring company's shareholders – that is, they do not create shareholder value for them. (The figures vary but on most estimates roughly 70 per cent of deals fail to **add value**.)

Therefore M&A were certainly driving growth while sacrificing risk and quality. We also need to bear in mind that the sheer scale of many of the businesses created inevitably raises questions as to how the enlarged entity can be managed. The integration risks are often very significant, let alone the obvious risk of buying at the wrong point in the cycle. While the market often looks at 'earnings dilution' to appraise deals (in itself a very incomplete method) 'management dilution' is often what leads to the deal being a disaster. This suggests a real need to examine the management skills and depth of management resource in any company making an acquisition.

So we have seen a retreat from growth and far more attention being applied to risk and quality. Investors are naturally responding well to those companies that can take risk out of their operations and of course out of their financial structure. Similarly, those companies with high-quality earnings – predictable earnings streams, high and consistent return on capital employed (ROCE) and strong pricing power – are attractive in the current environment.

Clearly, however, examining all the facets of these valuation drivers in as comprehensive a way as possible is a far more secure grounding for both running a business and deciding whether or not to invest. So let's look at the three key factors in more detail.

Growth

Growth is a key driver of value – a crucial determinant of the value of a business when we look at discounted cash flows and **P/E ratios**. However, we do need to be very careful when considering the growth of a company.

Growth in what?

One of the first things to be clear about is what growth we are talking about – whether it is growth in cash flow, sales or earnings. Measures such as price/earnings ratios will inevitably look at growth in earnings. However, if this is being driven by cost cutting this may be far less sustainable (and lower quality) than growth of sales. More cynically, if accounting policies are being interpreted favourably then again the underlying business is not delivering the results and so the business model may not be what we expect.

We also need to differentiate between organic growth (that is, growth from the existing business) from acquisition-led growth: the latter involves a much higher degree of risk. Organic growth that comes from growing market share off a low cost base with innovative new products that satisfy a real consumer need suggests a real momentum in the business. It also highlights a management team committed to healthy business growth while sustaining competitive advantage.

Looked at generally, growth can be delivered in a number of ways or from a number of sources:

- being in a growth market
- developing a new product or technology
- taking market share
- taking products/services into new regional/geographic markets
- investing in new facilities
- acquiring competitors.

The market takes different approaches to these growth generators largely because there may be more risks involved in, say, a new acquisition compared with an existing product that is taking market share in a growing market. Accordingly, the market will value more sustainable and lower-risk growth more highly than 'one-off' growth with higher risks attached.

Frequently, acquisitions may enlarge a business but not improve its longer-term growth potential (see p. 92 for a full analysis). The problem with cost reductions is that they again tend to be a one-off. They will boost earnings in the following year but not necessarily thereafter.

While growth is an attractive feature for making money in the long run, bear in mind that:

- it attracts a lot of capital, which depresses returns (how special is the product or service and what are the barriers to entry?)
- it may need a lot of capital in the early phases and not generate cash
- it may not mean that shareholder value is created

- you do not know when it will happen or how long it will last – growth may happen later and be of a much shorter duration than predicted
- the share price will tumble dramatically if it falls short of expectations.

Risk

When considering risk, what has been interesting in recent years has been the way it has been reduced to mathematical numbers or models: the use of **beta** for example (see p. 22). However, to get a more fundamental appreciation of the risks in a business we need to have a real-world sense of what is happening. Using the growth, risk and quality approach the key components of risk are:

- *Business risk* – the inherent risk associated with the **operating profits** and cash flows of the company and the competitive strategy which is being pursued.
- *Financial risk* – the risk associated with the type of funding used to finance the business, i.e. its capital structure. Financing the business with debt ('gearing') is riskier. It is the risk to the company of defaulting on its debt obligations.

Work done by Buehler, Freeman and Hulme[1] (HBR September 2008) suggests that the majority of risks (often up to 90 per cent) to the cash flow of a business are accounted for by five key factors: demand risk, operational risk, commodity risk, country risk and foreign exchange risk. These may vary from company to company but do give us a real sense of the importance of business and financial risk.

If we combine high financial risk (high debt) and high business risk then this is clearly going to be potentially very dangerous. Figure 1.2 demonstrates the potential pitfall of doing this.

As Figure 1.2 demonstrates, combining high operational gearing – where a small change in revenues leads to a massive change in profits because costs are mainly fixed – and high debt ('financial gearing') leads to a devastating impact on results.

While this is fairly simple to appreciate it is perhaps surprising how many cyclical and high-fixed-costs companies, such as those in the automotive,

---

[1] Buehler, L., Freeman, A. and Hulme, R. (2008) 'The New Arsenal of Risk Management', *Harvard Business Review*, September.

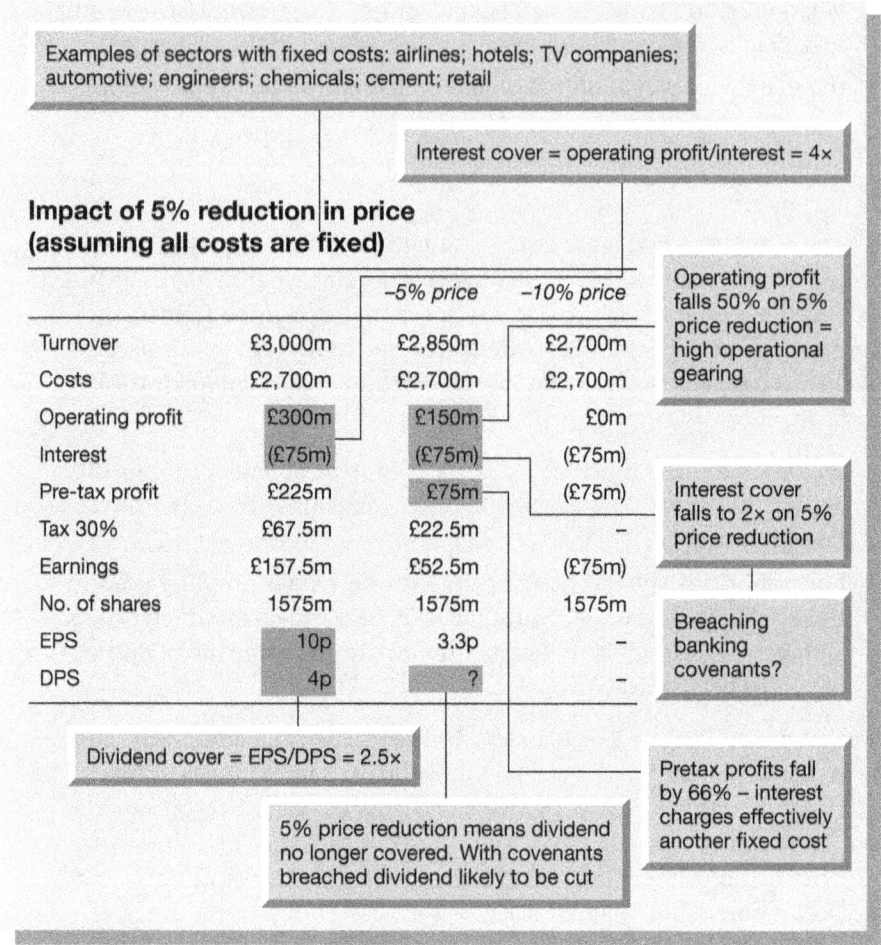

Figure 1.2 Operational gearing – how it works

engineering, housebuilding and airlines sectors, took on significant levels of debt during the boom. They are really paying for it now.

What Figure 1.2 clearly demonstrates is how important pricing power is for an industry or company as any price reductions come 'straight off the bottom line'. So in our example a 5 per cent reduction in price – £150 million of revenue – with costs being fixed leads to operating profits and pre-tax profits also falling by £150 million. Hence operating profits fall from £300 million to £150 million; a 5 per cent reduction in price and revenue leads to a 50 per cent drop in profit. The result is a gearing ratio of 10 to 1.

(At a practical level one can always look at the relationship between turnover movements and the related impact on operating profit in company announcements. This will not always be precise as currency and other cost-related factors will also be influential but it is always worth considering the relationship.)

Importantly, because the interest charges are high (reflecting high levels of debt) then at the pre-tax level the profits fall by 66 per cent rather than 50 per cent. In effect the interest charges are another 'fixed cost'.

This 5 per cent reduction cascades down the **profit and loss account** adversely impacting important and key ratios. So if we follow it down through the profit and loss (P&L) account we see that this relatively modest price can lead to:

- the company breaching its banking covenants (as **interest cover** falls to dangerous levels) and
- the **dividend** being cut (as cover for the dividend is reduced by below 1×).

Therefore because of the cost structure and debt levels of the business a 5 per cent reduction in prices is quite devastating. And as we can see, a 10 per cent reduction in prices and revenue leads to operating profit being eliminated and the company records a pre-tax loss of £75 million (the interest payments). The share price will either collapse on the back of this or already be at very low levels as investors express concern about just this sort of eventuality. While this is a simple example it is not too far away from the actual experience at General Motors, any of the airlines or other highly cyclical, fixed-cost businesses where price falls due to falling demand and/or intensified competition are all too likely.

with high debt levels a 5% fall in prices is devastating

Given how powerful the impact of this price fall is on the company, appreciating the industry dynamics, competitive structure and the company's product position that determines pricing is crucial to assessing the prospects and risk profile of the company (a topic we return to in the next chapter).

Risk as industry economics and corporate governance

While the debates over compensating investors for risk tend to revolve around the **cost of capital** (driven by the risk-free rate as an opportunity cost, the **equity risk premium** and the company's beta (see p. 22)), is this the right way to think about the risks involved in investing in a business in the real world?

A more fundamental and extremely effective risk appraisal procedure is provided by Warren Buffett. In this, risk is primarily determined by the economic position of the business and the quality of management. In particular, his comments on management are anchored in terms of good **corporate governance** suggesting this as key component of risk – something shareholders are increasingly conscious of given the governance concerns at such 'blue chip' companies as Marks and Spencer and Shell. Buffett's approach to risk, detailed in his 1993 letter to shareholders, focuses on:

- evaluating the long-term economic characteristics of the business – how certain are they?
- management
  - are managers running existing assets properly?
  - will they use cash flows properly (i.e. add-value)?
  - is management working for shareholders or for itself?
- inflation and taxes – the long-term impact on purchasing power
- purchase price.

This analysis is interesting in many ways. It emphasises that the real risks to shareholders are bound up with the company, its markets and management's decisions – something not necessarily captured by stock market volatility or 'equations with Greek letters in them'.

The first point highlights the need to get to grips with the **fundamentals** of the **sector** and the company's position within it. Market shares, quality of brands, pricing power, low-cost delivery and high barriers to entry are the sort of features that determine the economic strength of the business. Importantly, this long-term competitive focus (which is also at the heart of Porter's five forces model, see p. 45) is in sharp contrast to the market's preoccupation with short-term earnings targets. In effect it is deliberately focusing on the quality of earnings (that is, their predictability and sustainability) rather than quantity. We know that when a company has a weak competitive position and cannot control prices the impact can be devastating. The operational gearing example above highlights the dangers of falling prices to a business. Interestingly, Warren Buffett always tends to go for companies with considerable brand strength in his portfolio. Reflecting the elements of Figure 1.2 he reportedly quipped after an airline investment went very badly wrong that he was now a member of 'AA' – 'Airlines Anonymous'. If he felt moved to invest in an airline again he would phone a friend to talk him out of it.

The focus on management and its ability to run the existing business well is also a key element of risk. Being the lowest-cost producer and 'doing the ordinary things extraordinarily well' are demands a shareholder is entitled to make of a business. These characteristics are a crucial driver of value, especially in a low-inflation environment. Companies that constantly have to restructure reveal an inefficient cost base with clear risks to investors. An interesting example here is the impact of the low-cost airlines on the so-called legacy airlines or national carriers.

A key result of running the existing business well should, in theory, be strong cash flow. Using this cash flow to good effect – in a way that benefits shareholders – is crucial. This very much sums up how shareholders are currently viewing companies with strong cash flow providing funding for the business's growth without recourse to a stricken banking sector, while also enabling growing dividends which will help deliver returns in the long run.

Whether management is working directly in the interest of shareholders raises the key issue of corporate governance. Management must be working in shareholders' interests and not their own, and this is a crucial element for shareholders. Those companies (such as WorldCom, Enron, Ahold and Parmalat) most clearly associated with value destruction were invariably committed to policies of rapid growth achieved through aggressive acquisition policies, and aggressive accounting policies that enabled earnings targets to be hit, which in turn enabled bonus targets to be reached.

This aggressive approach to growth and desire to highlight how well the company was doing through flexible accounting (if not fraud) was driven entirely by what benefited managers not shareholders and the economic rationale for deals was highly dubious at best. Thus the increasing activism of investors for improved corporate governance is hardly surprising.

The failure of many financial sector firms has also also ensured that governance remains in the forefront of investors' minds. The International Corporate Governance Network refers to boards as having 'failed to understand and manage risk and tolerated perverse incentives',[2] and given the discussion of risk here, it also calls for institutional investors to 'consider the riskiness of a company's business model as part of their investment decision-making.'[3]

---

[2] Skypala, P. (2008) 'Time to reward good corporate governance', *Financial Times*, 16 November.

[3] Ibid.

While examining the cost of capital is important in assessing the risks faced by investors, it provides, at best, only a partial view of the potential dangers they are running. A more comprehensive view must embrace the competitive position of the business, the quality of earnings and, crucially, the quality of management. In particular, management committed to serving shareholders' interests rather than its own is a crucial aspect of risk minimisation. Accordingly, good corporate governance – where management really believes in and implements best practice – reduces risk and is an essential element in reducing the cost of capital.

Quality

The quality of cash flow and earnings is a vital component in valuing any company. While there is no one definition of quality, the following factors need to be considered:

- the sustainability and visibility of earnings in terms of the trading outlook which in turn derives from the volume, pricing and cost outlook: with high-quality earnings it is much easier to predict the earnings of a company
- high and consistent return on capital/creation of shareholder value
- that the profits are being generated by the core and are not coming from any one-off disposals or other (non-trading) benefits
- what management has control over and can influence (does the company have pricing power and can it influence input costs?)
- that earnings are coming through into cash flow cleanly/efficiently
- the use of very straight and conservative accounting policies by the company which ensures that the earnings number is a true reflection of what is really going on with the business, i.e. how it is really performing.

The more a company engages in accounting manipulation to 'hit' earnings targets, the poorer is the quality of its earnings. Critically, however, to the extent that earnings are benefiting from manipulation, its performance is less sustainable – at some stage it will run out of room for manoeuvre and the reality of the trading environment will catch up with it. A company that has, for example, been using provisions to hit earnings targets (by reducing the actual costs of doing business) may run into difficulties once all the provisions have been used up. The real costs of doing business will then reassert themselves. This was a feature of many of the acquisitive growth stocks of the 1990s.

A concern with companies that have aggressive earnings targets is that they will employ flexible accounting policies to hit those targets but ultimately the trading environment will catch up with them. Similarly, aggressive acquisitions policies can often camouflage what is really occurring within the core business and earnings may benefit temporarily from the acquisition. The key here is to ensure that earnings convert into cash. Earnings are a matter of judgement (i.e. it depends on an interpretation of accounting policies) while cash is a matter of fact. Accounting manipulation of earnings or sales recognition may flatter earnings but the earnings will not flow though into cash.

Another area to monitor is where a significant portion of profit comes from 'related' companies. This is where the main company has an investment in another company or venture. The former may book its fair share of profit but this will not necessarily correspond to the cash as the cash received will depend on the dividend received from such investments.

The IBM example (see p. 140) regarding disposals and its pension fund dramatically highlights the issue of **earnings quality**. The reason for scrutinising performance numbers is to assess the underlying (competitive) performance of the business. Critically, achieving earnings targets or expectations through one-off benefits, while the performance of the underlying business disappoints, will ultimately come to light and the share price will suffer. As these 'benefits' to earnings drop out of the equation, earnings growth will depend purely on business performance. If, for example, revenues have disappointed and the company has been losing market share, this will drive the valuation even if earnings have been on track. Investors should always be wary when scrutinising the results of companies that have a record of using dubious accounting policies to hit earnings targets. The valuation will reflect these concerns.

> earnings are a matter of judgement while cash is a matter of fact

The other important aspect for earnings quality is what management can influence. In commodity-based businesses, for example, earnings will, by their nature, be volatile. A timber trading company will be subject to the vagaries of price movements and the impact of currency movements in determining its profits. Both of these may be difficult to predict and lie outside management's control. This is not to say that management is not extremely good at what it is doing, but earnings are clearly going to be volatile. If the business benefits from sharp price rises, how much of the improved performance is attributable to good management and its control of the business? As well as lying beyond management control, the sustainability of these higher prices needs to be questioned. Conversely, a company with a strong market position and an excellent brand will be able to influence price, which translates into higher-quality earnings.

Shareholder value – the current debate

One of the responses to the recent financial 'crisis' has been a re-examination of shareholder value. This is a measure of the returns of the business and effectively assesses whether shareholders are being rewarded for the risks they are running, and whether management is using the assets under its stewardship to good effect and generating a good return from them. All the evidence suggests that generating these returns is the crucial driver of share prices longer term.

Jack Welch, former CEO of General Electric, stated: 'On the face of it, shareholder value is the dumbest idea in the world.'[4] It would be tempting to agree with him if this is what has been happening. Invariably, however, managers have been pursuing growth regardless of risk as a way of getting the share price up. In many cases management teams will sacrifice actions that improve the competitive position of the business to hit an earnings target. In effect management teams have been managing the share price not the business.

A study by researchers at Duke University and the University of Washington[5] found that 78 per cent of senior financial executives in the US said they would sacrifice shareholder value to hit an earnings target. Some 55 per cent said they would delay a (profitable and value-adding) project for the same reason. Interestingly, a greater percentage of companies in Q3 2003 were beating Wall Street estimates by a penny, compared to those missing by a penny, than was the case in 1999. The combination of the survey and subsequent earnings outcomes suggests a degree of accounting manipulation (notwithstanding recent accounting scandals) and an unhealthy focus on short-term earnings targets – crucially a target of questionable import as earnings targets have little to do with cash or economic value. Management is managing the target – earnings – not the business. But the business needs to be managed to generate the numbers in the long run.

---

[4] Guerrera, F. (2009) 'Welch condemns share price focus', *Financial Times*, 12 March.

[5] Graham, J., Harvey, C. R. and Rajgopal, S. (2003–04) 'The Economic Implications of Corporate Financial Reporting', Duke University/University of Washington.

This emphasis on hitting a target, therefore, distorts decision making. Examples of this might include cutting research and development or marketing budgets to ensure earnings meet expectations. Investors will not react favourably when they realise targets have been hit by the expediency of cutting marketing costs and thus damaging the franchise of the business. So what precisely is the advantage of these short-term decisions? The disappointing trading issues come into sharper relief (i.e. numbers would be below expectations save for the investment in marketing being cut) while management's judgement is called into question.

More importantly and far more damaging is where accounting policies are deliberately manipulated to ensure earnings do not disappoint. This is particularly likely to occur where companies have aggressive growth targets or where remuneration policies are linked with earnings. This is at the heart of corporate governance debates: decision making is distorted in favour of policies that generate growth (or the illusion thereof) but destroy shareholder value. This favours management through status and salary rather than shareholders. Linking salary to a short-term and arguably irrelevant performance metric engenders cynicism. Crucially, it also distracts attention from the key longer-term strategic issues that drive the company's performance and creation of value.

If shareholders subsequently find out that management has been manipulating its accounts or taking decisions detrimental to the company's long-term interests, then management's reputation will suffer irreparable harm. This may have far more damaging consequences than failing to hit a target – which may be for very good reasons.

Shareholder value properly implemented embraces the three pillars of growth, risk and quality rather than the one-dimensional focus on earnings growth. Shareholder value is, after all, only generated where investment returns compensate shareholders for risk.

There is much argument about whether shareholder value is focused on satisfying one, albeit crucial group (shareholders), at the expense of other stakeholders. This assumes that it is an either/or issue, but as ever in life things are not necessarily mutually exclusive. Our principal concern when looking at the fundamentals of a business is the competitive position of that business and its ability to generate sustained returns over time. The health of that long-term competitive position will determine the wealth created. Having a relentless focus on the health of the business (say the power and quality of the brand for a consumer business and therefore being alert to the needs of consumers first and foremost) is ultimately going to be a far more effective way of driving shareholder value than focusing on growth in earnings. Similarly, treating employees respectfully so they can deal with customers respectfully is also a way in which all the supposed competing interests actually converge.

Therefore a more comprehensive appreciation of shareholder value and an appreciation that it is how the business performs over time automatically take into account other stakeholders as a matter of course: how else can shareholder value be delivered?

A key concept

From an investor's perspective shareholder value is simply an effective way of ensuring the business generates returns that compensates them for the risks they are running (see p. 7 for an overview of risks). This then puts an explicit cost on the management for using your money. Can it generate returns on capital (after tax) that exceed the cost of capital to provide you with a positive return? A company which has high and consistent returns will have a higher valuation and perform better than one with a history of poor returns. A high return is a very good predictor of a high valuation and the ability to make money in the long run.

As one of the fundamental tenets of equity investment it is important to be aware of the concept of shareholder value. It provides us with

- an excellent way of evaluating management performance
- a way of relating returns to risk
- a means of deciding whether a business or division is competitive and being well managed
- the most effective way of assessing the effectiveness of mergers and acquisitions.

It is also at the heart of many of the debates on corporate governance. A management team may well be excellent at delivering growth and remunerated accordingly. However, if this is achieved through the aggressive use of debt (and therefore creating a lot of risk), a series of larger and larger acquisitions (which increase risk and rarely add value) or at the expense of returns, you as investors are losing out.

Shareholder value – an intuitive guide

If we look at the various categories of assets we can invest in, rank them for their likely risk profile and then see what sort of return we want from them, it allows us to benchmark the risk/reward profile of those assets.

As Figure 1.3 shows, we may want (say) a 5 per cent return from government bonds. Theoretically these are relatively low risk and so provide an indication of the return we can expect for taking relatively little risk (though the risk of inflation and the amount of government debt expected to be issued over the next few years needs to be borne in mind). This rate is often referred to in the jargon as 'the risk-free rate'. It becomes our base and other asset categories are priced off that – we have a 'spread' over that rate, depending on the alternative risks. This 5 per cent is received in the form of a 'coupon' which is paid by the government to holders of the debt. The debt is then redeemed 'at par' – if it was issued at £100 the government pays you back £100. The return is referred to as the **yield**.

So investing in the debt of an AAA-rated company (a very secure company in a safe sector, e.g. Nestlé) we are still in very low-risk territory. Accordingly, the 'spread' will be small and the yield may be, say, 6 per cent (though some companies may in fact be more secure in certain contexts than government debt!).

Clearly, for a company with a much lower **credit rating** (see p. 181) because it operates with a lot more debt and may be in a sector more affected by the fortunes of the economy than food, we want a higher return for the risks we are running. How much more will depend on just how weak its finances are and how volatile its business. In Figure 1.3 we have suggested a yield of 8 per cent is needed.

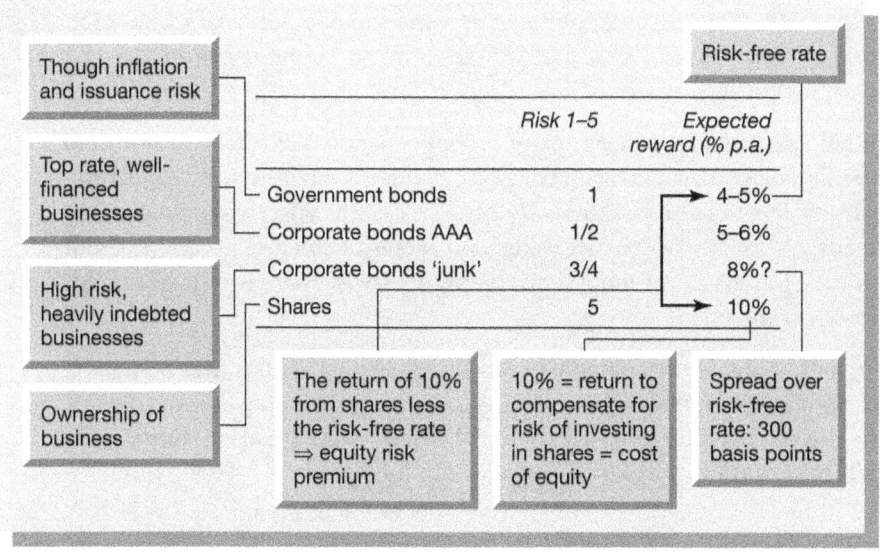

Figure 1.3 Suggested risk/reward profile for certain assets and sectors

For **shares** the risks are higher still – shareholders come last in the pecking order if things go badly wrong, as we have seen in recent times. In Figure 1.3 we have provided a number for investing in shares overall (risks will obviously vary from company to company). This is clearly very subjective and people may well have different requirements regarding the returns they want for persuading them to invest. I have suggested that a return of 10 per cent is required. Historically, shares have tended to generate a return of around 8–10 per cent (although I appreciate that the past decade has seen returns far lower than this).

If we use 10 per cent, then what we are saying is that we want a return of 10 per cent to compensate us for the risks of investing in shares. We know we can get 5 per cent for taking no risk so we need an additional 5 per cent to invest in shares. This is referred to as the 'equity risk premium'. It is normally in a band of 3–6 per cent.

Unlike a bond, however, this 10 per cent does not necessarily come from a 'coupon' or dividend. It is likely to be made up of some capital appreciation (the shares going up in value) and a yield from the shares as the company pays dividends. The precise mix will depend on whether the shares are growth companies which are using their cash flows to invest in their future – the capital appreciation will be the majority of the return. Conversely, a utility which has low growth but is mature and cash generative can afford to pay high dividends. The majority of the return here will be in the form of income from dividends. This combination of capital appreciation and income is known as 'total shareholder returns'. In effect it is the 'cost of equity' – you need a return of 10 per cent (on average) from investing in shares.

If the management of a company cannot generate that sort of return from the money you provide, you would be better off in another investment or getting 5 per cent for taking very little risk. So in effect you are charging management 10 per cent for using your money. Managers need to spend it in the business to get more than that or otherwise there is little advantage for the company.

To look at the returns obtained from the money in the business we look at the return on capital after tax. This is the operating profit generated divided by the assets required to get that profit. The assets are also referred to as **return on capital employed**. (For more on this see pp. 152–60.) Essentially:

$$\text{return on capital employed} = \frac{\text{operating profit after tax}}{\text{shareholders' funds} + \text{net debt}}$$

When we look at more individual shares we need to see what risks attach to them, their business models and their financial structures (as discussed on p. 7), and the sectors they are in. Figure 1.4 suggests the sort of returns one might expect from a variety of sectors.

As you can see from Figure 1.4, we have done a similar exercise to that in Figure 1.3. Clearly, for a stable sector like a utility where (economic) risks are relatively low we expect relatively low returns. And, as indicated, we would expect those returns to come in the form of income. Conversely, the rewards from a biotech company are incredibly challenging to predict and the returns are likely to be a long way off and come in the form of capital appreciation.

Again I have done these figures intuitively and you may have your own views on the validity of the numbers. Figure 1.5 offers a suggested spread of sectors' risks and potential rewards. In effect this provides the 'cost of equity' for these sectors: unless you get a return of 8 per cent or more you will not invest in a spirits company whereas you need a return of 25 per cent plus to be persuaded to hand over money to a biotech company.

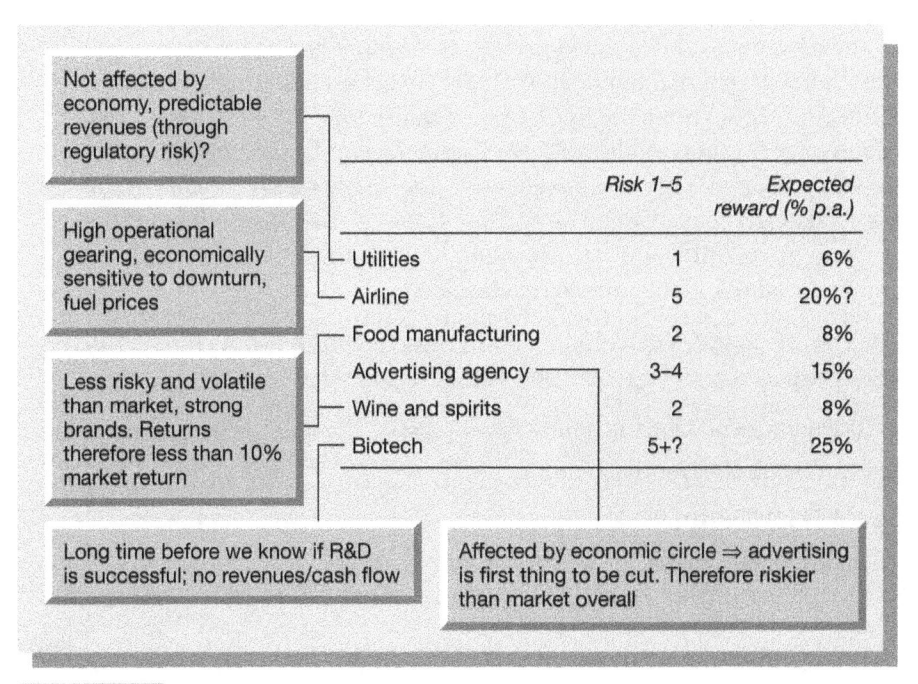

	Risk 1–5	Expected reward (% p.a.)
Utilities	1	6%
Airline	5	20%?
Food manufacturing	2	8%
Advertising agency	3–4	15%
Wine and spirits	2	8%
Biotech	5+?	25%

Not affected by economy, predictable revenues (through regulatory risk)? — Utilities

High operational gearing, economically sensitive to downturn, fuel prices — Airline

Less risky and volatile than market, strong brands. Returns therefore less than 10% market return — Food manufacturing, Wine and spirits

Long time before we know if R&D is successful; no revenues/cash flow — Biotech

Affected by economic circle ⇒ advertising is first thing to be cut. Therefore riskier than market overall — Advertising agency

Figure 1.4 Sectors – risk/reward profile

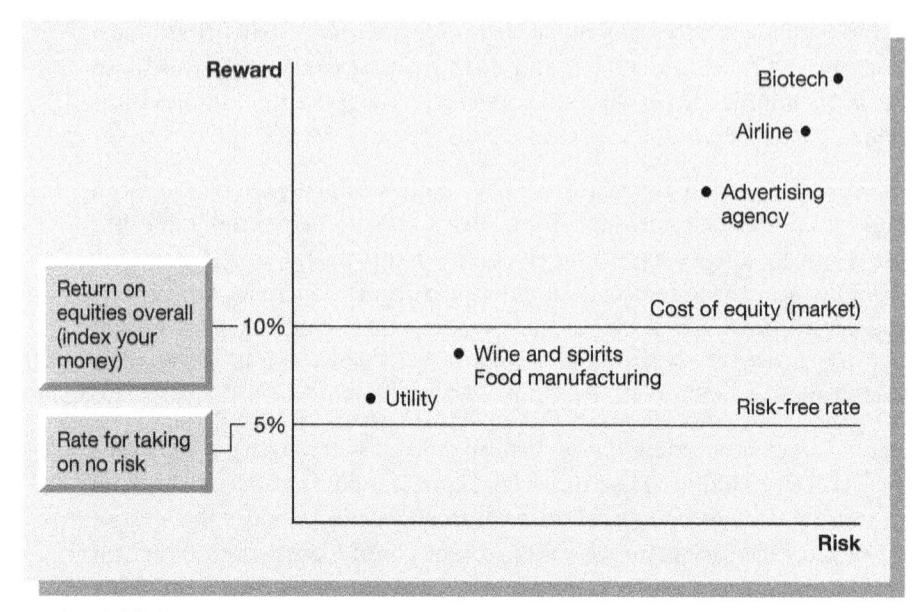

Figure 1.5 Relationship between risk and reward

As these examples are educated guesses, to be more precise we need to use the capital asset pricing model (CAPM). This is useful, although bear in mind that throughout the book I stress that a lot of the real-world risk comes from business models and events that cannot be predicted. The section on risk offers a more comprehensive assessment (see p. 7). One of the key weaknesses (possibly of many) of the CAPM is that beta is very much a measure of volatility and not risk – and while it tries to capture business and financial risk it does not do so adequately.

The cost of capital is determined by the structure of the company's funding – the balance between debt and shares. It is affected by:

- the mixture of debt and equity
- debt being cheaper than equity
- the tax treatment of debt.

These interrelated elements are considered below.

Cost of debt

The cost of the debt is straightforward to appreciate and to calculate. If the company can borrow from the bank or in the debt markets for, say, 8 per cent, this tells you the cost of servicing the company's debt. Importantly, the interest payments are tax deductible, which makes the debt even cheaper relative to equity. So, in this case the **cost of debt** would be 8 per cent × 0.7 or 5.6 per cent (i.e. deducting the 30 per cent tax charge).

The company's cost of debt will depend on its financial position, as discussed on pp. 164–203. The debt **rating** will have a major impact on the cost of debt. It is normally provided by a credit rating agency and is expressed in terms of letters, the highest being AAA (the so-called 'triple A' rating). The lower the rating, the more expensive the debt. In addition, when an agency downgrades a credit rating, not only does the cost of debt rise but the company's share price normally falls dramatically.

Cost of equity

As we have seen from example figures above, we can intuitively get a sense of the return we want from particular sectors and shares. Essentially, the **cost of equity** must reflect what rate of return an investor requires to compensate for the risks attaching both to shares in general and to a particular company (which may be riskier than the stock market overall).

Reflecting these considerations, the cost of equity is calculated by reference to:

- the risk-free rate of borrowing
- an equity risk premium to allow for the risks associated with investing in shares
- the volatility of the individual share, which is measured by its beta.

The risk-free rate of borrowing is normally based on the interest on a long-term government bond and reflects the 'opportunity cost' of investing in shares: the return you can get without risk. The use of a long-term government bond also ties in with the fact that it is the company's long-term cash flow projections that are being **discounted**.

The equity risk premium is the return required by share investors over and above the return on risk-free government bonds to compensate for the additional risks involved in equity investment. This is normally calculated by looking at the historic return of equities compared with government bonds, with the difference being deemed the premium required for investing in shares.

However, the use of historic data to determine the equity risk premium immediately creates a problem as investing in shares is a forward-looking activity. Generally, the equity risk premium is thought to be between 3 per cent and 6 per cent. Controversy has raged over the past few years as to what exactly the level of this risk premium is. The recent bear market has seen the premium rise significantly as investors have become very aware of the risks involved in shares. During the strong markets of the late 1990s many people argued that the risk premium was negligible – the risk was being out of shares.

> beta measures the degree of volatility a share displays against the overall market

The beta measures the degree of volatility a share displays against the overall market. Given how significant its impact is on the cost of equity it is worth gaining a better sense of what exactly beta is and the factors that determine whether it is a high or low number. It is also worth debating whether beta is in fact a sensible way of looking at risk.

Beta

What exactly is beta?

Beta is a measure of how volatile an individual stock is against the market. If the overall market rises 10 per cent and a stock rises 12 per cent, the beta would be 1.2. Conversely, if in a market that rises 10 per cent the stock rises only 8 per cent, the beta would be 0.8. The situation would be reversed in a falling market, with the stock on a beta of 0.8 falling 8 per cent in a market that falls 10 per cent.

To derive beta, the stock returns on a monthly basis are recorded, normally over a five-year period. This can cause problems for stocks new to the market, but considering a comparable company or looking at the company's characteristics can provide guidance. In the academic theory, beta is predictive, i.e. forward looking, and over time will trend towards 1 (i.e. the share ultimately moves in line with the market). This sounds complicated and indeed is – different methods and different providers of statistical data can and do provide different betas, which can affect the cost of capital materially.

Again in the technical jargon the 'stock-specific risk' of the shares is not included in this calculation. This is because the stock-specific risk can be diversified away by holding a portfolio of shares. Equity market risk and volatility against the market are what are being used to determine the cost of capital.

What determines beta?

Beta will vary across stocks and sectors. Essentially, the more cyclical a sector, the higher the beta is going to be. This is because the individual shares will be more volatile than the market overall. We have also seen, in Figure 1.2, the impact on earnings of a small fall in turnover. Conversely, more **defensive** areas of the economy such as utilities and food and drink will not be as sensitive to movements in the stock market. (See Figure 1.4 which shows how different sectors perform when the economy is affected by changes in interest rates.) Therefore 'defensive' shares will have a low beta while more **cyclical stocks** will have a higher beta.

Table 1.1 highlights the beta range across three very different sectors.

Table 1.1 Beta across different sectors

Sector	Stocks	Beta
Defensive	Unilever	0.4
Cyclical	BA	1.5
Growth	Logica	1.1

Clearly, in markets that are going through nervous times, the defensive, lower-risk characteristics of Unilever, the international branded food manufacturer, are going to be something of a 'safe haven'. However, as and when the stock market develops into a more positive mood, this may turn into a disadvantage.

High operational gearing v low operational gearing (profit sensitivity)

Again, high operational gearing (see p. 7) is likely to see greater volatility, which will see a higher beta accorded. Here for any given change in revenues a much greater change in operating profits will be recorded.

High financial gearing v low financial gearing (profit volatility)

Similarly, a company that is heavily indebted – high financial gearing – is a higher risk and will see its profits fall (rise) more dramatically if there is a significant rise (fall) in interest rates.

Liquidity

To the extent that we are looking at how volatile an individual share is against the market, as well as the factors described above, then how 'liquid' the company's shares are will influence the beta. Shares are liquid if they can be dealt with in large quantities without disturbing the share price. Conversely, a share where you can only deal in small amounts and this leads to a big shift in the share price are 'illiquid'. Clearly, if we are talking about the shares' volatility against the market as determining beta then **liquidity** or **illiquidity** will have a role in this.

Beta as a measure of volatility not risk?

It can be argued that beta as a measure of risk is not a reliable gauge. It measures volatility which may, or may not, be the same thing as risk. A fundamentally sound, quality company which represents good value may have a higher beta than a company which has a weaker market position and poorer prospects. Similarly, the shares may be volatile because they are illiquid but the financial and business risk are limited and well managed. Another issue with using beta is that it is a historic guide to the relationship of the shares and the stock market – this may or may not be useful for predicting future performance.

Certainly, shareholders in any of the fallen stars of Wall Street (Enron, WorldCom, Global Crossing *et al.*) are not worrying about the beta of those stocks. Focusing on the economic characteristics of the business and the quality and integrity of management are the fundamental issues when appraising the risk profile.

For those who are not algebraically inclined, the following quote from Warren Buffett is a source of reassurance:

> Read Ben Graham and Phil Fisher, read annual reports, but don't do equations with Greek letters in them.[6]

Calculating the cost of equity

Taking these three components of the risk-free rate, the equity risk premium and beta into account then:

Return on equity = risk-free rate + beta × (equity risk premium)

---

[6] Lowe, J.C. (1997) *Warren Buffett Speaks*, New York: Wiley.

Or the equation with Greek letters is:

$$R_e = R_f + \beta (R_m - R_f)$$

R_e = the return on equity: the required return on the shares to compensate you for the risks of share ownership.

R_f = 'The risk-free rate': the return you could get 'risk-free' by investing in (say) a 10-year government bond.

R_m = the return you expect to get from investing in the stock market overall.

$R_m - R_f$ = the return on the overall market (Rm) less the risk-free rate (Rf) of return.

This is known as the 'equity risk premium' – that is, the return required over and above the risk free rate to cover you for the risk of investing in shares generally.

So if you want 10 per cent for investing in shares then that is the 'cost of equity' for shares overall. The equity risk premium is then 10 per cent – 5 per cent (the risk-free rate) which gives you an equity risk premium of 5 per cent: the *extra* return you need to compensate you for the risks of share ownership.

The ERP is often measured over long periods and is the average amount by which the return on shares beats bonds. Historically it ranges anywhere between 3 per cent and 6 per cent. As a working assumption, therefore, the cost of equity being between 8 per cent and 10 per cent is a good rule of thumb.

To cover the cost of investing in different shares we need to take into account the risk/volatility of that particular share. We do that by using its 'beta'. So a very volatile company will have a high beta while a predictable company with little volatility will have a low beta.

If the risk-free rate is 5 per cent and the equity risk premium is 4 per cent, a stock with a beta of 1.2 would have a cost of equity of

$$5 + 1.2(4) = 9.8\%$$

A defensive stock such as a food retailer or branded food company may have a beta of around 0.5. This would then mean the cost of equity would be

$$5 + 0.5(4) = 7\%$$

A very volatile stock, say an airline with high operational gearing and lots of debt, would have a beta of say 3. Accordingly, the cost of equity would be

$$5 + 3(4) = 17\%$$

Therefore investors in a food retailer may want a return of greater than 7 per cent to cover them for the risks of investing while an investor in an airline wants at least a 17 per cent return to cover the extra risk.

Note that in the table of returns from certain sectors we had 8 per cent as a return from a food retailer as we intuitively realised that this sector is less risky than the market overall – for which we wanted a return of 10 per cent. So the cost of equity indeed comes in that ball park of 7–8 per cent: and for an airline we had 20 per cent.

Therefore we can see how sensitive the cost of equity is to assumptions about the equity risk premium and the dramatic difference in the cost of equity for a company with a low beta compared with a company with a high beta.

Much of this discussion on the cost of capital may feel unnecessarily arcane and obscure. However, the intuitive sense of which sectors or companies are riskier also plays a very useful role and provides a good guide to the required return without any detailed calculation (or indeed spurious accuracy).

The Buffett approach has great validity and focuses attention on getting to grips with the company's competitive position and its management quality. Nonetheless, the idea behind the cost of capital is crucial and the principle is quite straightforward. It is essentially saying that you as an investor need to be compensated for supplying risk capital. Importantly, this is the cost you want to charge to the company (and its management) for using your money – how else can we establish if management is doing a good job?

Other measures

You can always adopt your own rule of thumb by assessing the risks in the business as discussed by Buffett and in the section on what drives the beta (i.e. the combination of operational and financial gearing). If there are a number of risks you may want to use a cost of capital of, say, 15 per cent – i.e. this is the return you want from the shares. For less risky and less volatile situations you may feel that (say) a 10 per cent cost of capital is more appropriate; for emerging companies you may feel that 20 per cent is the sort of return you need to compensate for the greater risks you are undertaking; and so on.

Cost of capital – the WACC calculation

This then puts an explicit cost on the management for using your money. Can it generate returns that exceed the cost of capital to provide you with a positive return? This is one of the fundamental tenets of equity investment. Again, while you may not wish to use the jargon it is important to be aware of the concept.

Having worked out a method to calculate the cost of debt and the cost of equity we can now compute the weighted average cost of capital (WACC):

$$\text{WACC} = \left(\frac{\text{market cap}}{\text{market cap + debt}}\right) \times \text{cost of equity} + \left(\frac{\text{debt}}{\text{market cap + debt}}\right) \times \text{post-tax cost of debt}$$

Figure 1.6 shows that the WACC can range from 14 per cent when the business is 100 per cent funded by equity to 9.8 per cent when funded with half equity and half debt. This is a considerable difference. Where the WACC is reduced to its lowest is referred to as an 'efficient balance sheet'. We could have calculated that had there been an extreme 75 per cent funding by debt then the WACC would have been as low as 7.8 per cent. (In reality the debt would introduce so much financial risk that the beta would have risen significantly.)

Clearly, therefore, it is much easier to 'add value' if the business has lots of debt funding. This is why so many deals in the 2000–08 period were

```
Cost of equity  = Risk-free rate + beta (equity risk premium)
                = 5% + 1.5(6%) = 14%
Cost of debt    = pre-tax 8%; post-tax = 70% of 8% or 5.6%

Market cap      = £1,000m
Debt            = 0
Funding         = 100%; Equity @ 14%
Therefore WACC  = 14%

Market cap      = £750m
Debt            = £250m
Funding         = 75% equity @ 14%  = 10.5%
                  25% debt @ 5.6%   =  1.4%
WACC            =                     11.9%

Market cap      = £500m
Debt            = £500m
Funding         = 50% equity @ 14%  =  7%
                  50% debt @ 5.6%   =  2.8%
WACC            =                      9.8%
```

Figure 1.6 Weighted average cost of capital (WACC)

funded by debt. It also explains why **share buy-backs** were so popular with investors and companies. And private equity of course could create value more easily by funding businesses primarily with debt. We will return to funding structures, the advantages and risks of debt financing and efficient balance sheets in Chapter 5.

Increasing shareholder value – the key drivers

Having looked at the cost of capital element of shareholder value we can see that by increasing the amount of debt we can improve shareholder value, albeit with much more financial risk. Shareholder value can be improved with lower risk by getting the 'top line' right, i.e. by establishing a strong competitive business with low costs and pricing power generating excellent returns on capital employed. Increasing shareholder value through this route, especially enhancing the competitive position of the business, is the task management is charged with doing.

> shareholder value can be improved with lower risk by getting the 'top line' right

Therefore given that:

Price × volume – costs = operating profit

to improve shareholder value management can do three things:

- get higher prices for its products
- generate higher volume
- reduce costs.

Many companies tend to focus on cost reductions as the way to help create shareholder value. While this makes sense, care needs to be taken that the cost cutting does not compromise the ability to develop better products (or services) that can achieve higher prices and take market share. Also a cost-cutting culture can lead to the mindset where opportunities are overlooked as everyone is too busy reducing headcount. Cost cutting can therefore undermine the competitive position of the business.

Figure 1.7 highlights the key drivers of shareholder value. We can see that the key areas are the price volume and cost equation facing the company. Then there is the amount of assets needed to generate this operating profit. We have seen how devastating price reductions can be to returns, So it's vital to find companies with competitive advantage that can take market share off a low cost base and can influence price. That pricing

Increasing shareholder value – the key drivers

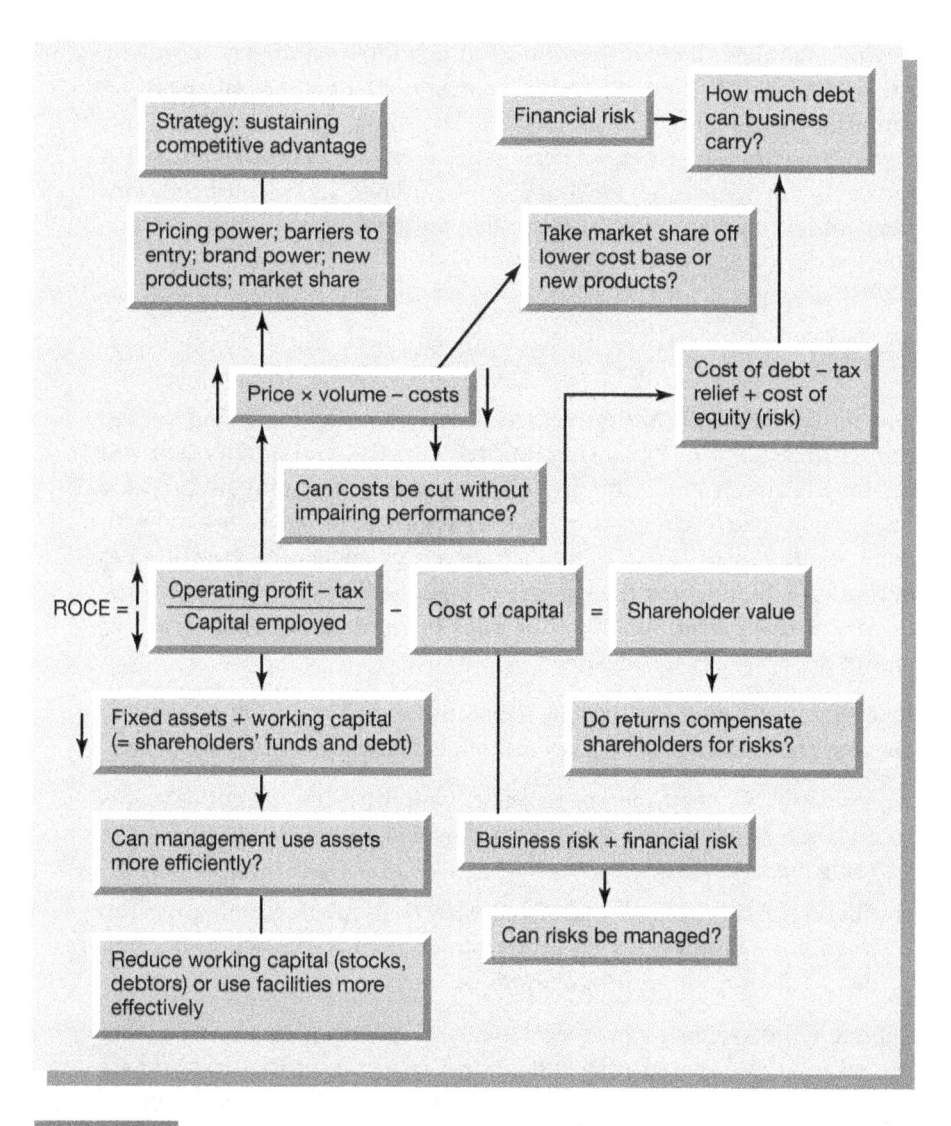

Figure 1.7 Ways to improve shareholder value

[Flowchart showing:

- Strategy: sustaining competitive advantage → Pricing power; barriers to entry; brand power; new products; market share
- Financial risk → How much debt can business carry?
- Take market share off lower cost base or new products?
- Price × volume − costs
- Cost of debt − tax relief + cost of equity (risk)
- Can costs be cut without impairing performance?
- ROCE = Operating profit − tax / Capital employed − Cost of capital = Shareholder value
- Fixed assets + working capital (= shareholders' funds and debt)
- Do returns compensate shareholders for risks?
- Can management use assets more efficiently?
- Business risk + financial risk
- Reduce working capital (stocks, debtors) or use facilities more effectively
- Can risks be managed?]

power and market share may be as a result of strong branding, new innovations that allow the company to take market share and preventing competition being on the basis of price.

Appreciating the factors that influence price, volumes and costs is therefore at the heart of getting to grips with the company's prospects, its competitive advantage and its ability to generate strong returns. We will return to these themes consistently throughout the book.

Having examined the Valuation Villa and the top-level drivers of growth, risk and quality, and established what shareholder value is all about, we can now start looking in more detail at the other elements of the Villa. Before doing that, however, we need to get a sense of the context in which the company operates by looking at the economic and sector conditions that influence pricing, volume and the cost environment – all of which affect performance.

Summary

The Valuation Villa is a very effective framework for identifying the key drivers of valuation. By considering growth, risk and quality you will establish a much more comprehensive view of the company you are investing in. The recent focus on looking at growth in isolation – and with many management teams very much driven by generating growth – has dramatically highlighted the dangers of being seduced by only one of the drivers of the Valuation Villa. The risks being incurred to deliver this growth are now only too apparent.

Investing is all about the balance between risk and reward and therefore assessing the risks involved is a key discipline. The key areas to monitor are:

- *business risk* – the inherent risk associated with the operating profits and cash flows of the company and the competitive strategy which is being pursued, and
- *financial risk* – the risk associated with the type of funding used to finance the business, i.e. its capital structure; it is the risk of the company defaulting on its debt obligations.

Therefore the key question when looking at growth is to assess whether the returns from that growth will compensate you for the risks you are running with your money. This is the cornerstone of 'shareholder value' – do returns compensate shareholders for the risks involved? Management is only creating shareholder value (or adding value) if the returns (on capital) exceed the risks (the cost of capital).

While there is often a great concentration on the growth in *quantity* of earnings, paying attention to the *quality* of earnings is also a vital component of valuation. In effect the quality of earnings is how predictable and secure the earnings and cash flow for the business are. Prudent accounting practices and earnings converting into cash are also a key element of earnings quality.

To drill down into more detail on growth, risk and quality you need to assess the management and strategy of the business, its financial position, the returns it generates and the outlook for the company's profits and cash flows. Taking all these together will give you a much clearer sense of whether the shares will make you money and the risks you running.

VALUATION VILLA CHECKLIST

Growth

Growth can be delivered in a number of ways. Is the company generating growth from:

- being in a growth market
- developing a new product or technology
- taking market share
- taking products/services into new regional/geographic markets
- investing in new facilities
- acquiring competitors.

Risk

In addition to business and financial risk we also need to consider the elements of Buffett's risk model which strongly emphasises industry economics and corporate governance matters:

- Evaluating long-term economic characteristics of the business – how certain are they?
- Management:
  - Is it running existing assets properly?
  - Will it use cash flows properly (i.e. add value)?
  - Is it working for shareholders or for itself?

Quality

Reflecting industry economics, looking at the quality of cash flow and earnings is a vital component in valuing any company. Consider:

- How easy is it to predict the earnings of the company?
- Does the company have high and consistent return on sales and capital?
- Are the profits being generated by the core and not coming from any one-off disposals or other (non-trading) benefits?
- What can management influence – in particular, does the company have pricing power?
- Do the earnings come through into cash flow cleanly/efficiently?
- Is the earnings number a true reflection of what is really going on in the business – how prudent are accounting policies?

Shareholder value

The basis of investing is risk/reward – as a shareholder you need to be rewarded for the risks you are running.

- What are the business and financial risks facing the company?
- While debt will reduce the cost of capital (it is cheaper than equity and has tax advantages), what level of debt is right for the business?
- What returns do you need to take on these risks?
- Has management got a track record in generating shareholder value?
- Are the corporate governance policies designed to protect investors?

2

Sector and market background

What topics are covered in this chapter?

- Why look at the sector first?
- What drives sector profits?
- What is the outlook for demand?
- What is the outlook for prices?
- What is the outlook for costs?
- General economic and stock market factors – how do they affect the sector?
- Summary
- Checklist

Why look at the sector first?

It is worth looking at the sector first as it gives you a quick sense of how difficult or otherwise it is for a company to make money. Historically, if the sector has found it difficult to make money and generate good returns, we must explore the reasons for this. This immediately may save you time as you can eliminate the sector as one where it is difficult to make money or, importantly, where the risks for you are too high.

What are the economic characteristics of the sector? What attributes does a company need to succeed in such an environment? Overcoming the difficult economics of an industry can be done, but it needs a special company with special characteristics to achieve this and it is quite rare. The sector may be prone to price wars, it may be cyclical or it may have a record of investing in huge amounts of capacity just as the economy turns down.

If you have found a stock that you find interesting in a sector that has historically failed to make money, you need to have a particularly good case for investing: what is different about the company that will enable it to succeed?

A number of sectors have historically failed to make money for shareholders over long periods. Steel, chemicals, paper and packaging, automotive and airlines spring to mind as areas that have been prone to losing investors' money on a long-term basis. This may reflect a combination of interrelated industry characteristics that profoundly affect the ability of a sector to create wealth. For example:

- *Overcapacity*. This leads to poor pricing and severe competition for market share. In theory if it is making no return this capacity should be withdrawn. In reality it tends to be the case that there are 'barriers to exit'. It may be expensive to withdraw or there is a temptation to wait for things to get better. When demand does pick up, there is too much capacity (and/or too many competitors) chasing the higher volumes. This leads to pressure on prices and will prevent a profit recovery.
- *Highly capital intensive*. The high fixed costs that are a feature of highly capital-intensive industries mean that there is a tendency for the companies in the industry to go for volume. Again this leads to pressure on prices. The high amount of capital employed combined with weak pricing will lead to very poor returns on that capital.
- *Commodity products*. An inability to differentiate between products means that competition is likely to focus on price. It may also mean that there are few barriers to entry. Prices are likely to fluctuate a great deal, with management having relatively little influence.
- *No pricing power*. This will be a feature of market structure and will be influenced by the factors outlined above. It may also occur where the consumer shops around and can bargain on price. The internet has made prices increasingly transparent and makes shopping around much easier.
- *Internationally competitive markets*. Again this intensifies competition.
- *Cyclicality*. Demand patterns which fluctuate widely mean that an industry goes through a series of good and very bad years. It can be difficult to generate long-term wealth in such conditions.

These factors are not mutually exclusive. Indeed they tend to be interrelated. What is crucial is that they all tend to undermine prices. Poor pricing and underperforming shares are a key relationship that will feature throughout the book.

To illustrate some of these issues we will look briefly at two sectors where the historic performance has been poor – automotive and airlines. The points made are simple and general but describe some of the key factors accounting for the industries' inability to make money. We will also look at the characteristics of a company that has managed to make money in each sector.

The automotive sector – factors driving poor returns

Figures 2.1 and 2.2 for the European and US automotive manufacturers illustrate a history of long-term underperformance relative to their respective local market. You would have lost a lot of money compared with just buying, say, an index fund that mirrored the overall market. The share price trend also shows great volatility, which suggests possible trading opportunities, although whether you have the skills to take advantage of that successfully is a different matter.

The automotive industry is a classic example of an internationally competitive market. Developing countries have encouraged indigenous car industries, often based on exports as an integral part of improving living standards. The industry has political importance in the developed world

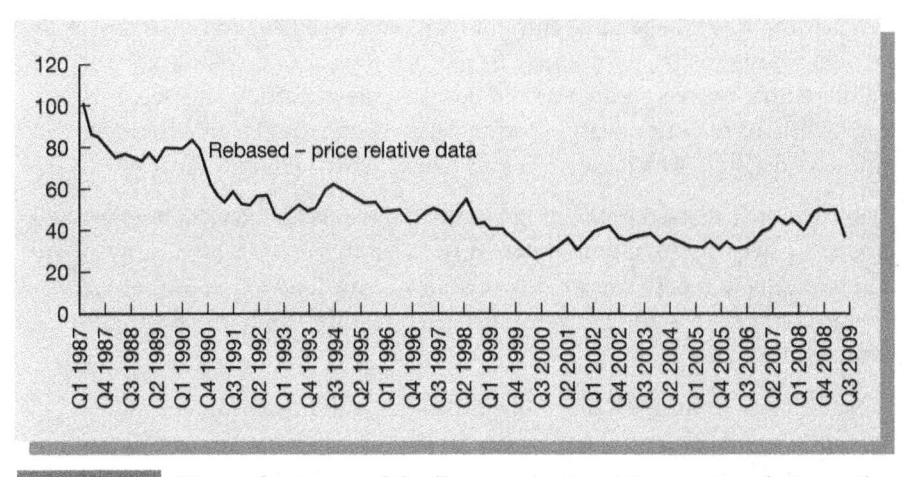

Figure 2.1 The performance of the European automotive sector relative to the overall European stock market (Eurotop 300) since 1987

Source: Thomson Reuters DataStream

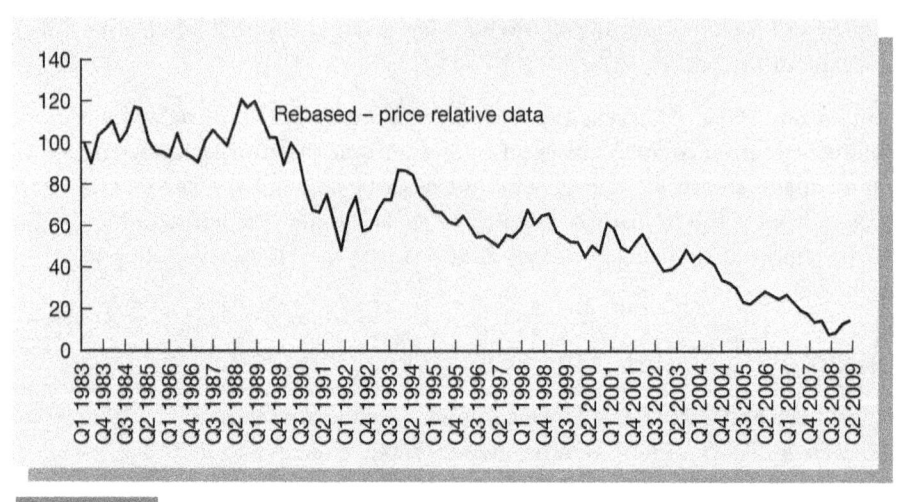

Figure 2.2 The performance of the US automotive sector relative to the US stock market since 1983

Source: Thomson Reuters DataStream

the automotive industry is a classic example of an internationally competitive market

too – it is a large employer and the local company is often seen as a national symbol. State subsidies or loans have been important historically, helping to preserve capacity, as politically and economically it is expensive to close capacity in advanced economies while new capacity is being installed in developing countries. This new capacity will be more efficient than older facilities and labour costs are often substantially lower. It may be that the prospect for volume growth and perennial recovery hopes in the industry mean participants feel it is worthwhile to retain capacity. Closing capacity can also be an extremely expensive decision, which accounts for a reluctance to withdraw capacity.

High costs are involved in building production plants and developing new products (these are sometimes referred to as 'sunk' costs). A high proportion of production costs are fixed. In addition, costs tend to rise as the cars produced have more and more sophisticated features while the real price of cars continues to fall.

These factors account for some of the difficulties with this sector. The industry tends to have permanent overcapacity, which leads to significant competition, domestic and international, which in turn serves to depress prices and margins. Volumes in the US automotive industry have been strong, but discounts to consumers and interest-free loans have cut margins to very low levels. Consumers are increasingly shopping around and, helped by the internet, are very price aware. This puts them in a position to negotiate keenly on prices. The weak pricing leads to weak margins which in turn put pressure on cash flow – a major problem for an industry with lots of capital to maintain, high costs and new product developments to undertake.

Therefore the combination of a high cost structure and a very competitive market makes for a difficult operating backdrop. This translates into poor pricing, high costs, low margins and poor returns on capital employed.

Porsche's outperformance

Given the issues surrounding the sector, Porsche's outperformance of the European equity market is quite exceptional (see Figure 2.3). The trend in its return on capital is also impressive in the context of its industry (see Figure 2.4). Its qualities and strengths contrast interestingly with the sector problems identified above. Porsche has clearly defined itself as a luxury product and has not compromised this by going down market. This has preserved the value of the brand.

Having had difficulties in the mid-1980s the company radically restructured and reduced capacity. Rather than add capacity it has been happy to manufacture to order and has waiting lists for its output – this keeps capacity under control, keeps costs down and removes the risk of falling demand or producing so many cars that the exclusive cachet is lost.

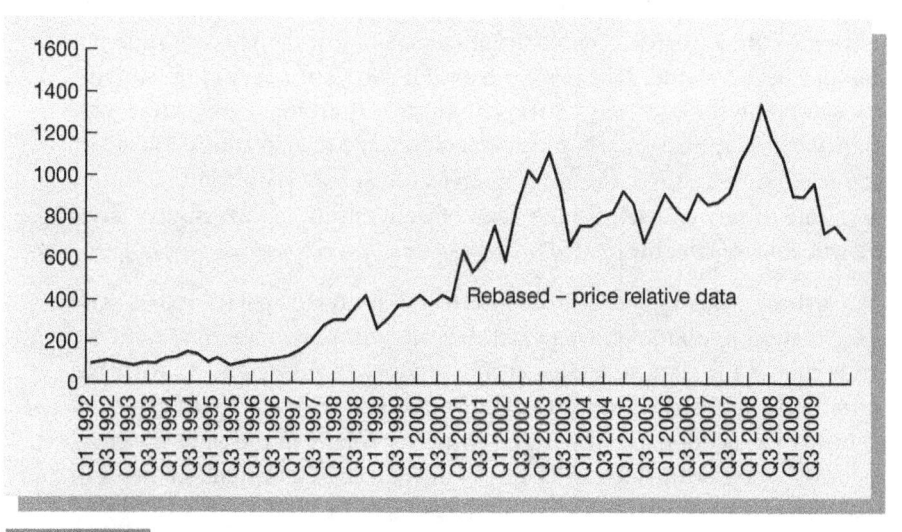

Figure 2.3 Porsche's share price performance relative to the European market

Source: Thomson Reuters DataStream

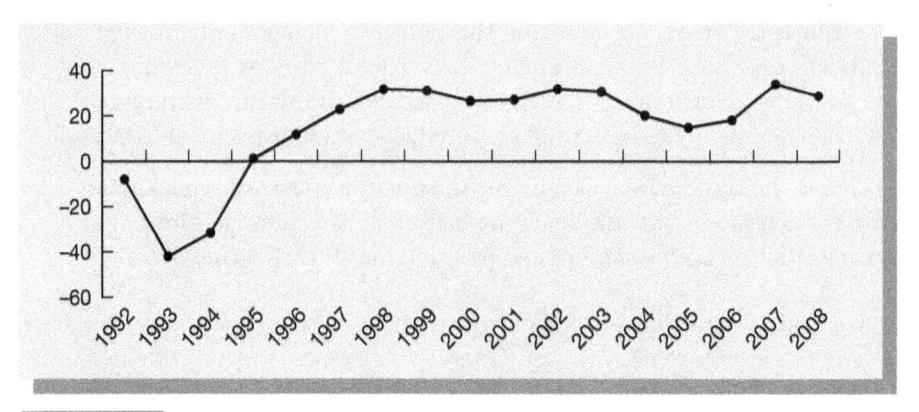

Figure 2.4 The trend in Porsche's return on capital employed since 1992

Source: Thomson Reuters DataStream

Therefore, by keeping capacity well under control and operating in a distinct segment of the market where competitive pressures are much lower, the risk/reward ratio is much more in shareholders' favour. However, maintaining exclusiveness of the brand is crucial in protecting sales and margins.

The airlines sector – factors driving performance

Figures 2.5 and 2.6 demonstrate that for both the world airline sector and the US sector there has been a clear, long-term relative underperformance against their relevant benchmarks. What is also a feature is the volatile pattern of these figures. Therefore the sector has lost money over time but has also been volatile. This may or may not suit your risk profile (an issue we will come back to frequently). If you feel that you have a thorough knowledge of the sector you may be able to trade it successfully. However, you need to be aware of the risks involved – you may want to have a short timescale or buy and sell on the basis of momentum (an investment style we will analyse later on p. 310).

The airline industry has also been affected by overcapacity issues. The combination of politics and the fact that an airline is a symbol of national pride makes for state subsidies and regulatory interference. As with the automotive industry, it tends to make it difficult for capacity to leave the industry. Costs are fixed in the sense that for each trip the same costs are incurred whether the aircraft is empty or full. Therefore small changes in passenger numbers can cause dramatic changes in profitability. Payments for landing slots and other fees to airport operators may also be unaffected by traffic. The cost of fuel oil is fixed and of course volatility in oil prices

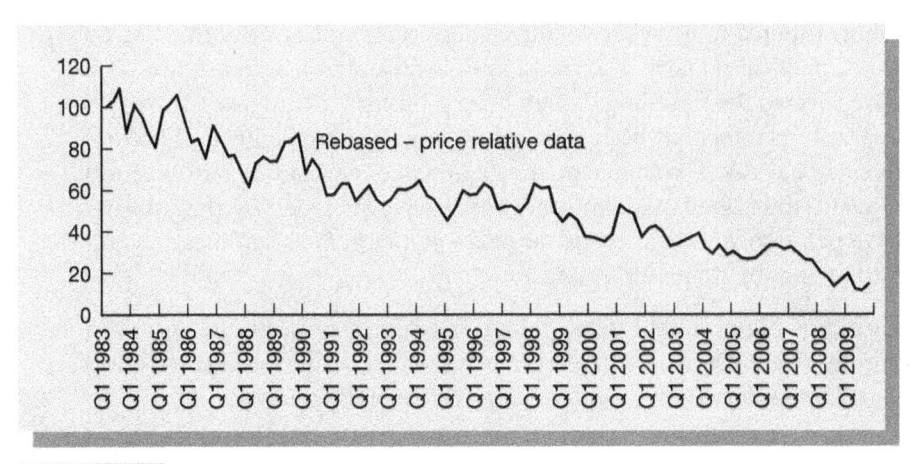

Figure 2.5 The performance of the US airlines sector compared with the US stock market since 1983

Source: Thomson Reuters DataStream

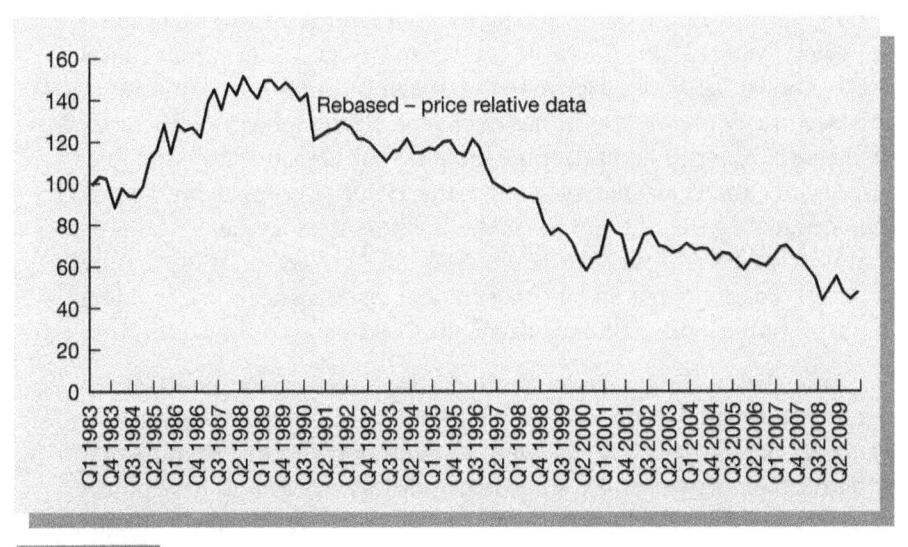

Figure 2.6 The performance of the world airlines sector relative to the world stock market since 1983

Source: Thomson Reuters DataStream

can cause major changes to sector profits. This might account for some of the sector's volatility. Capital employed is very high, although sometimes the aircraft may be leased, not owned (if it is a finance lease this will make no difference).

Demand tends to be cyclical – affected by economic activity but also by global political stability. The cutbacks in company expenditure since 2000 have affected the travelling of high-margin business customers. Growth for low-cost operators has been strong, however. This highlights that barriers to entry have been circumvented by companies with a different business model. These operators and the transparency provided by the internet have put a downward pressure on prices and customers can make significant savings by shopping around.

Therefore, high capital intensity, high fixed costs, overcapacity and price pressure again combine to make the sector a poor home for long-term savings. These returns are disappointing given the risks involved.

Southwest Airlines – a star performer

In a sector known for its highly cyclical nature and wide swings in returns, Southwest Airlines has been profitable in every year since 1973 despite having the lowest fares in the industry. It demonstrates an impressive earnings growth record and consistently high returns on invested capital and equity. While Figure 2.6 demonstrates a sorry tale, Southwest Airlines has been a star performer relative to the overall US market, let alone a very poor sector (see Figure 2.7). It has overcome all the industry difficulties cited above. Founded in 1971, it has provided the blueprint for other low-cost airlines that have emerged since the 1990s. The focus on costs is demonstrated by the fact that it has the lowest cost per available seat mile of any of the US airlines. This is achieved through 'no-frill' flights, only using 737s to economise on procurement and maintenance costs, avoiding the use of hub airports and maximising the fleet's usage.

The airline has also been driven to provide high levels of customer service and customer satisfaction, and has an excellent safety record. Clearly, as Figure 2.7 demonstrates, it has found a simple and effective formula that works for both customers and shareholders. Sales and earnings have grown strongly since the 1970s and the company has delivered excellent returns on equity. These returns historically have been between 18 per cent and 20 per cent before falling to 13.7 per cent in the year post September 11th.

The success of Southwest Airlines highlights what is wrong with many aspects of the industry. The focus on low costs and customer service has clearly created a significant amount of value for shareholders. The company has also been deliberate in choosing which segments of the market and which routes it believes will make money.

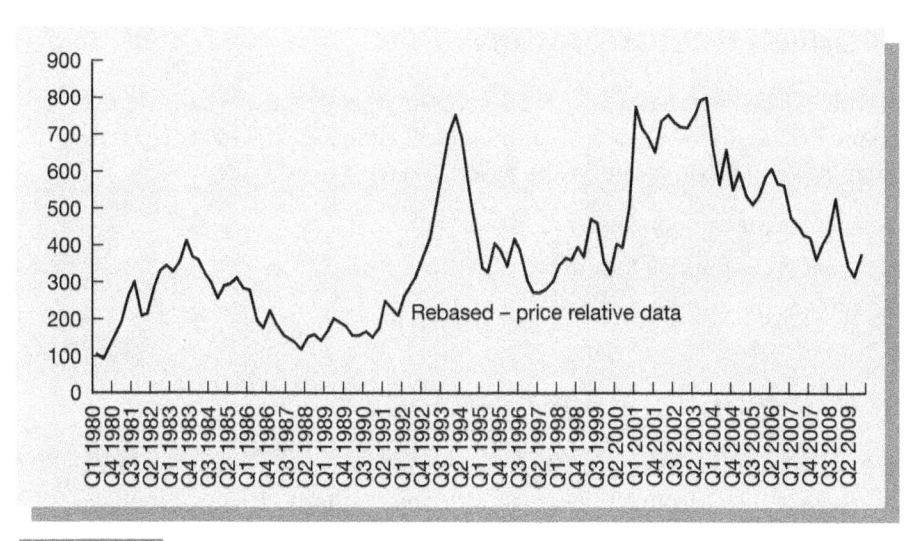

Figure 2.7 The performance of Southwest Airlines compared with the US stock market since 1980

Source: Thomson Reuters DataStream

Top down or bottom up?

This process of examining the prospects and issues facing a sector is often referred to as a 'top-down' approach. Many investing styles will contest this on the grounds that we buy stocks, not sectors. But sector knowledge is a good starting point for providing a framework for understanding the key factors influencing the likely performance of a share. If, from the sector's historic performance and economic characteristics, it is clear that it has rarely made money, you can save money and time by focusing on sectors with more compelling money-making characteristics. Alternatively, if there are certain trends and themes in the sector that appear attractive you will want to focus on those stocks that offer effective ways of playing these trends. Critically, you will be aware of the risks involved in investing in the sector. Porsche and Southwest Airlines clearly demonstrate that money can be made in sectors with a consistent tendency to lose money. However, the company must have special characteristics and a very different approach to the rest of the sector.

Once you understand what drives the sector you can then pursue a 'bottom-up' approach, focusing on the economics and strengths of a particular company. Chapter 4 deals with analysing the individual company.

What drives sector profits?

Having established that it is worth getting to grips with the sector context before drilling down to look at an individual company, the next step is to examine what drives profits in the sector. You need to ask:

- What is the outlook for demand?
- What is the outlook for prices?
- What is the outlook for costs?

What is the outlook for demand?

When considering the outlook for an industry or sector you must of course take into account the overall economic outlook. This will include the prospects for interest rates and consumer and business confidence, all of which will give you an idea of where in the economic cycle we are at present. You should also consider any predicted significant population trends, for example a baby boom or an ageing population, and any other social trends that are likely to change spending habits. Any research company or survey which provides well-thought-out predictions for the future will be widely reported in the financial press because it is exactly this sort of information all investors want in order to assess the prospects for one sector or company in comparison with another.

In assessing demand it is helpful to ask whether you are looking at a cyclical, mature or growth industry. This will immediately give you information about the outlook for demand regarding your target company. A cyclical industry is one that is known to have phases of doing well followed by lean periods; typically these follow the economic cycle or the interest rate cycle, which may be related. For example, the housebuilding industry tends to flourish during times of economic boom or low interest rates, but its investors and management expect it to do less well during a recession or when interest rates rise. This can mean that even if the economy is buoyant, if there is an expectation that interest rates will rise, housing shares may not perform as well as their business performance might warrant.

ask whether you are looking at a cyclical, mature or growth industry

What drives demand?

If the sector is cyclical, it is important to isolate what drives the cycle. In essence this is trying to establish whether company, personal or government expenditure is what determines the overall level of demand.

The economic difficulties at the beginning of the 2000s are interesting in this context. The difficulties experienced by the corporate sector and its high level of indebtedness have seen companies cutting back severely on any discretionary expenditure. This affected a whole range of sectors supplying the corporate sector, whether it be advertising or capital equipment. Conversely, consumers were surprisingly resilient as they used debt and rising asset prices to fund consumption. As a result consumer cyclical stocks have had a relatively encouraging demand backdrop. Similarly, in the UK public expenditure was strong, favouring companies supplying public projects (or public/private ones if funded in that manner).

However, as we entered the 'credit crunch' environment debt became a problem across personal, corporate and government sectors. With the corporate sector heavily indebted and the banks having their own financing problems to resolve, expenditure pressures here may be present for some time. This is likely to affect airlines with exposure to high-margin business travel, hotels, capital goods and machinery, media (with their exposure to advertising) and IT and software – all of which are affected by company spending.

Another factor that will determine how cyclical demand might be is whether the product is a 'high-ticket' or 'low-ticket' item: this means whether the item is costly or inexpensive. A major piece of **capital expenditure (capex)** would be 'high ticket' and likely to be deferred or cancelled in more difficult circumstances – especially when raising funds is so difficult. For the consumer, a car or new kitchen might be deemed high ticket while going out for a pizza might be deemed low ticket. In difficult economic conditions one would expect high-ticket areas to be especially vulnerable.

Where in the cycle are we?

If you are considering investing in a cyclical industry, you need to know at which point in the cycle the industry currently stands. This will give a good guide to the outlook for demand. How can you tell? If the sector's operating margins are very low and there have been several years of falling revenues, with prices depressed and poor demand, it is likely that the sector is close to the bottom of its cycle. Conversely, if margins are high and income (or revenue) is growing rapidly, it is likely that the industry is either at or approaching the top of its cycle.

Pinpointing the moment when the trend turns is by far the hardest part of the analysis for professional and small investors alike. Reading the cycle is not straightforward. In addition the sector may have 'structural' problems. These can include industry overcapacity, oversupply in the market, the impact of new entrants and problems among the customer base. All of these factors may mean that price, demand or profits do not recover when the economy or demand does and the share price continues to languish. The cyclical problems are prolonged.

The current situation is especially difficult, with debates about when and how sustainable any economic recovery will be given how much debt there is throughout the economy. This is compounded by the banks' financial position, which makes it challenging for them to increase lending to an economy that is already over-geared and where defaults are on a rising trend. It may take some time for this debt to unwind – for the 'de-leveraging' process to take place – so the economy can resume more normal conditions.

A *mature* industry is one in which investors expect steady demand (for its products or services) at all phases of the economic cycle but where the capacity for strong growth in the overall market is unlikely. The industry is likely to grow in line with, or a little below, **gross domestic product (GDP)**.

Examples of a mature industry in the UK would be food manufacturing or tobacco. Stable or gently growing profits over the whole of the economic cycle can be very useful, particularly during a recession. Mature industries are often good cash generators, which should mean a steady dividend. The strategic deployment of that cash flow will be a major issue at the stock-specific level.

A *growth* industry is one that is experiencing a significant increase in the demand for its products. The growth of the industry will considerably outstrip the growth of GDP. Often this is a young industry offering a new service or product, for example the mobile phone industry in the 1990s. It is also worth bearing in mind that in some instances growth sectors have turned out to be highly cyclical when the economy turns down. This has certainly been the recent experience of many technology stocks.

Growth industries are immediately attractive to the investor and will generate a lot of press and media comment. But a word of caution: high growth potential often attracts a lot of new companies which invest a lot of capital. This level of competition and high levels of capital investment make it difficult to generate the level of profits initially hoped for.

While the sectors have been broken down into cyclical, mature and growth components, a sector may have all these elements. The telecoms sector, for instance, tends to consist of mature fixed-line, conventional telephone operators as well as high-growth mobile operators.

What is the outlook for prices?

Prices are crucial to the investor. Falling prices are an effective method of destroying wealth. A price reduction comes straight off the 'bottom line', as revenues will fall sharply and so will profits as costs are relatively fixed. Take a company making operating profits of £10 million on turnover of £100 million. If prices fall 10 per cent, revenues will fall to £90 million – with costs unchanged, profit is eliminated. So an understanding of the key determinants of pricing in a sector is crucial.

We have already touched upon drivers of demand which are key elements in determining the outlook for prices. We now need to look at the other issues affecting the supply side and the competitive structure of the industry which influences price.

Porter's five forces

A really useful model to understand the competitive position of a company sector is Porter's five forces model (see Figure 2.8). Developed by Michael Porter in 1978 it provides an excellent framework for appreciating the competitive landscape and the pricing power of the company.

In the centre of the model we can see that competitive rivalry within the sector is a key determinant of pricing.

Competitive rivalry – industry or market structure

This is a major determinant of price. If an industry is fragmented, i.e. there are many small players, there is typically a lot of competition and prices are kept low. In Porter's terms the intensity of competition is high. As an industry matures it tends to go through a period of 'consolidation'. Companies merge with or buy each other, hoping to make it easier for them to keep prices higher and harder for new companies offering the same product or service to break into the market.

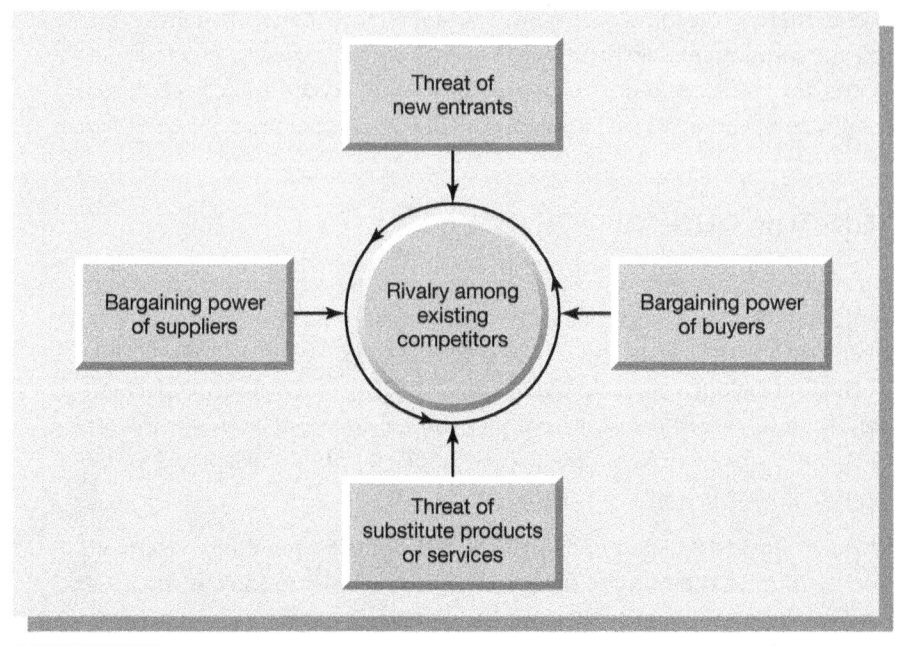

Figure 2.8 Porter's five forces model

Source: Reprinted by permission of *Harvard Business Review*. From 'How competitive forces shape strategy' by Porter, M., March/April. Copyright © 1979 by the Harvard Business School Publishing Corporation, all rights reserved.

Consolidation does not always lead to higher prices. If the larger companies are determined to win an even larger share of the market, they may depress prices to win customers. The extreme example of this is a price war in which prices are cut now to enable a company to dominate the market in the future. *The Times* newspaper famously did this when it cut its cover price to 20 pence at the beginning of the 1990s. Waging a price war costs money and depresses prices across the sector. It is rarely good news for the investor, at least in the short term.

consolidation does not always lead to higher prices

Competitive rivalry – market share aspirations and financial position

It is not just a consolidated market that is important – the participants need to be content with their market share as it is competition for market share that undermines prices. Therefore it depends on the aspirations and objectives of competitors. There may be a consolidated market, but if one of the competitors has a weak balance sheet and a need for cash, they may pursue a volume strategy to generate cash. This may or may not be sensible, but there is a danger it might happen.

Competitive rivalry – international competition

This is another important consideration. In general terms, barriers to foreign competition are coming down, encouraging new players into national markets, a process widely referred to as globalisation. This obviously undermines the market structure and will create a struggle for market share. International companies may have to target market share of the domestic market to make their presence worthwhile and to build a base for a longer-term push.

Some markets are already fairly international, for example car manufacturing, while others are still dominated by national players, for example high street (retail) banking. If foreign competitors are on the horizon it is likely they will depress prices.

Competitive rivalry – capacity position

Industries prone to large swings in demand are likely to see pressure on prices. The fluctuations in demand tend to be aggravated by the sector investing in new capacity at the peak of the market. The lags involved in bringing on stream new facilities invariably mean that demand has fallen by the time the new facility is ready. When demand does turn down, companies are keen to use this new capacity and tend to look for strong volume growth/market share. This inevitably depresses prices. It is perfectly understandable to look for volume – the new factories need to reach an efficient level of operation and this requires volume. In economic terms the 'marginal cost' of production is low so there is a temptation to go for volume as long as it makes a contribution to fixed costs.

This capacity concern can be applied to a whole range of sectors. Chemicals, airlines, insurance and paper are just some sectors that historically have seen capacity coming on stream to undermine pricing and hence sector performance.

Competitive rivalry – nature of the product or service

Clearly, a commodity product that cannot be differentiated will have less pricing power than a more sophisticated product (subject to the competitive conditions/market structure). A more sophisticated product has a greater array of features to compete on – the basis of competition is not just price but genuine performance benefits. Product differentiation should protect the company by building up brand loyalty and should provide a level of satisfaction that prevents consumers from switching to other suppliers.

Barriers to entry

If the structure of an industry changes, so will the outlook for prices. Investors must consider how likely it is that new entrants will appear that could significantly change the picture. Clearly the easier it is, the more fragile the profits of the existing players. There may be a technological development that means that a new competitor can establish an efficient, low-cost alternative to the existing players. The development of the technology to build 'mini-mills' in the US steel industry changed the economics of steel production. New players needed relatively small capital sums to enter the industry, compared with the established players which had huge amounts of capital committed. Similarly, the arrival of the internet has reduced entry costs for many businesses that may have previously required a widespread distribution network to service the client base. Amazon's impact on book retailing is a case in point.

In general, barriers to entry will be determined by such factors as the following:

- *Economies of scale* – the greater the economies of scale, the more difficult it will be for a new entrant. They will need a very large amount of market share to make it worthwhile. Attempting to get this market share would lead to a price war, making the desired returns on investment difficult to achieve.
- *Amount of capital* – generally if vast sums of capital are required to enter an industry, new players will feel less inclined to take risks.
- *Experience and steep learning curve* – in some industries the skills and experience of the industry will deter new entrants. Customers may not want to buy a product or service from a new entrant if there is a lot of technical know-how involved. If the new player were to get it wrong, the customer would be massively inconvenienced.
- *Presence of patents or licences* – these make it extremely difficult for new entrants to copy the existing player(s).
- *Distribution issues* – the existing players may have such strong control over distribution channels that it would be very difficult to get a new product into the market.

- *Product differentiation* – genuine branding differences or performance characteristics will make it difficult for any new players to gain market share.
- *Efficiency/low cost base* – the more efficient and effective the industry is in serving its market, the less likely it will be that new entrants will feel there is an opportunity to take market share.
- *Customer service* – evidence suggests that when levels of customer satisfaction are very low, customers are more likely to try a new supplier.

An interesting and important example of where barriers to entry have been circumvented is the emergence of low-cost airlines. They have made a big impact on the industry and taken a significant degree of market share. If such airlines can lease the aircraft, then the barrier to entry – the capital limit – is avoided: that is, the company can rent the aircraft rather than having to find the substantial sums needed to purchase a very expensive piece of transport. There may have been a feeling that the industry's cost structure was not sufficiently competitive, which meant there was scope to undercut the existing players. Similarly, the level of consumer satisfaction and the value for money equation provided by the existing players may have encouraged the low-cost airlines. If customers were very loyal to the existing players it would have made entering the industry much more challenging.

Threat of substitutes

Competing with a substitute product inevitably puts a limit on the pricing of the company's products. This is especially true if there is a cheaper price but comparable product performance. This may be true for buying books second hand rather than new, for example, or it may be that many people see mobile telephones as a direct substitute for 'fixed-line' telephony. This will then limit the pricing power of fixed-line services as customers will migrate to mobile services.

This then raises the question as to how far the company can differentiate its product or services from the 'substitute' in a real sense. This must mean that the performance is somehow differentiated as being a lot better and the marketing creates a 'brand' that connects with people (see Buffett's comments on Gillette on p. 62).

Bargaining power

Another useful question to consider is who has the bargaining power to determine prices in the industry. This will depend mainly on the relative sizes of the customer and the supplier. The food retail sector sees power rest with the distribution end of the system. Much has been said and written about the ability of the supermarkets to control prices. Companies supplying the food retailers will, in general, have little influence on pricing.

Another important example is the automotive industry. The size of the multinational car manufacturers means they place extremely large contracts which are very important for the supplier to win. These orders may also be placed on an international basis so that the supplier must meet that requirement to be able to fulfil the contract – a contract that will often stipulate that prices will fall on an annual basis over the contract's life.

The price competition for the end product (witness the prices and dealer discounts, including 0 per cent finance offered in the US), however, means that operating margins for the car manufacturers are very low. Accordingly, there is significant pressure on them to reduce costs which will be felt among all their suppliers. The danger for component suppliers is that while they may have to have the infrastructure to be able to supply their customer globally, and a commitment to research and development (R&D) to make the products attractive to the customer, the price received from the customer does not enable them to generate an appropriate return on the extensive assets required or compensate them for the costs involved. Therefore it costs a lot to secure this contract but the pressure on prices may mean that profitability is severely affected. This may not be an attractive situation for an investor.

Where distribution is more fragmented and customers are placing relatively small orders with a limited number of suppliers, the power may rest with the manufacturers.

Regulatory issues

For some sectors, such as utilities, there may not be any direct competition. To prevent monopoly profits the government may restrict pricing freedom by imposing a cap on price or restrictions on the returns the industry can generate. This is done by appointing a regulator who will determine the prices and returns that the industry can achieve in the absence of competitive pressures.

Summary

From the investor's point of view there are clear advantages to having 'pricing power'. This is arguably becoming even more important (and even rarer?) given the twin concerns of globalisation and deflation.

What is the outlook for costs?

Given the impact of globalisation and an increasingly competitive environment, tight cost control and an ability to manage costs effectively are a key requirement for any company. In addition, a much stronger position is established where a company can differentiate its product so price is not the major consideration when customers buy.

The costs an industry faces are often broken down into three categories: variable, fixed and sales.

Variable cost

The cost of raw materials is a *variable* cost because it will rise and fall depending on supply and demand in the raw materials' market. Where variable costs are a large proportion of the overall costs, the investor needs information about the outlook for prices of the raw material in question. For example, the plastic pipe industry will see its profits significantly affected by movements in PVC prices, so some research into the outlook for PVC production would be useful. Fuel costs are often a significant proportion of overall costs and may need watching. Rising fuel costs adversely impact the airlines sector. A key issue is whether these cost increases can be passed on to customers, which will be dependent on several factors.

Fixed costs

One of the most important factors an investor needs to understand is what proportion of an industry's costs are *fixed*. In a sector where fixed costs are a high proportion of overall costs, small movements in the volume of goods (or services) sold will have a relatively big effect on profits. One aspect to watch out for is a tendency for a management with high fixed costs to adopt a strategy of selling large quantities of goods (high volume) to spread the costs. To do this it may be tempted to drive down the price. However, competitors may retaliate to regain market share, leading to a price war in which only the consumer wins.

In some sectors, such as the service sector, wage costs can be a key fixed cost. If there is a scarcity of the skills needed to perform this service, costs may rise sharply. An obvious example is the football sector, where shareholders have suffered as players have prospered.

The balance between fixed and variable costs is an important relationship. This determines what is called the 'operational gearing' of the sector and tells you the relationship between a change in revenues (price × volume) and the impact on profit. For high fixed cost companies, say those involved in manufacturing, a small fall in revenue will have a significant impact on profit. A 5 per cent revenue fall might lead to anything up to a 40–50 per cent fall in profits. The impact is greater if the fall in revenues is driven by a reduction in price. There is a fuller discussion of operational gearing on p. 219.

> the balance between fixed and variable costs is an important relationship

Sales cost

The third main element of costs is *sales* costs. These are important in assessing the cost structure of a sector to get a feel for what proportion of overall costs needs to be spent on advertising and marketing, or research and development. These costs can be high when supporting an existing brand/consumer good is important, when new product launches are a regular feature or in a start-up situation. Many internet companies, which had relatively low fixed and variable costs, had a very high level of sales costs.

These costs are *discretionary* costs – they can be increased or decreased as the company sees fit. In a recessionary period a company may be able to cut back on sales and marketing without severely undermining its long-term competitive position. However, the company needs to be sure that it will not lose competitive advantage.

The net effect of demand, prices and costs is to determine the profits and returns of the sector – which is what you are investing for.

General economic and stock market factors – how do they affect the sector?

Defensive v growth sectors

Knowing where we are in the economic cycle and the outlook for economic activity is an important factor in determining the attractiveness of a sector. A period of rapid and sustained economic growth, such as that which occurred during the mid- to late 1990s, will tend to favour growth-oriented stocks. This was indeed a period in which growth stocks outperformed **value stocks**, with the value stocks tending to occupy the more cyclical or low-growth areas of the economy.

The deteriorating economic environment, especially for companies supplying the corporate sector, has severely undermined the attractions of growth. The extent of the indebtedness facing the corporate, consumer and government sectors, combined with the poor position of the banks, means that the shape of any economic recovery is even more difficult to predict than normal.

This has been an environment for more 'defensive' stocks, i.e. stocks that are traditionally considered to be not materially affected by the economic cycle. They should face a steady outlook for demand and prices. Often they are focused on the domestic economy and not subject to pressures from exchange rates/imports. Examples of defensive stocks include: food manufacturing and food retailing; pharmaceuticals, utilities (note that political/regulatory risk is important in these two areas); and tobacco (where political/litigation risk is a major concern). These areas have on the whole been very good for investment since 2000, with tobacco a notable winner. The issue then becomes, given their excellent performance over recent years, whether the 'defensive' element is already in the price.

The difficulty for these areas is that demand tends not to grow as the economy/people's incomes grow – they become a lower proportion of household expenditure and the economy. It is difficult to see long-term growth for these businesses. Nonetheless, in difficult economic circumstances their attractions are clear. The low growth is outweighed by stability. In addition, the financial attractions of being in a defensive or mature area of the economy can work to shareholders' advantage. Strong **balance sheets** and cash flow can either be used to invest in new areas of growth – for example emerging markets – or be returned to shareholders through dividends or share buy-backs.

There may also be specific difficulties for these sectors that undermine their defensive characteristics. This includes the purchasing power of the big food retail customers, which has caused margin pressure on food manufacturers.

A 'defensive growth' play, which is where growth is not dependent on the performance of the economy (e.g. in pharmaceuticals), may also look interesting in such an environment. Demand for pharmaceuticals is underwritten by an ageing population, the fact that using drugs is a much more cost-effective solution than hospitalisation and the need to alleviate illness and disease. These trends are relatively independent of what is happening to GDP. Risks tend to focus on the failure of drugs to gain regulatory approval, the number of drugs coming off patent, the length of time drugs spend in R&D, the recent lack of 'blockbusters' and the need for governments to control health care costs, which may lead to pricing pressure.

Impact of interest rates

Falling interest rates will affect sectors in different ways. Housebuilders, for example, tend to have a strong correlation with interest rate trends, though in the current climate it is the availability of credit rather than its price that is the issue. See Figure 2.9 for various buy and sell options in an economic slowdown.

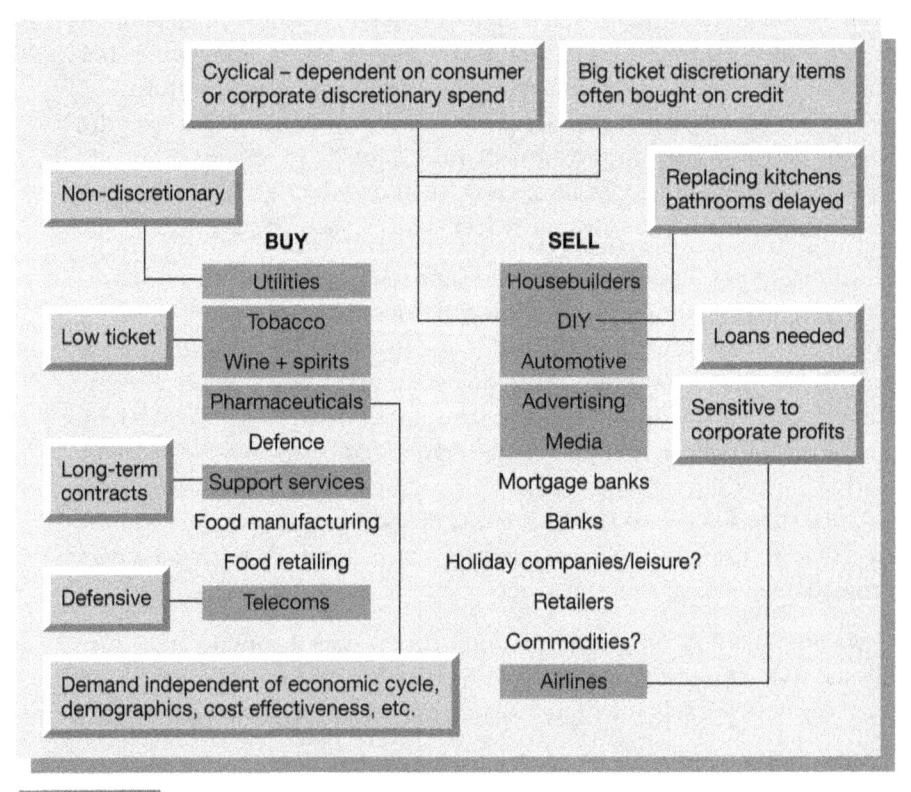

Figure 2.9 Sectors to buy or sell when interest rates rise (or no credit is available) and the economy slows down

BUY
- Non-discretionary
  - Utilities
  - Low ticket
    - Tobacco
    - Wine + spirits
  - Pharmaceuticals
  - Defence
  - Long-term contracts
    - Support services
  - Food manufacturing
  - Food retailing
  - Defensive
    - Telecoms

Demand independent of economic cycle, demographics, cost effectiveness, etc.

SELL
- Cyclical – dependent on consumer or corporate discretionary spend
- Big ticket discretionary items often bought on credit
- Replacing kitchens bathrooms delayed
  - Housebuilders
  - DIY — Loans needed
  - Automotive
  - Advertising — Sensitive to corporate profits
  - Media
  - Mortgage banks
  - Banks
  - Holiday companies/leisure?
  - Retailers
  - Commodities?
  - Airlines

The performance of cyclical stocks depends on the trend in the cycle and the trend in interest rates. While cuts in interest rates should benefit a cyclical stock, it may be that demand does not revive or industry overcapacity threatens pricing – the structural difficulties we referred to earlier. However, there is a 'Catch 22' situation for cyclicals with respect to falling interest rates. A cut in interest rates is good for cyclicals for the following reasons:

- Profits are very sensitive to GDP and falling rates should stimulate economic growth in time.
- Often these companies are highly geared financially so their interest burden is likely to be reduced.

Be aware though that the reason interest rates are coming down may also be important. If interest rates are cut because the economy is slowing rapidly and inflation is under control, this may well see volumes and pricing come under pressure. Deflation has been a particular concern to the manufactured sector for some time. Globalisation and the transparency created by the internet have been competitive and deflationary forces for many internationally traded goods.

This concern is particularly acute in the current environment – a downturn characterised by falling company expenditure, excess supply, inflation well under control and prices for many products on a downward trend. On the cost side these have been squeezed by higher raw material commodity and energy prices.

Growth

Falling interest rates are positive for growth stocks as they reduce the rate at which future earnings are discounted. Historically, growth stocks (and especially 'cyclical growth' stocks such as software) have performed well coming out of a bear market. This might suggest that good-quality, lower-risk growth stocks with some GDP sensitivity would be an excellent way of playing the current market recovery. This is, of course, subject to the caveat that this economic cycle is very different and overcapacity exists in many cyclical growth areas that may weaken the earnings recovery this time round.

The investment style guide (p. 301) provides more on the pros and cons of defensive and growth stocks/sectors.

Global sectors and currency

Increasingly, due to globalisation and the consolidation of many sectors, it is becoming less and less appropriate to think about sectors on a national basis. Sectors are being driven by events and developments all over the world. The technology, media and telecoms (TMT), pharmaceuticals, oil, automotive and chemicals sectors, to name but a few, are all increasingly international. This has profound implications when examining trends and valuing these sectors (which we will turn to later). As a matter of interest the investing institutions have adapted to this environment by increasingly looking at sectors on a global basis (or at the very least a pan-European basis). Many of the larger US investing institutions are already structured along these lines.

With this perspective, looking at and/or comparing GlaxoSmithKline and AstraZeneca in the UK context may not be appropriate when there may be more attractive, better-value opportunities in the US or European pharmaceuticals sector. This may be important if it is a sector with overseas exposure. Different constituents will have differing exposures to the various regions. This may well be relevant to your decision in that you may feel that prospects are better in, say, Europe than in the US. It will also be important in terms of the impact of currency movements.

The impact of currency

When assessing the impact of currency it needs to be established how currency movements affect the company or the sector. There are two key ways in which profits are affected by currency movements, normally referred to as the translation and transaction effects.

The translation effect

This is straightforward as it is simply the impact of a rising or falling domestic currency and how it affects the recording of the profits of an overseas subsidiary. Let us take a company reporting its profits in sterling with a substantial part of its earnings from European subsidiaries. If the euro is very weak, profits will be lower when translated into sterling. Conversely, if the euro were to strengthen, profits might rise.

These movements may be mitigated by a company's hedging policies. It may be that the company has a lot of euro-denominated debt. Then the servicing cost of that debt would fall, which would reduce the impact of the currency depreciation. The company might also enter into contracts in the currency markets by buying or selling the currency in the futures market.

The impact of translation on a share's value should be relatively short-lived as the movement may be a one-off boost (or reduction) to the company's profits. In that sense the improvement is a low-quality source of earnings (see earnings quality on p. 13). If you choose to gain overseas exposure to a particular country or region you should do it on the basis that the prospects for volumes and prices in those regions are attractive.

The transaction effect

The transaction effect is far more complex and can have a profound impact on the value of the business. This is because it affects the competitive position of the company. It also affects those sectors which deal in internationally traded goods and sectors. Manufacturing sectors such as engineering and automotive are the most obviously affected.

If the domestic currency strengthens, imports are more competitive and exports less so. This leads to a decision for the domestic producer – whether to lower prices and protect market share or to try to maintain prices and margins. This is a difficult decision and will depend on a number of factors, such as how big a threat import competition is going to be and whether importers, distributors or consumers will be attracted to these products. It may be that increased promotional spending will highlight the benefit of the domestic product or will try to get customers to focus on non-price areas of competitiveness. This marketing will reduce margins at least in the short term, but with the obvious intention of protecting longer-term market share and seeing off the import threat.

If prices are cut, the impact on operating margins and profits will be severe. If volumes fall, profits will also fall but perhaps by not as much as allowing prices to fall. However, as always, it is not as easy as that. Once market share is allowed to slip, there is the danger that importers will use this base to take even more market share.

Many of these issues are of a long term-nature and will be more costly if there is a prolonged strengthening (weakening) of the domestic currency. In a worst case scenario this could see the progressive erosion of market share for the domestic companies.

As the transaction effect could have such a profound impact on sales, long-term market share, operating profits and operating margins of a sector, it clearly could also have an enormous effect on its valuation.

Summary

The impact of the current economic downturn upon certain sectors has been very marked. Those sections of the economy exposed to interest rate rises and slowing economic activity such as banking, automotive, steel, housing, business travel and media (through advertising cut-backs) have been particularly hit. This is especially true when we are talking about 'big ticket' items (a house, a car, new kitchen or bathroom) that are financed with a loan. Conversely, low-ticket items that are 'defensive' such as utilities, food retail, alcohol and tobacco have held up relatively well.

Therefore having an appreciation of how the economy impacts on a sector is vital. This sets the 'macro' context within which a company is operating and will determine the amount of activity in a sector that will influence how much it sells (volume) and at what price.

The other key aspect to be aware of is the competitive structure of the industry. Using Porter's five forces model we can get a strong sense of the likely pricing and margin environment for the company. This model also allows us to analyse how those forces are changing or may change in the future: Are new competitors emerging? Are customers and suppliers consolidating? Is a major player looking for market share or to generate cash?

Taken together, demand, prices and costs determine profits. Understanding the outlook for each of these elements in your chosen industry will give you a strong background against which to begin the analysis of your target company.

SECTOR CHECKLIST

Demand

- Is it a growth, mature or cyclical sector?
- How do movements in interest rates and GDP affect it?
- If cyclical, is it the business (capital expenditure) or consumer cycle that drives demand/profits?
- How discretionary is this expenditure?
- Is it 'high ticket' or 'low ticket'?

Pricing

- How consolidated is the sector?
- What are the barriers to entry and how high are they?
- How powerful are its customers?

- Is there overcapacity and/or fierce struggles for market share?
- Is there significant international competition in the sector?

Costs
- How operationally geared is the sector?
- Are trends in raw material costs likely to make a big hole in sector profits?
- Are employment costs a key component and are the skills scarce?

General economy and stock market influences
- Is it a defensive or growth sector ... how will it perform in difficult economic environments?
- How is it affected by interest rates?
- Are there structural factors such as overcapacity as well as cyclical factors that need to be considered?
- Is the sector dominated by a few major companies?

Is it a global sector?
- How do currency movements affect the sector?
- Does this impact on the translation of overseas profit or on the competitiveness of the sector (transaction effect)?
- Is political and/or regulatory risk a feature?

3

Management and strategy

What topics are covered in this chapter?

- Why are management and strategy so important?
- What is the company's market position?
- What is the company's strategy?
- What is the quality of management?
- Is its corporate governance best practice?
- Does management need to change and will it make a difference?
- Strategic issues – disposals, mergers and acquisitions: do they add value?
- Why deals are done
- Types of deal being done
- Evaluating the deal: what to look for
- Why deals do not add value for shareholders
- What is the market's reaction to the deal?
- Summary
- Checklist

Why are management and strategy so important?

When buying a share in a company you are essentially buying a stake in the competitive position of the business – if the business is competitive and selling products and services people want to buy then the shares have a very good chance of making money. This position will have been attained by management over time and the key role of strategy is to 'sustain the competitive position of the business'. Therefore there is a clear link between 'shares' – buying a stake in the competitive position of the business – and 'strategy' – which is all about how that competitive position is maintained and enhanced over time.

With all the changes that occur over time, management's ability to read developments in the economy and sector it operates in and then position the business accordingly is crucial. When asked to cite on an unprompted basis the most important influence on their investment decisions, 70 per cent of investors cited management.[1] So can management consistently take decisions that maintain and enhance the competitive position of the business?

Sustainable competitive advantage is the essence of strategy. Michael Porter comments that: 'the job of the strategist is to understand and cope with competition.'[2] This will involve a combination of decisions around developing the top line – generating volume and price growth to protect and drive revenue. This requires that the company has both a clear customer value proposition regarding what makes its products or services distinctive so that they really appeal to customers, and the resources and capability to consistently deliver on that proposition. This may be by creating an effective brand or new product that gives a real edge over competitors.

The key then is to ensure that competitors cannot compete – by establishing 'barriers to entry' (as discussed on p. 45 as part of Porter's five forces model) or what Warren Buffett refers to as a 'moat' around the business: 'In business I look for economic castles protected by unbreachable moats.'[3] This has led to Buffett investing in companies such as Proctor and Gamble (P&G), Coca-Cola and Gillette (until its takeover by P&G). His comments

---

[1] MORI Poll (2005) Based on 145 interviews between June and July 2005.
[2] Porter, M.E. (2008) 'The Five Competitive Forces that Shape Strategy', *Harvard Business Review*, January.
[3] The 2007 letter to shareholders explains his views on 'moats'.

on Gillette are interesting and reveal much about Porter's five forces model and the competitive importance of the moat:

> There are 20 to 21 billion razor blades used in the world in a year. Thirty per cent of those are Gillettes, but 60 per cent by value are Gillettes. They have 90 per cent market share in some countries. Now when something has been around as long as shaving and you find a company that has both that kind of innovation in terms of developing better razors all the time, plus the distribution power, and the position in people's minds ... here's something you do every day ... and get a terrific shaving experience. Now men are not inclined to shift around when they get that kind of situation.[4]

Therefore, in this sense, strategy is investing in widening and deepening the 'moat'. This will not only give the company pricing power but also crucially allow it to defend itself against the structural shifts that will inevitably happen in any market over time. This very much ties in with Porter's analysis of competitive advantage. In his *Harvard Business Review* article[5] in January 2008 marking the 30th anniversary of the first publication of the five forces model, he argues that understanding industry structure is crucial for investors as well as managers. Analysing the forces that drive sustained profitability, the competitive landscape and the changes that are likely to happen is far more important than focusing on short-term projections of earnings.

Combining the wide and deep moat with low costs will lead to superior returns on sales and assets and this will drive the share price higher over time. (The top management team keeping a consistent eye on costs is another obvious source of competitive advantage. The less scope for differentiating a product the more crucial low costs will be.)

Crucially, the 'moat' reduces risks, improves returns and improves the quality of earnings because of the pricing power the company has. As the Valuation Villa suggests, this will lead to a higher valuation for the company's shares.

The key components

So what are the key components of a good strategy? In effect it is a road map of where we are, where we want to be and how we are going to get there. In *Good To Great* (2001) Jim Collins found that those companies

---

[4] Lowe, J.C. (1997) *Warren Buffett Speaks*, New York: Wiley, p. 151.
[5] See note 2.

that went on to great success had real clarity about what they were doing. He comments that all companies have strategy – the key to the great companies is the 'simplicity' of their strategy.[6] The simple concept behind the strategy is then used as a frame of reference for all decisions, making it much easier for the strategy to be implemented. Importantly, great companies were never motivated by fear (competition, looking foolish, others having short-term success, etc.) but by a very clear sense of what they wanted to create. By creating this the company will make money for shareholders.

Interestingly, in great companies there was an absence of talk about competitive strategy.

Collis and Rukstad in the *Harvard Business Review*[7] summarise the issues around strategy very effectively. The essential components are as follows:

- *Mission* – why the company exists, its purpose.
- *Values* – what the company believes in and how it will behave, its culture and priorities.
- *Vision* – what it wants to be.
- *Strategy* – what the competitive game plan will be.

The strategy component itself breaks down into three elements:

1. *Objective* – what is the company trying to achieve and what is the end goal?
2. *Scope* – clarity on what the company will do (and what will it not do) regarding type of customer or product offering, geographic location and vertical integration (where the company may be involved in different stages of the supply chain).
3. *Advantage* – what is the competitive advantage, how does the company excel and how will it be sustained? There are two key parts to this: the customer value proposition (what makes the company distinctive in the marketplace?); and its unique characteristics, capabilities, resources or activities that allow the company to deliver that proposition. This is what will create the 'moat' and ensure it is very difficult for competitors to take market share.

---

[6] Collins, J. (2001) *Good to Great*, New York: HarperCollins, p. 39. Copyright © 2001 by Jim Collins. Reprinted with permission from Jim Collins.

[7] Collis, D. and Rukstad, M.G. (2008) 'Can You Say What Your Strategy Is?', *Harvard Business Review*, April.

Having a clear mission and a defining set of values creates a level of clarity that helps to drive the business forward. These components contribute to the competitive position of the business and its long-term strategic success by driving differentiation, brand development, innovation and new product introduction. Clarity about what the company does well, for whom (a real insight into the customer and what they need) and what is needed to excel makes decision making much easier and more effective. Resources are then allocated to support the development of these unique attributes to ensure the company remains competitive. The vision and values help motivate and create momentum for management and employees alike as well as contributing to the development of clear recruitment policies.

For many companies, having clarity about mission and values delivers an effective set of management principles that helps define not only the direction of the business but how business is going to be done and the appropriate behaviours necessary to fulfil the company's objectives. This creates an ethical blueprint for the business. If we contrast the approach and fortunes of companies such as Apple and Enron we can clearly see the difference that clarity about mission and values makes. Indeed, in *Good to Great* Jim Collins comments: 'Enduring great companies preserve their core values and purpose while their business strategies and operating practices endlessly adapt to a changing world.'[8]

values create an ethical blueprint for the business

This enduring greatness very clearly derives from an effective implementation of the mission, values, vision and strategy hierarchy above. This structure is used by Steve Jobs, co-founder of Apple, when he asks questions like 'Who is Apple?', 'What does it stand for?', 'Where does it fit in this world?' Apple's core belief is that 'we believe that people with passion can change the world for the better'.[9] Accordingly, Apple is a company that 'does not make boxes' (which would make it a very commodity-oriented business competing on price) but a company with 'a passion for doing things differently'. As a result it is one of the top brands in the world.

Therefore, while it may seem somewhat abstract talking about 'mission' and 'values' when examining the potential for making money from an investment, the absence of values (or presence of values that were detrimental to society and reflected callous disregard of others) was a major factor that led to the demise of Enron. The self-styled 'smartest guys in the room' had a value around demonstrating how clever they were and, as the

---

[8] See note 6, p. 195.
[9] Steve Jobs on YouTube, 'Being Meaningful'.

phrase suggests, all their attention was directed to themselves – they were inward looking and not connecting with the consumer. This 'cleverness' also extended to wanting the numbers to 'look' good to reflect their smartness so the accounting policies were 'flexed' to support that illusion. According to the 'Smartest Guys in the Room' documentary,[10] one of the philosophies of the senior management team was 'earnings before scruples'.

Another very successful and highly regarded company that implements its mission and values effectively is Proctor and Gamble who looks to improve the lives of the world's consumers with high-quality products that represent good value. This then leads to a company with a very innovative approach to consumer products.

The mission and vision statements of many companies can be very pedestrian and cloaked in the language of large corporations. But as we have seen, when thought through and genuinely believed in they can have a very motivating impact and create great results. However, putting mission and values into action is vital and, as is often quoted, 'vision becomes hallucination without implementation'.

Given the importance of management and strategy as described above we now need to establish how well management and strategic issues are being addressed in companies that you are interested in.

You need to ask yourself:

- What is the company's market position?
- What is the company's strategy?
- What is the quality of management?
- Is its corporate governance best practice?
- Does management need to change and will it make a difference?
- Strategy – disposals, mergers and acquisitions: do they add value?

We will consider each of these questions in turn.

What is the company's market position?

Having looked at the factors influencing the sector, the company's market position is another key consideration when assessing how well a company is likely to do in the future. The company's current market and competi-

---

[10] Director Alex Gibney, 2005.

tive position needs to be evaluated before assessing its plans. Investors should expect every company to have a believable strategy for growth as a means of increasing shareholder value. However, such plans should not be taken at face value. It is worth considering the following questions:

- What is the company's market position?
- Is it gaining or losing market share?
- What is the company's profile?
- What is its strategy?

We could then drill down further and consider more detailed questions, such as:

- Is it a market leader?
- How consolidated or fragmented is the market?
- Is it a low-cost producer?
- Is there a single customer that dominates sales?
- What are the barriers to entry? How might they be broken down?
- What is the record for innovation and introducing new products?
- Does the company have the ability to move into new markets?

Examining market position

Is your target company one of the top three in the industry? If so it should be able to influence industry trends and prices. An ability to influence prices is a huge advantage and should secure both higher profits and a greater degree of stability. The issues surrounding pricing power/profitability are discussed elsewhere (see p. 8). It is worth stressing that barriers to entry and a high degree of product differentiation (branding) are likely to establish a strong economic franchise or 'moat' that should face little threat. The sustainability of this franchise is critical to long-term share performance and how we value the shares.

Conversely, where there is little product differentiation (a commodity product), price wars or struggles for market share may well be a feature. This tends to be avoided only if the market is highly consolidated (very few players) and the market shares have reached a level where the players or other interested parties believe they have a natural market share. The competitive position of the company and its ability to translate this into high margins will very much depend on the market structure.

As discussed when examining the prospects for the sector, margins are likely to be threatened if there is a customer that accounts for a large proportion of sales or that is such a significant purchaser that they can bargain down prices aggressively.

Smaller companies may face some disadvantages in terms of pricing power but alternatively may be more nimble at exploiting industry trends. You should also consider whether the company has a track record as an industry innovator. Particularly if it is a large organisation, you will want to know whether it can still move quickly to meet changing market circumstances. A track record of introducing new products/services and responding to developments in the marketplace is a crucial indicator of the company's ability to look outwards to the needs of the market. (You may want to see whether you can establish what proportion of sales comes from products that were not part of the portfolio say five years ago.)

> consider whether the company has a track record as an industry innovator

Being a low-cost player is also a key element of a company's market position. Again this is one of the issues identified by Warren Buffett when he cites that management should 'exert tight cost control at all times'[11] (see management culture, p. 74). Again this can be crucial not only for competitiveness but also for deterring new entrants. If potential competitors can see that a major player has an inefficient cost structure it may well encourage them to think they can serve the market in a more cost-competitive way and establish a strong market position relatively quickly.

Is it gaining or losing market share?

Winning market share can be a very obvious way of growing the business (assuming that the company does not have a monopoly position). This is particularly true of smaller or medium-sized companies. The danger is of course that competitors react aggressively and a price war ensues (the newspaper market in the UK has gone through various price wars, for example). This can be costly for an industry and ruinous for investors.

There can be a lot of sense in building market share on a long-term basis. To do this the company needs to be a low-cost producer and financially strong enough to take a long-term view. The US computer equipment company Dell has had a clear policy of building market share by being a low-cost producer. Being a dominant player when the market has matured can be a very attractive position.

---

[11] See note 4.

Market share can also be developed by focusing on segments of the market that offer higher growth potential. Again the culture of the company is important here. It needs to be very market aware and focused, enabling it to exploit new trends and developments in the market, a move which is far less likely to cause a price war. If the segments of the market are performing well and have slightly different requirements, addressing these needs may even command higher prices and margins. So a combination of new product development and changing product mix can be an effective way of both gaining share and enhancing margins.

Growth from the gaining of market share and new product introductions is sometimes referred to as 'organic growth'. Similarly, when people refer to 'like for like' expansion they are also referring to organic growth. Essentially this means growth from existing operations and is used to differentiate it from growth achieved via acquisition.

The risks attached to growth by acquisition tend to be much higher than organic growth, so the market tends to value organic growth more highly than acquisition-led growth. (The risks and issues surrounding acquisitions are detailed on p. 109.)

What is the company's profile?

A good way of quickly getting to grips with the company is to get a feel for its overall profile. By this I mean a balance of operational and financial characteristics that will determine whether it is likely to make money. Some of these factors will be determined by the characteristics of the sector.

The following is a brief list of questions you may want to consider.

- Is it a one-product company?
- Is it focused or diversified?
- What is the geographic profile of earnings and is one of those regions about to run into trouble?
- Does the business generate cash?
- What is the balance between cash-generating and cash-absorbing businesses?
- Is there a significant need for capital expenditure (**capex**) in the business?
- What is the relationship between growth and replacement capex?
- Is the company growing organically or through acquisition?

Product and divisional mix of profits

If the company is reliant on one product, this can be both an advantage and a disadvantage. Thus depends on the strength of that product and its economic characteristics, such as the degree of market dominance, quality of the brand, low-cost production and barriers to entry. Focus has been increasingly seen as an advantage over the past decade or so as companies increasingly stick to what they know. The downside is if the product becomes out of date due to technological change, becomes unfashionable or is subject to a competitive threat from another product or service. Profits are likely to come under severe pressure in this situation, what the famous industrialist Lord Weinstock referred to as 'a niche becoming a tomb'. Again this stresses the need to know the economic and market position of the company.

Analysing the divisional breakdown of profits (normally Note 1 to the report and accounts) is important. This will help establish how focused or diversified the company is. It is worth getting a sense of whether the activities are related to each other and if so how. If the skills required for the divisions vary enormously, does management have the requisite skill set to manage this portfolio effectively? The divisional mix of profits will also point out some strategic issues. If a division is a small percentage of profit and it has been owned for some years, what is the case for keeping it? Similarly, you will want to check the growth, risk and quality characteristics of each division as this will mean that each one will be valued differently. You also want to examine the returns of each division to see if they are **adding value**. If the returns are low, again we must question why the division is part of the company.

Geography – well positioned for growth?

The geographic profile of earnings may be important as prospects may vary between different countries. Is the company over-dependent on one country and does this country offer reasonable prospects? If the business is cyclical this can be crucial. The building company RMC had a strong position in the German building industry, the largest in Europe. This was a major advantage in the late 1980s and early 1990s as the UK market was suffering from weak volumes and prices, and Germany was enjoying a reunification boom. However, from the mid-1990s German construction activity entered a downturn that lasted for many years. With pressure on prices as well as volumes, the business became scarcely profitable.

In the first of these periods RMC shares were a reasonably good investment, but they became a very poor one in the second period. RMC allocated a lot of capital to these German operations when things were going well; arguably it should have been diversifying into other regions. This is not being wise after the event but illustrates that the geographic profile of earnings and how those markets are performing will directly affect the performance of your investment. It is also worth stressing that the cyclicality of the business, its operational gearing and the sensitivity to price falls are all economic characteristics that need to be taken into account.

A good spread of regional/country operations may be an effective way of diversifying risk as you are not dependent on the fortunes of any one market.

a position overseas may be relevant to ensure a lower cost base

Increasingly in internationally competitive markets a position overseas may be relevant to ensure a lower cost base. In the case of a company with a number of overseas subsidiaries, it is important to check what its market position is in each market.

Presence in emerging markets can provide good long-term growth potential, but earnings can also be affected severely if the country runs into trouble. It can take a long time to build up an effective position in these markets and results can be disappointing for a number of years. In the initial stages the company may generate very low returns. However, the emergence of the so-called BRIC countries (Brazil, Russia, India and China) has seen these regions and other areas of Asia (excluding Japan) being the most important drivers of the world's economic growth. For many companies operating in mature western markets exposure to the growth potential of these markets is very important long term. Of course for many companies there will be very low-cost and effective competition from these parts of the world and concerns regarding overcapacity as they invest aggressively in developing their businesses. Finally, with respect to the company's geographic profile you will need to consider the influence of currency, as discussed on p. 56.

Cash generation and investment

As well as examining the geographic profile, you may want to consider the balance of cash-generating and absorbing businesses. You are trying to get a feel for whether there are businesses that have a good market position with good margins which consequently generate a lot of cash (sometimes referred to as 'cash cows'). While attractive, these businesses may not offer any growth. Therefore, if there are other products or areas that offer good growth potential, cash can be allocated to these to improve the growth outlook. As ever, with any investment it is not just the growth but the return it generates that is important.

The need for capital expenditure within the business also needs to be determined as it influences many other elements, such as the dividend, that affect you as a shareholder. This might be detected by looking at the relationship between capex and **depreciation**. If capex has been systematically and significantly below the depreciation charge, this may suggest the company has been underinvesting in assets, which may well catch the company out at some stage. It may become less and less competitive as it uses equipment that is progressively more inefficient. The risk then is that a massive catch-up investment programme is needed and that all the available cash and management time will go into this project. Then regaining lost market share can be a difficult process.

The **capex/depreciation ratio** can also be a useful way of determining company growth. If the capex number is significantly higher than the depreciation ratio, this can be an indicator of potential growth. Again it needs to be considered in the context of what the company is investing in and what the returns are likely to be.

Organic or acquisition-led growth?

The other aspect of the company's growth profile to monitor is the extent to which growth is achieved by acquisition rather than organic growth. The reliance on acquisitions for growth can be an issue of potential concern. The record of acquisitions adding value is on the whole poor (see p. 109). Ideally one would like to see high organic growth rates supplemented by low-risk, in-fill acquisitions that improve the company's market position and range of capabilities.

What is the company's strategy?

Top management teams make strategic decisions. They decide on the allocation of resources – capital and personnel – that will deliver shareholders the best returns. This involves deciding which divisions should be kept, which will prosper and which are best disposed of. Getting this right is crucial in making money for shareholders.

Supporting the right divisions with appropriate capital expenditure and investing in product support and R&D should generate returns on investment that reward shareholders for taking on the risks involved. The returns generated from these decisions will influence share prices and consequently return on investment.

Key to longer-term value

The allocation of capital to add value for shareholders will drive the share price in the long term. There is of course an assumption that the current portfolio is performing effectively and is run properly.

If a discounted cash flow valuation is used to appraise capital investment, 50–60 per cent of the value is normally generated after the first five years, highlighting the longer-term importance of strategy. Share prices are often depressed because a company is perceived to be ex-growth and to have no strategy. Alternatively, there may be a perception that the management has no credible strategy or does not have the resources (financial or managerial) to execute a winning strategy.

Effective implementation is crucial

Once the strategy is decided, there remains the key issue of implementation. The board will need good people to run the key divisions and carry out the board's instructions and objectives. Indeed, the whole workforce needs to be motivated to see effective implementation of strategy.

This combination of strategic and implementation skills is critical for setting the company on the right long-term course for adding value. The management's track record (see p. 90 for an evaluation of performance) will provide an immediate check on what management has been delivering. The best plans in the world are likely to fail if management is poor or inexperienced and cannot deliver. Conversely, simple and/or conservative strategies executed by competent managers may do well for investors.

Different skills required

Different businesses may need very different managerial approaches to be successful. A highly regulated utility, for example, requires a very different approach from a highly cyclical commodity business, which in turn requires very different skills from a fast-growing technology business. Similarly, companies at different stages of development (start-up, high growth, mature, declining or recovery) may require very different skill sets. This can often be seen in recovery situations where the skills and approach needed to cut costs and reorganise the portfolio may not be those needed to start developing a growth strategy.

The blend of skills on the board should also be consistent with, and complementary to, the strategy. The financial implications, risks and impact on returns from any given strategy will require a detailed and thorough examination by the finance director (FD). The FD should be an effective check on the chief executive officer (CEO) to ensure that the financial aspects of the strategy make sense. The FD will need to address issues such as:

- Can the strategy be funded?
- What returns will it generate?
- What is the cash flow profile of the move?
- How will it affect the share price?

What can happen is that the FD is very good on matters of financial control and reporting but not as good at appraising the strategic aspects of what the company is undertaking. The debate on strategy then becomes less effective.

The ability to delegate and empower people is critical if the strategy is to be implemented effectively. So strong divisional and operational management that can drive the strategy through and ensure the required results are delivered is needed.

Do the skills match strategy?

This raises the issue of whether the skills of the board match the strategy the company is pursuing. Reading the biographical notes in the **annual report and accounts** may help with this. Do the board members have a lot of experience in what the company actually does? Marconi expanded and focused on its telecoms operations when both its CEO and FD had little experience of this market. This was not the only problem that Marconi ran into and perhaps not its major one. But the relationship between skills and strategy is an important issue here and needs to be taken into account. It should also be noted that there was a fashion for both focus and the telecoms sector at this time and the moves were initially well regarded, as evidenced by a soaring stock price. Again sensible business strategies and doing what is right for a business may be divorced, short term, from stock market trends.

Management – the scarce resource?

The shortage of high-quality management is a major constraint on corporate performance and the implementation of strategy. This has been highlighted dramatically by the high-profile corporate failures of recent years. It is now also very much an issue with the failure of mergers and acquisitions to add value. While earnings dilution is always the number people focus on when deals are done, 'management dilution' is often a much greater determinant of whether the deal is successful in creating value for shareholders and the impact on share price performance. (This is discussed in more detail on p. 92.)

In conclusion, the availability of high-quality management will have a crucial impact on the longer-term performance of the company and its shares.

What is the quality of management?

This answer to this question is critical for the success of your decision. The recent failings of corporate management have spelt out only too clearly the need to identify businesses that are well run and where management has a commitment to the creation of long-term value.

To get a sense of management's quality and the extent to which managers are working for you, it is worth examining management culture, corporate governance and management change. Another critical issue in assessing the quality of management is the results and returns it delivers. This will be covered in detail on p. 90.

Management culture

While difficult to define, it is nonetheless important to have a sense of what the culture of the management/company is. This can be decisive in whether it is successful at what it does. Warren Buffett has neatly encapsulated the key elements of a successful corporate culture. This is a management that:

- behaves like owners
- exerts tight cost control at all times
- does ordinary things extraordinarily well.

This sounds and indeed is wonderfully straightforward: however, it is rarely found. Management often loses sight of these key guiding principles. It may be that as companies get larger they lose the ability to think and act like 'owners'. The important thing is that a management that is working on this basis has its interests firmly aligned with the shareholders'. This is a key requirement for avoiding many of the management scandals and corporate

> as companies get larger they lose the ability to think and act like 'owners'

governance issues that have dominated the headlines in recent years. For investors it is crucial to ensure that the management culture is driven by adding value for shareholders.

Reckitt Benckiser, a company that has been very successful, exemplifies the low-cost approach as well as the benefits of as having an entrepreneurial and accountable culture. Having a focus on household products and health care and a limited range of 'power brands' also keeps things very simple. Its record for innovation is outstanding – in 2007 40 per cent of its revenues came from innovations developed in the previous three years. The percentage of sales coming from new products is a useful key performance indicator (KPI) to assess whether the culture of a company is, for example in this case, innovative – but crucially translating that into action. (We discuss KPIs in more detail on p. 213.)

The need for tight cost control at all times is interesting in the context of companies that have periodic major restructurings to deal with an uncompetitive cost base. This clearly implies that they allow costs to get out of hand until they decide that a massive attack is needed. This inevitably tends to mean big write-offs, exceptional charges and a related cash outflow on redundancies. All of these things impair the net assets or cash position of the company to the detriment of shareholders. Restructurings are often an integral part of recovery stories, but caution should be exercised.

Long-term business perspective

Taking decisions in the long-term interests of the business is an important factor in delivering returns to shareholders in the long run. As we will discuss when we come to look at earnings, decisions to hit short-term earnings targets may, in an immediate sense, please the market. However, if this is being achieved by reducing discretionary expenditures on marketing and R&D, or under-spending on critical investment that the business needs, then the long-term position of the business is likely to be undermined.

If management is driven by short-term financial goals, this may jeopardise the value of the investment in the longer term. So, if hitting an earnings target is important to management, the decisions it takes to do this may not be in your interests – and this may involve decisions that do not support the business and/or the accounting is flexed to hit the goal. There may not even be a short-term benefit: if the market sees that earnings have benefited from the reduction in marketing or R&D, the shares are likely to be marked down.

What do management target and why?

This leads us to examine what management targets for performance and why. There is a legitimate question as to whether targets should be set in the first place. As mentioned above, the danger is that targets are hit by decisions that harm the business. Even worse is fraud. The accounting scandals of 2001–02 invariably revolved around numbers being manipulated to hit sales or earnings growth targets. (The other principal reason for accounting trickery was to conceal the extent of the company's debt levels.)

It is interesting to note how management is remunerated, which will normally be detailed in the report and accounts. If performance bonuses are linked to growth in earnings per share (EPS) or, even worse, earnings before interest, depreciation and **amortisation (Ebitda)**, this immediately suggests a potential conflict of interest between management and shareholders. This will be explored in more detail later, but essentially actions that deliver growth do not necessarily create added value (i.e. returns compensate shareholders for the risks they are undertaking by exceeding the cost of capital). Earnings and EBITDA may also bear no relation to cash generation, another crucial driver of long-term wealth creation.

Mergers and acquisition (M&A) may well deliver growth in EPS (and are guaranteed to increase EBITDA), but M&A has a poor record of delivering shareholder value. The other great danger is that if debt is taken on to fund the deal and deliver an increase in EPS and/or EBITDA, the risks will increase considerably. This is on top of the risks of the deal itself (overpaying, buying a poor business, buying at the wrong point in the cycle, etc.).

These actions benefit management as they help reach performance targets, thus triggering bonuses and the higher remuneration that goes with running an ever-larger business.

Another danger of targets is the impact when they are missed or no longer relevant. This can cause disappointment in the market. Targets that are absolute are also likely to cause problems. For example, setting an earnings target of 15 per cent when inflation is 6 per cent becomes a totally different proposition when inflation is 2 per cent.

So targets can be dangerous in a number of ways. They may encourage accounting gimmickry, which must be avoided. Again this is putting a gloss on the company's performance and position, which distorts the reality of its real performance and position, which in turn is what drives value. Targets may also encourage management to take decisions which destroy shareholder value but help hit targets – and of course trigger managers' bonuses.

This suggests that targets should reflect the long-term health and wealth of the company and linking remuneration to cash generation or value creation is far more appropriate than measures such as earnings or EBITDA which do not reflect returns, cash or the level of risks incurred – the things that serve shareholder value.

Bullish v conservative

If possible it is worth getting to know whether management normally takes a cautious view of developments and likely profits (conservative) or whether it tends to be optimistic and upbeat about prospects (bullish). This enables you to form a sense of how realistic the company's announcements and assessments of the outlook are likely to be. Reading the report and accounts and results announcements and seeing what the chairman's statement indicates will give you a clue, as will reading the financial press. If the management is perennially bullish you may want to 'aim off' its indications of future results. It may also be the case that a company that is conservative by nature will also be conservative in how it presents its numbers and will not attempt to distort the numbers through flexible accounting policies. Companies that are bullish by nature may be tempted to flex the numbers to reach their bullish targets (though this is certainly not always the case).

Growth culture – organic v acquisition

If the company has a growth culture and relies heavily on acquisitions to achieve this, the risks may be much higher than in a company with a culture of expanding its core operations organically. Again it is worth stressing that many of the companies that have crashed following the boom years were highly acquisitive by nature. Often this was to disguise difficulties in their core operations and to provide growth and the accounting flexibility that often goes with integrating acquisitions. The destruction in value that acquisitions often deliver will be discussed on p. 98.

Growing a business organically tends to be lower risk and more likely to deliver higher value. Accordingly it will be valued more highly by the market.

Production or technology driven, cost or market driven?

It is always worth trying to establish whether there is a particular bias in the company towards production or marketing. In effect you are trying to establish how inward or outward looking the company is. Many companies have developed a new product or production process but have not had a sufficiently strong marketing culture or distribution network to exploit the product. Many technology companies have historically been guilty of this. This can be particularly important if there is a relatively short product cycle as the company may not capitalise on the product and before it realises the situation another product has taken its place.

Importantly, many companies make the mistake of emphasising technology or production skills when actually it is a focus on costs and/or marketing that is the most critical requirement to ensure competitiveness. The majority of consumers buy a product on the attractiveness of its features, how it performs, and not the technology. It is also easier to understand what the market is likely to be for a product than for the technology.

Monopoly culture

Another potential problem exists in companies that have historically enjoyed a dominant or monopoly position in a market. This can breed inefficiency and a culture of not having to try too hard and not having real insight into the market and the consumer. Arrogance towards the market can alienate the customer base. If an alternative competitive product or provider emerges, customers are more likely to switch allegiance. Market share can then fall sharply as the management has never had to deal with this encroachment on to its territory.

The attitude and performance of many newly privatised companies in the UK has been interesting in this regard. Arguably, BT had a large bureaucratic structure with a lack of commercial awareness that is not surprising in a company that had been in the public sector for so long. Accordingly, it has missed potential market developments or, in some instances, not made the most of its position.

Culture of privatised companies

Partly related to this monopolistic culture is the culture often found in recently privatised companies. Having been previously government or local authority owned, utilities are often bureaucratic and not commercially oriented. Interestingly, when they find that the regulator is looking to control and regulate their core business, their natural reaction appears to be to buy overseas utilities or to diversify domestically. This has tended to lead to them overpaying for acquisitions, not running them effectively when they have them and then finally selling them at a loss.

Culture determines whether management will make money for you

It can often be difficult to assess something as intangible as 'culture'. Nonetheless, it is well worth thinking about it when looking at a company as it can be critical in whether you make money. As we discussed earlier, the values of an organisation and the ability to 'live them' will create a culture that generates a commitment to value. In this sense the most important aspect is that management is clearly and emphatically working for shareholders. A focus on doing what is right for the long-term benefit of the business – in Buffett's terms 'acting as owners' – is going to deliver returns to you in the long run. An openness and directness in its dealings with you is also an indicator of a culture that is conducive to treating owners properly.

Is its corporate governance best practice?

The spate of scandals over the collapse of many household names, the accounting fraud that dominated the early part of the decade and management receiving massive salaries while companies perform poorly and share prices slump has put the issue of corporate governance firmly on the agenda. How and why this is allowed to happen and why the checks and balances to protect the interests of shareholders (who happen to own the company) have so often failed are the crucial issues that corporate governance must seek to address.

One of the interesting issues in many instances has been the power of dominant chief executives whose ambition has gone unchallenged by the board. The absence of debate and ideas being tested thoroughly has led to poor decisions being taken.

Buffett's rationale for managers to behave like owners becomes abundantly clear in this context. While one can legislate for 'best practice' in corporate governance matters, there is no substitute for a management with integrity that is fundamentally committed to acting in the interest of shareholders and who culturally acts in a way that serves shareholders. This then becomes part of the company's values rather than a response to legislation and concern around 'box-ticking' and being 'seen' to do the right things rather than instinctively just 'doing' the right things.

The principal–agent problem and conflicts of interest

The issue of why shareholders' interests are sometimes poorly served reflects the twin issues of the 'agency' problem and related 'conflict of interests'. The agency problem refers to the fact that there is an effective separation of owners (shareholders) and those who are employed to manage the company on their behalf. Will they really, as agents of the owners, manage in the interests of shareholders? Conversely, the owners may be disinterested or feel they have little impact on influencing the management team. As a result there are few constraints on management.

The decisions taken by the board may well be taken in its interests rather than to benefit shareholders. That it is in a position to decide things immediately raises the 'conflict of interests' element of the equation. If it appoints non-executive directors (NEDs), there is immediately a conflict of interests. Does the loyalty of the non-executives lie with the chief executive who appointed them or with the shareholders they should be representing? If these non-executives are on audit committees this conflict arises again. It might be compounded by the fact that the board may hire remuneration consultants to deliver evidence to the remuneration committee. Again the consultants' interests lie with the executives who hire them.

Clearly from a legal perspective the NEDs are responsible to shareholders, as are auditors whose appointment is voted for by the shareholders at the AGM.

Conflicts and bonuses: what triggers the bonus?

The other area where major conflicts arise is that of pay, the award of stock options and bonuses. Bonuses in particular have been and remain a key concern. Remuneration packages are often triggered by hitting earnings or EBITDA targets (which arguably have very little relevance to long-term shareholder value), an acquisition being completed successfully or the company's shares outperforming the market. The problem is of course that these targets may have nothing to do with good management and may not be consistent with shareholders' interests. In particular, acquisitions can help you hit EBITDA or earnings targets while increasing risks dramatically and subtracting a lot of value for shareholders (i.e. the returns from these deals are massively below the cost of capital).

In certain sectors there may be a boom in volumes and prices that has nothing to do with good management performance and adding value. In effect, in a bull market anyone would be able to hit targets set in absolute terms. So you need to think about how demanding the targets are. Let's say bonuses are triggered by earnings growth of 7 per cent. In a company with high operational gearing these payments could be generated by relatively small trading improvements. If there is a 3 per cent uplift in profit for each 1 per cent increase in revenue, a 3 per cent revenue uplift could trigger a 9 per cent uplift in earnings. For some industries this could be easily achieved if volumes and prices are on a rising trend. Alternatively a company facing poor volumes and weak pricing, or where there are high variable and low fixed costs (i.e. low operational gearing), might find it incredibly challenging to have a 7 per cent earnings trigger.

Therefore these targets will encourage strategies and policies that are likely to hurt shareholders in the long term. In the meantime the remuneration package for the board can rise dramatically. An acquisition being completed should not be a source of extra pay; generating a return on capital that compensates for the risks involved and making the deal work is where management should distinguish itself. Similarly, linking rewards to the shares' performance against the market overall may not be appropriate. In many respects the shares may perform by default against the market – defensive shares may perform brilliantly in difficult economic environments but that may owe little to management performance.

> the remuneration package for the board can rise dramatically

Good examples of these policies include Vodafone where remuneration has been triggered by EBITDA targets and where the CEO did receive payment for successfully completing the Mannesmann acquisition in 2000. Similarly, GlaxoSmithKline ran into controversy during 2000 over an attempt to reward its CEO more generously. This has revolved around earnings targets being 9 per cent over inflation over a three-year period, the shares' performance relative to the FTSE and being in the top third of a group of chosen drug company peers. The issue is whether these targets are relevant and how challenging they are. Similarly, might an acquisition be undertaken to help with these targets? It is far from clear whether previous acquisitions have added value. Indeed, the poor performance of the company's drug pipeline might suggest that a further acquisition would make this problem even worse. In effect it may be that there are diseconomies of scale in the company's R&D division – a key driver of long-term value.

Best practice is to use a combination of internal targets which are difficult to achieve and targets set against the performance of competitors (if you happen to be in a growth sector it might be easy to beat the market or FTSE; you are certainly not comparing like with like). And given the factors that drive performance and wealth creation in the long run it may be far more effective to reward returns on capital and cash generation or KPIs that are genuinely lead indicators of improved long-term returns.

Therefore the issues of agency and conflicts of interest lie at the heart not just of the corporate governance issue but also of profitable investing in shares. While this is increasingly a feature of the regulatory environment, it works far more effectively if the culture of the company is deeply committed to adding value for shareholders, i.e. it is part of the company's culture and not a box-ticking response to regulators.

Governance and strategy

Strategy must reflect the vision, mission and values of the company. To arrive at it therefore requires a very considered and debated process which asks the right questions that are answered with complete honesty. These questions need to establish with clarity what the unique proposition the company delivers is, how it can be improved and what skills and resources are needed to do that. Given the complexity of the world and the markets the company operates in, these issues need careful consideration. This clearly requires a board that constantly challenges and tests those ideas with scrupulous attention to the evidence of the company's performance. For this to happen it implies that there is a CEO who is sufficiently committed to the mission that they accept it is a project that is beyond them and therefore one that requires everyone's intelligence and input to be successful. Best practice corporate governance is designed to ensure that these discussions occur and the risk and rewards of decision making are carefully analysed.

An autocratic, over-bearing and ego-driven CEO is often a prime trigger of corporate failure. The recent collapse of much of the banking industry is one area that arguably suffered from strategic decisions not being challenged or dissenting views not listened to. The evidence appears to be that there was little scope to challenge the CEO on their views and the strategy they were embarked upon. Decisions are going to be much riskier without a more rounded view of the issues and the insight of other experienced executives.

What can happen in this situation is that the strategy is to 'grow rapidly'. Growth is not a strategy but an outcome – an outcome of a clear and compelling vision about how to excel in a market where the company has a unique proposition and the resources to deliver on that offer. Having these characteristics firmly in place then generates growth. Interestingly, a significant number of banks seemed to have a 'grow rapidly' strategy with no thought of the risks of such a policy. Very often such strategies are driven by large acquisitions, even though the evidence of such deals is that they fail to add value.

The characteristics of CEOs who produce sustainable long-term results is very effectively summarised in Jim Collins' concept of a 'Level 5' leader as featured in *Good to Great*.[12] They 'embody a paradoxical mix of personal humility and professional will' and their ambition is to build a great business not their own aggrandisement. As a result they realise that for the business to have ongoing success there needs to be a very clear succession plan with their successors taking the business on to even greater things. Collins also points out that such leaders often have the characteristics of 'compelling modesty, are self effacing and understated'.[13]

It is interesting to reflect that many CEOs associated with not only failed strategies but ones that led to the brink of collapse in the financial sector certainly did not embrace the qualities of a 'Level 5' leader. This has led to the Walker report[14] on corporate governance which recommends much more scrutiny of the risks attached to the board's decisions and where necessary getting external investigation of them. Additionally, many companies with dominant CEOs certainly seem to have problems developing a clear and sensible plan for succession yet this is a key sign of any well-managed organisation.

With the need to create shareholder value increasingly being recognised, one of the key areas where shareholders will engage with management is in the strategy domain. This is an area where shareholders are increasingly trying to influence company boards. This influence tends to revolve around the company's portfolio and the pressure either to sell underperforming divisions or to ensure that value-destroying acquisitions are prevented – especially if it is a case of 'growth for growth's sake'. Clearly this pressure implicitly suggests that there is little confidence in management's ability to allocate cash in value-added ways. The track record generally on acquisitions adding value is poor and if a particular company has consistently subtracted value, it is likely to come under pressure.

---

[12] See note 6, p. 94.

[13] Ibid.

[14] *A review of corporate governance in UK bank and other financial industry entities*, 16 July 2009, Norwich: The Stationery Office.

Ensuring good governance

Focusing on corporate governance, therefore, is crucial to ensure that management is acting in your interests and developing a strategy to build the long-term 'health and wealth' of the company. In effect it is another way of reducing risk. There may be one or two instances of founder owners breaking the codes on good governance which do not harm the returns to shareholders – the managers are owners to a significant extent. The founder may hold such a large share of the equity that their interests are aligned with those of the shareholders. More generally, however, it is crucial to ensure that 'best practice' is being followed.

The best practice checklist should cover such matters as:

- quality and integrity of management
- separation of chairman and CEO roles
- ratio of non-executive to executive directors
- independence of non-executives
- contract length
- remuneration policies
- what triggers performance-related bonuses
- open and timely communications to shareholders.

This list is to ensure a proper board structure, with a split between the roles of chairman and CEO and high-quality, independent non-executive members of the board. The splitting of the roles of chairman and CEO is important in order to avoid an overly powerful and influential figure who proceeds to make decisions without sufficient scrutiny from and debate with the board. The chairman's role is managing the board and considering higher-level strategic issues while the CEO is responsible for the running of the company on a day-to-day basis. Someone once said that the art of being a good chair was to 'promote competition between ideas and cooperation between people'. This competition between ideas has been sadly lacking in many organisations.

Similarly, independent non-executives are important to represent the interests of shareholders on the board and to challenge the executive members to justify their decisions. It is normal to have three independent non-executives on the board, although some commentators are now advocating having a higher number of non-executive to executive directors.

The independence aspect is clearly crucial – non-executives should not be dependent on work coming from the business or have commercial relationships with the CEO or chairman. Otherwise they will not provide an independent check to boardroom discussions. This is why there is so much concern about the number of directors who sit on each other's boards. If you have a non-executive director (NED) on the board where you are CEO and you are a non-executive on their board, there is an obvious conflict of interests and lack of independence (I do not challenge you, you do not challenge me).

> the independence aspect is clearly crucial

The importance of a board having high-quality and independent non-executive directors was the focus of the review by Sir Derek Higgs entitled 'Review of Role and Effectiveness of Non-Executive Directors' – commonly called the Higgs review.[15] This addition to the combined code and suggestions for improvement to best practice was instigated by government in February 2002 in response to the fallout from Enron and other financial scandals. At the same time Sir Robert Smith[16] was asked to look into the role of the audit committee.

While there has not been anything on the scale of Enron in the UK there have been many instances of companies pursuing strategies which have destroyed value on a grand scale. On this basis improving the quality and independence of the debate over strategy and whether the allocation of capital will create value has to be beneficial for shareholders.

In terms of improving the functioning of the board and the decision-making process, the Higgs review focuses on avoiding concentration of power on the board. Here the independence of NEDs is crucial. To this end the proposals revolve around having a higher proportion of independent and well-informed NEDs on the board with their role defined more clearly. To achieve this, the review suggests that the selection and appointment process needs to be broadened and made more rigorous. There also needs to be a step change in the provision of training and development of NEDs to maximise their contribution to the decision-making process.

An important aspect of the Higgs proposals is the appointment of a senior NED whose responsibilities would include chairing meetings of NEDs

---

[15] *Review of the Role and Effectiveness of Non-Executive Directors*, January 2003, Norwich: The Stationery Office.

[16] *Audit Committees, Combined Code Guidance: A report and proposed guidance*, September 2002, Norwich: The Stationery Office.

where the chairman is not present and, significantly, to act as a link with shareholders. The senior NED may sit in on regular meetings with shareholders and also act as a point of contact for shareholders if they feel grievances are not being dealt with effectively by the chairman or CEO.

The proposals in the Higgs review are an updating of best practice and are incorporated into the combined code. A critical part of the approach is that rather than focusing on legislative requirements the onus will be on best practice, with the board having to 'comply or explain'. There may be good reasons why a company cannot comply with best practice but these must be explained to shareholders. If you as an investor feel that management is not operating in your interests by complying with best practice, you need to think through the implications.

Some of the key features of the Higgs review are as follows:

- The division of roles of chair and CEO should be clearly defined, written down and agreed by the board.
- The CEO of a company should not become chairman of that company – an issue that has been important in financial companies.
- NEDs must be independent – that is, the individual should not be receiving fees from the company or have a business relationship with it, should have no family connections, should not represent a major shareholder or have been on the board for more than ten years.
- Half of the board, excluding the chairman, should be NEDs.
- NEDs should lead audit, nomination and remuneration committees.
- A senior NED should be identified.
- If shareholder concerns are not addressed effectively by normal channels and fail to be resolved, the senior NED should be used.
- NEDs, and in particular chairs of committees, should attend the **annual general meeting (AGM)** and answer relevant questions.
- A full-time executive board member should not have more than one NED role.
- No individual should chair more than one board of a major company.

Concerns and objections to the review have centred on potential conflicts between the senior NED and the chairman. Some critics argue that in some instances the senior NED might emerge as an alternative power base and this would disrupt the 'unitary board' that characterises the UK's approach to corporate stewardship. It is also feared that confusion will arise if the message from the senior NED to shareholders differs from that of the chairman/board. While this may occur in some instances the potential upside of the proposals, if managed properly, far outweighs any downside.

One of the features of the accounting scandals in the US has been complicity or negligence by the auditors. In some cases this has been because of auditors earning non-audit consulting fees, which makes the rocking-the-boat option a costly one. In such a case the auditors' independence is severely compromised. The auditors should be representing shareholders, not executive management.

Reflecting these concerns the Smith proposals revolve around the audit committee being made up of the non-executives, ensuring the independence of auditors and the enforcement of accounting standards. As with the Higgs review, a 'comply or explain' approach is adopted.

Some of the key features of the Smith proposals are as follows:

- The audit committee should comprise at least three members, all independent NEDs.
- At least one member should have significant, recent and relevant financial experience.
- The role of the audit committee is clarified to include monitoring the integrity of the financial statements, reviewing financial reporting judgements and reviewing the company's internal audit function and financial controls.
- The audit committee is also responsible for making recommendations to the board concerning the appointment of the external auditor and for monitoring the external auditor's independence, objectivity and effectiveness.
- The audit committee should develop and implement policy on the engagement of the external auditor to supply non-audit services.

The length of employment contract for key executives is another area of concern. If they are on a long-term contract (say three years), it can be expensive to get rid of a poorly performing board member. Not only have they destroyed value, they receive a payoff for leaving the company. Accordingly, the code advocates that contracts should be of 12 months' duration and no longer.

The use of share options and bonuses that are triggered by certain targets should also be monitored carefully. This can lead to massive payouts but, as discussed earlier, this may be for achieving objectives that do not assist shareholders, and indeed may be positively harmful to their interests. Again there is a temptation to use sharp accounting practices to help hit these targets. Clean accounting should be a fundamental part of the quality and integrity of the management team.

An open communication policy is not necessarily part of any strict governance code but it is an important part of how your company is run. Critically, it tells you a lot about the culture of the management – that it is interested in doing the job properly for all those who employ it: the shareholders. The company being open with all its shareholders at the same time is a legal requirement.

Many companies do in fact talk to analysts and brokers to guide expectations one way or another. You can see this from the way share price movements in stock market reports in the papers are described. Again this is not best practice. A **trading statement** at the end of the half-year and full-year trading periods is a more effective way of communicating fairly to all shareholders.

Upside of good corporate governance

The benefits to you as a shareholder/potential investor of good corporate governance are considerable. At the very basic level, the quality and integrity of the management will be a crucial determinant in the success or otherwise of your company. Knowing the company is being run in your interests is critical. Increasingly, good governance is being taken seriously and large shareholders in particular are keen to ensure that boards are more aware of their views on these key issues. Evidence is also starting to show that valuations are benefiting from good governance practices. Crucially, weak governance and the impact of dominant CEOs at companies leads to higher risks, which increases the cost of capital.

> knowing the company is being run in your interests is critical

Activism and good governance

Another aspect of corporate governance is the criticism that institutional owners have received for their part in the demise of many household names by not cross-examining the directors more effectively, especially with respect to the risks presented by the business models. In fairness many claim they did but were not listened to. An area identified by both Walker and Myners[17] is the need for investors to ensure that the board has the skills necessary to discharge its duties which, given the complexity of some of the risks and decisions being taken, is clearly crucial.

---

[17] *Myners Report on Institutional Investment*, 6 March 2001, Norwich: The Stationery Office.

Another area investors arguably failed to monitor was in allowing remuneration packages to go unchecked and rewards for failure to be paid. This has raised legitimate questions as to whether institutions are exercising their rights as owners (or acting on behalf of owners). While many **hedge funds** are very vocal about the company's plans and business models, and often receive criticism for this for being too short term, it is important to note they are acting like owners. Many longer-term funds on the other hand have been far less forthcoming (although there are many who operate very effectively behind the scenes). There is evidence, however, that institutions are responding to these pressures and seeking to have a more constructive and engaged dialogue with the board to ensure their views are effectively represented.

While it is often the case that activist investors, especially hedge funds, are seen as being aggressive in this situation it needs to be borne in mind that if the shares have been languishing for some time then management should have been alive to the issues and responded much earlier (rather than watching over the poor share price performance without doing anything to credibly reverse it). Invariably the activist analysis will have been well thought through and will therefore stimulate a useful debate.

It is normally quite easy to spot where the activist investor will apply pressure as it will be something that creates a 'catalyst' for change and actions that will create shareholder value. (We do need to be careful here that we are discussing long-term shareholder value and not a short-term share price hike as discussed in the shareholder value section.) Some of the activism may be to ensure that the company complies with best practice corporate governance such as separating the roles of chairman and CEO – as is happening at Marks and Spencer. On more strategic matters it may be that pressure will be applied to (say) disposing of a business, improving the returns from the core business (which may be lagging the peer group), merging with a competitor, a share buy-back (albeit far less common these days), or increased dividends. Ultimately, of course, the issue may well be to change the management.

This is not to say that active investors' views are necessarily correct – but management should be anticipating their views and creating a momentum story of its own. One of the concerns about activist investors' pressure is that decisions are taken in favour of one particular (and vocal) group of shareholders. They will have a specific agenda which may or may not create value for all shareholders in the long run. This is again where the benefits of management having a clear and compelling strategy and how it is attending to the long-term health and wealth of the company are very apparent. If it is clear how the decision-making process is supporting the value of the business there is less scope for pressure from activists. Delivering on the strategy will be in the long-term interests of all shareholders. If the strategy has been communicated clearly then investors will have a real sense of what they have invested in.

Does management need to change and will it make a difference?

Management teams and chief executives are judged on how well they use the money shareholders have invested and what subsequently happens to the share price. If management has consistently failed to deliver and change is needed, what issues must be addressed if you are to continue to hold the shares or consider buying them?

News of management changes

When returns have continually disappointed and this has been reflected in a sharp fall in the share price with little prospect for a recovery, things need to change. A new management focused on generating higher returns is very much needed. This may be a buy signal if the new management has a realistic chance of turning the company around.

How does poor performance show up in the figures?

The return on sales and capital employed are likely to have fallen to low levels in absolute terms and will certainly be a lot lower relative to others in the same sector or industry. The return on capital may be so low that it is not covering the company's cost of capital and it would be better putting money in the bank. This may have occurred over a long period. The share price is also likely to have underperformed both the sector in which the company operates and the broader market. (We will discuss the returns issue in more detail later.) A collapsing share price will inevitably lead to close scrutiny of management and its failings.

Are the key problems endemic to the industry/business itself or to management failings?

Poor corporate performance, or even failure, is often ascribed to deficiencies in the trading environment rather than to a poor management team or performance. It needs to be considered, therefore, whether the market conditions are genuinely difficult, with both prices and volumes under significant pressure.

It might be the case that returns are low due to significant overcapacity and weak pricing across the industry. In this instance it may not be a demand problem and may well require action across the industry before returns register any improvement. However, it might be that blaming a poor trading environment is a diversion from more long-standing and deep-seated problems within the company. We have continually stressed the need to take long-term decisions to protect and enhance the company's competitive position. If management has consistently failed to do this, ultimately the company will lose market share and see returns on sales and capital come under pressure.

Careful analysis is needed to determine whether this weak position is due to any of the following:

- Has the company lost touch with what is going on in its markets and what its customers want?
- Has an acquisition gone badly wrong (a strategic error)?
- Is a particular division seriously underperforming its peer group?
- Is the cash flow seriously deteriorating?
- Have the returns on a large investment programme disappointed?

Who decides management should change?

This is a complex question and realistically represents a variety of factors/issues coming to a head. If the performance has been poor for a significant period, then shareholder pressure combined with media coverage should galvanise the NEDs to initiate change. This presupposes that large shareholders are ready to wield their influence. Alternatively, the threat of being taken over may lead either to action to improve performance or to the management deficiencies being remedied by a takeover.

What management needs to do and can it do it?

In essence, the key options to raise returns and hence the share price that are open to management are to:

- improve revenues (prices and volumes)
- reduce costs
- reduce the amount of capital that is used in the business.

Improving the revenue side of the equation requires either extra volumes or higher prices to be achieved. This may be problematic because the market is too difficult and/or the response of competitors prevents extra volume or higher prices being obtained. This may be especially true if one of the players in the market is driven by gaining long-term market share. Problems will also arise if there is a lot of competition from imports. If the company has seen a long-term erosion of market share, generating higher revenues may be far more difficult to achieve. Significant investment in the product and marketing will be required to regain market share. This will take time and success is not guaranteed.

Costs are the one variable within management's control and so tend to feature prominently in recovery stories. The cutting of overheads, closing of factories and discontinuance of loss-making or poorly performing product lines/divisions are the first port of call for any restructuring programme. This arguably represents the easy first stage of the recovery. If prices or volumes continue to fall, however, this may not be sufficient for a profits recovery. So buying shares for a profit recovery in these circumstances may well fail to make you money. In addition, it is worth stressing that these restructuring charges and asset write-offs will have a negative impact on shareholders' funds/net assets and cash flow (to pay for the redundancies, etc.).

If massive restructuring charges are taken, it may well be future earnings that benefit from this action. One needs to be careful in these circumstances to determine how much of the uplift is a benefit of accounting matters rather than the underlying performance of the business. The danger is, of course, that **shareholders' funds** are written off to benefit earnings growth so that shareholders are in effect paying for the earnings growth.

Strategic issues – disposals, mergers and acquisitions: do they add value?

As well as trying to rectify a poor trading performance, the management may need to address the company's strategic position. This may involve selling off poorly performing or non-core activities. However, as recent evidence has amply demonstrated, this is far from straightforward. Selling companies at a sensible price in a bear market when companies are highly indebted and have little access to new funds is very difficult.

Assuming disposals can be achieved, this should allow management time to be focused on the core and raising its performance (as well as improving the financial position of the company). As indicated earlier this may be a long-term process. Improving its operating performance may then allow growth opportunities to be considered. Acquisitions may improve the product coverage and growth profile (subject to the caveats about acquisitions made in the M&A section on p. 109).

Culture

One of the great difficulties in turnaround situations is gauging how far the culture of the organisation needs to be changed and how long this will take. This can be especially true when once-great companies have underperformed for years but still believe themselves to be great. A bureaucratic structure may have evolved during the years of success: but this invariably prevents the radical change that is needed. This can also be the case when a company had monopolistic control over a market and has come under pressure: BT being a classic case. The important thing to bear in mind here is that any investment on a recovery basis will take time to come through.

> a bureaucratic structure may have evolved during the years of success

How long will it take? How long should they be given?

These questions are almost impossible to answer as each situation will be different and the complexity of issues will vary enormously. Is it just a cost problem or are there fundamental problems with the company and/or the marketplace? Critically, both the external environment and the extent of the internal problems will have a big bearing on the success of the turnaround – and the time required. A turnaround in a stable market where revenues are not under pressure may be much quicker and easier to effect than in a cyclical commodity business with huge overcapacity, high import penetration and price weakness. Where the culture has become bureaucratic and unresponsive to developments in the market and the needs of customers (leading to a significant loss of market share), combined with pressure on volumes and prices, there is a much stiffer challenge – a turnaround will not be achieved quickly.

Is it an internal or external appointment and is this significant?

Some CEOs have good reputations as agents of change. It may be that a fresh approach is just what a company needs. Track record is important here. The new members of the top management team, if brought in from outside, will have no loyalty to past decisions or to any particular division where they cut their teeth, nor will they have been affected by a possibly inefficient or lazy corporate culture. This will hopefully counteract any inertia blocking the implementation of change.

What skills does the new CEO bring?

Is the new CEO a cost cutter, a product/marketing expert, or do they have skills in restructuring portfolios? What does the company need? If the CEO has a proven record in cost cutting, what happens when the company needs to grow? Similarly, if their track record is in running dynamic growth businesses, what happens when the company matures? In most recovery situations a blend of these skills will be needed to transform the company's fortunes.

Again it is worth stressing Warren Buffett's dictum on management, which is particularly relevant in situations where there are management changes in companies that are struggling:

> with few exceptions, when management with a reputation for brilliance tackles a business with a reputation for poor fundamental economics, it is the reputation of the business that remains intact.[18]

Waiting for a takeover?

It can be tempting when holding the shares of a severe underperformer to wait for a bid approach (indeed you may consider that the shares are attractive on the basis of a likely bid and be a potential buyer). The danger is, of course, that the company's market position and performance have deteriorated to such an extent that the company is no longer as attractive as it was. It no longer enjoys the market share that may have made it a genuinely attractive bid candidate. Indeed, the competition may have been so successful in gaining market share from this weakened competitor that they, correctly, feel they can gain even more market share by undercutting the company (the customers are also those most likely to have noticed poorer performance). Furthermore, there is no desire to take on the difficulties of an ailing company.

This is not to argue that potential takeover situations cannot be a potentially profitable investment area. However, it is important to be aware of the risks involved and that a bid may take a long time to materialise (if ever). In the meantime you may be invested in a company that is going

[18] See note 4.

through a difficult time and as a result you may lose a lot of money while waiting. So if you are thinking of buying shares in a company on the basis of a potential takeover, try to ensure that its underlying performance is reasonable, that it genuinely has features (high market share, good technology, brands, distribution network) that make it still attractive to potential suitors and that the takeover hopes are not the only reason you are holding the shares. A takeover should be the icing on the cake.

Management change and recovery stories – will you make money?

All in all it is quite complex to assess whether new management coming into a company will reverse its fortunes. A key issue is the extent to which the company's market position and returns have deteriorated – the steeper the descent, the more difficult the turnaround. Another key issue is the stability of the markets in which the company operates. The more volatile the pricing and volume environment, the more difficult it will be to improve returns. In an environment where prices are falling rapidly, any cost-cutting initiatives will be needed just to stand still.

Doing your homework to assess the company's market position and performance is crucial as there are significant risks involved. The changes are likely to take a long time to implement and correspondingly it may be a long haul for the shares.

Making sense and creating value out of mergers and acquisitions

A merger is when two companies of roughly the same size join forces. An acquisition is when one company takes over another. Mergers and acquisitions remain an important part of the financial landscape even though much of the academic and empirical evidence casts serious doubts on whether they fulfil the promises made at the time of the deals, and more than half destroy, rather than enhance, shareholder value.

In the light of this evidence it is worth exploring:

- why companies are keen to do deals
- the types of deal being done
- what to consider when evaluating deals
- why deals do not add value for shareholders.

We will now explore each of these factors in turn.

Why deals are done

The principal drivers of acquisitions tend to involve attempts to improve earnings and returns on investment by:

- controlling costs
- influencing prices
- growth from new product or geographic areas.

In theory, deals done for these reasons should benefit shareholders. A stronger business with a better earnings outlook and long-term growth potential should deliver a higher share price. Considering these objectives, the most common reasons advanced to justify deals include to:

- improve the growth outlook for the company
- enable costs to be cut
- improve pricing power
- increase market share
- take out excess capacity
- gain access to a new product area
- gain access to a new geographical area
- gain access to a key technology
- gain control of key raw materials or inputs
- gain a stronger control of the way the product/service is sold.

It could be argued that the risk/reward profiles differ with the various reasons for doing a deal. A move that is made because it enables costs to be cut and gives the combined entity greater market share (and better pricing power) is arguably lower risk. It should be easier to implement the required actions as the management is working in an industry it knows. It might be that these benefits are one-off and improve the earnings growth for a couple of years. This may limit the longer-term rewards but then the risks are also lower.

The more growth-oriented deals may involve more risk. Moving into a new product or geographic area will inevitably pose the management with more unknowns and potentially therefore be higher risk. For example, moves into new geographic regions often prove to be disappointing, or at the very least take a lot longer to deliver value than originally anticipated. This can be the case especially when the deal leads to a very small market position being established.

Types of deal being done

The probability of a deal 'adding value' may well depend on the type of deal being undertaken. As mentioned earlier, the risks increase dramatically as more unknowns are taken on. It may also be the case that the larger the deal, the more risks are likely to be present, certainly in terms of the management resource needed and the size of the 'bet'.

The type of deal can vary enormously and might include the following.

- *Strategic* – this might be a very large acquisition to take the company into a new regional market in a business it is already in. For example, a company entering the US market for the first time might make a 'strategic' acquisition to gain access to that market. Alternatively, it might take a company into a related product area where the technology is different and the technological know-how is as important as the product.
- *Vertical integration* – this is when a company acquires a supplier (sometimes referred to as 'upstream') or a customer ('downstream'). Reasons for doing this might be to gain control of a critical raw material to ensure a regular supply, or to gain market share through a distributor to ensure an outlet for the product instead of that being given to a competitor.
- *Horizontal integration* – this is when a company acquires a competitor in the same market or industry and might be referred to as 'industry consolidation', as discussed earlier. This should be lower risk, although the competition authorities may express an interest.
- *In-fill acquisition* – this is normally a low-risk way of expanding. A company buys a small competitor that operates in an area of the market to which it does not have exposure. This may be a region or a certain segment of the product market. By their nature these deals should be lower risk and fit into the existing business very easily.
- *Agreed/hostile deals* – whether a deal is agreed between the two boards or whether it is hostile may make a difference to the outcome. A premium paid to secure agreement may depress returns, but if it means that key personnel do not leave and the integration process is conducted efficiently and effectively, the premium might be worth paying. Alternatively, a hostile deal might avoid the need for a premium and allow the aggressor the freedom to do exactly what they want as quickly as they want.

Evaluating the deal: what to look for

While management may make all sorts of claims when looking to do deals, investors should focus on:

- the impact on earnings
- the economic return from the deal.

One of the most commonly used phrases in statements accompanying deals is that the 'deal will not dilute earnings in the first year' or the 'deal will enhance earnings in the first full year'. This reflects the focus that is placed on earnings per share by the management and the market.

Earnings are one of the key numbers monitored by investors and the growth in earnings is a key driver of valuation and hence share prices. Therefore, when a company is doing a deal, attention inevitably focuses on the impact it has on the company's earnings outlook. Whether this is the correct number to focus on is highly debatable. In the wake of the degree of value destruction that followed the deals of the boom years, attention has correctly turned to the returns on investment and the value added of the transaction.

The return on capital that a deal is expected to generate is crucial for shareholders. If the company is going to be allocating capital to a deal, it is important that it generates an appropriate return to compensate shareholders for the risks involved. Again there is a clear correlation between the return on capital a company generates and its valuation/performance relative to the market.

So how does the impact on earnings and returns flow through? This very much depends on:

- the price paid
- how the deal is financed
- the benefits of putting the two businesses together
- how effectively these benefits are realised.

The price paid

Clearly, paying an appropriate price is the critical cornerstone of any successful deal. Even if the deal makes all the commercial sense in the world, if it reduces earnings and generates a very poor economic return, shareholders will lose out heavily.

How the deal is financed

Debt finance

If the deal is paid for out of debt, the earnings effect is simply:

> The profit from the new business + the cost-saving benefits from combining the businesses + the pricing/revenue benefits from the combination − the cost of paying the interest on the debt

There may be a complication in the form of whether the deal influences the tax charge − earnings being struck after tax. (Indeed, sometimes deals may be done because of the tax advantages that a target brings, but on the whole doing deals simply for the tax benefits may not be beneficial in the long run.)

Equity finance

When shares are used, the calculation becomes a question of adding the overall profit impact from the deal (as detailed above) and dividing by the enlarged number of shares (adjusting for any tax impact). If the deal is done part way through a year, the profits for that part of the year are included and a weighted average of the number of shares is used.

Cost of capital

This is important for assessing the economic impact of any investment project or deal. A company must generate a return that exceeds its cost of capital to make the deal worth doing when set against the risks involved. This is referred to as 'adding value'.

The cost of debt is relatively straightforward and is effectively the rate of interest at which the company can borrow. This will normally be at a premium to long-term government bonds, which is regarded as the risk-free rate. Therefore an investment or acquisition that is funded by shares needs to generate a much higher return to exceed the cost of capital, i.e. generate a positive economic return.

The **weighted average cost of capital (WACC)** simply reflects the extent to which the company is funded by equity or debt. If the ratio is 70 per cent equity and 30 per cent debt and the cost of equity is 10 per cent and post-tax cost of debt is 4.9 per cent, the WACC is:

$$(10 \times 0.7) + (4.9 \times 0.3) = 8.47$$

To show the impact of debt on reducing the cost of capital, if we say the company is funded 50 per cent equity and 50 per cent debt, the WACC is reduced to:

$$(10 \times 0.5) + (4.9 \times 0.5) = 7.45$$

Therefore a company that is more heavily funded with debt will have a lower cost of capital.

The problem is of course that the risks go up the more heavily indebted the company is. In this case the beta would rise and this would increase the cost of equity to reflect the greater risk (see the factors influencing beta on pp. 22–23).

The benefits of putting the two businesses together

Debt v equity finance – the impact on earnings and returns

To consider the impact of the various methods of financing an acquisition, let's consider a takeover by company A of company B. The total consideration (or **enterprise value (EV)**) is detailed in Table 3.1. You need to ask yourself the following:

- What is the impact on earnings per share?
- Will the deal add value?
- What will be the financial position of the company after the deal has gone through?

The equity value on takeover takes into account the premium needed to secure the control of the target company. The provisions reflect liabilities that would be inherited when the acquisition is completed. It may relate to environmental responsibilities the company has or the need to fund pension payments to current and former employees. The costs of the transaction will relate to such things as the documentation needed, legal advice and fees for getting the share issue underwritten.

Buying company B would bring operating profit of £65 million. It is assumed that the benefits of putting the two businesses together, the merger effect, is an incremental operating profit of £25 million. These benefits may come from a range of cost-cutting measures: removing head office costs, purchasing economies, and economies of scale of putting extra volume through the operations. These benefits are often referred to as the 'synergies' of the deal. Clearly at this stage they are hypothetical and management has to deliver these benefits.

Table 3.1 The cost of buying B (£m) with 70% funded by equity and 30% by debt

Pre-bid value	600
Equity value on takeover	780
Debt	100
Provisions	40
Costs of transaction	20
EV	940
70/30 equity/debt	
Shares	£658m
Debt	£282m (at 8 per cent)

Share price of A = 650p, market cap = £1.95bn
Share rights issue at a 20 per cent discount to share price, i.e. 520p
Therefore the number of shares that need to be issued = £658m/520p = 126.5m

Table 3.2 A takeover by Company A of Company B

	Company A	Company B	Merger effect	70/30 equity/debt	All shares	All debt
Operating profit	150	65	25	240.0	240	240.0
Interest	10	10	22	32.0	10	85.2
Pre-tax	140	55		208.0	230	154.8
Tax	−42			−62.4	−69	−46.4
Post-tax earnings	98			145.6	161	108.4
No of shares	300		126.5	426.5	481.0	300.0
EPS	32.7			34.1	33.5	36.1
P/E	20×					

The central case assumes that the deal is financed by the issue of shares for 70 per cent of the cost of the deal and 30 per cent by extra debt. The shares are issued in a **rights issue** at a 20 per cent discount to the prevailing market price. At a share price of 520p the company needs to issue 126.5 million shares to meet 70 per cent of the acquisition consideration. The debt component of £282 million is financed by debt with an interest cost of 8 per cent.

Table 3.2 demonstrates the impact of financing the deal entirely with debt and entirely through the issue of shares, where the assumption is that the shares are issued at 520p. This is perhaps unrealistic given how many shares are being issued, which might suggest a bigger discount than the 20 per cent. If it was, say, 30 per cent, 207 million shares would need to be issued and not the 181 million shares in the example. This would reduce earnings to 31.7p, representing **dilution** of a relatively modest 3 per cent. Table 3.2 demonstrates that the deal improves EPS (enhancement) in all the proposed financing methods.

The advantages of 'gearing up', i.e. using debt, are clearly illustrated in the all-debt option. Earnings rise by 10.4 per cent when the all-debt option is pursued. The tax efficiency of the debt option is evident as the tax charge increases by only 10 per cent despite a 60 per cent uplift in operating profit. With no extra shares in issue, the EPS benefits significantly.

The danger of the all-debt option is of course the financial position of the enlarged company post the deal. In this instance we can see quickly that interest cover falls to 2.8× (240/85.2). Whether this is comfortable is very much dependent on the type of business it is (i.e. how cyclical or stable the revenues are), the need for capital expenditure and the cash generation expected of the enlarged business. (See financial position, interest cover on pp. 177–180 for a fuller discussion.)

If the business was cyclical with a high level of fixed costs, where volumes and prices are subject to significant swings, this level of interest cover would be a source of some concern. A relatively small fall in revenues could reduce interest cover to dangerous levels. The risks to shareholders in such a scenario rise dramatically. However, if the business was very stable with strong pricing and good visibility of revenues, one might feel more relaxed about the all-debt option.

> we need to see whether the deal actually 'adds value'

As the impact on earnings is positive for all three options, management could argue that as growth is enhanced by the deal it represents a sensible move for shareholders. However, we need to see whether the deal actually 'adds value'. We also need to bear in mind that there are considerable risks that the deal will not deliver the hoped-for results.

Looking at the value added we need to assess the cost of capital and see whether the returns exceed this. The returns are relatively straightforward. We are buying £90 million of operating profits (£65m of operating profit plus the £25 million of merger benefits) for a total outlay of £940 million. This gives a pre-tax return of 9.6 per cent. With tax at 30 per cent the return falls to 6.7 per cent.

The cost of debt we know to be 8 per cent in this instance. However, as discussed above there are tax advantages of debt – the interest payments are deductible before arriving at the pre-tax number. Accordingly the cost of debt is 5.6 per cent.

The cost of equity is more complicated. In this case we are assuming it is 12 per cent.

For the central proforma case we take the 'weighted average cost of capital'. Here we simply take into account that we are funding 70 per cent of the deal at 12 per cent and 30 per cent at 5.6 per cent. This gives an overall cost of 10 per cent.

Table 3.3 demonstrates that economic value is added only when the deal is funded by debt. This is because debt is cheaper than equity and crucially the tax deductability of interest payments reduces the post-tax cost of debt considerably. As discussed earlier, the issue here is what happens to the risk profile given the higher financial gearing associated with this option. As an investor you would have to feel confident with the higher risks being undertaken.

Table 3.3 Value added

	Pre-tax (%)	Post-tax (%)
Returns (90/940)	9.6	6.7
Cost of debt	8	5.6
Cost of equity	12	12
WACC (70/30)	10	10

The other two options clearly destroy value. The only way they might add value is if the 'synergy' benefits are much higher than the planned-for £25 million. Obviously the higher the assumption, the greater the risk of not realising the benefits. In this case it would take a further £45 million of synergy benefits to ensure the deal did not destroy value: £130 million/£940 million = 14.4 per cent. Taxed at 30 per cent this gives a post-tax return of 10.1 per cent. In the context of a company making £65 million, a further £65 million would be a very tall order.

The other way of trying to make the deal more beneficial in terms of economic added value is to reduce the extent of the premium that has been paid. In this case it is 30 per cent, which is a fairly standard premium to secure a takeover. Trying to secure the company with a 15 per cent premium would save £90 million. Whether the management and shareholders agree to this is a moot point. It does illustrate that the problem with acquisitions is that they are good for the shareholders of the company being taken over but not so good for the shareholders in the acquiring company.

Earnings growth or returns?

Therefore, when evaluating the success or otherwise of the deal, you need to be clear about what is being delivered and what you feel is an appropriate way of assessing the deal. Conventionally there has been a tendency to focus on the impact on earnings. However, following the raft of poor deals in the past few years and a disillusionment with management and their far from shareholder-friendly policies and actions, there is much greater focus on deals delivering value. With balance sheets constrained and the appetite for risk having fallen significantly, this again argues for an approach based on value being created for shareholders.

The issue of growth is also perhaps even better understood if one considers the aggressive acquisition policies of companies in the 1980s and early 1990s. The 'trick' here was to use 'highly rated paper' (i.e. shares standing on a very high P/E) to acquire lower-rated companies. This would both deliver the growth needed to justify the high rating and ensure a re-rating of the earnings acquired. The higher the rating, the less paper you need to issue.

By way of example, look at the previous case and assume the stock was rated at 30× earnings rather than 20×. Let's consider the all-share option in this case (Table 3.4). On 30× earnings the share price would be 981p (32.7 × 30). If we are issuing shares at a 20 per cent discount we need to issue only 120 million shares (120 × 784p generates the required £940 million) rather than the £180 million for the all-share option with the share price on 20× earnings.

Here we can see that the earnings enhancement is dramatically better – 38.3p of earnings represents an uplift of 17 per cent compared with the 2.4 per cent increase in the first example. This obviously drives a great earnings growth story. Critically, however, there is absolutely no difference to the value added of the deal. The returns on the price paid are exactly the same: £90 million on an outlay of £940 million. The cost of capital is 12 per cent because of the all-equity nature of the deal.

Table 2.4 The all-share option (using highly rated paper)

	All shares
Operating profit	240
Interest	10
Pre-tax	230
Post-tax earnings	–69
Earnings	161
No of shares	420m
EPS	38.3p

This provides an even more dramatic conflict between the two ways of evaluating the deal. Earnings are boosted dramatically but the economic result of the deal is precisely the same.

Benefits of the deal

How much profit is to be added when performing this calculation? This figure depends crucially on the 'integration benefits' of adding the new business. This will depend on the scope for cost cutting and/or generating extra revenues from combining the two businesses.

Costs

If there is significant overcapacity in an industry and this has led to weak pricing (with the target company especially aggressive in looking for market share), then taking over a competitor may make a lot of sense. If fixed costs are high and the number of factories can be reduced, then costs will benefit from the closure of uneconomically performing factories and greater efficiency at the factories that are now producing greater volume at lower costs. In addition, there may be cost savings as a result of bigger discounts when buying greater quantities of raw materials/supplies ('procurement economies'). These procurement economies can be an important saving for retail or distribution-related businesses as they will give them a much more effective hand when dealing with suppliers.

The issue with costs is whether the benefits are just a one-off and do little to improve the longer-term growth outlook for the business. As a result earnings growth over a (say) two-year period will be valued relatively low by the market. An interesting example here is the merger trend in the pharmaceuticals sector. There can be many savings in R&D and marketing in such situations. However, if investors have been investing for growth through new product introductions they may fear that the cost-cutting initiatives (and indeed the merger itself) are being implemented to conceal the poor performance of the drug portfolio. Therefore the cost cutting will be valued differently compared with the earnings growth that may be generated from 'top line', i.e. revenue, growth.

Another important issue to bear in mind with cost cutting is whether the benefits are offset by price or volume weakness post the deal. In our earlier example of taking capacity out of an industry the danger is whether the deal does enough to lead to price stability. If the industry remains fragmented, with a number of players committed to gaining market share and import competition a key threat, the prices are likely to remain weak. In this case weak pricing will offset the cost reduction programme.

Price benefits

Revenues will obviously benefit from the contribution of the acquired company. However, the removal of an aggressive competitor will hopefully lead to a less competitive marketplace. This will help pricing stability. This process is often referred to as consolidation: the industry sees fewer players with greater market shares. In theory this is beneficial to pricing, although there can be exceptions as mentioned above. (A powerful competitor may still be driven by market share considerations and/or cash flow to service a high level of debt or need for income, in a family-run business for example or more simply when there is an economic downturn.)

Therefore the removal of a disruptive competitor and the subsequent improvement in industry pricing could see quite a significant benefit to the company and its shareholders. It is worth bearing in mind that the benefits of higher pricing have a 'geared' impact on the bottom line – a few percentage points increase in prices can dramatically improve profits. This would reinforce the cost savings benefits described above.

These cost and revenue benefits are why a company is prepared to pay a premium to acquire the business in the first place. If it is the case that the pricing environment has improved, this makes a crucial difference. Post the deal the management has a greater influence on the market and this helps to improve the 'quality of earnings', that is to say the earnings stream is more stable and management has greater influence on matters that affect its profits. (Quality of earnings is discussed in more detail on p. 131.) Deals which help improve the pricing and revenue potential tend to be the most successful.

Volume benefits

The benefits from extra volume can also have an important impact on both revenues and the bottom line (again the impact of operational gearing). The extra volume also equates to an enhanced market share which will improve the quality of earnings. Volumes may benefit from access to a bigger and better distribution network or to different distribution channels.

Revenue benefits

These volume and pricing benefits of acquisition combine to generate an overall revenue impact. The ability to grow revenues, the 'top line', and not just enable one-off cost reductions to be made will make a crucial difference as to whether the deal adds value. These revenue benefits will be valued much more highly by the market as they will improve the quantity and quality of earnings.

Timing of benefits

Some deals will inevitably be more complex than others. Therefore it may take time for the full benefits of a deal to come through. The company may well make it clear that the deal will take time to yield the maximum benefit and that it will incur short-term earnings dilution. This sort of deal is often referred to as being 'strategic'. If the company has a good track record in delivering returns and living up to its promises (as well as having a clearly articulated long-term strategy), the investment community will support the deal. Alternatively, if the management has a poor record and a reputation for subtracting 'value' when doing deals, it will be hard pressed to convince investors.

When deals work

Given the high risks attached to acquisitions and their poor record in adding value, it is worth having a sense of when they have a good chance of working. Clearly, management track record is crucial here – a history of not overpaying and then making sure the acquisition is effectively integrated is essential. While it sounds easy, the number of deals that do add value suggest very few do it well.

A checklist of factors that give the deal a chance of succeeding would include the following (although this list is not necessarily comprehensive):

- a sensible price is paid which enables the weighted average cost of capital (WACC) to be exceeded
- acquisition made at right point in cycle
- consistent with stated strategy
- acquisition is part of an overall strategy ... the strategy is not to acquire
- core business is performing well with few problems
- management not trying to avoid difficulties within core
- management fully understands the business/market – the acquisition is part of core business
- known target company well for some time
- management has the resources to ensure integration is done effectively without the core being adversely affected
- pricing in the industry is improved
- revenue growth is delivered
- genuine cost benefits/economies of scale
- improves quality of earnings
- improves growth profile of business
- adds a key capability, a new product, new region or technological skill
- balance sheet not too stretched post the deal
- bolt-on deals more likely to add value than strategic deals.

As the list demonstrates, management discipline and focus are essential. The demise of many of the high-fliers in the technology, media and telecoms (TMT) boom was interesting in that many were highly acquisitive. They often used highly rated paper which would immediately have boosted earnings but not necessarily added value (as discussed in the example on p. 104). A number of acquisitions occurred at the peak of the cycle at valuations that could never possibly have added value.

Therefore companies that are continually acquisitive may well be trying to hide a far from flattering performance of their core operations. Interestingly, in *Good to Great* (2001) Jim Collins argues that great companies use acquisitions to accelerate not create momentum.[19] This suggests that the core is working really well and there is a very clear strategy and sense of direction – the acquisition then helps accelerate that. However, for many companies the acquisition is the strategy or is seen as a way of transforming a company running out of growth and ideas. It won't work.

Companies that are highly acquisitive may also be prone to engage in accounting practices that put them in the best possible light and give the illusion of growth. This raises serious questions over the risks being run and the quality of those earnings both from an accounting and sustainability standpoint. Accordingly, if you are invested in such a company you are running a much higher degree of risk than you may appreciate and your chances of making money are much more restricted.

Why deals do not add value for shareholders

The academic evidence suggests that few deals add value or work to the benefit of shareholders in the acquiring company and it is worth examining why the above theory does not appear to work in practice.

The most common dangers tend to be:

- the price paid is too high, making it impossible to generate an appropriate return
- the company is bought at the wrong point in the cycle – earnings from it immediately drop dramatically
- the strategy is ill-conceived
- management takes on too many unknowns (e.g. a business it doesn't know in a region/country it doesn't know)
- management is overstretched at the acquiring company – 'management dilution'
- the business is not integrated as effectively as planned – does not deliver promised benefits
- culture of the two companies is radically different preventing a smooth integration
- diseconomies of scale – the enlarged company is too big to run effectively

---

[19] See note 6, p. 104.

- target is in a weaker position than envisaged
- loss of more revenue than anticipated
- loss of top people in acquired company.

The price paid and the point of the cycle at which the company is bought are the key drivers of a successful deal. Having bought the company, however, it has to be managed and integrated to deliver the appropriate returns. Good-quality management is a scarce resource and while the strategy may be well conceived much can go wrong in the integration process. While we have discussed the importance (or otherwise) of earnings dilution, many deals fail due to 'management dilution'. This dilution is likely to be more exposed if the company has gone into product areas or regions that it has no knowledge of – the risks are much greater. Management is spread far too thinly across the enlarged company, resulting in problems in the entire business in a worst case scenario. This can be especially true if the acquisition is in a much poorer position than was envisaged originally. It may have a weaker market position than thought and be in need of a lot of catch-up capital expenditure. These weaknesses may well be why the company was very happy to sell out, of course. It is always worth trying to find out why the acquired company was selling.

> many deals fail due to 'management dilution'

Also, it often appears that among some management there is a size for size's sake approach and an attraction to the glamour and excitement of doing deals. Running the number one business in an industry confers status – returns to shareholders may be a less important item on the agenda.

More cynical reasons for deals being done include:

- size for size's sake
- to protect jobs of top management/boost their salary
- fear of being taken over
- to cover up problems in the core business
- it is easier/more exciting to do a deal than run the existing business.

What is the market's reaction to the deal?

Given the potential benefits and drawbacks of doing deals, how will the stock market react to a deal being announced by a company in which you are interested? This will depend on the interplay of the factors determining why deals work and why they conspicuously fail.

A good test is to ask yourself how far you trust the management. If it announced a deal, would you immediately think it deserves the benefit of the doubt or would you be concerned? This view will be formed by its track record in doing deals that add value, the performance of the existing operations and the financial position.

The market's reaction will also be very much determined by the financing of the deal – how much is financed by the issue of new shares and how much by debt? Again a useful checklist would cover such factors as:

- Is the deal consistent with stated strategy?
- Is there compelling commercial logic... does it fit?
- Management track record – is it trusted, will it deliver?
- What is the size of the deal (in-fill v strategic)?
- What is the price paid? What is the valuation of the target?
- How is the deal financed?
- What is the post-deal financial position... gearing and interest cover?
- What will be the financial impact – effect on earnings and returns v cost of capital?
- What will be the impact on longer-term growth potential?
- What will be the impact on quality of earnings?
- Are the main benefits due to cost savings, pricing power or extra volumes?
- What is the quality of the target?

Summary

The combination of the economic slowdown and the credit crunch has seen many famous and well-established companies go bankrupt or perilously close to bankruptcy. Many others would have failed had it not been for government intervention. A common factor in company failure is the role of management and its strategy.

Many companies failed because a strategy of aggressive growth achieved through acquisition led to companies being too large to run effectively. Overpaying, poor integration and a clash of cultures are just some of the contributory factors that led to the companies being exposed. These factors, allied with an economy turning down and high debt levels (reflecting the fact the deals were funded by borrowings), led to devastating consequences.

Another key element in all this has been the role of boards in effectively challenging (often dominant) CEOs and improving the quality of debate and scrutiny of the company's strategic priorities. Not surprisingly, good corporate governance has emerged as a key area to prevent these mistakes occurring in the future. The balance of power on the board needs to be assessed and the presence of independent non-executive directors is necessary to ensure management acts in the interest of shareholders. Evidence suggests this is of paramount importance. Clearly, not having a board committed to shareholder value in practice (actually doing it, not just talking about it), and where growth is used as a proxy for shareholder value, increases the risk profile considerably.

MANAGEMENT AND STRATEGY CHECKLIST

What is strategy?

- When you own a share in a company you are investing in the competitive position of the business.
- Building and sustaining that competitive advantage is the essence of strategy.
- There are two key elements of strategy:
  - customer value proposition – what makes the company distinctive in the marketplace and how does it excel?
  - resources to deliver – what are the unique characteristics, resources or activities that allow the company to deliver that proposition?
- Does the management team have the blend of necessary skills to appreciate and deliver what the customer requires?
- Mergers and acquisitions rarely add value. They work most effectively when they 'accelerate momentum' whereas when they are driven by size for size's sake they invariably destroy value.

The company's competitive position

Combining a wide and deep 'moat' with low costs will lead to superior returns on sales and assets and this will drive the share price higher over time. You need to establish:

- Is the company a market leader?
- Is it a cost leader?
- Is it gaining or losing market share?
- Are there strong barriers to entry and how have they been strengthened?
- Is it investing in improving its competitive position?
- Does the company have a good record for introducing new products?
- Has the company established a track record in moving profitably into new markets?

4

Performance and returns

What topics are covered in this chapter?

- Why performance and returns are so important
- The five-year trading record
- Sales
- Profits
- Earnings
- EBITDA
- Key performance ratios: profitability and returns
- Operating profit margins
- Return on capital employed (ROCE)
- Economic value added – exceeding the cost of capital
- Summary
- Checklist

Why performance and returns are so important

By getting to grips with the underlying performance of the business we can see whether the company has a genuinely competitive market position and if management is delivering good results from the assets it has under its stewardship. Generating a good return on capital and creating shareholder value as a result tells us whether management is efficient and doing a good job. Critically, it is a key predictor in the long term of whether the shares will make you money.

There are three key elements here:

- the performance of the business in terms of sales, profits, earnings and cash flow
- how that performance measures up against competitors
- the returns those activities are generating – that is, how much money we needed to spend to get those sales and profits.

The sales and profits may look impressive but if we have spent a fortune on developing the product and marketing it then the returns may tell a far less compelling story. Without the crucial reference point of the returns the company generates we do not know whether it is worth all the effort.

Evaluating the trend in sales, especially when we break it down into the price and volume components, provides an excellent guide as to how the company is performing both in absolute terms and relative to its peer group. If we know how an industry is doing in terms of volumes we can tell whether the company is gaining or losing market share. If we can see prices going up it may reveal that the company enjoys strong pricing power or that new products are being introduced that can be priced more highly. This tells us whether the company really does have a competitive advantage. If the sales performance is good we then need to ensure that the returns on those sales (operating margins) are also attractive.

Earnings performance is a number that receives a lot of attention and we often refer to deals that have been 'earnings enhancing' or 'dilutive'. It is also the denominator in the widely used valuation technique of price/earnings ratios. We look at the growth in earnings and whether or not earnings are in line with expectations. In effect earnings performance is a post-tax guide to how price, volumes and costs have been performing.

While widely used and therefore an important number to be aware of, there is a lot of scope for earnings to be manipulated and, as we saw when looking at earnings quality, we need to see how the earnings correlate with cash to provide a true measure of the underlying performance of the business.

Returns v growth

One of the issues that comes up frequently is whether growth is really attractive. A lot of value was destroyed by the 'growth' companies of the dot-com boom. A classic case here is a business that is growing sales or earnings rapidly – but at the expense of return on sales (operating margins) and return on capital employed. To rub salt into the wound the company could be seeing significant cash outflows to generate this growth (and require a series of fund raisings to stay on track). The other key element of returns is of course shareholder value – it may be the company is generating good growth but the risks of the strategy are very high (which might be true when acquisitions are used, for example).

This is not to say that growth is not a key determinant of long-term share price performance. However, we need to have a more comprehensive view of the situation by looking at growth in conjunction with risk and quality as well as the other elements of the Valuation Villa – especially returns.

The other element to consider is timescale. There may be a strong case for building market share in a growth phase to enjoy subsequently the pricing power that position gives the company longer term. This case should be made very clearly in the strategy statement.

> the other element to consider is timescale

In the long run it is high returns on capital, cash generation and value-added growth that will drive the share price higher. This demonstrates that you have bought into a business that has real competitive advantage and is using your money effectively and compensating you for the risks of investing.

All the statistical evidence suggests that the key driver of share price performance over time is return on capital employed (ROCE). Reflecting the importance of cash generation, many investors prefer to look at 'cash flow return on capital'. Importantly, the higher the return on sales, the higher the return on capital will be and the more cash the company will be generating. This cash allows the company to fund its strategy and rising dividends (another key driver of share price appreciation). The high returns give us confidence that the company can reinvest its strong cash flows to grow and create value for sustained long-term returns.

We will now look at the key elements of performance in terms of

- the five-year trading record
- sales
- profits
- earnings
- EBITDA.

This is then followed by an analysis of the key performance ratios.

The five-year trading record

The five-year trend in sales, profits and earnings relative to the sector will tell you a great deal about the characteristics of the company and its performance. Has the company demonstrated consistent growth in sales, profits and earnings? Have there been wide swings in sales and profits? Have sales grown rapidly while profit growth has been slow, implying progressive deterioration in operating margins?

There will be a five-year record in the report and accounts (R&A) which will detail the trend in the key numbers and ratios. This is a useful and quick way of getting to grips with recent trends. Hopefully this five-year record will reveal the performance of all the company's divisions. This will enable you to see the contribution of those various divisions and whether they have been a spur to, or a drag on, performance.

This will immediately tell you whether the company is a growth or highly cyclical company. Alternatively, if sales and profits have been on a steady downward path this might reveal a company in long-term decline. A rapid growth in sales but falling margins may reveal a company looking to grow market share at all costs.

The company's performance relative to its sector will demonstrate whether the company has been performing better or worse than its peer group. You will need to ask:

- What has been the trend in sales, profit or earnings?
- Has it been losing market share?
- Has it witnessed an erosion of margins due to costs increasing, or prices falling, more than its peers?

This track record is a good starting point for quickly getting a sense of what has been going on and how the company has been performing. For a more thorough view, looking at its key performance ratios (see later) will reveal a great deal.

Sales

Sales are a good indicator of how the company is performing – are they growing reflecting organic growth in the market? Or taking market share from a competitor or from introducing new products that are appealing to consumers? And of course we need to break the sales performance down into what is happening to prices and volumes. Are prices going up as the company has pricing power, is developing higher-value new products with better features or reflecting cost increases?

In sectors such as retailing, 'like for like' sales growth is monitored closely. This is the performance of existing outlets and strips out the impact of acquisitions. The level of sales will indicate the health or otherwise of the market – or whether the company is taking market share (i.e. the company's sales exceed those of the market overall). This performance relative to the industry peer group is obviously a key indicator of both the company's competitive position and management's ability to deliver.

The performance of sales does need to be put in context, however. The profitability of those sales is crucial. If sales are growing but at the expense of operating margins or the risk of causing a price war, this is potentially very dangerous.

If sales are growing rapidly while margins are falling sharply, the value of those sales is clearly deteriorating. However, if there is a long-term strategy of taking market share, this may make sense, especially if the company has a very low cost base and a strong financial position. These characteristics make the longer-term strategy far more credible.

To get a clearer perspective on the performance of sales you need to ask yourself what the key drivers of sales have been, in particular:

- To what extent is sales growth organic and what has been the impact of acquisitions?
- How much of the sales growth is driven by new products?
- To what extent has the revenue figure been influenced by volume or price?
- Has the company been chasing volumes and market share?
- Is the sales pattern stable? Are sales sustainable and easy to predict?
- What is the divisional breakdown and performance – which division has been contributing most to the sales performance?
- Are there any noticeable leaders and laggards?
- What is happening to the mix of sales and the margins generated?

As a general point it is best to be careful when company statements start with proudly announcing record sales. This often tends to mean that the profits and earnings generated by those sales are disappointing. The company may have pursued volumes at the expense of margin.

Accounting for sales

Historically it has been felt that the sales figure was one of the few numbers not subject to widespread accounting manipulation. However, recent accounting scandals, especially on Wall Street, have tended to revolve around sales manipulation. Indeed, in 2000, 70 per cent of Securities and Exchange Commission (SEC) accounting and audit enforcement cases were problems of revenue recognition – either recognising future revenues too early or recording revenues that did not exist at all.[1]

Therefore you should try to understand the company's policy on sales recognition. It is a particular concern where there are long-term contracts involved such as building or software contracts. The photocopier company Xerox was forced in June 2002 to restate its sales and profits to a significant extent. The SEC alleged that it had inflated revenues by more than $3 billion and earnings by $1.5 billion over a four-year period. Revenues were being booked well before sales actually took place.

The manipulation of sales was also a feature of the technology and telecommunications sector, with 'hollow swaps', where telecoms companies sold capacity to each other and booked it as revenues even if no money changed hands. Related-party transactions, selling to companies in which you had a significant stake, were also undertaken to boost the sales figure. These devices gave the appearance of high growth and reflected the fact that sales were featuring increasingly as a valuation driver.

This manipulation of sales tends to boost profits as there is a 'mismatch' – the costs related to those sales are invariably not recognised until they are incurred at a much later date.

Profits

As with sales, assessing the trend in profits over a five-year period (and longer if possible, especially in highly cyclical businesses, to establish what a complete cycle might look like) enables you quickly to get a sense of the characteristics, quality and performance of the business. Used in conjunction with sales, profits provide a major performance measure (operating margins) which we will explore in detail on p. 146.

---

[1] Turner, L. E. (2001) 'SEC and Financial Reporting Institute', 31 May.

Similar issues with sales need to be explored:

- To what extent is profit growth organic and what has been the impact of acquisitions?
- To what extent has profit been influenced by volume or price?
- To what extent has profit benefited from cost reductions?
- Is the profit pattern stable? Are profits sustainable and easy to predict?
- Are there any one-off boosts to profits?
- Are profits depressed by investing in marketing or R&D to foster long-term growth?
- What is the divisional breakdown of profits?
- Are there any noticeable leaders and laggards?
- What is happening to the mix of profits and the margins generated?

It is important to have a sense of the divisional contribution to overall profits. The value attaching to the different divisions will vary depending on their economic characteristics, returns, growth and quality of earnings. Therefore a company can hit profit expectations, but that is not the end of the story. How did it do it? If it is achieved through the help of a one-off contribution, such as a property disposal or selling an asset or a volatile, low-quality business doing extremely well while a better-quality one disappoints, the share price will suffer.

The benefit from disposals and the impact of exceptionals are important issues. They influence the quality of earnings. We will discuss these factors in detail when exploring the trend and influences on earnings. Earnings are an important measure of performance and influence on valuation.

Profits can be made to grow through acquisition while earnings per share can fall correspondingly (as more shares are issued). Accordingly, we will concentrate the discussion on earnings rather than on profits. The issues and concepts are applicable to both.

Earnings

The trend in earnings per share, defined as earnings attributable to ordinary shareholders divided by the number of shares in issue, is often regarded as a key measure of a company's performance. Much of the stock market's attention is focused on the projected earnings of a company. Analysis of corporate results invariably revolves around an assessment of

> the growth in EPS is a critical guide to how well a company is doing

what earnings have been reported compared with what had been expected. Whether this focus is correct is perhaps debatable and we will explore other important measures of performance later. Nonetheless, the growth in EPS is a critical guide to how well a company is doing. This will normally drive the share price. Poor earnings results or downgrades will put pressure on the share price. The growth in EPS, especially when compared with the market overall, is often a key component of management bonus and option arrangements.

Given the crucial importance of this figure it is worth being aware of:

- the various definitions of earnings per share that can be used
- how companies may distort the numbers to hit targets.

Earnings definition

The calculation of earnings per share is in principle very straightforward. You take the profit left after tax that belongs to ordinary shareholders. This is sometimes referred to as **attributable profit** as it is profit that is available to ordinary shareholders. The earnings per share figure is then derived by dividing the attributable profit by the number of ordinary shares in issue.

Example – EPS calculation

> A fictional brake-unit manufacturer, Full Stop, had operating profits of £7.5 million in 2010. Let us assume that interest costs were £2.5 million, so deducting that from the operating profits gives a pre-tax profit of £5 million. If the standard tax rate of 30 per cent is applied, post-tax profits, called earnings, are £3.5 million.
>
> If there are 30.5 million shares in issue, the earnings per share number is 3.5 million/30.5 million, or 11.5p per share.

It should always be remembered that the numerator (earnings or attributable profit) must be that which belongs to ordinary shareholders. Therefore, if there are any preference dividends due to preference shareholders, these must be deducted before arriving at the earnings figure. Similarly, if there are any minority charges these must also be deducted. Minority charges relate to outside shareholders' claim on the profits of the company – again they are not attributable to the ordinary shareholders in the company. So if an outside company has a 25 per cent investment in the company (or a subsidiary), it is entitled to 25 per cent of the earnings of the company. In this situation ordinary shareholders do not own and therefore are not entitled to 100 per cent of the earnings generated by the company.

The denominator

The number of shares can be found in the notes to the earnings number in the accounts. There will normally be the weighted average number of shares used for the period in question. To calculate the year-end position you may need to check the called-up share capital note to the accounts. This will detail any changes in the number of allotted shares in the year.

As well as considering any distortions to earnings from exceptional or amortisation charges, you will need to ensure there are no distortions arising from the number of shares in issue. In particular, there might be **convertible shares (convertible loan stock)** that need to be taken into account or outstanding share options.

If there is a convertible issue, you need to work out what the conversion terms are. This is normally stated in the accounts. For example, each £1 of convertible may convert to four ordinary shares. Then this is multiplied by the outstanding amount of convertibles. This gives you the number of shares on conversion. To get to the earnings number, you need to add back the interest on the bond or the cost of the preference dividends to the earnings amount (as the bonds or **preference shares** are 'converted' to ordinary shares there would be no need for these payments). The new earnings per share will normally be lower than the original one. This is called dilution and you will usually find that the 'fully diluted earnings' calculation is done in the R&A.

What earnings are we using?

There is often an abundance of earnings numbers (and hence P/Es, the share price divided by the earnings per share, which we will come to later) and potential misunderstanding as different methods of computing and using earnings are employed. To avoid confusion, it is important to be clear about the two ways of looking at earnings. It is crucial to define carefully:

- the time period to which the earnings relate
- the accounting definitions used.

Prospective v historic

Investment is a forward-looking business. Therefore, wherever possible it is important to look at what the future earnings of a company are likely to be.

There is clearly risk in doing this (the forecast may prove to be far from accurate), but again this is an integral component of investment – the confidence you have in the forecast is also an important element in your decision.

When looking at P/Es it is extremely important to differentiate between forward-looking multiples – often called prospective P/Es – and historic (earnings for the last fiscal year) or trailing P/Es (i.e. based on the past 12 months or the last four reported quarters). While many information sources such as newspapers quote historic and/or trailing P/Es, this is far less useful than a forward-looking measure – investment is about the future. The prospective P/E takes into account how well a company is expected to do in the current and subsequent financial years. So wherever possible try to use the prospective multiple.

These forecasts are available on some financial websites, normally in the form of the 'consensus earnings'. The consensus earnings figure is the average of the numbers expected from stockbroking analysts covering the company. They will be reached using their forecasts for the companies' key markets and in consultation with the companies. In addition, when a company has reported results the financial press will often carry a guide to what profits are going to be in the current year or for the next full year.

The forecast is useful when looking at the growth rate in earnings delivered by the company and how that compares with both the company's sector and the overall stock market. The valuation of the share will depend on the company's earnings growth rate compared with the market average.

Calendarised earnings

This refers to the earnings of a company when adjusted to a calendar year basis. This is done to ensure comparability of companies with different year ends. For example, to arrive at this number for a company with a March year end you would take a quarter of the last financial year's earnings and three-quarters of the current year's earnings to establish the earnings in the calendar year. This would be done on the same basis for future years so it is crucial for using prospective earnings. The numbers are then broadly comparable to companies with a December year end.

Pre-exceptional pre-amortisation earnings v stated earnings

When looking at P/E multiples it is critical to compare like with like. What can sometimes confuse investors is when analysts or commentators use different methods to compute the earnings. The simplest and easiest way to compare earnings on a standardised basis is to use **pre-exceptional pre-amortisation** numbers. The rationale for using this definition is that exceptional charges, by definition, are one-off by nature and should not be allowed to distort the earnings series of the underlying business.

Exceptional items

Exceptional items (exceptionals) can come from a variety of sources. It could be the costs associated with closing a factory or division, or the writing down in value of assets. These items would appear as a negative in the profit and loss (P&L) account. Exceptional credits might derive from the disposal of investments or a piece of property. These charges/credits will not be related to the underlying performance of the business. Also, a really large credit will lead to an abnormally low P/E, while a significant charge will lead to a very high P/E which is not representative.

As well as comparing across companies, using pre-exceptional earnings makes for a fairer and more effective assessment of a company's earnings progress. Again it is important to be aware of the earnings number being used. For example, if a company has a large exceptional credit in one year, if you do not strip this out of the earnings number it might appear that the next year's earnings are going to fall. This could lead to a wrong conclusion about how the company is doing.

What should be deemed exceptional?

There is a danger, however. Companies may be tempted to include (usually large) items that are in fact normal costs of doing business. So you need to ask yourself, is the exceptional charge really exceptional and what does it relate to? A danger sign is if these charges occur year in year out – so that they are hardly an exceptional occurrence. In addition, if the costs relate to the core business, some commentators would tend to ignore them on the basis that they are not exceptional.

> a danger sign is if these charges occur year in year out

The Institute for Investment Management and Research (IIMR) has its own definition of earnings. The broad rule is that if the items relate to 'capital' items they are legitimate exceptionals, whereas if they relate to operating events within the core business they are not exceptional items. The capital item may refer to profit or loss on a disposal of an asset such as an investment, a subsidiary or a property. It may also reflect a change to the value of that asset.

You will often see in the R&A, in the note relating to earnings, an explanation as to how they have been calculated (a note is always worth looking at, especially if there are exceptional items). This will normally include an IIMR definition also sometimes referred to as 'headline' earnings. The IIMR definition will normally be lower and stricter if there are exceptional charges than the definition used by the company. This will essentially reflect the exclusion of exceptional charges that relate to the core business, such as large restructuring or redundancy charges.

An interesting example is the UK food retailer Sainsbury's. The company had an exceptional debit of £20 million in the 2002 R&A debited from the UK stores' performance. This figure was down from £37 million in 2001. The reason for this charge was cited as being due to:

> *The costs in Sainsbury's supermarkets relate to the business transformation programme which involves upgrading its IT systems, supply chain and store portfolio. These costs are exceptional due to the scale, scope and pace of the transformation programme. These costs primarily relate to the closure of depots and stores and associated reorganisation costs. (p. 24 of the 2002 accounts)*

Are these charges really exceptional? On a strict IIMR definition they would not be as they relate to the core business. In addition, it is worth looking at this in terms of the position of the underlying business. The reason these costs are exceptional relates to the scale of the charges and action needed to upgrade the IT systems, supply chain and store portfolio. However, as discussed when looking at the company's economic and market position, spending to maintain the competitive position of the company is crucial. One interpretation of the scale of this needed upgrade is that the company failed to invest properly on a consistent basis, hence the need for 'catch-up' spending. The company had fallen behind its main rival Tesco, partly attributable perhaps to this lack of investment in its 'IT systems, supply chain and store portfolio'. On this basis, it seems inappropriate to treat this item as exceptional.

Exceptionals and earnings comparisons

Exceptional items can distort performance comparisons. A competitor that consistently invested in these crucial areas for a food retail company would have incurred these costs. This would have depressed its operating margin compared with a company such as Sainsbury's that did not invest regularly. Similarly, taking the charge as an exceptional means that the operating margin does not suffer if you use a pre-exceptional number to calculate it.

Performance comparisons can also be distorted if a company makes a major restructuring provision, which might be deemed exceptional due to its sheer scale. This then will flatter future performance as the use of provisions means costs are lower than would otherwise be the case. A company that has consistently kept costs low and incurred redundancy costs as a regular feature would not have the advantage of this provision to help its future performance. But its continuing focus on low costs at all times is a much more effective management approach (as identified by Buffett. The subsequent figures are much cleaner.

So what has started out as a simple issue of earnings per share has become complicated by the issue of exceptionals. The message is that care needs to be taken and just because a company calls it an exceptional item does not mean you have to agree with it. Indeed, a company's frequent use of exceptionals may be worth investigating in detail to make sure this does not reflect a historically overinflated cost base that is finally being treated or a systematic underinvestment in the business. This approach to exceptionals may not be one that will make you money in the longer run.

Amortisation

Prior to IFRS (see below) a company was obliged to write off the goodwill that arises when it acquires another company at a premium to assets. The premium to **book value** is called the **goodwill** and reflects the value of the group's brand names, market shares, etc. Some businesses, most notably service-related businesses, have little by way of assets, so goodwill on acquisition can be quite considerable.

This goodwill was then 'written off' over the course of its 'economic life'. This may be ten years. So if a business with £20 million of assets is purchased for £100 million, the goodwill is £80 million. If this is written down over ten years it generates an £8 million per annum charge to the P&L. It should be stressed that this charge to the P&L does not involve an outflow of cash (referred to as a non-cash item).

Therefore when comparing a company that had made an acquisition with one that had not, the acquiring company is penalised if you use a post-amortisation charge. Similarly, a company may have made a series of acquisitions prior to the introduction of the accounting policy of writing off goodwill to the P&L. This company will have higher earnings growth as the goodwill was written off to the balance sheet.

Using a pre-amortisation definition irons out these difficulties and means that you can compare like with like. Therefore, whenever looking at quoted P/Es try to be clear as to whether they refer to the past or the future and whether they are before or after various exceptional charges. You should also question the legitimacy of charges deemed exceptional.

The impact of IFRS

From 1 January 2005 some 7000 European Union listed companies have had to prepare their accounts under International Financial Reporting Standards (IFRS). Historically there has been a difference in accounting approaches and often accounts have been prepared for different groups – in the UK it might be the shareholder that takes precedence while in parts of Europe minimising tax may have been the objective and so there was more focus on what is presented to the tax authorities. Different government policies may also have meant that it was advantageous to interpret things differently.

As we saw when looking at sectors, investors are increasingly focused on comparing companies globally. Therefore it is important to be able to rely on the consistency of financial reporting to make international comparisons. This requires a uniform set of high-quality accounting standards. One area that is helpful to investors is the suggestion that there is greater disclosure and detail in divisional breakdowns. This will help promote greater understanding of the business and what drives the different elements within it.

The policies that have greatest impact on the earnings and balance sheet of the company are discussed below.

Earnings

As far as 'exceptional' items are concerned there is not a major difference between the old accounting methodology and IFRS. However, UK standards specified the term 'exceptional' and provided a tight definition of these items, whereas IFRS defines items that need to be separately reported and deemed special. Such material items that might be deemed 'special' include restructuring costs, write-down costs, litigation settlements, as well as any provision reversals – all very similar to the definitions of exceptionals above. Again the distinction between capital and operating items is still very much worth making.

One of the issues that will influence sectors such as technology and software companies, banks and media companies are rules on share-based payments. These differ substantially from previous UK policies in the expenses treatment of employee stock options. A higher recognised employment cost is likely to arise which will depress profits and earnings.

Another element where there might be some changes is when costs can be capitalised (that is, charged as an investment in assets and therefore not charged to costs). The policy will be to expense items immediately unless the costs incurred will result in future economic benefits (that is, the project becomes commercially viable) when capitalisation is permitted. Where development costs and patents are capitalised this will lead to a higher amortisation charge and depress earnings (though there will be no impact on cash flow).

Mark-to-market

One of the most controversial elements of IFRS has been IAS 39. This is the standard on fair value or 'mark-to-market' accounting for financial instruments, including **derivatives**. Gains and losses that arise from the changing market price of these assets will be reflected in the P&L and hence impact the earnings reported by the company. This will make the reported earnings from these companies much more volatile.

The banks have been challenging this because of the impact on their business of holding financial assets that have seen their prices fall dramatically as a result of the credit crunch. They argue that sometimes the market price is far from useful because the market is too illiquid to give a real indication of what the asset is worth. They also contend that they may hold the asset until maturity and so again the mark-down is neither relevant nor appropriate. Lloyd Blankfein, chief executive of Goldman Sachs, has argued[2] that there is a strong rationale for mark-to-market accounting as it forces managers to see the 'early warnings' of the crisis as market values adjust quickly to the environment. This flags up issues emerging for the banks in the holding of these assets and to investors of the trend in asset backing. He also touched upon the need to ensure that off-balance sheet items and any involvement in structured investment vehicles (SIVs) were visible in the accounts (an issue we touch upon in the financial position chapter on p. 175).

This mark-to-market controversy was also highlighted by David Einhorn, the hedge fund manager who made considerable amounts of money

---

[2] Hughes, J. (2009) 'Goldman Chief Backing for Fair Value', *Financial Times*, 11 June.

shorting Lehman shares. He has referred to mark-to-market when applied by some companies as being 'mark-to-myth' or 'mark-to-fantasy'. This can happen when financial institutions use their own models (and own favourable assumptions?) to arrive at a valuation. Einhorn analysed Lehman's issues with great precision and clarity and was proved right. Interestingly, many of his comments appeared to be about not carrying assets at appropriate values and therefore presenting an overinflated view of Lehman's asset backing. So while there appears to be a lot of controversy about IAS 39 it is clearly a crucial area. (It is also interesting how much analytical intelligence was conveyed by Einhorn 'shorting' Lehman – information that if acted upon earlier by the company and the authorities could possibly have made a difference to the eventual outcome.)

One also wonders, given that Enron used mark-to-market to boost its earnings (but had a tendency to manipulate markets) and was delighted at its availability, whether some of the financial institutions did indeed use 'mark-to-market' on the way up; naturally they became very reluctant to have the same discipline on the way down. This certainly serves to reinforce the wisdom of Blankfein's comments. Clearly this will depend on the type of financial instrument, whether it has a certain income stream and how long the investment will be held: will it be held until maturity and was that the original intention? If companies have different policies or reclassify their holdings then comparing the performance of differing financial companies will be very difficult.

Impairment reviews

An important change is that goodwill arising on acquisition will no longer be amortised. Instead, the asset will remain on the balance sheet subject to annual reviews of its value. Any change to its value will be charged to the P&L – although as with amortisation the write-off is a non-cash charge. An **impairment review** provides a far more rigorous regime where management must assess the business's value based on a **discounted cash flow (DCF)** methodology. Clearly, any deterioration in the volume and pricing environment will (especially if operational gearing is high) have a major impact on value. This will favour deals that enable pricing discipline to be improved. Conversely, sectors where international trade is significant will face continuous pressure on prices thus threatening impairment reviews.

More importantly, an 'impairment review' will inevitably lag the decline in the subsidiary's value (e.g. as with Vodafone). That is, the market will discount the poor contribution in earnings and cash flow terms from the acquired subsidiary very swiftly and so the market cap will have already fallen. The company will then (in nine times out of 10) recognise this after the event. The financial effect is negligible at that point – the real issue is of course that the market will have decided that it was a very poor management decision to acquire this business and question its strategic/operational credentials. The valuation effect (as opposed to the impact on reported numbers) is negligible at this point.

> an 'impairment review' will inevitably lag the decline in the subsidiary's value

While many commentators have focused on the extra volatility of earnings due to impairment reviews, the real issue becomes the strategic and operational credentials of the management team. This explains why such reviews are normally done by a new management team, as happened at Ahold. A new management team confronting the reality of poor acquisitions, poorly integrated, made dramatic impairment reviews. As the price already discounted such difficulties, the shares actually went up on the announcement.

Provisions and acquisitions

Under IAS 37 provisions can only be established if the provision

- is a present obligation
- can be reliably estimated
- relates to a past event and
- requires a cash outflow to settle the obligation.

Importantly, the timing between establishment and use is likely to be shortened and unused provisions will have to be released back through the P&L.

Prior to IFRs, provisions were based on management intention and not actual events. This leaves huge scope for manipulation as provisions can be set up in good years or on acquisition and then released to 'smooth' earnings. In common with many aspects of IFRS such smoothing will be far more difficult.

This change regarding provisions appears to rule out providing for post-acquisition integration and reorganisation costs charged against the acquired assets. The use of such provisions has generated huge scepticism towards acquisition-driven growth. The flexibility allowed by making significant provisions and asset write-offs will be greatly reduced as setting up the provisions will be far more difficult. This is perhaps not surprising given that many accounting scandals revolved around highly acquisitive growth stocks with aggressive earnings targets. Preventing such excesses and presenting a more realistic view of both corporate performance and the financial health of a company – what it owes and owns in a real sense – are at the heart of IFRS.

Balance sheet

Many of the changes proposed by IFRS revolve around making the balance sheet (what the company owns and owes) reflect 'fair' not historic values. This means the numbers will more closely reflect invested capital – an excellent discipline in a more returns driven market (this will also impact the P&L).

The balance sheet will also reflect more fully the debt and liability profile of the company as well as its asset usage. If the economic risks of ownership and management control reside with the company, the assets should be recognised on the balance sheet. More operating leases will be classified as finance leases – which need to be capitalised, bringing more assets on to the balance sheet. As some operating costs will now be allocated to the finance line, so operating margins will increase but return on capital will fall. Sectors affected by such changes include hotels, general retailers, transport and airlines.

Special purpose entities (immortalised by Enron but arguably still an issue with the financial sector who have many special investment vehicles (SIVs) where liabilities may reside) will be consolidated where management control is exerted. If this curbs the use of dubious related-party transactions and provides shareholders with a real sense of what the company owns and owes (and the associated risks) it will be very much welcomed. Of course with off-balance sheet debt, the liability for pension deficits and preferred capital all being treated as debt, the impact on gearing ratios will in some instances be considerable. These changes will impact gearing ratios and interest cover, which in some instances may trigger covenants being renegotiated or credit ratings altered. Crucially, all of these liabilities need to be recognised in the company's debt and therefore will appear in the company's enterprise value (which we will discuss on p. 273).

The earnings calculation

In Table 4.1 (later), Company A demonstrates a more complex example of earnings and earnings per share. Here one can see that there are effectively three earnings per share that have been used. The a, b and c references are to both the pre-tax profit number and the corresponding earnings per share figure.

(a) **Stated earnings** – these are earnings post all charges for whatever reason. So this number is struck after amortisation and exceptional charges. It is also struck after the appropriate deduction for minority charges and preference dividends, but this is done for all earnings measures.

(b) **Pre-exceptional profit** – here the exceptional debit of £15 million is reinstated. In this case we have assumed it will be taxed at 30 per cent when calculating the earnings number. (Often this can be quite complicated as there may be different tax treatments of the exceptional charge.)

(c) **Pre-exceptional pre-amortisation profit** – as well as adding back the exceptional charges, we add back the amortisation charge.

The question as to which earnings number you should use is dependent on the issues discussed above. Normally, to get at the underlying performance of the business we would use the pre-exceptional and pre-amortisation definition. However, it does depend on the nature of the exceptional charge. If it is for an ongoing restructuring of the core business, we would be sceptical about treating it as an exceptional – it is an ongoing charge against the core business. This would be reinforced by the fact that the same charge occurs in consecutive years. We should be wary if large exceptional charges are a recurring feature. If, however, the debit relates to a loss on disposal, then this would be very clear cut and we would use the pre-exceptional pre-amortisation level.

We will discuss again the earnings profile of Company A when we examine the quality of earnings below.

Quality of earnings

While all the focus on whether earnings are hitting targets and what the growth rate is tends to grab the headlines, it is crucial to identify the quality as well as the quantity of earnings. The quality of earnings is a vital component when valuing any company. While there is no one definition of earnings quality, the following factors need to be considered:

- The use of very straight and conservative accounting policies by the company which ensures that the earnings number is a true reflection of what is really going on with the business – how it is really performing.

- The sustainability and visibility of earnings in terms of the trading outlook, which in turn derives from the volume, pricing and cost outlook. In this sense it is much easier to predict the earnings of the company.
- That profits are being generated by the core and not any one-off disposals or other benefits.
- What management has control over and can influence.
- That earnings coming through into cash flow cleanly/efficiently.

The first two are clearly related. The more a company engages in accounting manipulation to 'hit' earnings targets, the poorer the quality of its earnings. Critically, however, to the extent that earnings are benefiting from manipulation, its performance is less sustainable – at some stage it will run out of room for manoeuvre and the reality of the trading environment will catch up with it. A company that has, for example, been using provisions to hit earnings targets (by reducing the actual costs of doing business) may run into difficulties once all the provisions have been used up. The real costs of doing business will then reassert themselves. This was a feature of many of the acquisitive growth stocks of the 1990s.

This situation is especially true with the onset of a recession or more difficult sector trading conditions. The economic slowdown since 2008, combined with overinvestment in many areas, has cruelly exposed the lack of earnings quality in many growth stocks. With growth stocks the management may hope that the high rate of growth or benefits from new acquisitions will prevent the problems ever coming to light – either continued growth or a recovery will bail them out.

The IBM example (p. 140) regarding disposals and the pension fund dramatically highlights the issue of earnings quality. Critically, achieving earnings targets or expectations through one-off benefits, while the performance of the underlying business disappoints, will ultimately come to light and the share price will suffer. As these 'benefits' to earnings drop out of the equation, earnings growth will be dependent purely on the performance of the business. If, for example, revenues have disappointed and the company has been losing market share, this will drive the valuation.

The other important aspect for earnings quality is what management can influence. In commodity-based businesses, for example, earnings will, by their nature, be volatile. A timber trading company will be subject to the vagaries of price movements and the impact of currency movements in determining its profits. Both

the other important aspect for earnings quality is what management can influence

of these may be difficult to predict and lie outside management's control. This is not to say the management is not extremely good at what it is doing: but earnings are clearly going to be volatile. If the business benefits from sharp price rises, how much of the improved performance is attributable to good management and its control of the business? As well as lying beyond management control, the sustainability of these higher prices needs to be questioned.

In our case study comparison of the manufacturing company Tin Can and pharmaceutical stock Pink Tablet we can immediately identify that there are many things beyond the control of Tin Can's management that can seriously affect the company's earnings. These include the potential for higher raw material prices, falling selling prices due to industry overcapacity (and the threat from foreign competition) or a major customer taking away a contract. Pink Tablet, with patent protection, a diversified range of products and stable to rising demand, enjoys better-quality earnings.

Earnings and cash flow relationship

The ability to generate cash is crucial to a company's health and wealth. It is also the ultimate driver of value, which we will discuss in more detail later. Therefore it is important that earnings growth translates into cash generation.

There are a number of ways that the earnings growth can be registered (on top of accounting duplicity) without cash flowing into the company. One of the most important is where earnings growth may be achieved through the performance of what is called an **associate company** or related company. This is where the company has an investment of over 20 per cent but below 50 per cent. In this situation the company 'equity accounts' its investment, i.e. it books its share of that company's profits. If the investment is growing rapidly, the company's P&L will show this. If it accounts for all the growth being achieved, we need to consider what is going on within the core business.

Critically, the impact on cash flow is very different. The cash received from this investment will only be the dividends paid out – something the management of the company may not be able to influence. If the investment is growing rapidly there may be no dividend at all – the cash will be invested in the business.

Therefore strong earnings growth is not generating any cash. The quality of earnings is further reduced as the management has no control over the investment/source of the profit. The sustainability of the performance of this investment must also be questioned.

As well as related companies, there can be situations where management has a subsidiary of which it does not own 100 per cent and hence does not exert full control over the cash flows. This can occur with an investment in an overseas market where the culture and approach may be different from the domestic market.

Another key area to watch is the use of provisions and cash flow. If earnings growth is being achieved through aggressive write-offs so that the cost base is reduced, there may be a lot of cash going out on redundancy payments or other costs associated with the provisions. This can be particularly true for highly acquisitive companies and needs to be monitored carefully.

Problems with earnings quality and cash may occur where profits are generated in overseas markets where inflation and currency issues may complicate the picture. In addition, repatriation may be a problem from countries with exchange controls or where weak currencies make it uneconomic to bring funds back to the home market. The volatility of earnings from emerging markets, albeit that there may well be a good long-term growth story, raises question marks over earnings quality.

Analysing earnings quality

To illustrate the issues that are relevant when assessing the company's earnings, let's take two companies with similar pre-tax profits and explore the differences in their quality of earnings. We can also see how the EPS number is calculated.

Companies A and B are identical in size in terms of turnover, pre-tax profit and the number of shares in issue: 545 million. However, the business and earnings profiles differ in certain key respects. Company B is focused on one core business in which it has strong market positions in the key developed countries. Company A has a spread of businesses in both advanced and emerging markets, many of which are not wholly owned. The exceptionals for company A relate to costs of the ongoing downsizing and restructuring of the company's core operations. This reflects the fact that the company has invested less in its facilities and has seen its cost base grow more rapidly than its rivals.

Both companies have an amortisation charge of £5 million.

The P&L schedules detailed in Tables 4.1 and 4.2 reveal the financial differences. The results for 2009 have been declared and are referred to as actual (abbreviated to A) while the numbers for 2010 are forecasts and are therefore 'expected' (abbreviated to E).

Table 4.1 Company A's P&L schedule

£m	2009A	2010E
Turnover	1500.0	1600.0
Depreciation	15.0	17.0
Amortisation	5.0	5.0
Operating profit	135.0	155.0
Associates	30.0	35.0
Investment income	15.0	10.0
Interest cost	−12.0	−13.0
Redundancies	−10.0	−10.0
Exceptionals	−15.0	−15.0
Pre-tax(a)	143.0	162.0
PX-PTP(b)	158.0	177.0
PXPA PTP(c)	163.0	182.0
Tax	−42.9	−48.6
Tax rate (%)	30.0	30.0
Minorities	−20.0	−25.0
Preference dividend	−8.0	−8.0
Attributable	72.1	80.4
No of shares	545.0	545.0
Stated EPS(a)	13.2	14.8
PX EPS(b)	15.2	16.7
PXPA EPS(c)	15.8	17.3

Table 4.2 Company B's P&L schedule

£m	2009A	20010E
Turnover	1500.0	1600.0
Depreciation	20.0	22.0
Amortisation	5.0	5.0
Operating profit	160.0	180.0
Associates	5.0	5.0
Interest cost	−12.0	−13.0
Redundancies	−10.0	−10.0
Exceptionals	0.0	0.0
Pre-tax	143.0	162.0
PX-PTP	143.0	162.0
PXPA-PTP	148.0	167.0
Tax	−42.9	−48.6
Tax rate (%)	30.0	30.0
Attributable	100.1	113.4
No of shares	545.0	545.0
EPS	18.4	20.8
PX EPS	18.4	20.8
PXPA EPS	19.0	21.4

Looking at the two businesses, some of the key differences are as follows:

- *Where the profits come from.* When considering how the pre-tax figure is arrived at, the principal trading difference is that Company B is generating a greater contribution from its core business, and its operating margins at 10.7 per cent compare favourably with the 9 per cent achieved by Company A. For Company A, 17.5 per cent of trading profit (i.e. income including associates and investment income) derives from associates, while a further 9 per cent derives from investment income. Furthermore, the exceptional debit of £15 million makes for a less 'clean' contribution. Importantly, these debits may be helping the subsequent year's operating performance.

- *Earnings calculation*. When calculating the earnings per share, apart from the exceptionals, the difference in earnings per share is accounted for by the debit of the minority and preference charges. These need to be deducted to arrive at the amount of earnings available for ordinary shareholders.

- *Exceptional charges*. The fact that the restructuring charges occur in successive years immediately raises suspicions as to how 'exceptional' they are. In addition, they clearly relate to the core business and so while more work is needed to reach a firm conclusion, they certainly need to be challenged. An IIMR EPS measure would exclude them as they relate to the core business. It might be that these charges reflect a cost base that has slipped out of control and is belatedly being brought back into shape.

- *Earnings quality*. Crucially, the earnings quality varies significantly between the two companies. The profile of the businesses immediately raises issues over earnings quality. Company B is clearly focused on its core operations with strong market shares which, in theory, should produce some influence on price/price stability in its markets. The higher return on sales highlights these strengths. The emerging market exposure of Company A may make earnings less easy to forecast (i.e. lower quality) given issues over exchange rates (possible translation and transaction risks), inflation and the higher risks that often attach to emerging markets (though offering good growth potential in the longer term). The exceptional charges may also be benefiting the numbers by reducing costs in subsequent years.

- *Sustainability of profits*. The proportion of earnings coming from investment income and the difficulty of assessing its sustainability also raises issues over earnings quality. If the investment income is partly made up of disposals, this may not be repeatable. The same may be true of the associate income where there is also a cash flow issue (see below). Effectively earnings are being influenced by a number of things beyond the control of management (value of investments, currency, performance of associates, etc.).

- *Cash flow*. There are major differences in how the earnings convert into cash. Company A will only receive a dividend from its associate contribution. It may also have cash costs related to the exceptional charges. There may be repatriation issues from some of the emerging markets to which it has exposure – exchange controls or unattractive exchange rates may make it impossible or uneconomical to bring back the cash to the company's HQ. In addition, the cost of servicing its preference dividends and also its minority holders make its cash flow profile less attractive than that of Company B. The higher operating margins will also enable better cash generation.

Comparing these two companies it can be seen that Company B has a much better-quality earnings stream and the earnings and cash flow profile are much 'cleaner'. On a fundamental basis, therefore, Company B would be far more attractive.

Not all earnings growth is created equal

Thus, when looking at earnings it is important to look at the quantity and quality of those earnings. The source of earnings growth is crucial to the quality and hence valuation of those earnings.

Earnings growth achieved by a one-off gain due to a one-off contract, currency movements or an asset disposal (if not deemed exceptional) will be valued very low. This is because it does not represent a repeatable source of earnings. The example of IBM meeting expectations through the disposal of a business saw the share price fall and question marks raised over its quality of earnings. (Those results had seen sales come in below expectations which pointed to difficult trading conditions and perhaps a loss of market share.)

The same reservations might apply to reduction in costs, though of course these are critical to the efficiency and competitiveness of the company. The problem is that they may be responsible for providing a one-off boost to earnings but not contribute to sustainable long-term growth. (It is not quite as straightforward, as the lower cost base enables extra market share to be won.) Market comment on US retailer Home Depot's third quarter 2002 figures indicated that, while the company's earnings met market expectations, the shares fell 13 per cent as this was achieved entirely through cost-cutting initiatives. It can be seen that the market is very aware of where earnings growth has come from and will adjust its valuation accordingly.

In both the IBM and Home Depot examples the market's disappointment revolved around the performance of the business. Despite the fact that numbers were in line with expectations, the 'top line' or revenue performance suggests things were not quite as encouraging as one would hope. It is wrong to focus just on earnings – it also depends on the underlying performance of the business and the returns being generated.

Growth achieved through volume and price growth, if sustainable, is indicative of a company performing well. However, in a commodity business large, unsustainable hikes in price may increase earnings but would not be valued highly by the market as they are of poor quality. Again the concern here is that the uplift is one-off or unsustainable – prices will fall back to previous levels in due course.

Another sensitive area is growth in earnings following provisions. This might occur if there has been an acquisition or a major exceptional charge. In the case of a large exceptional charge, shareholders will see shareholders' funds written down. In addition, there is likely to be a cash outflow to pay for this earnings growth. It is always worth checking post a large exceptional charge whether the subsequent earnings growth has been offset by a decline in net assets per share. In the case of acquisition-related provisions there may well be problems when the provisions run out. This may lead to the company pursuing another acquisition to maintain momentum.

Earnings from acquisition growth will tend to be valued far lower than those generated organically. As discussed in the M&A section, earnings growth can be achieved easily via acquisition while failing to add value – doing deals that are against shareholder interests. The risks attaching to growth through this route are also much higher. So it is important to ensure that growth is not being achieved at the expense of economic returns or through an increase in the risk profile.

Therefore while people correctly monitor earnings and how they may measure up to expectations, it is important that the issues of what has been driving the earnings are fully taken into account and understood. Critically, the make-up of earnings will be a key influence on how the shares are valued.

How earnings might be distorted – the accounting

When considering the accounting methods used to arrive at the earnings number, it pays to be sceptical. Management's credibility and rewards are intimately connected with delivery of earnings targets. This scepticism may be especially warranted if any change in accounting policy or one-off items of a dubious nature allow a company to hit market expectations.

> it pays to be sceptical

Below is a list of areas in which a flexible approach might be adopted to flatter the earnings number. It is by no means comprehensive but covers some of the key areas of concern.

Things to watch out for include the following:

- *Profit smoothing* – this may not be a bad thing necessarily. The stock market/investors prefer to see a smooth earnings trend rather than experiencing huge volatility. This at least gives the impression of earnings quality even if the reality is rather different. This may lead to profits being stored away in good years and released in lean years. This may involve provisioning or recognising costs earlier in a very good year. This then reduces the current year's profits, which means that the benchmark for the following year is set at a lower, more 'realistic' level. If trading conditions in the next year are more difficult, then due to the provisioning and transferring of costs into the previous year the company can meet its profit expectations.
- *Sales recognition* – an aggressive policy on sales recognition can bring forward future profits (while not recognising the costs) and boost earnings. This is a major issue when long-term contracts are involved.
- *Asset disposals* – while this should be clearly stated separately, it may not be immediately apparent that the company has disposed of an asset or business. It may be netted off cost of goods sold. This was done in IBM's fourth quarter 2001 profits when a business was sold to JDS Uniphase which generated a profit of $280 million, which added 10c a share to earnings. Importantly, in this example revenues were below expectations, suggesting that the focus should be the underlying performance of the business – not just the earnings target.
- *Pension benefits* – again this may be legitimate but if there is a change of policy it should be clearly stated. Again, a reduction in the cost of goods sold can obscure this, with the pension credit being buried deep in the notes to the results/accounts. CAP Gemini Sogetti did this in the summer of 2000.

Optimistic assumptions about returns from the pension fund may flatter earnings as pension contributions are lower than they would be on the basis of more realistic assumptions. IBM, under its previous chief executive, assumed future returns of 10 per cent. A downgrading of this assumption to 9.5 per cent in March 2000 was likely to increase costs (and hence reduce earnings) by $350 million in 2002. With many commentators expecting returns to be much lower than this, there is likely to be pressure on the 9.5 per cent assumption in the future.

- *Option costs* – this has been a big area for debate, with Warren Buffett stressing that as far as he is concerned, the granting of options is an employment cost. Interestingly, IBM (along with many other tech companies) would see its earnings reduced by 15 per cent if the granting of options was taken into account. Some have suggested that the technology sector would see a reduction in earnings of up to 50 per cent if option costs were expensed as IFRS proposes.

- *Provisions* – a fairly common way of boosting earnings is to make big provisions in one year which then effectively allows costs to be lower in subsequent years. This may involve provisions for cost reductions or the write-down of asset values. If earnings are deemed more important than assets, asset write-offs may be used to help reach earnings numbers. (To make sure a company is really creating wealth it may be worth checking that the **net asset value (NAV)** grows as well as earnings.)

- *Acquisition accounting* – when a company acquires another company its accounting policies may be less conservative than those of the target company and this will benefit earnings. In addition, big provisions may be set up to fund the integration of the two businesses. Stocks may be written down and then sold at a higher level, with a benefit to profits.

- *Capitalisation of interest* – instead of charging interest costs associated with a large investment project to the P&L as a cost, they might be capitalised as part of the cost of the whole project. This would then be depreciated in the normal way.

- *Depreciation policy* – this might be lengthened (suggesting that the useful life of the asset would be longer than anticipated) to reduce the depreciation charge. This would lower costs and hence boost earnings (it makes no difference to cash flow).

- *Deferring marketing/advertising or capital projects* – this gives a short-term gain as costs are reduced but inevitably leads to potential market share issues. Some investors may feel that a more long-term approach is required to investing in the product and supporting market share. Ironically, companies may do this because they do not want to disappoint investors' short-term earnings expectations.

- *Currency* – this can have a big impact on earnings for companies with sizeable overseas activities. The translating of these overseas profits into the reporting currency can cause earnings to be a lot better or worse than expected. Cynically, a company with a policy of using a year-end rate may change to an average rate if the drop in the overseas currency occurs in the second half of the year. This will result in a higher earnings number being recorded. This may indeed be a fairer reflection of the performance of the subsidiary during the course of the year – it is the change in policy that generates the questions.

- *Tax charges/policy* – the tax charge is another variable that impacts upon the earnings per share number. Therefore it is always worth monitoring whether there has been any change in the underlying tax rate. This may reflect, for example, a changing geographic profile of earnings (different countries have different rates and allowances) or a change in the tax rules in any of the areas of operation. Changing policy may cover such areas as deferred tax and again it is worth noting if the policy changes. Sudden rises in tax charges can have an impact on share prices as they lead to downward revisions in earnings growth.
- *Low tax charges* – a very low tax charge can be an indicator that the earnings are being considerably overstated and not just due to the low tax charge. The tax authorities' view of (taxable) profits may be that they are considerably lower than the company is reporting. This immediately raises question marks as to the company's accounting policies and its approach to profit recognition. The other danger is that the tax charge at some point rises towards the standard level, which reduces the earnings growth quite dramatically.

EBITDA

Ebitda stands for earnings before interest, tax, depreciation and amortisation (see Table 4.3).

Many of the issues explored under the quality and quantity of earnings apply equally to EBITDA; the issues over accounting policies are especially relevant.

Table 4.3 Calculating EBITDA

	Year 1
Pre-tax profit	£20m
Interest	£2.5m
Forecast operating profit (EBIT)	£22.5m
Depreciation	£20m
Amortisation	£2m
EBITDA calculation (in millions)	22.5 + 20 + 2
EBITDA	£44.5m

Why it's used

EBITDA developed as a performance number partly because it strips out the effect of different depreciation and amortisation policies that companies may have. In particular, with the growth of investment on a pan-European or global basis, it became important to avoid the distortions of different countries' accounting policies. For example, some countries had tax regimes which encouraged the accelerated depreciation of assets. This would lead to a very high depreciation charge because it was tax efficient but would correspondingly depress earnings. Therefore comparing across countries was rendered invalid at the earnings level. It should also be borne in mind that companies in the same country, and indeed the same sector, might have different policies with respect to depreciation, hence making comparisons very difficult. Similarly, amortisation of goodwill and the treatment of goodwill vary across countries.

> some countries had tax regimes which encouraged the accelerated depreciation of assets

EBITDA is also struck before exceptional items, thus avoiding another potential accounting distortion to comparisons (see p. 123 for an analysis of exceptionals).

The other (contentious) reason for using EBITDA is that it serves as an approximation for cash flow and it is often referred to as a cash flow-based measure of performance/valuation. This is because depreciation and amortisation are non-cash costs, i.e. while they are deducted before arriving at a profits number there is no actual payment that goes out of the company. Accordingly it gives an indication of gross cash flow. (Cash flow, as we will discuss in more detail later, is regarded as the key driver of value.)

The other advantage of using EBITDA when comparing companies is that it takes into account the different capital structures the companies may have. As we have seen, there are advantages to using debt over equity, so a company that has used a lot of debt in its capital structure can be compared with one that has used very little debt.

EBITDA is also used and indeed promoted as a performance measure by companies that have no earnings. This may reflect a company with cyclical earnings being at the bottom of the cycle. The other situation of course is where a company is at an early stage of development and has yet to generate a profit. If it can generate a positive EBITDA, this will hopefully reassure investors. It might be that a major programme of capital expenditure has been completed to get the business under way. These assets will be depreciated so the business is generating cash though not earnings.

What is driving EBITDA?

As with the section on earnings it is crucial to assess what is driving EBITDA. Investing in the business can certainly help EBITDA grow. The investment will hopefully improve revenues and lower costs and of course will attract additional depreciation charges as the asset base expands. However, in the first few years it may be that the depreciation charge increases but profits (earnings) do not. So EBITDA grows but profits do not. The real issue is that earnings need to increase.

However, the EBITDA measure of performance excludes the financing costs of this extra investment – the interest charge. If the interest component is rising rapidly, the investment is not actually improving the earnings available to shareholders. It may be that both the depreciation charge and operating charge do in fact rise, but that rising interest costs prevent this coming through to profit or EPS. Many companies using EBITDA are at an early stage of development and are in precisely this sort of situation. This is not to say that they are bad investments but that care is needed to ensure that the investments will generate appropriate returns. This brings us back to a central concern when looking at performance – that growth is not driven at the expense of returns on investment or value added (i.e. the returns on the investment exceed the cost of capital).

Another key concern is when the focus on growth in EBITDA leads to an aggressive acquisition policy, i.e. the growth is achieved through buying other businesses rather than through the underlying performance of the company. (We have already discussed why acquisitions rarely add value.) Such acquisitions have been very destructive of shareholder value. Bought at the top of the cycle, at very high valuations, these businesses failed to deliver. While the growth failed to materialise, the funding, whether debt or equity, needed to be serviced. The (often severe) deterioration in companies' financial position then left them in much weakened positions and dramatically increased their risk profile.

While the fashion in the mid- to late-1990s was that debt was good (it reduced the cost of capital and helped improve earnings growth), deteriorating economic conditions and weak financial markets have made overstretched balance sheets a major concern. This is especially true for those companies suffering from poor volumes and price. Debt servicing has become increasingly difficult and has led to a serious downgrading of credit ratings and higher debt servicing costs as a result. Inevitably this undermines the company's competitive position and makes investing for growth impossible.

Aggressive accounting policies have also been a factor. As discussed under corporate governance (see p. 80), EBITDA has been the trigger for remuneration packages. On the basis that if it is targeted it can be manipulated, care needs to be taken. The evidence is clear that accounting policies have been extremely aggressive (if not in some instances fraudulent) to ensure that performance targets were hit.

Not a true measure of cash flow?

Another of the major disadvantages of EBITDA is that depreciation is a very real cost of doing business in many industries and should be taken into account. It is crucial for the company to protect its competitive position and maintaining capital expenditure is critical in this regard. This, combined with the need for working capital and movements in provisions to be taken into account, prevents EBITDA from being a useful proxy for cash flow.

A performance measure in disrepute?

As a result of all these factors EBITDA has fallen into disrepute in the post-bubble years. Many of the companies, especially in the US, that championed it as a performance metric have either run into serious financial trouble or have been very poor investments. The demise of many of these companies has raised serious issues over its use as a performance measure.

Given the importance accorded to EBITDA, its complexity and the publicity it has generated, it is worth summarising the pros and cons of this performance measure.

Advantages of EBITDA

- It takes the whole funding structure into account (unlike P/Es).
- It allows comparisons between companies with different accounting policies towards depreciation and amortisation.
- It ignores exceptional charges, again allowing comparison.
- It is a cash flow-based measure.

Disadvantages of EBITDA

- Is it being used when all other measures are disappointing?
- Maintenance capex is a key cost and working capital also requires cash, so is it a true measure of cash flow?
- What does it measure – neither cash nor profitability?

▶

- Earnings can still be manipulated.
- Earnings before interesting things ... are we missing the story?
- Investment can grow EBITDA (EBIT, depreciation and amortisation), but what is the rate of return on that investment v the cost of capital?
- What is happening to interest costs?
- What is the impact on gearing and risk?
- It is used in capital-intensive, high-growth industries where no profits/EPS are generated ... but what about overinvestment and low returns?

Key performance ratios: profitability and returns

Checking the performance of a company against others in the sector is a useful way of assessing how well the company is positioned, how efficient it is and how well the management is performing. There are three key ratios you should concentrate on:

- **operating profit margins**
- **return on capital employed (ROCE)**
- **economic value added.**

Operating profit margins

The company's operating profit margins will be available from its P&L. Some companies spell this out while for others you will have to divide the operating profit by the turnover. Operating margins are the proportion of revenue that is pure profit.

Operating margins are essentially the outcome of changes in volume, prices and costs and therefore these crucial drivers of margins should always be considered. They convey a wealth of information about how well positioned, how efficient and how well managed a company is. They can also raise issues of strategic importance – is the company ex-growth or are there likely to be new entrants attracted to the industry? Prices are a key influence on margins, as discussed in Chapter 2 (p. 45) and the company position.

In terms of the message and information that may be deduced from operating margins it is important to consider the following.

How does the profit margin compare with that of similar companies?

Comparing margins with the peer group provides an excellent way of judging the performance of a management team. However, care needs to be taken to ensure that 'like for like' comparisons are being made. For example, one company may include an overseas subsidiary in a division that distorts comparisons with a company operating solely in the domestic market. One business may be 'vertically integrated' (performing many functions between its suppliers and its customers rather than outsourcing them) while the other concentrates on one element of the process. Company reporting does not always facilitate easy comparisons.

If margins of one business are consistently higher than those of another very similar company in the same sector, then clearly as a business and as a management they have found a winning formula. The investment issue is then whether to go for the winner or whether there is a 'catch-up' story in the weaker-margin business. If it is a strong winning formula, the scope for catching up might be far more limited than it may appear. This is especially true if the higher-margin business has built up a dominant market position, an effective way of generating higher margins and a culture that enables it to continue to do well. Conversely, the weaker-margin business may have a weaker product offering and market position, and a less attractive formula and a management culture that is not as effective at generating value. Overcoming these weaknesses is far from easy and so buying the company on hopes of restoring margins to those of the competitor can be a risky policy.

What has been the trend in margins?

Have margins been improving, static or declining over the past five years? What is the longer-term trend? Steadily rising margins are usually a good sign that the business is performing well, while declining margins are a cause for concern. As ever, care needs to be taken before reaching firm conclusions. A higher-quality, and higher-priced, product and/or progressively lower costs should see margins going higher to the advantage of shareholders. However, a company with a good-quality product and tight costs may consciously and perfectly sensibly decide to be very price competitive as it looks to increase its market share. This will see short-term margins decline but overall sales and profit increasing. This strategy will benefit the longer-term position of the company as it develops its market share position.

Conversely, a company may cut back on product development and marketing expenditure and boost short-term margins. However, this may progressively erode its long-term product offering and market position. The business and shareholders are likely to suffer.

If margins have been moving about widely (say from very low to high and back again), volatility is clearly a feature of the business. This suggests that the quality of earnings is very low. If you invest when margins are at the top of their historic range, there is a serious possibility that margins and earnings are about to fall. Accordingly the shares are likely to fall in value.

What has been driving margins?

It is important to have an understanding of what forces have been driving margins. This will affect the sustainability of those margins and the potential risks. If, for example, margins have risen following a rise in prices due to a shortage of the product or a temporary price hike in a volatile commodity, the higher margins will prove to be temporary – they will reverse as prices decline. Importantly, as discussed in the section on quality of earnings (p. 131), in these cases management or the actions of the company are not the driving force behind the higher margins.

Similarly, temporary boosts to margins from lower raw material costs are likely to unwind relatively quickly and owe nothing to management action. However, a concerted effort by management to improve its purchasing policies and source more cost-effective/higher-quality components is likely to offer sustained benefits.

If margins are being boosted by solid volume growth, firm pricing, new product developments and improved product quality, this augurs well. Not only will margins expand but the company's position and profile in the market will be enhanced.

If margins are low, can they be improved? Is this a recovery stock or just mismanaged?

buying margin recovery stories is fraught with difficulties

Low margins relative to the peer group may provide potential upside. However, they may reflect years of underinvestment in both plant and machinery and product range/development. This will inevitably lead to a worse cost structure and an inferior product offering than the competition and a continuous erosion of market share. Restoring margins and market share in this scenario is likely to be extremely difficult and take a long time (if ever) to achieve. Buying margin recovery stories is fraught with difficulties. Often the weak market position of the company or the degree of mismanagement is underestimated by outsiders – the company is in a much weaker position than anticipated.

One of the classic difficulties is a situation where costs are cut dramatically to restore margins. However, rapidly falling prices offset the improvement in the cost base. If you are going to invest in a margin recovery story, ensuring a stable revenue background is an important part of the equation. Alternatively, if it is a more simple case of an inflated cost base that can be addressed easily, then a margin recovery story is possible (though typically this will require a different management approach to the one that presided over the initial inflation of the cost base).

If margins are low due to start-up costs, investing in new product development or sales and marketing, this will reverse in due course. This may be a buying opportunity if these initiatives are part of a sensible long-term strategy.

If margins are low, is there a risk of going into loss?

If margins are low this can be a significant source of risk as there is little scope for anything to go wrong. If margins are low because things are already going wrong, it may not take a lot to see profits swing into loss. A contractor with operating margins of 1 per cent, for example, may run into problems with a large contract and quickly run into loss.

The risks are higher if the business is highly volatile and subject to wide swings in volume and price (high operational gearing).

Industry structure a big influence on pricing and margins

The degree of consolidation in an industry is a big influence on margins. At the obvious extreme a monopolist will enjoy very high margins, though this should not necessarily be construed as the result of good management. A high degree of industry consolidation – i.e. a few players accounting for the vast majority of the market – should lead to a better pricing environment than a fragmented industry where a large number of small players are jockeying for position.

There can be exceptions. In some industries with high fixed costs, for example steel, chemicals and cars, profits may be very sensitive to volume. Accordingly, some players may decide to ensure they protect/increase market share by increasing volumes/cutting prices, which will inevitably hurt margins. Similarly, a company that takes the view that, in the long term, it will be better off by increasing market share may achieve its objectives by cutting prices aggressively in the short term. It may want to be seen as the most competitively priced player in the sector at all times. This again may cause margins to fall for all the industry as others try to compete.

Changes in industry structure which allow pricing, and hence margins, to improve can be a buy signal. Therefore watching industries where the market is fragmented (shared by a high number of players) for signs of consolidation may alert you to some potentially interesting possibilities.

If margins are a lot higher than competitors', can the figures be believed? Is the accounting prudent?

On the basis that 'if something looks too good to be true, it probably is', margins that are significantly greater than the competition should be closely scrutinised. They may genuinely represent the superior efforts of management – better products produced at much lower cost generating a much higher price. However, they may reflect a less prudent approach to accounting – low depreciation charges, valuation of stock, recognising profit earlier than is sensible or capitalising costs that other companies expense. Therefore it is well worth being aware of any accounting issues that are flattering operating margins. The policies adopted may be entirely within accounting guidelines, but they might be stretching the rules to the limit and far from conservative.

Similarly, if a company is generating high margins for producing a basic commodity, care needs to be taken.

If margins are low, does it indicate pricing power lies elsewhere?

Companies that supply big, powerful customers, for example the automotive industry or food retailers, will inevitably find that prices and margins come under pressure. The car manufacturers themselves tend to earn low margins and are almost permanently engaged in driving down component prices.

To counteract this trend, companies need to be able to display a tight control over costs and/or improve product or service quality. Large contracts from the car companies can be critical to the long-term future of suppliers and this can lead to poor margins as prices are cut to secure the contract. Alternatively, a company producing plastic products might find its supplier of petrochemicals can increase the prices for its products but these higher costs cannot be passed on to the customer. This may reflect a very competitive market for the plastic products or the importance of very large customers, such as the big DIY chains. In both these instances shareholders need to be aware that improving margins is likely to be difficult.

In the automotive supplier example, lower prices may have to be accepted given the purchasing power of the carmaker. However, it may well be that significant R&D and other costs were essential to meet the order and provide goods of a satisfactory design and quality. If margins are too low, all this effort is failing to add value. In these circumstances a shareholder is, in effect, subsidising the customer and is unlikely to make money from the investment.

Are margins so high they will attract new competition?

One of the potential dangers of high margins is that they encourage competitors to copy what you are doing. The ease with which people can do this will obviously vary, depending on the barriers to entry. An industry may have high barriers to entry due to patents or technical know-how, high capital costs, significant economies of scale, regulatory hurdles or a high level of brand recognition. Conversely, low barriers to entry are likely to characterise products/industries that are commodities by nature, have low set-up costs and few economies of scale.

If margins are high, is there little prospect for future growth?

A company that has hit a certain level of margin may find it very difficult to go beyond that point. This may mean there is little growth left in the business. There is also the risk of attracting competitors. This may be a warning sign and can be a good time to sell if the company's core business is ex-growth. Attention should then turn to the management's strategy. The high margins will lead to the company being highly cash generative and if it has reached a 'natural' market share beyond which it is difficult to grow, the requirement for capital will be limited.

The dilemma at this point is whether the cash flow is returned to shareholders or used to find other avenues for growth. This carries a degree of risk subject to the transferability of the management's skills to other products or other regions. Merger and acquisition activity is a strong possibility in this situation, but whether this adds value is a moot point (see pp. 109–110 for an analysis of the risks and issues to be monitored in this area).

Do the margins reflect the capital intensity of the business?

(See also return on capital employed, below.) It is important to make sure that operating margins a company achieves reflect the capital employed in the business. In theory the higher the capital employed in the business, the higher the margins should be.

If a very capital-intensive business has low margins, returns on investment will be very low. So cement or chemical plants need to generate high margins to get a return on the big outlay involved in the plant. Conversely, it might be quite all right to have a low-margin business if it generates a high return on capital by using very little capital, or the capital is 'turned over' very quickly. For example, food retailers have margins of around 5 per cent but they use relatively little capital. Suppliers fund their working capital which they turn over quickly. Therefore, because they efficiently turn capital into sales, returns on capital can be very attractive.

Where are margins going in the future?

As with any investment issue, we are concerned with the future trend and direction on margins. This is what will determine whether the company (and ultimately the shares) will make money. By bringing together the issues identified as being important in the margin equation you should have a good sense of the factors influencing margins. Where margins are going in the future may bear no relation to where they have been in the past if the industry dynamics and structures have changed.

Return on capital employed (ROCE)

The return on capital employed (ROCE) is a critical figure that tells you how well management is using shareholders' money.

There are a number of ways of calculating this. The simplest is to divide operating profit by shareholders' funds plus net debt. If the level of debt moves sharply during the year you may want to think about the average level of debt employed. You can always look at the interest payments and divide these by the rate of interest the company pays (there will be some notes in the accounts that should help you). Net debt should also include any preference shares or convertible bonds that the company may have.

Shareholders' funds plus net debt effectively give you the amount of resources the company is using. To improve the ratio obviously requires an improvement in operating profit and/or a reduction in the amount of capital needed to produce it.

The level of returns is critical as the value of any asset depends on the amount of income it generates. Therefore high returns on capital are strongly linked with share price performance and valuation. The ratio, and more critically its future trend, is crucial for the performance of your investment.

The factors driving the operating margins (p. 146), given that they drive operating profit, will also determine the return on capital. Again the influence of prices is crucial. As with high margins, a high return on capital employed may encourage new competition as competitors/new entrants seek out the profits available.

Example – calculating ROCE

Blogg's Cement

Take a fictional company, Blogg's Cement. We will assume it has invested £150 million in a cement works. The works has the capacity to turn out 1.5 million tonnes of cement a year, the cement sells at £60 per tonne, and the operating margin is 10 per cent.

Investment in works	£150 m
Capacity	1.5 million tonnes
Price per tonne	£60
Revenue calculation:	
Capacity × price	1.5 m × 60
Revenue	£90m
Operating margin	10%
Operating profit calculation:	
Revenue × operating margin	90 m × 10
Operating profit	£9m
Return on capital calculation:	
Operating profit/investment	9m/150m
Return on capital employed	6%

This shows us that the return on capital employed is 6 per cent.

Joe's Widgets

Compare that with another fictional company, Joe's Widgets, which has also invested £150 million and has the same operating profit margin of 10 per cent. It produces 3 million widgets a year, which it sells at £50 each. This gives revenues of £150m a year. This equals a return on capital employed of 10 per cent.

In both examples the margins are the same at 10 per cent, but the ROCE clearly shows that money invested in Joe's Widgets has generated a much better return than that invested in Blogg's Cement. This is because the revenue generated by the invested capital in Joe's Widgets is a lot greater than for the cement plant – £150 million compared with £90 million.

The relationship between margins and ROCE can be seen clearly from these figures. A 10 per cent operating margin from the cement investment generates a low return of 6 per cent. If we say the cost of capital is 10 per cent, you can see this is a far from effective investment.

Investment in works	£150m
Capacity	3m
Price per widget	£50
Revenue calculation	
Capacity × price	3 m × 50
Revenue	£150m
Operating margin	10%
Operating profit calculation	
Revenue × operating margin	£150 m × 10 per cent
Operating profit	£15 million
Return on capital calculation:	
Operating profit/investment	15m/150m
Return on capital employed	10%

An operating margin of 17 per cent would be needed to generate a return on capital of 10 per cent (£150 million of investment @10 per cent is £15 million. £15 million/£90 million is 16.7 per cent). Therefore much higher margins are needed to compensate for the capital that is needed in the business to generate the level of sales. (Alternatively, the prices charged are too low to generate the returns required. Whether they can be increased of course depends on market conditions and the market structure.)

Analysis

Therefore, the greater the amount of capital/investment needed per £ of turnover, the higher the margins need to be to ensure an appropriate return.

In Blogg's case, each £ of turnover needs £1.67 of investment. However, Joe's Widgets needs only £1 of investment for each £ of turnover. A 10 per cent margin in both cases produces an acceptable return of 10 per cent on capital for Joe's Widgets but an unsatisfactory 6 per cent for Blogg's Cement.

Risk and returns

Investing in any enterprise clearly involves a degree of risk – how much will vary from industry to industry, company to company, and is likely to be different for different countries. Companies at an early stage of development are likely to have a higher risk profile than more established companies. Companies diversifying into new products or regions will be taking on higher levels of risk than those staying within their existing area of expertise.

Shareholders shoulder the risks of the business and therefore should be appropriately rewarded – the greater the risk you bear, the higher the returns you should receive. Being aware of the risks involved is important for you to assess the returns you want.

So if the ROCE is only, say, 6 per cent, you would have been better off putting your money in a high-interest deposit account. The return would be similar but without any risk. Another key problem with such a low return is that if the trading environment deteriorates, this could drop returns to extremely low levels. (The importance of risk is incorporated in the cost of capital where beta is used to reflect the volatility of an investment, see p. 22.)

High returns

A high ROCE normally tells you that management is using your resources efficiently. This generates confidence that any investment programmes or acquisitions undertaken will reward shareholders. This improves the quality of the earnings and gives confidence in the longer-term growth outlook. The key is to evaluate the sustainability of those returns.

If returns are very high, there is a risk that potential competitors will be casting an envious eye at the company's market and looking to enter the industry/product segment to capture some of the returns. How easily they can do this will depend on the barriers to entry that exist. If relatively low, new entrants may trigger a battle for market share and lead to a significant erosion of return on capital.

Another potential problem if returns are very high is that there is no room for improvement. If the industry is mature, or the company has reached a market share that is difficult to expand upon, there may be concerns that the company is ex-growth. Management may be tempted to raise the growth profile by acquisitions or moves into other business areas. These initiatives may increase the risk profile of the company and lead to a lower rate of return in the new areas.

Low returns

If ROCE is low, has it been low for a long time or fallen recently? This can be important when returns are low for a long period of time. The conclusion may be that these assets are considerably overstated in the balance sheet. This may lead to the company having to write down the value of these assets.

Alternatively, low returns may mean that poor management is underutilising the asset base. This may trigger a call to change the management or a hostile takeover if the considered view is that the asset value is right and the returns (through poor management) are wrong. This may lead to viewing the stock as a recovery or takeover story.

Is it poor management or poor industry?

If returns are consistently low, it is worth exploring the extent to which this is a feature of the industry in which the company operates. This is especially so if the returns are low even when the company is in an up-phase of an economic or industry cycle. If it appears that returns are indeed low but they are in line with the rest of the company's competitors, it is clearly an industry issue. This may well suggest that the shares, and indeed the sector, are best avoided.

To be a buyer of the shares you need to believe that something is about to happen that will raise returns – either for the company or across the industry – or that the shares are so lowly rated that the low-achieved returns are 'in the price'. Returns may be set to improve due to a significant increase in demand and/or firmer pricing. This may involve, for example, some capacity closure or mergers that improve the pricing power of companies in the sector. Such recoveries often fail to materialise and it is worth examining future prospects closely and realistically. The risks of investing in such a situation are high.

How much capital (and what type) is needed?

It is also worth considering how much capital is needed in the business. The valuation will depend on the amount of capital needed to grow. Some businesses may be capital intensive while others may be able to generate high levels of revenue growth on the back of relatively small investments. In some businesses that require a lot of working capital (stock, for example), it may be possible to use capital provided by suppliers. Food retailing is a good example of this. Here the capital required is relatively low as there is 'negative' working capital because suppliers fund this element of the business.

The relatively low level of capital employed in this instance leads to relatively low margins. Employing a lot of capital is not a bad thing per se – it just has to generate an appropriate return. One would, therefore, expect to see in capital-intensive businesses higher operating margins, which then ensure that the all-important return on capital is high enough to add value.

In some industries the 'asset' base may be more people-oriented (e.g. service-related industries such as advertising). In this case there may be a high rate of return on capital, reflecting the fact that very little capital is employed. You will need to ensure operating margins are at healthy levels.

ROIC – assets written off the asset base

When looking at the return on capital figure it is important to ensure that the definition of assets is comprehensive. A company may have invested in an acquisition that necessitated a considerable write-off of goodwill (the amount paid for a business over and above its net assets). The total investment clearly needs to generate an appropriate return. However, the shareholders' funds figure will exclude the amount of goodwill written off and so flatter the ROCE (often calculated by adding debt to shareholders' funds) figure. The **return on invested capital (ROIC)** ratio, by adding back this goodwill, provides a more reliable guide to how management has been allocating resources. Look in the notes to find the cumulative goodwill that has been written off: this then needs to be added back to generate the invested capital.

look in the notes to find the cumulative goodwill that has been written off

Examining the numbers

To look at the difference that this can make to returns let us consider the two companies A and B we discussed when examining quality of earnings (pp. 134–138). From this example we know that company B is generating a greater proportion of profits from its core operations and has higher operating margins. We also know that Company A has preference capital as a preference dividend was deducted before arriving at earnings per share. This we will treat as debt and so it will form a part of capital employed.

We can see that Company A has written off goodwill of £90 million in 2002 following an acquisition. We will assume that the acquisition was contributing from January 1 so there is a full year's contribution. Shareholders' funds are therefore reduced by a corresponding amount (the year-end figure is partially offset by **retained profits** in the year). You can see immediately that lower shareholder funds imply lower capital employed if we ignore goodwill. On a capital employed measure, the capital employed falls from £964.3 million to £953 million despite a £50 million increase in debt. But this goodwill was an integral part of the money spent on the acquisition. Table 4.4 calculates the ROCE on the basis of shareholders' funds plus debt and ROIC where the goodwill written off is added back. We can see that the ROIC is much lower in 2010 at 13.6 per cent compared with the ROCE at 16.3 per cent. Clearly this makes an enormous difference when assessing the management's performance.

Table 4.4 Calculating the ROCE on the basis of shareholders' funds plus debt and ROIC including goodwill written off

	Company A	
Balance sheet data	2009	2010E
Equity shareholders' funds	575.4	510.0
Minority interests	68.9	68.9
Total shareholders' funds	**644.3**	**583.0**
Net debt	200.0	250.0
Preference capital	120.0	120.0
Capital employed	964.3	953.0
Goodwill written off	100.0	190.0
Invested capital	1064.3	1143.0
Gearing (%)	**49.7**	**64.0**
ROCE (%)	**14.0**	**16.3**
ROIC (%)	**12.7**	**13.6**
Post-tax ROCE (%)	9.8	11.4
Post-tax ROIC (%)	8.9	9.5
NAV (p)	118.2	106.9
No of shares (m)	545.0	545.0

	Company B	
Balance sheet data	2009	2010E
Equity shareholders' funds	575.4	620.0
Minority interests	–	–
Total shareholders' funds	**575.4**	**620.0**
Net debt	200.0	180.0
Capital employed	775.4	800.0
Goodwill written off	100.0	100.0
Invested capital	875.4	900.0
Gearing (%)	**34.8**	**29.0**
ROCE (%)	**20.6**	**22.5**
ROIC (%)	**18.3**	**20.0**
Post-tax ROCE (%)	14.4	15.8
Post-tax ROIC (%)	12.8	14.0
NAV (p)	105.6	113.8
No of shares (m)	545.0	545.0

Company B benefits from a higher operating contribution from its core business and does not have the investment and associate income distortions to its overall performance. Very importantly it also employs fewer assets to achieve that operating contribution. It does not have the preference capital or the level of goodwill employed by Company A in 2010. As a result in 2009 it is using invested assets of £875.4 million to generate operating profit of £160 million rather than A's use of £1064.3 million to generate £135 million of operating profit.

In 2010 the gap widens even further as the capital employed by Company A increases to reflect the goodwill increase following acquisition. Significantly, in 2010 B's cash generation leads to lower debt levels (which have fallen by £20 million) and hence capital employed.

Pre- or post-tax figures?

The other issue is whether to use pre- or post-tax figures for the return on capital or invested capital calculation. In Table 4.4 both are included, taxing the operating profit at 30 per cent. What is left for shareholders is clearly post-tax and so this is perhaps the most useful way of computing the return. In addition, when looking to assess whether a company is adding value a post-tax return is used. This reflects the fact that the post-tax cost of capital is used for the debt figure. This is covered in more detail on the economic value added section (below) and when we look at the cost of capital in more detail when considering discounted cash flow valuations.

Return on equity

A similar and very important alternative to return on capital is to look at the return on equity (ROE). This is, in many ways, a more logical way of assessing the use to which shareholders' funds are put as it looks at what is left for shareholders in relation to what they have invested.

It is calculated by dividing the profit after tax and any deductions due to non-equity holders (e.g. minority charges or preference dividends) by the amount of ordinary shareholders' funds. Sometimes this is calculated by including any goodwill that has been written off because this has been deducted from ordinary shareholders' funds.

Again this provides an important way of assessing whether the company's management is using resources to best effect. If returns are low, the alternative would be to put the money in a (risk-free) deposit account.

As we will see in the next chapter on financial position (Figure 5.1 p. 166), ROE can be improved by 'gearing-up' the business. By having lots of debt to drive the business there is less equity issued and so the returns generated are spread over less equity increasing the ROE. However, this also introduces a lot more risk.

Economic value added – exceeding the cost of capital

Having looked at how to calculate ROIC and the factors that influence it, we are halfway to assessing whether the company is adding value. Adding value refers to how the return on capital relates to the cost of that capital – which in turn reflects the risk of investing in the company. This can appear complicated but is an extremely important concept to understand. In essence, it is the minimum return you would expect from a business given the need to be compensated for the risks involved. It is also charging management a proper cost for all the resources they are using to ensure that they focus on exceeding this very real cost of doing business.

Adding value depends on the company's economic position, its efficiency and the returns generated by its assets and how these compare to the cost of capital. This in turn depends on the proportion of equity and debt capital as equity is more expensive than debt and does not have the same tax advantages. We have seen in analysing the returns from acquisitions that economic value added is crucial for shareholders and helps reduce the emphasis that is commonly put on growth in earnings (or EBITDA). Whether a company is adding or destroying value will be a crucial driver for both valuation and share price performance. It is also crucial to give you a return that compensates for the risks you are taking.

Cash return on invested capital (or CROIC)

Given the critical importance of cash as a driver of value and the need to generate an excellent return on the assets employed in the business, the cash return on invested capital (CROIC) provides an excellent catch-all measure. Many investors and brokers use models that use this number as there is strong evidence of its good predictive power as a performance measure. There is also an intuitive sense that it is useful to get a cash rather than profit return on the money the company has invested. It would be far more preferable to have a business that is generat-

earnings are a matter of judgement and cash is a matter of fact ing a lot of cash without the need for lots of investment. And remember that earnings are a matter of judgement and cash is a matter of fact. Companies in heavy growth phases, or in less attractive circumstances companies being creative with accounting numbers, can see earnings growing rapidly whilst experiencing significant cash outflows. This may not be sustainable and monitoring any discrepancies between earnings and cash is very worthwhile.

There are many ways of defining cash flow in this context. One of the most common is to use **operating free cash flow** (see p. 230).

Depreciation and amortisation are added back as they are what are called 'non-cash costs'. This means that while these amounts are deducted to arrive at a profit number, they do not involve an outflow of cash. (The difference between them is that basically we depreciate assets we can touch (tangible) and amortise assets that we can't (intangible).)

Capital expenditure explicitly recognises that this is a critical component of the company both achieving the forecast growth targets and maintaining its competitive position through maintaining the quality of its assets.

Maintenance capital expenditure is often used in more slowly growing environments or phases of a company's development. This ensures that the fabric of the business is protected, recognising that maintenance expenditure is a real cost of doing business (a weakness discussed when considering EBITDA as a performance number). Similarly, working capital is required as the higher sales over the growth period will require cash to fund the expansion of working capital.

The assets used in the business then provide the denominator. So here we are looking at

Capital employed = shareholders funds + net debt

Here we need to remember to add back any assets the company has written off – we need to have a sense of what the cash investment has been – not the book value. (Sometimes we refer to this as 'invested capital'.)

What represents a good return?

A good return, as ever, will depend on the risks in the investment. The higher the risk the greater the return we need. We know that for a company with an 'average' level of risk we need a return of 10 per cent. If the company is financed with a lot of debt the WACC will be lower than this (see p. 27 in Chapter 1).

Generally the lower the return the more vulnerable the company might be – low returns are more fragile as anything that affects the business can see returns fall dramatically. Similarly, if returns are very low there is very little point reinvesting in the business.

Given the importance of the company's financial position in terms of the cost of capital and valuation of the company and the risks posed by poorly financed businesses, we now turn to examine how to assess the financial position of a company in the next chapter.

Summary

The performance of the business needs to be assessed both in absolute terms and relative to the competition. The level of returns – especially whether the company is creating value and generating a good cash return – is an important predictor of share price performance in the longer term.

The performance of key measures such as sales and earnings gives us important information about the company's markets and how it is performing in those market conditions – is it beating the peer group? It is important to bear in mind that some measures are more useful than others. A company can increase sales by sacrificing margin or being aggressive in accepting longer payment terms from customers so that the money is slow to come in.

Of particular concern is the emphasis on earnings growth. While a very useful measure, it must be borne in mind that the focus on earnings has led to many companies taking decisions that boost earnings but may be detrimental to the competitive position of the business. So, for example, a company could cut back on its marketing expenditure to hit an earnings target – but what might this do to the brand value if the cut is sustained over time?

As we have seen, earnings growth does not necessarily mean value creation. A healthier picture emerges if we focus on those ratios that assess how effectively the management is using your money by looking at the returns on investment being generated. Given the critical importance of cash, focusing on the cash being generated in relation to the amount invested is a very effective way of assessing performance. When comparing this to the risks being incurred a picture emerges of whether the management team is really generating value for their shareholders.

The higher the returns (whether that be on sales, capital invested or shareholder value), especially when consistent over time, the more competitive the business is. When buying shares you are in effect buying a share in the competitive position of the business. Building and sustaining competitive advantage is management's key role and it is a key driver of long-term wealth creation: looking at returns in detail allows you to tell whether management is delivering.

PERFORMANCE AND RETURNS CHECKLIST

How well is the business performing in absolute terms and relative to the peer group?

Trends

Performance trends to monitor include:

- Sales – trends in price and volumes will tell you whether the company is taking or losing market share, has pricing power or its revenue is being driven by new products commanding a higher price.
- Earnings – is growth being generated from the core business, acquisitions or one-off contributions? What is the quality of earnings?
- EBITDA – adding back non-cash costs gives a sense of cash generation (though depreciation is a real cost of doing business).
- Cash – is the company generating cash after funding its capital expenditure requirements? This will be vital for the future success of the business and the performance of the shares.

Returns

How well is management running the business?

The key return ratios are:

- Operating margins – how profitable is each pound of sales?
- Return on invested capital – how much has been spent to generate the earnings?
- Cash returns on cash invested – cash is the key driver of value and less easy to manipulate than earnings.
- Economic value added – do the returns compensate for the risks involved?

Issues when looking at returns:

- If returns are much higher than competitors, can the numbers be believed?
- Are returns so high that new competition will be attracted? What are the barriers to entry?
- Are returns so high that the company is ex-growth?
- If returns are low, can they be improved? If so, how – and is this credible?

5

Financial position

What topics are covered in this chapter?

- Why financial position is critical
- What is the company's financial position?
- Gearing – the debt/equity ratio
- Pension deficits and other liabilities
- Interest cover and other measures of financial strength
- Credit ratings
- Covenants
- Why high gearing may hurt the company and its share price
- How much debt should the company have? Efficient balance sheets
- Raising fresh capital: rights issues
- Cash flow
- Summary
- Checklist

Why financial position is critical

As the current financial environment has made abundantly clear, the level of debt in a company (often referred to as 'gearing' or 'leverage') is a key element of risk – and, as we have seen, financial risk is a key driver of valuation. One of the key lessons from the credit crunch is that while debt is fine when the economy/business is doing well, when the economy slows down then it can be disastrous for certain sectors.

Financing businesses with debt became widespread during the boom years of 2004–07. Indeed, the advantages of using debt were seen to be so obvious that the private equity sector grew considerably while using debt aggressively, while the company sector, often under pressure from private equity or shareholders wanting more efficient balance sheets (see p. 185), engaged in massive share buy-backs.

Similar to when you buy your house with a very large mortgage (so you can buy a bigger, more expensive property) the impact on our wealth is dramatic if house prices rise significantly. If we buy a house for £500,000 financed entirely with a mortgage, a 20 per cent price rise generates a £100,000 profit. Provided we sell while house prices are still rising this is all very easy and profitable. So in an economic environment of strong growth and, crucially, rising asset prices, funding businesses with debt delivered very strong results. Importantly, it is vital to remember that this is a function of strong economic and asset growth and debt funding – not individual brilliance – because, as they say, a 'rising tide lifts all boats'.

Of course if the economy turns down things can become very challenging very quickly. Rising interest rates – or the absence of credit, which has characterised this recession but has the same effect – not only slows the economy but also reverses the trend in asset prices. This causes havoc with balance sheets for the personal and corporate sector, as we have seen. The 'toxic assets' consisting of asset-backed loans to housing and commercial property have been a crucial component of the problems facing the banks. At the company level there is a similar exposure to economic activity although there may be lots of other risks to consider as well – the impact of competitors, imports and exchange rates, dependence on certain customers, etc.

Figures 5.1 highlights the advantages to earnings and return on equity of funding a business with debt. And of course as debt is cheaper than equity it will, on the face of it, be much easier to create shareholder value. However, as Figure 5.2 makes clear, if things turn down the highly geared companies are in trouble very quickly.

In the figures we have three identical businesses that have chosen three different funding options. To illustrate operational gearing and for simplicity we assume all costs are fixed. Company A is funded with 100 per cent equity while B has half equity and half debt, and C has funded the busi-

	A	+10% T/O	B	+10% T/O	C	+10% T/O
Turnover	£1,000m	£1,100m	£1000m	£1,100m	£1000m	£1,100m
Costs	(£800m)		(£800m)		(£800m)	
Operating profit	£200m	£300m	£200m	£300m	£200m	£300m
Interest	£0m	–	(£64m)		(£96m)	
Pre-tax profit	£200m	£300m	£136m	£236m	£104m	£204m
Tax	(60m)	(90m)	(40.8m)	(70.8)	(31.2m)	(61.2m)
Earnings	£140m	£210m	£95.2m	£165.2m	72.8m	142.8
No. of shares	400m	400m	200m		100m	
EPS	35p	52.5p	47.6p	82.6p	72.8p	142.8p
ROIC (post tax)	8.8%	13.1%	8.8%	13.1%	8.8%	13.1%
ROE	8.8%	13.1%	11.9%	20.7%	18.2%	35.7%
Interest cover (Operating profit/interest payable)	–		3.1×	4.7×	2.1×	3.1×

A ⇒ £1,600m invested = all equity, 400m shares @ £4.00
B ⇒ £1,600m invested = 50% debt at 8% = £800m
C ⇒ £1,600m invested = 75% debt at 8% = £1200m

Figure 5.1 Debt and equity funding – the upside

ness with 75 per cent debt. As we can see, company C has much higher earnings per share (as there are far fewer shares in issue) and much higher return on equity. It is also worth noting, given the tax-deductibility of debt, how company C is paying about half as much tax as company A.

It is when turnover rises 10 per cent that we can see the even greater 'benefits' of the high gearing. Earnings for company C almost double compared to a 50 per cent uplift at company A. Interest cover for company C also expands to a healthier 3.1×. So if the turnover continues on an upward trend the debt-funded business will continue to enjoy better earnings growth and returns on equity.

However, as Figure 5.2 shows, if turnover comes under pressure for whatever reason then company C is suddenly in real difficulty. A 10 per cent reduction in turnover almost eliminates pre-tax profit (and hence earnings) as all the operating profit services the interest bill. Interest cover falls to just over 1.0×. Therefore debt is excellent if everything is going well!

	A (–10%)	B	C
Turnover	£900m	£900m	£900m
Costs	(800m)	(800m)	(800m)
Operating profit	£100m	£100m	£100m
Interest	–	(£64m)	(£96m)
Pre-tax profit	£100m	£36m	£4m
Tax	(£30m)	(10.8)	(£1.2m)
Earnings	70m	25.2m	2.8m
No. of shares	400m	200m	100m
EPS	17.5p	12.6p	2.8p
ROIC	4.4%	4.4%	4.4%
ROE	4.4%	3.1%	0.7%
Interest cover		1.6×	1.04×

Figure 5.2 Debt and equity funding – the downside

So when considering the financial position of a company it is critical to establish the type of business it is and the risks it is likely to face. As Figure 1.1 shows, certain sectors are very sensitive to the movements of interest rates (or in the current situation the availability of credit) and the subsequent impact on the economy.

Similarly, as Figure 5.2 shows, the impact of operational gearing – that is to say the impact when turnover falls on profits when fixed costs are high – is also pretty devastating. Combining high debt with a company sensitive to economic forces and high fixed costs is a recipe for disaster – as was well illustrated by the plight of the automotive and airlines sectors as well as banks, housebuilders and construction companies.

With companies going bust or needing rescue rights issues, the risks of financing certain types of business with debt all too apparent. You need to pay attention to the amount of debt in a business (and whether the business profile will support that debt) – but also the type and term structure of debt (i.e when does it have to be paid back?). If all the debt has to be paid back within (say) the next 12 months and banking conditions are unfavourable the company may run into trouble. This is a far riskier proposition than companies with a long-term debt maturity profile with money being paid back evenly over the next decade (and preferably much of it owing at the end of that period). The company having to pay back debt may have to sell off key assets at less than favourable prices (because no one else is in a very strong position to fund the purchase of the assets) to stay afloat.

The other key area to focus on is the fact that the interest bill is paid out of cash flow. Without cash flow the game is up as the debt cannot be serviced. The company may have a reasonable asset backing but if those assets are not generating cash then covenants, many of which will be linked to interest cover or the performance of EBITDA, are likely to be broken. This will almost inevitably mean that the dividend will be cut as this is also paid out of cash flow and the banks may well stipulate that this be suspended until they get their money back.

without cash flow the debt cannot be serviced

Furthermore, given that our main concern is the competitive position of a business, a company with a lot of debt may not be investing in its product offering and reducing its costs. Decisions will be distorted as it focuses on running the business for cash to stave off the banks rather than serving customers effectively in the short and long term. Clearly this is not sustainable in the medium term. And as the company loses its market share it will be making less money to service the debt, let alone invest in the business.

Therefore getting to the bottom of the company's financial position and its cash flow profile is crucial to minimise the risks in investing and to ensure you are investing in a sound business with long-term potential off the back of a strong competitive position.

What is the company's financial position?

There are a number of key figures to look at when considering the financial health of a company:

- gearing – the debt/equity ratio
- pension deficits and other liabilities
- interest cover and other measures of financial strength.

Gearing – the debt/equity ratio

Gearing is the most common way of measuring a company's financial position. The normal way to derive this is to first work out the group's net debt. Net debt is the total debt a company has minus any cash it holds.

You then divide that figure by shareholders' funds. Shareholders' funds are clearly listed on the balance sheet and are basically the book value of the company's assets at that point in time. This would include the value of buildings and plant, stock held and any profits retained over the years. A common definition of gearing is net debt/shareholders' funds, the latter including **minorities** (although some investors may exclude minorities which gives a more prudent view). Minorities are the portion of assets owned by outside shareholders when a company has a majority holding but does not own 100 per cent of the company.

You then multiply your answer by 100 to give you the gearing figure, expressed as a percentage. So if net debt is £100 million and the company's shareholders funds are £200 million, the company is said to have gearing of 50 per cent.

Gearing, then, is a measure of how much of the capital employed in the business is provided by shareholders' funds and how much by debt. A company with low gearing has a small proportion of its capital supplied by debt, whereas a highly geared company has a high proportion of its capital funded by debt.

Companies that are in sectors where there are few **fixed assets** or where assets tend to be 'intangible', such as the value of brand names, can be disadvantaged if you look just at gearing to evaluate their financial position. The same is true of highly acquisitive companies that write off a lot of goodwill on the 'assets' they acquire. These companies will tend to have a high level of gearing even if they have very little debt. In these cases a better guide to the companies' financial position would be to look at interest cover (see p. 177).

There is no 'correct' level of gearing (as it depends on the type of business), but above 50 per cent is normally considered on the high side. A company operating in a stable industry, with a clear view of its revenues and little need for new investment in the business, will be able to live with a much higher level of gearing than a company in a cyclical business that has no visibility in its revenues (i.e. it is extremely difficult to predict the volumes and prices of the company's output) and needs a lot of cash to update a large factory or piece of equipment.

The main questions to ask are:

- How is the company affected by the economic cycle?
- How predictable is the revenue?
- Does the company have pricing power?

- Is the company dependent on one client?
- How much cash is the company generating?
- Does the business need a lot of investment?
- Is the interest rate charged on the debt fixed or variable?
- Is the debt short or long term?
- Are the shareholders' funds (assets) realistically valued?

Example – calculating gearing

Milk Pops

Let us take another fictional company, Milk Pops, which produces breakfast cereal. We assume it has debt of £60 million, shareholders' funds of £100 million, so it would be said to have gearing of 60 per cent. Milk Pops has total sales per year of £200 million and a 10 per cent operating profit margin, so its operating profit is £20 million. One of the features of the business is the predictability of its sales, which have grown consistently at around 4 per cent per annum even in periods of recession.

Debt	£60m
Shareholders' funds	£100m
Gearing calculation	
Debt/shareholder funds	60/100
Gearing	60%
Total sales	£200m
Operating profit margin	10%
Operating profit	£20m

Full Stop

Compare that with Full Stop, a fictional brake-unit manufacturer that makes brake units and sells them to a nearby large car manufacturer. Full Stop also has debt of £60 million and shareholder funds of £100 million and so like Milk Pops has gearing of 60 per cent. Its sales are currently £150 million, having fallen from £200 million last year. Its profit margin is 5 per cent, having fallen from 10 per cent last year. This year its operating profit is £7.5 million.

Debt	£60m
Shareholders' funds	£100m
Gearing calculation	
Debt/shareholder funds	60/100
Gearing	60%
Total sales	£150m
Operating profit margin	5%
Operating profit	£7.5m

A key feature of this business is that it is highly cyclical in nature (as demand for cars goes up and down with the business cycle). In addition it is vulnerable to the loss of one major contract with a car manufacturer. This raises uncertainty over its future performance.

> **Analysis**
>
> While the two companies both have relatively high gearing it is evident that Milk Pops has a higher level of operating profit and a more stable performance than Full Stop. Full Stop has the same relatively high debt but makes less money, less consistently. This would be likely to cause concern for investors.

When does the debt mature?

Another step, especially relevant in the current environment, is to check the 'term structure of debt' – that is, when does the debt mature? Ideally the company should have debt maturing in a number of years' time as a reliance on short-term debt may make renegotiating that debt difficult and expensive if it is all due to mature in (say) the next six months.

Pension deficits and other liabilities

To get a comprehensive view of the debt profile of the company as well as looking at the level of short- and long-term loans (less any cash on deposit or cash-like investments) we need to check any other liabilities the company may have responsibility for. Here we need to examine pension and health care liabilities, off-balance sheet debt, and outstanding preference and convertible shares. The new IFRS accounting standards mean all these are now recognised as debt and the credit rating agencies also factor them into their assessment of a company's rating.

Pension fund deficits

The importance of pension fund deficits in corporate valuation continues to dominate the headlines. According to the Pension Protection Fund in the UK, the insurance scheme for the underfunded pension plans of insolvent employers, the aggregate gap between the value of scheme assets and the value of liabilities it guarantees rose to £253.1 billion.

The arrival of IFRS brings the issue to the fore as the impact of deficits will be felt directly on the balance sheet. This will affect the net assets of the business through distributable reserves and hence dividend-paying capacity. In effect this makes explicit the fact that shareholders are exposed to risk through pension guarantees to current and previous employees. The company's financial position is very much weakened as the deficits are treated as debt.

Crucially, the funds required to make good such promises (and they are often substantial) are funds diverted from the potential income of investors (dividends are being cut as a result of this) or funds potentially invested in the business which help maintain and enhance the company's competitive position. Clearly both of these drastically undermine the attractiveness of the company as an investment. Similarly, there have been situations where companies looking to reduce their debt through disposals have discovered that the pension fund trustees have a say in how the disposal proceeds are used – and clearly it may be their legal duty as trustees of the pension scheme to insist that the funds make good a deficit.

The accounting for pension funds was also put under the spotlight by a Securities and Exchange Commission enquiry into the assumptions made by US firms on the expected returns from shares. The higher the assumed returns the lower the deficit and the less the need to pay into the fund. As a result earnings benefit or are manipulated. Some companies have been assuming equity returns as high as 10 per cent. The wisdom of doing this when such a high rate has never been delivered over a sustainable period is clearly questionable – let alone given the actual return from equities in recent years.

As well as the 'flexibility' of assumptions on expected returns, the other variable that can influence the size of the deficit is the **discount rate** used. The lower the rate the greater the liability (as future liabilities are discounted to present value at a lower rate) – this may lead to companies choosing a higher rate to lower the deficit. So the choice of discount rate is actually very important. With 'quantitative easing' seeing long-term gilts rise in price (and yields correspondingly fall) this can have serious repercussions for the size of the deficit.

> the choice of discount rate is actually very important

The other key assumption is how long the liabilities will run for – i.e. how long will the pensioner live? These longevity assumptions can make a dramatic difference to the size of deficit as the company's liabilities are running for much longer. It was estimated that Boots' pension fund deficit would increase by about £350 million if longevity assumptions were changed by three years.

Another aspect that needs to be considered is the asset allocation of the pension fund. The extra volatility of shares as an asset class introduces uncertainty as to returns, and with the introduction of the new IFRS accounting standards this will be evident on the face of the P&L. The risk of this equity exposure and the associated extra volatility results in a higher cost of capital. At the company-specific level companies such as BT and Diageo have high equity exposure within their schemes.

Therefore when assessing the value of a target company the pension fund deficit has to be incorporated into the enterprise value (see p. 273) – the deficit is effectively a liability akin to debt. This is reinforced by the fact that the credit rating agencies take the liability into account when attributing ratings. The link has been made explicit by the bond issues made by many companies (including the largest ever, GM's $13 billion capital raising) deliberately undertaken to plug a hole in their pension funds. In the UK, Marks and Spencer has also issued a bond specifically to help fund its pension fund deficit.

Sectors susceptible to deficit problems have the characteristics of being mature and labour intensive and often have been government-owned enterprises in the past. Periods of heavy redundancies/early retirements may also create liabilities. Accordingly engineering, automotive, national airlines, brewers, utilities, fixed-line telecomms and support services are sectors where care needs to be taken.

With recent returns from equity markets being so disappointing, companies undergoing 'triennial reviews' of their pension funds' capacity to service future liabilities are likely to see a big mismatch between assets and liabilities. Smiths Group warned (on 24 March 2009) that it may see its contributions rise significantly as it undergoes its review. Its deficit has risen from £11 million to £500 million. On the day it announced this 14 per cent was knocked off the share price. Formerly nationalised businesses such as BT and BA have significant deficit issues as well. BT could be forced to double its annual pension contributions to £560 million a year under a legally binding agreement it signed with the trustees of its pension scheme in 2006 and approved by the Pensions Regulator. BA has on paper a £600 million deficit and is paying £320 million into the scheme – this is a considerable increase in risk given the company's debt profile and high operational gearing. The probability of its dividend being restored looks very slim on that basis.

One of the key issues has been the deterrent effect the pension deficit has on deals. The deficit is increasingly appreciated as a debt obligation and can add considerably to the take-out value for the deal. This happened in Permira's proposed acquisition of WH Smith. Similarly, uncertainty over the extent of pension liabilities was an issue in Philip Green's bid for M&S. On the other hand, one of the reasons Balfour Beatty could take over Mansell was that it had the resources and financial strength to absorb its pension liabilities. Mansell was concerned it would not have the resources both to meet this liability and fund the growth of the business.

Health care liabilities

Another area of particular importance, especially in the US, is the company's liability for the health care of its employees (past and present). Again assumptions made on the inflation of health care costs and the discount rate used will have a big impact on reported earnings. For the domestic US automotive companies the cost of health care per car is often greater than the cost of steel per car (this is true for both GM and Ford). As well as being a liability that needs to be taken into account when computing economic value, it clearly has a profound impact on the company's economic competitiveness. Many overseas players without such heavy 'legacy' costs are therefore far more competitive. It may also mean that given the need to service these 'interest' or liability expenses there is a temptation for the US producers to go for volume to generate cash – hence the discounting in the new car market although the fixed-cost nature of the business also suggests there may be a tendency to go for volume too.

The inevitable impact on margins from such a volume-led strategy (the US majors make very little (if anything) from manufacturing cars) will also heavily influence valuation. Similarly, a poor competitive position undermines the credit ratings of the companies. Interestingly, both S&P and Fitch cited pension and health care deficit concerns (and the risks to the projected returns being used given the actual performance of equity markets) whenever they downgraded GM's debt.

A company's liability to its employees in terms of both pensions and health care is a major financial issue. With shareholders shouldering this responsibility it must be factored into valuation. As we have seen with the US car sector, these liabilities really affect the competitive position of the firm and therefore the attractiveness of the company as an investment. The treatment of these liabilities as debt also raises profound questions when examining the appropriate financial structure for a company. These have been very real concerns for some time but the arrival of IFRS accounting standards will crystallise the issues for investors, lenders and dealmakers alike.

Off-balance sheet debt

It always pays to make sure that the company has declared the full extent of its liabilities and that this is incorporated in the debt number. The company may have debt in a joint venture that is not consolidated in the overall debt numbers. This is referred to as off-balance sheet debt. Similarly, the company may have leasing obligations that are, in effect, debt.

The use of off-balance sheet debt was of course a major feature of the demise of Enron, the energy trader. The company flattered its balance sheet by parking debt off balance sheet in joint venture companies. These companies were set up specifically to conceal the debt. An important lesson from this saga was that the off-balance sheet companies had assets equivalent to their liabilities. These special purpose entities (known as special purpose vehicles or SPVs or in the financial services area as structured investment vehicles or SIVs) therefore had gearing of 100 per cent. It can be difficult to unearth this information, but a close look through the notes to the report and accounts is crucial in order to find related-party transactions and liabilities.

The banks have had many of these SIVs which were not apparent to investors as they were not on the balance sheet. However, they were classified as liabilities when things got difficult. Some consider this one of the major regulatory oversights of the banking crisis.

Convertible and preference shares – also debt?

When looking at the gearing ratio you should also consider whether the company has any convertible shares or preference shares that may be to all intents and purposes debt. This may be because the shares are redeemable or will never become equity. Many companies will exclude these from their gearing figures, which gives a much more flattering view of their financial position. Most analysts will treat these as debt and this will give a more conservative view of the financial position.

It is always worth taking a cautious view of overall indebtedness and being as comprehensive as possible in assessing the debt number.

Short- and long-term debt

An important issue to bear in mind when looking at a company's financial position is the maturity structure of the debt as well as the overall level. If it is all short-term debt at variable rates of interest, profits will be hit hard if interest rates rise sharply. Also the banks may call in the debt when it is up for renewal rather than extending it, which could cause other lenders to panic. Longer-term debt at fixed rates will offer a more stable financial profile. The impact of changes in short-term interest rates would be minimised and there would be no need for constant refinancing. This would also allow for greater stability, liquidity and flexibility than shorter-term debt.

The other important thing to consider in terms of the time profile of the debt is the assets that the debt is used to finance. If the company has invested in factories and capital equipment that have a long economic life, it would be inappropriate to finance this with potentially volatile short-term debt. Debt of long-term maturity or a bond would be far more appropriate (with bank loans and overdrafts funding short-term working capital requirements). It is not dissimilar to buying a house: a mortgage over 25 years is infinitely more appropriate than an overdraft. You could argue that very long-term assets should be financed with equity.

An aspect of the credit crunch and the lack of finance available from the banks is the extent to which companies will now issue more long-term bonds to fund the business rather than loans or overdrafts from the banks.

The valuation of assets and shareholders' funds

When you have got to grips with the level of debt, you need to ensure that the value of shareholders' funds is appropriate. In most instances this should not be a problem. However, there are situations where the assets on the balance sheet might be considerably overvalued, such as where an acquisition has been bought at the top of the cycle at a very high price. If the industry then turns down and remains in the doldrums for some time, the value of the asset is likely to be overstated. If the performance of the business has fallen by 40 per cent and the likelihood for improvement is limited, in theory the value of the asset should be 40 per cent lower. It could of course be worth even less, subject to how overpriced the acquisition was in the first place.

A very important aspect of asset valuation at the moment is the valuation of housing and property assets. Banks having made loans to fund the purchase of these assets (or invested in securitised portfolios of assets) may inherit assets which are worth considerably less than the outstanding loan amount if the consumer or company defaults. So the asset backing of banks with big exposures to housing and commercial property may be considerably less than the current book value. Clearly in this case the shareholders' funds are considerably overvalued.

Similarly, if we take the situation where an acquisition accounted for 50 per cent of assets and those assets, following an 'impairment review', are deemed overvalued by 50 per cent, this 50 per cent falls to 25 per cent, while the overall assets fall to 75 per cent. Gearing on this basis would rise dramatically. If the stated gearing is 60 per cent, then on the basis of the real value of the assets this rises to 80 per cent (60/75). Crucially, because the impair-

gearing on this basis would rise dramatically

ment review is done on the back of lower cash flow projections there is a lot less profit and cash flow to service the debt.

An obvious way of checking whether the assets are appropriately valued is to check the return on assets (the assets are worth only what they are generating in terms of cash and returns on investment). So if the return on assets is 5 per cent and has been for some time, the assets are likely to be overvalued. This may apply to certain divisions or to the whole company.

The asset side of the equation is very important to the companies. Often there will be net asset covenants which stipulate that assets should not fall below a certain level or gearing must not exceed 100 per cent. In this situation the temptation is to maintain an asset base as high as possible. The reality of the worth of the assets is clearly very different. Therefore the asset side of the equation is very much worth taking on board.

Interest cover and other measures of financial strength

One of the issues with looking at debt to equity ratios is that the assets may not be generating the income needed to service the interest payments. Other measures of financial strength tend to look at the income and cash flow that is being generated (from that asset base) and seeing how comfortably the company can meet its liabilities. As we have seen with the operational gearing examples, the key here is whether those income and cash flow streams are sustainable.

Interest cover

Interest cover is a measure of how easily the company can pay interest on its debt. This is measured by taking the operating profit and dividing it by the annual interest payments. Both these items are listed in the P&L statement.

Example – the interest cover calculation

Returning to the example of Milk Pops, its debt stands at £60 million and its operating profit at £20 million. Paying 5 per cent interest a year on its debt gives an annual interest payment of £3 million. So, to calculate interest cover we take £20 million (operating profit) and divide by £3 million (interest payment) to give a figure of 6.7. This means that the operating profit could pay the interest 6.7 times over ... and it's expressed just like that, 6.7×.

This is a simple to calculate and widely used method of assessing a company's financial position. As a rule of thumb, figures below 3 are viewed with caution, while those above are seen as safe. One of the advantages of using this measure is that it provides a much more reliable guide to a company's financial strength than conventional gearing (debt/shareholder funds) when a company has very few assets.

Where a company has few assets

The use of interest cover is particularly relevant in areas of the service economy where there are few assets ('people businesses') and situations where assets have been severely affected by the write-off of goodwill. Consumer products companies that have been involved in a series of acquisitions may have written off substantial amounts of goodwill (where the price paid for the deal considerably exceeds assets on the balance sheet). Diageo, the international drinks company, normally presents its financial position through the use of interest cover because a debt to equity measure would be meaningless as considerable amounts of goodwill have been written off – i.e. shareholders' funds are relatively low, having been reduced significantly by goodwill written off.

How volatile are the operating profits?

As with the debt to equity ratio, the degree of danger in any given ratio depends on the economic characteristics of the business. As the numerator is operating profit, the key issue to focus on is the sensitivity of operating profits to changes in prices and volumes (operational gearing, see p. 219). If we consider the example of the manufacturing company Tin Can, we know from the characteristics of its markets – overcapacity, a commodity product and competition from imports – that prices are likely to be volatile. With turnover of £250 million, a 5 per cent reduction in price will reduce turnover by £12.5 million. With costs fixed, this then reduces profits by £12.5 million (50 per cent) as well.

Similarly, its cost structure, given a high proportion of fixed costs, makes profits highly sensitive to changes in volume.

If we say that operating profits are £25 million and interest payments are £5 million, interest cover is 5×. However, on a 5 per cent price reduction, profits halve (from £25 million to £12.5 million) and accordingly interest cover falls to 2.5×. This is falling to dangerous levels. This deterioration is on an all too plausible assumption of a 5 per cent reduction in prices. If prices fell more than 5 per cent and a key contract was lost, the financial position would deteriorate even more sharply. A 10 per cent price reduction would eradicate profits and leave no interest cover at all.

By contrast, for Milk Pops (or Pink Tablet) a stable volume and pricing scenario suggests that the risks are much lower. Accordingly, interest cover ratios could be a lot lower and one would still be comfortable with the company's financial position.

The danger level for interest cover

Companies with this sort of cover are in a difficult position, especially if operating profits are volatile as discussed above. At 2× or below, the company's bankers will be keeping a close eye on its developments and indeed it may well be that debt covenants (agreements undertaken by the company with its banks) are being broken. This may lead to a downgrading of the company's credit status and force the company into disposals or a rights issue, or quite possibly both. In an environment as difficult as the current one, it is likely to be only the best parts of the business that will attract buyers. Following the disposals, what is left of the company may not be what originally attracted you to invest. Therefore, when evaluating a potential investment idea, the risks attaching to a company with such a low level of interest cover are very high – it can cost you a lot of money. A simple and effective ratio, such as interest cover, which can be quickly and easily computed, can help you avoid potential disasters.

a simple and effective ratio can help you avoid potential disasters

Cash flow pays interest costs not asset backing

When we looked at the company's assets we had to consider the possibility that the shareholders' funds element of the balance sheet was overstated. The assets might be worth far less than their book value. This will inevitably be because the cash flows they are generating are dramatically lower than has been the case historically. But of course it is the cash flows that service the interest costs. Therefore using measures which deliberately take into account the current (and likely future) cash generation of the business is far more effective. The measures cited below are useful because they allow for this.

Cash flow cover – EBITDA/interest payable

A variant on interest cover calculated by using operating profit over interest payable is to compute a cash flow cover. This adds on depreciation and amortisation to operating profit as they are non-cash costs. This obviously means that the cash coming into the business can also be used to meet the interest payments. However, the danger is that funds are diverted from replacement capital expenditure and investing to maintain competitiveness, to servicing the interest. Nonetheless it may be that you wish to take into account the cash flow cover of interest payments.

An important feature to monitor in the calculation is that interest is not being 'capitalised' and thus excluded from the interest payable figure. Interest may be capitalised when it is included in the cost of building plant or facilities for long-term use (the interest is treated as an important cost of the development and is therefore included in the total cost of the project, i.e. capitalised). Food retail outlets, property developers and hotels are some of the businesses that may capitalise interest. There is nothing necessarily wrong with this practice, but it is worth monitoring if the company is capitalising interest and it is worth checking how much interest is being capitalised. The cover would then be calculated on the interest the company actually pays to banks as opposed to the amount declared on the P&L.

Net debt/EBITDA

This also looks at the cash flow element but looks at how many times the debt exceeds the cash flow. The higher the **multiple** (i.e. if debt is say more than four times EBITDA) obviously the more uncomfortable the position. The other issue of course is the predictability or otherwise of the EBITDA – which again takes us back to the type of business.

After the lax lending of the earlier part of the decade banks are now being much stricter on these multiples. Future covenants are likely to limit debt at less than three times EBITDA for many sectors.

Fixed charge cover

Also worthy of note is whether there are preference shareholders that have to be paid or other providers of debt to the company such as convertible bonds. The payments to these people effectively constitute interest or a fixed charge, where the providers of this money have a priority claim on funds before the shareholder. Some of these payments may occur 'below the line', i.e. after the profits figure has been struck. As a result, they may not feature in the interest line. Accordingly, they should be added to the interest payments when calculating cover. Sometimes this is referred to as a fixed charge cover ratio. Some people take into account other fixed charges, such as lease payments, as this is in effect a form of interest on an asset used in the business.

Credit ratings

A credit rating is a measure of the issuer's ability to service and repay its debt. This will depend on:

- its financial position (the amount of debt, the liquidity position and other liabilities such as pensions and healthcare liabilities); and
- the performance of the business which after all is generating the cash flow to service the debt and ultimately redeem it.

These ratings are provided by the major credit ratings agencies such as Standard and Poor's (S&P), Moody's and Fitch. Table 5.1 highlights the range of ratings from S&P.

Table 5.1 S&P ratings

	Ratings	*Grade*	*Status*
AAA	Highest	Investment grade	Rising star
AA	Very strong		
A	Strong		
BBB	Adequate		
BB	Speculative	Non-investment grade	
B, CCC, CCC, CC, C	Speculative		
D	Default		Fallen angel

A company with very sound finances – very little debt and strong and predictable cash flow – will have an AAA rating. This means it can raise money much more easily and cheaply. Anything above BBB is regarded as 'investment grade'. When a company is below BBB it is not investment grade (rather it's 'junk') and then the costs of raising money increase dramatically as the risk of the company defaulting on its payments is so much greater.

The 'cult of debt' experienced in the past decade has seen the number of AAA-rated companies decline dramatically. The share buy-backs, leveraged buy-outs and debt-fuelled mergers and acquisitions of this period have inevitably seen credit ratings come under pressure.

Strikingly, the number of companies rated A and higher has tumbled to just 11 per cent, from 17 per cent in 1998 and from 50 per cent in 1980. In the US only five AAA-rated stocks are left: Automatic Data Processing,

Exxon Mobil, Johnson & Johnson, Microsoft and Pfizer. Therefore, given the much higher proportion of debt below BBB grade, the risk of companies defaulting in the current environment is so much greater, especially given the weak economic outlook.

Over time the proportion of US industrial companies (excluding utilities and financial institutions) in the B rating category account for nearly half of all S&P's corporate credit ratings whereas this category made up just 7 per cent of ratings in 1980.

According to S&P, 75 entities worldwide, representing debt topping $174 billion, were identified as potential fallen angels in January 2009. This compares with an average of 47 potential fallen angels per month in 2008.

A number of concerns have been voiced about the independence of the credit ratings agencies as a result of the credit crunch and the poor performance of many instruments that had been assigned AAA ratings. Crucially there has also been an issue that a downgrade of a company's debt comes far too late. This makes the debt rating a lagging indicator whereas the shares are likely to be an effective way of anticipating the troubles ahead.

Covenants

There has been much concern about highly indebted companies breaching their banking covenants. This reflects the fact that their financial positions have deteriorated and some key ratios such as interest cover (operating profit/interest payable) that will have been stipulated in the covenant have fallen below prescribed levels.

We saw in the operational gearing example that if prices for the companies fall 5 per cent then profit could halve. Clearly then interest cover would halve. In that example interest cover fell 2×. This represents a level at which the providers of debt will be getting very nervous, especially if the prospects for the company's revenues remain uncertain. It would probably be in breach of its covenants.

Not only will a covenant stipulate the level of interest cover required, it will stipulate the method of calculation. Otherwise companies could use favourable interpretations of accounting policies to try to keep the numbers on the right side of the line.

Breaching the covenants means that the debt providers can demand immediate repayment. However, in most instances discussions will take place to renegotiate the terms of the debt and if this is agreed then the company will be paying much higher interest costs as a result. Obviously, in a worst case scenario the company will default on its debt and go bankrupt. (The banks may then go for a debt–equity swap if that is deemed worthwhile.) These discussions may see the company agreeing to sell off assets – this may be good for the banks but less attractive for equity holders if they are key assets of the company and are sold at distressed prices. In other situations the debt may be rolled over only if equity holders inject additional funds.

> in a worst case scenario, the company will default on its debt and go bankrupt

Why high gearing may hurt the company and its share price

Generally speaking, a higher level of gearing suggests a higher level of risk. Below we detail some of the problems associated with high gearing and the adverse impact it may have on a company and its share price performance.

- *Higher risk.* An important aspect of the higher debt levels is that the risks are greater. This will put off potential investors who might have been interested in the situation if debt was at lower levels (i.e. they have low risk thresholds and may invest only in companies with low gearing). Clearly if interest rates are expected to rise, investors will be wary of getting involved.
- *Cash flow servicing debt – cannot invest.* This will undermine the valuation of the shares, especially when combined with the risk of a rights issue. A company with a high level of gearing may find that it cannot fund investment in maintaining the quality of assets or the growth of the business. This could be very dangerous competitively. Good commercial opportunities may be missed as the company takes too long to raise the money or cannot raise it all. This will undermine the valuation of the shares, especially when combined with the risk of a rights issue.
- *Business run for creditors not for shareholders.* One of the central problems if gearing is at very high levels is that the management will be taking decisions favoured by the bankers, which may well not be in the long-term interests of shareholders. Discretionary costs such as marketing and R&D are likely to be reduced and capital expenditure cut back. In addition, promising projects may have to be abandoned. Creditors anx-

ious to get their money back may also force the company into selling off its most valuable assets. As a result shareholders may not be invested in what had attracted them to the company in the first place.

- *Risk of rights issue.* The higher the level of gearing and the weaker the cash flow, the much greater the risk of a company having a rights issue. This may be avoided by selling off assets, although that involves the risk that the most saleable assets are the most profitable. A rights issue in itself may not be a major depressant on a share price, but the laws of supply and demand suggest a lower share price.

- *Cost of debt.* Another problem for a company with high debt levels is that the cost of borrowing will tend to rise to reflect the higher risk of default. Bond issues by telecoms companies following their heavy investment in expansion in the late 1990s saw the cost of servicing their debt rise sharply as lenders, concerned about their poor financial position, demanded higher rates. This problem is compounded if much of the existing debt is at variable rates and interest rates are generally rising.

- Obviously, if there are substantial amounts of debt, if the cost of that debt rises by 3 or 4 percentage points this will have a big impact on debt costs and hence reduce profits significantly. When this works through to earnings, the dividend is likely to be cut (especially as the trading environment is also likely to be difficult in these circumstances).

- The credit ratings agencies have had a significant impact on this concern. Indeed, the ICI rights issue in 2001 was very much driven by debt ratings agencies warning of what would happen to the cost of debt if action was not taken to reduce debt and of course in the current environment many rights issues are taking place for the same reason. This led to a deeply discounted and underwritten rights issue. The downgrading of companies' credit ratings can have a severe impact on share prices and again highlights the risks involved for shareholders.

- *Low dividend growth.* The need to service high debt levels will mean that the ability to grow the dividend is limited. This may be a deterrent for those investors that have a requirement for a growing income. This, combined with the inability to invest in the business, leaves the shares looking very unattractive.

- *Bankruptcy.* If the financial position deteriorates dramatically, ultimately a company may be forced into bankruptcy. If the business prospects are poor and it cannot service its existing debt, it will prove impossible to continue to fund the business on an ongoing basis. The fate of Marconi is salutary here – while it has not gone bankrupt, shareholders have ended up with a mere 0.5 per cent or so of the equity, as bondholders converted their bonds into shares.

How much debt should the company have? Efficient balance sheets

The increasing use of 'economic value added (EVA)' approaches to investment analysis in the 1990s led to a lot of attention being focused on 'balance sheet efficiency'. This means that by having the right level of debt and equity you will minimise the cost of capital. Indeed a very large investor based in the UK, Hermes, has as one of its principles for companies the following:

Lowering the cost of capital
Principle 6 'Companies should have an effecient capital structure which will minimise the long-term cost of capital.'

Gearing and returns

The notion of efficient balance sheets highlights that gearing can be a good thing – as demonstrated by Figure 5.3. It is much cheaper and more tax efficient to fund businesses with debt (the debt payments are deducted before arriving at pre-tax profits). This improves returns. In many cases it is similar to the advantage of buying a property with a mortgage accounting for 100 per cent of the value of the property. Any increase in the value of the property then belongs entirely to the mortgage holder.

It can also be the case that the debt ensures that the business is run efficiently. There is the discipline of making sure the debt can be serviced and that there is extra left over for shareholders.

High gearing and volatile income to be avoided

A high level of financial gearing, however, combined with a high level of operational gearing can be extremely damaging in a downturn. If volume and/or prices fall in a business with high fixed costs, operating profits and cash flow will fall dramatically. This might make it very difficult to service the company's debt and may well lead to the dividend being cut. In a prolonged downturn this may lead to a period of poor performance and conceivably bankruptcy.

Adding value is defined as producing rates of return over and above the cost of capital. Companies with low levels of debt were encouraged to engage in share buy-backs to improve their cost of capital by increasing the proportion of (cheaper) debt in their financing mix. Gearing generally in the corporate sector has been on a rising trend, partially due to this drive for balance sheet efficiency.

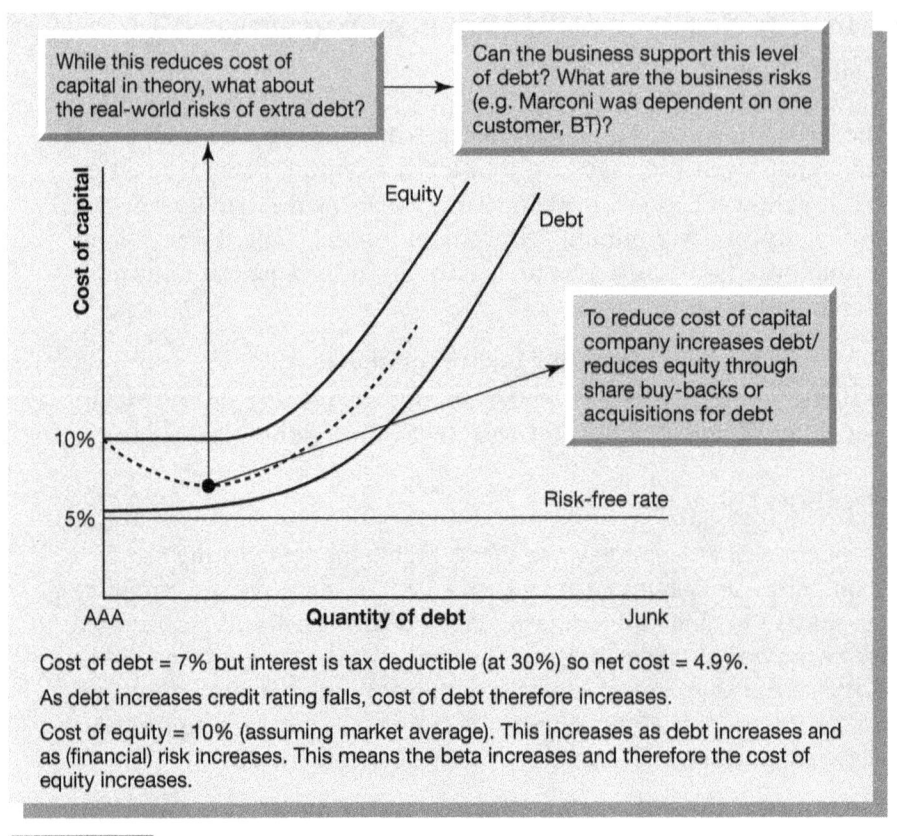

Figure 5.3 Efficient balance sheets

Callouts on figure:

- While this reduces cost of capital in theory, what about the real-world risks of extra debt?
- Can the business support this level of debt? What are the business risks (e.g. Marconi was dependent on one customer, BT)?
- To reduce cost of capital company increases debt/ reduces equity through share buy-backs or acquisitions for debt

Axes: Cost of capital (y) vs Quantity of debt (x, from AAA to Junk). Curves labelled Equity, Debt, and Risk-free rate. Reference lines at 10% and 5%.

Cost of debt = 7% but interest is tax deductible (at 30%) so net cost = 4.9%.
As debt increases credit rating falls, cost of debt therefore increases.

Cost of equity = 10% (assuming market average). This increases as debt increases and as (financial) risk increases. This means the beta increases and therefore the cost of equity increases.

It is also worth bearing in mind that (debt) capital was not only cheap in the 1990s and early 2000s, it was widely available. Therefore there was a strong climate that encouraged share buy-backs and of course the private equity industry was very busy taking companies off the stock market and loading them with debt. Indeed, what would happen was that a company that was bid for by private equity would use share buy-backs as part of its bid defence as this was seen as being shareholder friendly.

The current environment is far less supportive of share buy-backs but that does not mean to say that they should not be considered: it does mean that the case for buy-backs has to be rigorously applied and the reasons behind them confirmed as ones that will create shareholder value.

So companies with very strong balance sheets – stable low-risk businesses which require little new investment – may well have a case for a buy-back. In the oil sector, for example, Exxon has been judiciously using buy-backs.

Therefore having an efficient balance sheet means having the right level of debt to minimise the cost of capital. (It should be borne in mind that this only works if the conditions cited above – stable revenues, strong cash flow, low operational gearing, etc. – are all in place.)

So a company that has cash on its balance sheet or no debt would be deemed to have an 'inefficient balance sheet'. To make the balance sheet efficient it needs to increase the amount of debt (reduce the amount of cash) and it can do this by:

- investing in the business
- making acquisitions for cash
- a share buy-back
- a special dividend
- increasing ordinary dividends.

However, before engaging in any of these activities it is worth considering the following questions.

What type of business is it and how competitive is it?

A key issue is whether the business is capable of having higher gearing – what type of business are we talking about? The advantages of gearing up in terms of reducing the cost of capital and the disciplines of higher debt are confined to companies with predictable revenues (especially price stability) and cash generation. A high proportion of fixed costs (high operational gearing) is also a significant deterrent to debt. Combining high operational gearing and high debt levels is very dangerous – relatively small movements in revenues significantly impair the company's ability to service debt.

The retail, property and hotels sector saw significant buy-out activity during the boom of 2004–07. The asset backing provides a major opportunity to secure lending – banks will often lend up to 90 per cent against property as opposed to around 70 per cent for an operating business. In some deals this has seen the operating company split off from the property assets. The ongoing rental liability services the debt secured on the property assets. However, given the severity of the downturn many retailers, property companies and hotel companies have run into serious financial trouble.

Questions inevitably arise as to whether operating businesses in these sectors have the degree of visibility of revenue and cash flows to service the high rents and/or high interest payments involved in higher debt levels.

This reinforces the notion that it is the visibility of the revenue streams and cash flow that is crucial when gearing up, not the asset backing.

If the company has a high debt burden and a significant amount of cash flow is servicing debt, there has to be a major concern that the company's competitive position, due to underinvestment in the business or its brands, is severely undermined. These concerns have been manifest with buy-outs returning to the equity market. Given the high leverage and the implications this has for investment in the business, investors were, not surprisingly, very wary about buying these assets back from private equity and very circumspect about the price they would pay. There were concerns, for example, at Premier Foods that the brands had been starved of advertising, which in a very competitive marketplace may result in an erosion of long-term market share. Clearly such a fall in market share severely affects the company's long-term ability to service debt.

Therefore, while the financial structure of a company is a key determinant of its cost of capital, in the long run it is the company's competitive position that will determine its ability to add value and service its liabilities. This requires a clear strategy and the managerial and financial resources to compete effectively. While there are advantages to debt finance, it can be self-defeating where competitive pressures need to be met with significant investment.

How will the cash be returned?

If the balance sheet is inefficient and the business can support higher debt without incurring extra risk or undermining the competitive position of the business, the main debate centres around the most effective way of returning the money to shareholders: via a buy-back, a dividend increase or a special dividend. Each has merits in different contexts. As well as the impact on the cost of capital, the other main issue is what each action 'signals' to investors.

The tax implications for shareholders will differ and also need to be taken into account. Typically capital gains are taxed at a lower rate or have scope to be managed in a way that income cannot. Buy-back programmes often have structures such as 'A' and 'B' shares which enable investors to defer crystallising a capital gain.

Another important factor in determining how to remedy the inefficient balance sheet are the different objectives of shareholders – a register that contains mainly 'value' shareholders may have very different views from a register mainly populated by 'growth' investors. In the current market 'growth' appears to be returning to favour – these growth investors on the register may prefer the company to engage in M&As or significant capex programmes.

What is the cost of capital?

A share buy-back corrects an inefficient balance sheet – that is where the company has too much cash (or too little debt) on its balance sheet given the business it is in, the cash it generates and its need for capital for investment. Having more debt on the balance sheet will reduce the cost of capital as debt is both cheaper than equity and enjoys the advantage of being tax deductible. (This is sometimes referred to as the 'tax shield'.)

By substituting cheap debt for expensive equity the cost of capital is reduced thereby creating value for shareholders. One of the main advantages of a buy-back is that by reducing the cost of capital, future cash flows are discounted back at the lower rate. This can produce significant changes in the value of the business which is then spread over fewer shares in issue.

Are the shares 'cheap'?

The traditional reasoning favouring a buy-back is that management is demonstrating it believes the shares are significantly undervalued given the company's excellent prospects. The management is buying an asset it knows. Importantly, the share buy-back is not a cash return to shareholders – it is an investment in the company and shareholders can choose whether to take cash by selling their shares or not.

As the buy-back is a capital allocation decision/investment, it needs to be done at an attractive share price. As Warren Buffett argues, it hardly makes sense to pay $1.10 for a $1 bill. Investors retaining their shares will own a greater proportion of the company and have a greater stake in its future. As a capital allocation decision, share buy-backs only make sense if the shares are cheap. This does of course raise a key issue: does management have the ability to identify whether the shares are cheap or 'fairly valued'?

If the shares are 'intrinsically' cheap (see p. 192) then management by engaging in the buy-back is 'signalling' to the market that it believes the company to be undervalued on a long-term basis and that there is no better home for the surplus capital than its own shares. Many shareholders (including Warren Buffett) do look at it this way – and for good reason.

Clearly if the shares are 'up with events' or expensive then a buy-back may not be appropriate. A company buying your shares at an overinflated level will destroy value. In which case a 'special dividend' or an increase in the ordinary dividend is far more appropriate.

It is not about earnings per share – is it?

Often companies who should know better will refer to the benefit of the share buy-back as having a positive impact on EPS. This is *not* the rationale for the share buy-back. Any impact from a rising EPS is offset by the higher risk of financial gearing which will reduce the P/E. Crucially, given the change between the equity and debt components of the company's funding, it is far more appropriate to consider enterprise value when assessing the company's value (see p. 273). This obviously in theory remains the same (the business is just funded differently): the EV/sales ratio (say) would stay the same and this should only improve if the company's operating margins or sales growth improve. As we stress below, improving the strategic and operational performance of the business is a crucial element in successful buy-backs.

On a corporate governance note, here it might be that the buy-back is helping the company meet earnings target which also happen to be the key trigger for the executives' remuneration packages. Again having a target like earnings – which does not necessarily reflect the performance of the business or the creation of economic value – does not make a lot of sense.

What about capital allocation and returns?

In many instances the main reason for the share buy-back may be to reduce the cost of capital and thereby increase shareholder value. However, it may also be desirable from a shareholders' perspective to ensure that a company with a poor track record in doing deals – acquisitions that consistently fail to add value – does a share buy-back rather than engage in further value-destructive deals. In effect, shareholders are saying that 'we do not trust you to add value when doing deals'.

This does, of course, beg the question as to why shareholders should trust the management to run the existing assets in the first place – which of course may actually trigger a change in the management team, especially if they are not responsive to shareholder demands.

It is crucial to use shareholder value in evaluating M&As so you should also consider them when doing buy-backs: buy-backs are clearly a form of capital allocation in the same way capex or M&A is. The buy-back must 'signal' a commitment to shareholder value when deploying shareholders' money.

What about capital discipline?

Shareholders are effectively putting an important capital discipline on management. This discipline comes about as (arguably) greater gearing concentrates the mind and makes management far more focused in generating cash returns to service the debt. In addition, as there is little capacity for extra debt, management has to be very selective in capital allocation decisions. In theory, therefore, this rationing ensures management will only engage in projects that generate the best returns. (The ultimate gearing discipline is of course being taken over by a private equity firm where the firm is substantially backed by debt. Thinking of share buy-backs and private equity as part of a continuous spectrum is a useful way of thinking about company funding. Clearly the private equity approach pushes the efficient balance sheet/cost of capital argument to its limit.)

Will there be an increase in the ordinary dividend?

Interestingly, anecdotal evidence seems to suggest that for some very large companies, buy-backs do not seem to have much impact on the share price. This may reflect the fact that the company is of a size where it is indeed ex-growth and the buy-back merely confirms that.

However, what may be more important is that the share price effect is probably reflecting a cross-over point between growth and value investors which will take time to correct. (Growth investors are selling the shares as they no longer offer the prospect of above average growth. However, the yield on the shares has not risen to a level – i.e. the share price has not fallen far enough – to entice value investors.) This is not for one moment to say that the company is all of a sudden a 'bad' company, only that its investment appeal has changed significantly as it moves beyond a certain point in its life-cycle. The enhanced ordinary dividend 'signals' the board's confidence in its long-term cash generation capabilities. It also suggests that maybe income rather than capital gain will be the key component of total shareholder return (TSR).

In this situation some might argue that a sharp increase in the ordinary dividend is therefore a better 'signal'. This is because it commits the company to an increased payout ratio in the future. This 'permanent' payout will impose greater discipline on management. If the company is offering lower growth (but is highly cash generative) this makes perfect sense. All

> this 'permanent' payout will impose greater discipline on management

the statistical evidence suggests that it is in fact growth in dividend – not a high starting point – that makes money for investors over time. One could argue that Vodafone moved from being a growth stock to a utility. Accordingly, its yield needs to reflect this – and increasing the ordinary dividend and payout ratio would help this process.

Value shareholders (who put more emphasis on the certainty of income rather than the uncertainty of capital growth when assessing total shareholder return) would then find the shares more attractive. Inevitably, however, in some situations management teams are invariably reluctant to acknowledge such a dramatic change in the status of the company.

What are special dividends?

Given that share buy-backs work most effectively if the shares are below their **intrinsic value**, returning cash to shareholders if the shares have had a strong run or are 'fairly valued' by the market poses a different problem. If the shares are fairly valued and management does not feel it appropriate to commit itself to a permanent increase in dividend levels, a 'special dividend' may be the most effective way of dealing with surplus cash.

Often special dividends accompany a disposal or a 'one-off' gain for the company. (As it is a one-off gain an increase in the ordinary dividend is not appropriate.) A good example is Carillion which has declared that it will pay a special dividend whenever it makes a disposal from its portfolio of private finance initiative investments. As these are one-off events and may occur infrequently a special dividend is an effective way of dealing with the cash proceeds of the disposal.

Clearly if the shares have had a very strong run – perhaps anticipating a major disposal – then this tilts the argument in favour of a special dividend instead of a buy-back.

What about company performance and strategy?

Rather than just focusing on the 'financial engineering' of share buy-backs, real value is driven by making the core business more efficient and competitive. A clear and credible strategy that will deliver improved competitive performance, cash flow and earnings is absolutely critical – the benefits of this are then magnified for long-term shareholders with the improved performance being spread over fewer shares. Similarly this suggests that there may be a case for higher investment in a business or small bolt-on acquisitions rather than returning funds to shareholders. This obviously assumes you trust management to deliver value from such initiatives!

A disposal of a non-core business accompanied by a share buy-back may be greeted positively as it means management can focus on the core business and generate better returns from it, and these improved results will be spread over fewer shares. The cost of capital is reduced but management time is freed up to improve the performance of the core business which will now be valued more appropriately rather than being dragged back by the underperforming non-core operations. Future improvements in performance will then see share price growth.

In this situation, take a shareholder with a 10 per cent stake. A non-core division is disposed of, realising 25 per cent of the market cap. If the shares are bought back then there are now (say) 25 per cent fewer shares in issue. If the shareholder believes that the management is now focused on generating value for them and is making the right decisions about the core that will create a more competitive position for the business, they will hold on to their 10 per cent. (This presupposes that management has done an excellent job convincing investors it can effect a turnaround.)

If the performance of the business improves significantly the shareholder now has 10/75 or 13.3 per cent of the equity. This can be viewed as the opposite of the dilution you get with a rights issue. Therefore this shareholder is entitled to 13.3 per cent of the enhanced EPS and cash generation of the improving business. As mentioned above, the DCF calculation will also make the business more valuable as the discount rate will be lower reflecting the lower cost of capital – not only is the debt higher but the increased focus on the core business should also reduce risks.

Too many management teams just focus on the buy-back. For many large companies engaging in a share buy-back the share price response will be very disappointing if it is not accompanied by actions to improve the underlying performance and/or growth of the business. Clearly, for very large companies this may be a 'Catch 22' as they are handing the money back because they do not have major value-creating growth opportunities open to them. (Maybe in this case they should consider the ordinary dividend route discussed above?) Nonetheless, a clear strategy needs to be explained to the market regarding what returns are likely to be delivered in the future.

When do share buy-backs work?

Share buy-backs therefore make sense for a company when:

- the business profile – visibility of cash flows – means it can cope easily with the higher levels of debt
- it has an 'inefficient' capital structure – that is, the company does not minimise the cost of capital because it has lots of cash or very little debt on the balance sheet
- the company does not require lots of investment to ensure it remains competitive or is missing out on growth opportunities – investments that, if made, will generate shareholder value
- the company's share price is undervalued
- it creates value.

Critically, all of these conditions need to apply if the buy-back is to make sense – overpaying is hardly in shareholders' interests, while incurring extra risk of higher debt finance when it is not appropriate is hardly sensible.

Buy-backs must not be seen as an isolated, short-term response to a flagging share price but as part of a committed, long-term approach to shareholder value. Management must have a clear and credible strategy for delivering improved returns, earnings and cash flow, which spread over fewer shares will benefit those long-term shareholders that have supported the management and its strategy.

There is still a negative association regarding share buy-backs. The situation is often interpreted as indicating a company that is ex-growth with few value-added opportunities for investment or lacking strategic direction. This is particularly important in high-growth sectors where investors are expecting the company to exploit growth opportunities. (Interestingly, buy-backs in the high-tech area are often to avoid the dilution that accompanies employee share option schemes.)

However, buy-backs should be appraised in terms of value creation not growth. Many capital allocation decisions grow earnings but destroy value. Similarly, buy-backs do not excuse a company from having a credible strategy.

Therefore, while the financial structure of a company is a key determinant of its cost of capital, in the long run it is the company's competitive position that will determine its ability to add value. This means that it can generate the profits and cash flows to service its liabilities. Higher levels of debt – especially if competitors are more conservatively financed – may well undermine the ability to compete. Being competitive requires a clear strategy and the managerial and financial resources to position the company effectively. While there are considerable advantages to debt finance, it can be self-defeating where competitive pressures need to be met with significant investment.

During the boom years of 2003–07 debt was fashionable and available – the 'cult of equity' was very much replaced by the 'cult of debt'. This helped facilitate the move to higher gearing and encouraged companies to use debt finance.

However, the impact of the recession, the 'credit crunch' and the widespread use of debt by companies without the quality of earnings/visibility of revenues to service that debt has inevitably led to companies needing to refinance through the equity market.

The fashion has swung back towards low gearing and ensuring a sensible debt profile – i.e. a long-term structure of debt. This has seen many companies – some with more choice than others – engaging in rights issues.

Raising fresh capital: rights issues

The 'credit crunch' has seen access to bank loans and in some instances the bond markets closed off as a source of finance for many companies. Given the severity of the recession and the impact on profits banking covenants have either been breached or close to breaking. This has put many companies in a very serious financial position.

For companies with lots of debt that sell goods to consumers who are both in debt and need to raise debt to purchase the product (selling 'high-ticket' items), the challenging trading conditions may persist for some time. The process of 'de-leveraging' (cutting debt levels) may take a considerable period to work through for both the corporate and consumer sectors.

So with access to debt so difficult companies need to raise finance from their shareholders to ensure their survival – although of course companies in healthier positions can raise capital to fund growth plans too. In extreme cases, if the company is in trouble the debt of the business may be converted into shares if the company cannot survive any other way. In this situation the original shareholders may be left with nothing, paying the ultimate price for the risks of investing in shares as shareholders come bottom of the pecking order.

A 'rights issue' is a way in which a company can sell new shares in order to raise capital. Shares are offered to existing shareholders in proportion to their current shareholding, respecting their pre-emption rights. Pre-emption rights simply means that as an existing shareholder of the company your are entitled to have first say as to whether you want to support the fund raising and preserve your share of the business. It would obviously be very unfair if the company found a fantastic investment opportunity and to fund it decided to give shares to a new shareholder who had not supported the company in the past. Given that equity means fairness this would be a completely inappropriate way to act. For example, there was has controversy over the way in which Barclays raised money from sovereign wealth funds in the Middle East at very attractive rates for the investors.

> a 'rights issue' is a way in which a company can sell new shares in order to raise capital

There has been some suggestion that both the rights issue process and the role of pre-emption disadvantage certain companies. So, for example, small technology and bio-tech companies may have greater flexibility raising money through a series of placings where a smaller amount of shares is 'placed' with investors prepared to back the fund raising. In terms of the process the very heavy rights issues by the UK banking sector arguably caused many problems. The length of time it takes to raise the money meant that hedge funds could effectively sell the shares 'short'.

With the pre-emption principle being maintained shares are offered in proportion to an existing holding. So, for example, there may be one share issued for every two shares held. This is referred to as a one-for-two. Clearly the more money that needs to be raised the more shares will need to be issued.

The price at which the shares are offered is usually at a discount to the current share price, which gives investors an incentive to buy the new shares – if they do not, the value of their holding is diluted (they will be holding a lower proportion of the company than before the rights issue). The extent of the discount will depend on stock market conditions and the 'heaviness' of the rights issue (i.e. how much is being raised and does that mean we are looking at a one-for-one rather than a one-for-five issue). In recent times many companies have engaged in 'deep discount' rights issues where the shares may be at a 50 per cent discount (say) to the previous share price. This is done to ensure the shares are attractive and so raise money. In the past this was also often done so that the company could avoid having to underwrite (or insure) the rights issue to ensure it got the money. However, given market conditions even deeply discounted issues are being underwritten.

Example – how rights issues work

> Company A needs to raise £150 million. It has a share price of £2.00 (the pre-rights price) and there are 200 million shares in issue. Its current **market capitalisation** (shares in issue × share price) is therefore £400 million. The company is going to do a deeply discounted rights issue at £1.00.
>
> It therefore needs to issue 150 million shares at a £1.00. There are 200 million shares in issue so by having a rights issue of three new shares for every four shares held there will be 150 million new shares created. The rights issue is therefore three-for-four at £1.00.
>
> You as a shareholder can then buy three shares at £1.00. Given that you hold four shares at £2.00 you would then have £8.00 worth of old shares and £3.00 worth of new, or £11.00 invested in seven shares. Each share is then worth £11.00/7 or £1.57. This is known as the 'theoretical ex-rights price' or TERP.
>
> The new shares are being sold at a 50 per cent discount to the pre-rights price or a 36 per cent discount to the TERP.
>
> Technically the money is regarded as being raised at the current market price and there is then a bonus element to the rights issue and so previous year's earnings per share are adjusted by the TERP divided by the last day of dealing cum-rights price (i.e. the shares are still entitled to take part in the rights issue). If this stayed at £2.00 then the adjustment factor would be 1.57/2.00 which is 0.785. More realistically the shares may drift off towards the TERP. Alternatively, we know that there are now 350 million shares in issue and 75 million shares would be issued at £2.00. This means that the scrip element is 75 million/350 million or 0.214. So the previous year's earnings would be 21.5 per cent less than previously stated.

For investors there may be a significantly greater reliance on rights issues in the future so knowing the options and impact of them is clearly very important.

Example – options for investors

> Following on from the above example, let's say you have 1000 shares. Originally worth £2000 these are now worth £1570 at the TERP. There are three options:
>
> - **Take up rights** – If you accept the issue in full then you will be investing in 750 new shares at £1.00 or £750.00. You then have 1750 shares at 1.57 or £2747.50 in total and have the same proportion of the company as you did before so you have not been 'diluted'.
> - **Sell enough to be cash neutral** – If you cannot afford this you could sell enough rights to take up the remaining rights: you can sell rights at 57p if the shares fall to the TERP. The rights are therefore worth £427.50 (which almost takes you

> back to the value of your original investment). So by selling half the rights this would generate £213.75, enough to buy 214 shares when rounding. You now hold 1214 shares.
>
> ■ **Let the rights lapse** – If you do not subscribe for your shares the company will sell your rights at the market price on your behalf.

Do you hand your money over?

As ever, when a company and its management team are asking for money the key issue is whether we trust that management team to use the funds to make a real difference to the business and make money. So you need to ask yourself:

- Why are they raising the money?
- What will they do with it?
- Will this generate an appropriate return?

Of course it is complicated with some rights issues because there may be very dire consequences if we do not support the company. However, if we do not have faith in the management team then a change of management may be a condition of the money being raised. Here larger investors will have to play a role to effect the changes needed.

Work done by Morgan Stanley suggests that rights issues are most successful – that is, the shares go on to perform well – when

- the shares have been very poor performers
- the company raises a significant sum relative to its market capitalisation
- the funds raised are used to reduce debt.

Why does this happen? One way of explaining this is to say that the poor share price performance means that the share price already reflects the considerable risks of the poor financial position. By removing the financial risk completely – because the size of the issue means the company will not be coming back with the begging bowl again in the near future, we can 're-price' the shares on the basis of the company's now much clearer prospects and lower financial risk. This of course means we still have to see if the company's competitive position will now make us money. The improved financial position does now, however, mean it can invest more effectively in its franchise and take longer-term decisions.

Interestingly, the corollary of this is that raising smaller amounts of money for purposes other than to reduce debt – let's say to make acquisitions –

have been less successful. We do know of course that the vast majority of acquisitions fail to create shareholder value, so maybe this explains why the paying down of debt is a better reason for supporting the issue.

Implicit in this is that you believe in management to use the breathing space both to invest in the business to improve competitiveness and to implement the business strategy effectively. Therefore using the components of the Valuation Villa provides us with a basis to appraise the rationale for supporting a rights issue.

Cash flow

There is no one definition of cash flow. Nonetheless it is critical to monitor this aspect of corporate performance, for assessing both the operating health and valuation of a business.

Changes to cash flow within a business are a far more straightforward guide to the reality of its position than, say, earnings. Focusing on earnings quality and how earnings convert into cash is a key consideration here. As we have seen, earnings can be very much influenced by the favourable interpretation of accounting policies and distortions such as the use of provisions.

A commonly used measure of cash flow is EBITDA. This can be worked out by taking the operating profit (from the P&L account) and adding back the non-cash costs of the business, depreciation and amortisation. However, as discussed on p. 145, there is some dispute as to the usefulness of this number.

Gross cash flow comprises operating cash inflow (operating profit adjusted for the impact of the movement in working capital) with non-cash items, depreciation and amortisation being added back. Net cash flow adjusts for the impact of tax and the cost of the dividends. This is sometimes used to generate a cash earnings per share number by dividing retained profit plus depreciation by the number of shares in issue.

Operating free cash flow is defined as net operating profit after tax plus depreciation and amortisation, less maintenance capital expenditure (with an adjustment for any necessary movements in working capital). This recognises that funds are needed to maintain the fabric and quality of the asset base and to meet the working capital requirements of higher turnover. This offsets one of the weaknesses of EBITDA in that it explicitly recognises maintenance capital expenditure as a real cost of doing business. This is a definition we shall come back to when looking at discounted cash flow valuations (p. 230).

While all these definitions may be used to analyse or value a company, it is worth bearing in mind that what actually is left for shareholders will be after taxes have been paid and after the servicing of the capital within the business.

Why cash flow is important

A healthy cash flow is crucial. At the very basic level a company will go bust without it. Cash enables a company to maintain and grow the business by providing funds to:

- maintain quality of assets
- invest for growth
- service debt
- pay a growing dividend.

If cash flow deteriorates sharply, this can have serious repercussions. This is particularly true if the company is highly geared. The ability to service the debt can diminish rapidly and can lead to a lot of uncertainty (and high risk) for equity holders. The cost of debt is likely to rise, possibly sharply leading to lower profits and earnings for equity holders. Assets may have to be sold to reduce the debt. This may result in a weakening of the business and its prospects. In addition, the price received for any assets may be low as the company is a forced seller. Remember, shareholders come bottom of the pecking order if a company runs into financial difficulties.

shareholders come bottom of the pecking order

It is, therefore, very important to monitor this deterioration in cash flow and the financial position of the company. Sometimes the continued growth of earnings per share can conceal this deterioration. Earnings can be manipulated by accounting policies or adjustments; the cash flowing in or out of the business provides a more effective and straightforward guide to the real performance of the business.

It can also be true that a company is seeing heavy outflows of cash without it being a major concern. It may be investing aggressively for growth or be replacing a particularly large piece of plant and equipment. The important thing in this situation is that the capital expenditure can generate a return that is appropriate for the risks of the project.

You might want to consider the 'lumpiness' of the capital expenditure programme – is it one large item or a collection of small discrete items? – and the timescale – i.e. how long will it be before the investment generates a return? The longer the timescale, the greater the risk of a change in economic circumstances. A lumpy investment must be finished to have any value, while small incremental additions have the advantage that they can be curtailed in response to changing circumstances.

A worst case scenario might be a process plant which takes two to three years to build. It is started at the top of the cycle (when there is a shortage of capacity) but comes on stream when volumes and prices are dramatically lower at the bottom of the cycle. Clearly the returns on the investment are likely to disappoint, at least in the short term.

In terms of risk profile, the size of project in relation to the size of the company is worth bearing in mind. Large projects can be plagued by delays and overruns and this can have a material impact on the cash flow and earnings of a smaller company which a larger entity might accommodate more easily.

The higher expenditure will lead to a sharp increase in the depreciation charge which may limit earnings per share growth in the short term. This is not a problem in terms of cash generation. (This is one reason why many start-ups with high capital requirements are valued on an EBITDA basis.)

What to look for

When looking at the cash flow profile of a business it is important to see that the company is generating cash, where it is being generated and where it is being spent. Tracking the movement in net debt is one way of seeing whether the company is generating cash (making sure debt is not coming down due to one-off financing items such as disposals or share issues). It is also always worth making sure that the cash is being generated from the ongoing business and not from, say, a one-off disposal of assets. Discarding peripheral or non-performing assets can be an important and sensible way of running the business, but it may also conceal a poor underlying performance and a response to deteriorating cash flows. Finally, you need to take into account the quality of earnings and the efficiency with which earnings convert into cash. This is particularly important if a high proportion of earnings comes from associates.

A fall in operating cash flow may come about because of money going into working capital (traditionally defined as stocks, plus trade debtors, minus trade creditors). This may not be a problem if it is to meet an anticipated expansion of the business. However, it may herald serious problems if stock is being accumulated involuntarily because of a sharp slowdown in demand.

A key driver of value

Cash flow is one of the (if not the) most important drivers of value – any asset is effectively worth the cash return it can generate. The ability to generate cash is critical for any business to be successful. It is no good growing rapidly and investing aggressively in a business if you are not generating cash – bankruptcy will inevitably follow.

Summary

A company's financial strength can be examined by looking at its debt to equity (gearing) ratio, its interest cover and the degree to which the company is generating cash. In practice it is worthwhile considering all of them, as they are clearly interrelated, to provide a reliable picture of a company's financial position. If a company is highly cash generative, then a high gearing ratio may not be a major source of concern. Conversely, a high gearing ratio and a poor cash flow profile are a recipe for trouble.

The fashion changed considerably from the mid- to late 1990s when the desire for balance sheet efficiency and cutting the cost of capital saw gearing levels rise (often as a result of share buy-backs). However, the combination of the 'credit crunch', more difficult trading environments and uncertain equity markets has ensured that the fashion has swung back to low gearing and strong cash flow as the desirable financial attributes.

One of the key lessons of this period is the dangers of excessive debt or leverage when the economy turns down. Companies with (a) high exposure to the performance of the economy, (b) high operational gearing or (c) high business risk should not engage in high financial risk by having significant amounts of debt. The plight of the airlines, automotive companies and housebuilders provided ample evidence of the need to ensure that where there is high business risk it needs to be combined with low financial risk.

When looking at the financial ratios it is important to remember that while looking at the debt/equity ratio is very useful, cash pays the interest bill, not asset backing. Therefore looking at interest cover or net debt/EBITDA ratios is also important to establish an effective overview of the company's financial position.

It is also vital to make sure you get a comprehensive view of all the company's liabilities. Pension fund and health care deficits can be really sizeable and off-balance sheet liabilities also need to be monitored closely.

FINANCIAL POSITION CHECKLIST

In considering what is the right level of debt for a business ask yourself:

- What are the economic characteristics of the business?
- How predictable are revenues and profits?
- Are volumes likely to fluctuate?
- Are prices subject to severe competitive pressures?
- How strong is the company's pricing power?
- Is the company dependent on one main customer?
- Are there high fixed costs and so high operational gearing?
- How much cash is the company generating?
- Does the business need a lot of investment to be competitive?
- Is the interest rate charged on the debt fixed or variable?
- Is the debt short or long term?
- Are there preference shares or convertible bonds that need to be included?
- Are there off-balance sheet liabilities that need to be considered?
- Is there a pension fund deficit and what are the assumptions (longevity, investment returns and discount rate) used in arriving at that deficit?
- Are the shareholders' funds realistically valued?

The measures of financial strength include:

- debt/equity – the amount of debt including preference shares, pensions, and off-balance sheet liabilities divided by shareholders' funds (the company's net assets)
- interest cover: operating profit/interest payable
- cash cover: EBITDA/interest payable. (Cash flows service the debt, not asset backing.)
- fixed charge cover: operating profit/interest payable, preference share costs and lease payments
- net debt/EBITDA: expressed as a multiple, so a low multiple is attractive.

The dangers of high gearing include:

- the company is incurring higher risk
- it cannot fund investment in the business to maintain competitive position or grow
- the business is run for creditors not in the interests of shareholders
- reflecting the higher risk the cost of debt will be higher – higher interest payments
- a risk of a rights issue depresses the share price
- risks of dividend cuts and no dividend growth in the future
- risk of bankruptcy and a debt for equity swap renders the shares being effectively worthless.

6

The outlook

What topics are covered in this chapter?

- Why outlook drives valuation (and share prices!)
- What are profits and earnings going to do?
- Management's view of the future
- Operational gearing
- Forecasting operating margins
- Sanity checks
- Summary
- Checklist

Why outlook drives valuation (and share prices!)

Investment is all about the future. When valuing any asset it is the future cash flows that determine its worth. Therefore the outlook is a crucial component of valuation. We have seen in Chapter 2 how looking at the macroeconomic factors and sector characteristics provides a useful 'top-down' framework for predicting what may happen. We can then attempt to predict what might happen to industry volumes, prices and costs.

A key aspect of the outlook understands how the competitive landscape might change. This involves assessing the potential risks and any potential structural changes in an industry – what is going to happen to the industry and how will management respond? Here Porter's five forces model can be very helpful to see how the industry dynamics might shift and how the competitive landscape might change. This will have crucial repercussions for the future cash flows of the company. A new competitor or a company's customers merging so they have a better bargaining position will affect pricing power considerably. Conversely, the harsh trading environment in retail, for example, has seen many large players exit the sector enabling others to take market share. Management analysis of these trends and having a credible strategy to navigate the company's way through the changing landscape will be a key determinant of whether you will make money or not.

Combining these elements together is done with the purpose of predicting future profits, earnings and cash flows. Here it is important to remember that we do not know what the future holds and that we have a tendency to be either overoptimistic or too gloomy as the pendulum swings between 'fear and greed'.

Share prices, driven by the future outlook, are always looking ahead. Typically they will be anticipating or 'discounting' what might happen in the next 18 months to two years. Therefore share prices contain a mix of the market's hopes and fears for the next two years and the balance of sentiment and how that influences buyers and sellers. If a company announces record profits for the year just gone but is cautious about the next 12 months, the share price will fall. What can often happen is that the company's current trading is absolutely fine and in line with expectations. The share price, however, is falling and creating a very low valuation. This reflects the fact that the market is looking beyond the next 12 months. This also highlights why the more forward looking the report and accounts can be the more useful they are as a source of information.

In 2007, for example, housebuilders' and banks' shares were on very low valuations including a low P/E. Trading was still very good leading managements to think that the shares were cheap. However, the key here is that the shares were anticipating a sharp slowdown in the economy and especially the housing market, and reflecting the high risks in the sector, especially for those with a lot of debt. The banks had seen loan books for long-term assets increase dramatically, funded by short-term wholesale money market deposits. Often the lending criteria and multiples of income were not as disciplined as was historically the case. House prices were at unprecedented levels and affordability correspondingly really stretched. Banks were also lending aggressively to many segments of the population who may have had no history of servicing their debts and paying off the loan. This seems to have been one of the many perverse aspects of incentives as they were purely based on volumes and not on the underlying risk or long-term profitability of the loan. This clearly highlights a critical failure of management.

On this occasion, therefore, share prices were accurately anticipating the looming problems – valuations were not cheap but merely reflected that these sectors were either ex-growth and/or at the top of an incredible boom. In addition the risks of so much debt in the system and poor management decision making also conspired to suggest that these companies were heading for a very difficult time. The market is not always correct as it may become excessively optimistic or pessimistic. Nonetheless it is always worth reflecting that a low valuation means the market has concerns about the future and potential risks. So we need to ask: is something cheap or is it correctly anticipating poor trading and reflecting high risk? This anticipating the future and reflecting the risks is often referred to as 'discounting' or examining what is already 'in the price'.

We are in an economic environment where the degree of earnings visibility is very low and the timing and extent of any recovery highly uncertain. It is extremely difficult knowing what the next three months – let alone the next 12 – have in store. Extrapolating further out to ten years and beyond (which we need to forecast if we are to do discounted cash flow analysis) becomes highly conjectural to put it mildly.

This uncertainty combined with a genuine desire to focus more on the long-term 'health and wealth creation' of the organisation has seen many companies ceasing to give any 'earnings guidance' to the market. Provided the management has a clear and compelling strategy for long-term wealth creation, which it communicates effectively, then the absence of guidance may not be too problematic. As well as a clear strategy, however, there also needs to be a very open and transparent sense of

- what drives the company's profits
- what the key risks and sensitivities are, and
- how they are managed.

In particular the key performance indicators (KPIs) that management monitors to signal whether it is on track to achieve its goals should be outlined. These indicators should be selected because they are at the heart of its long-term 'health and wealth'.

While we cannot predict the future we can stack the odds in our favour by selecting companies with a quality franchise and management teams committed to improving and sustaining long-term 'health and wealth' through the company's competitive position and generating value for shareholders.

What are profits and earnings going to do?

The reason for getting to grips with the characteristics of the sector, the competitive and financial position of the company and appraising the performance of management is to establish a sense of what future profits and earnings the company might make. Gaining an understanding of the company, its track record, its operating and financial performance and financial position will be of great value.

The company's future profits 'simply' depend on the outlook for volumes, prices, costs and margins. However, as the whole spate of profit downgrades in recent years has testified, this is not as straightforward as we might like. Future profits are a crucial driver of share prices and again getting a sense of what can go wrong is a critical part of the investment process.

The risks in forecasting

The stock market hates uncertainty and valuations and/or share prices will fall sharply to reflect the degree of uncertainty. In terms of forecasting operating profits, it is important to get a sense of perspective on the degree of uncertainty affecting the principal drivers of profit, volumes, prices and costs.

Volume

A large drop in investment and a cut-back in discretionary expenditure by the corporate sector have driven the economic difficulties experienced at the time of writing. This affects the types of company being hit by profits warnings. Therefore the slowdown in companies' spending on technology and software has caused great problems for the part of the technology sector serving those markets.

The increasing maturity of the market for mobile telephony is a good example of the concerns and uncertainty over future demand levels for this sector. The prospect of growth from 3G and the use of handsets for data as well as voice holds out the prospect for longer-term growth. This has changed the perception quite rapidly from its status as a key growth area into one where there is a lot of debate about short- and long-term prospects. Similarly, with advertising being a discretionary item, cutting back on this can be done almost with immediate effect (helping the company to reduce costs and preserve cash). Again this has hit the media sector hard on a worldwide basis.

When considering the factors affecting the outlook for volume it is worth asking:

- How sensitive is demand to a slowdown in the economy?
- Is demand cyclical, mature or growth?
- Is it a capital good, i.e. part of companies' investment plans?
- If it is company expenditure, how discretionary is it? (For example, capital projects can be deferred while advertising can be cut relatively quickly.)
- Is it a consumer good?
- Is the government the main consumer?
- Is the purchase discretionary?
- Is it a 'high-ticket' item?
- Market share assumptions: is forecast volume growing more rapidly than the market?
- Is the company in an outperforming segment of the market?

Price

Prices have an enormous impact on profitability and margins – hence the importance of Porter's five forces model and Buffett's concept of the 'moat'. The slowdown in the economy has seen demand weaken which will tend to reduce prices of its own accord. In many areas there are also sector-specific reasons for price trends. This invariably depends on the market structure, how competitive the industry is, and the degree of overcapacity.

In many of the technology areas, investment during the late 1990s boom saw capacity in many product areas increase dramatically. This caused all sorts of pricing problems in the downturn, especially given the extent of the sharp drop in demand. The elimination of industry overcapacity is fraught with difficulty and invariably takes longer than expected. Judging the robustness of pricing in such an environment is clearly very difficult.

The increasing globalisation of markets and the use of technology (and especially the web) to enter into traditional markets has brought new competition into many areas of the economy. This again creates huge uncertainty over the pricing environment. The concern over deflation reflects precisely these sorts of factors. The impact of online retailers on the pricing of cars, books, travel, holidays, banking and financial products has been dramatic. With the help of the web consumers are increasingly better informed on pricing and able to negotiate a better deal.

Overoptimism on price is one of the major issues behind profit downgrades. When considering the factors affecting the outlook for price it is worth looking at the issues affecting both demand and supply:

- The economy – what is the impact on demand?
- What is the industry structure and is it changing?
- What are the barriers to entry?
- Are there new forms of competition?
- Will globalisation affect pricing?
- Is there industry overcapacity and if so how much?
- Are there fierce struggles for market share?
- How differentiated is the product or service?
- Are there changes in product mix affecting prices?
- If announced, why will price increases stick?
- What will the customer reaction be to those increases?
- What will be the competitor reaction and what are their objectives?

Costs

The cost side of the equation can be disrupted by a sudden increase in the price of a key raw material. The impact of the surge in oil prices on the airlines and haulage sectors has been considerable. Similarly, the surge in energy and electricity price hikes has caused major cost pressures for many manufacturing-type operations, an issue which is affecting large parts of the industrial economy. Rising agricultural and commodity prices have been an important factor, squeezing margins in the food and beverage sectors.

The proportion of costs that are variable will determine the impact on profits. The impact on profits will also be dependent upon the ability to pass on the increase in costs in the form of higher prices. This will vary enormously from industry to industry.

Costs associated with new projects or product launches have a notorious tendency to overrun and this can cause disappointment. However, by their very nature they tend to be one-off and would be expected to generate returns in the longer run.

When considering the factors affecting the outlook for costs the following should be considered:

- What is happening to raw material costs (variable costs) and what proportion of total costs are they?
- What is happening to the cost of bought-in goods and services generally?
- Are there costs associated with a new project or product launch?
- What is the cost structure, i.e. the relationship between fixed v variable costs?
- What is happening to labour and/or employee costs and what proportion are they of total costs?
- Is there a sharp increase or decrease in such discretionary costs such as marketing or R&D?

Profits

The outcome of all the issues affecting volume, price and costs is profits. Given the uncertainties and difficulties in forecasting all of these components, it is hardly surprising that forecasting profits can be such a hazardous exercise. Furthermore, there is a geared relationship between revenue and profits, operational gearing, where a small change in revenue can lead to a significant rise or fall in profits.

With any downgrade it is worth finding out whether the reduction has been driven by disappointing volumes, pricing or an adverse trend in costs. This may help form a view of the depth of the problems. If there is a small slippage in demand for easily understandable reasons, this may not pose too much of a long-term threat. Falling volumes, significant price erosion and industry overcapacity suggest much deeper concerns and a high degree of uncertainty.

The complexity of these factors and the difficulty in quantifying the extent of the profits fall lead companies and analysts to underestimate the seriousness of the downgrade required. This so often leads to a whole series of downgrades occurring – undermining confidence in the company and its ability to read what is happening in its markets.

there is always a danger of hope springing eternal

There is always a danger of hope springing eternal. Optimism rather than hard analysis may be determining the following year's forecast. Hence the health warning that accompanies all forecasts.

Management's view of the future

As we have seen, investing is all about what is going to happen in the future and the outlook is a core driver of valuation. Companies can help investors with these issues by improving their communications with shareholders. The report and accounts (R&A) as currently drawn up is far too retrospective for shareholders basing their decisions on what is going to happen in the future. An operating and financial review (OFR) that looks forward and explains the key performance indicators (KPIs) of the business, the key risks and sensitivities involved, and the company's performance relative to the peer group, offers companies a major opportunity to inform investors of the key factors influencing the outlook for the business. A key issue for understanding the outlook more fully is having a good appreciation of the company's strategy. This is referred to as 'narrative reporting' and is referred to as 'the management discussion and analysis (MD&A) section' at the front of a US company's report and accounts, and the operating and financial review (OFR) or 'business review' in the UK.

Such information will make the R&A a far more effective document for investors by creating a more comprehensive assessment of the company's competitive position, where it is going and the potential risks and how they are being managed. The analysis required should basically be an extension of what the board's analysis of the business involves and how it arrives at both tactical and strategic decisions. As a result it will be easier to make an assessment of the outlook for the company as investors will better understand the business.

Embraced positively the OFR will ensure best practice in corporate governance which delivers improved long-term returns to shareholders. It provides a welcome opportunity to differentiate the company in terms of management quality, the clarity of its strategy, ability to read its markets and how to respond to change.

In particular, it should embrace an openness and transparency to help investors (i.e. the owners of the business) to understand the business, where it's going, the risks involved and how they are being managed.

The sort of information investors need to assess the company's prospects includes:

- the key trends and factors driving the company's markets and its future performance – the real drivers of business performance

- the value drivers of the business
- key risks and how they are being managed
- key sensitivities
- performance relative to competitors across the chosen KPIs
- which customers/regions are delivering the highest proportion of profit
- whether this will continue
- which divisions are adding value and when those not adding value will do so
- balance sheet and capital structure – especially valuable in the current environment
- treasury policies and objectives
- environmental, employee and non-financial factors.

A requirement of IFRS is to provide more comprehensive segmental data and this should be used within the OFR. In particular, analysing which divisions are adding value and which are not will shed light on key strategic issues. The allocation of capital is a key management responsibility, so having to account for the decisions taken seems perfectly sensible. If a division is in a start-up phase then explaining the factors that will make it successful and an expectation of when it may cover its cost of capital should reassure shareholders of the long-term merits of the investment. This is precisely the sort of area to which the forward-looking requirements of the OFR are ideally suited.

The OFR also requires more information on the balance sheet structure – the debt profile, liquidity, treasury policies, etc. In the current environment this is to be welcomed. That the rationale and risk attaching to funding decisions must be explained is a major step forward, helping both equity and debt investors take a view on the wisdom of the decisions. For bond investors especially, the term structure of debt is a critical driver of value. This requirement for more detail in and explanation of the balance sheet provides another link to IFRS as certain liabilities such as pension funds, health care or environmental liabilities, leases and off-balance sheet debt are more explicitly recognised with the new accounting standard. Again this provides for a much clearer assessment of the company's financial and competitive position, potential risks and its ability to face the future. This also makes eminent sense as balance sheet structure determines the cost of capital – a crucial driver of economic value added.

A more forward-looking R&A will helps investors understand what is driving their business and how management is allocating resources. This provides a far more effective basis for taking investment decisions. The costs of OFR have to be seen in the context of creating a far more relevant value added document. Rather than thinking of IFRS and OFR as a regulatory and reporting burden they provide a welcome opportunity to differentiate the company in terms of management quality, the company's strategy and progress towards its stated goals, and the ability to read its markets. Crucially, it enables management to open a far better informed dialogue with all investors and establish best practice in shareholder communication.

Key performance indicators (KPIs)

The value of KPIs is crucial to improved narrative reporting by companies. In terms of the components of the KPI the crucial elements are:

- Key – when it is of fundamental importance to the business. Crucially it is 'key' because it is demonstrating that the business has a competitive advantage or is developing it. It should be a ratio that really highlights the success of the business and is central to strategy.
- Performance – when management performance can directly influence it and it can be quantified.
- Indicator – it is forward looking and provides leading information on future performance. This may be the development pipeline for new products, for example.

KPIs make it a lot easier for the company to be understood by investors (what are the key variables that need watching?) and also provide important benchmarks to evaluate management performance. With performance measurement systems in place management and investors can keep track of the progress of the business. This provides vital information about what is happening in the business. A company that is seeing continual improvement in its KPIs is clearly on track and reflects the fact that management is on top of trends. (Conversely, if management is falling short of hitting KPI targets or the trend is declining, it is an important signal that attention is required and issues need to be addressed.) This also helps establish a management track record. KPIs should reflect measures that enable us to appreciate if the company's strategy is being delivered and risks and uncertainties are being attended to.

> KPIs enable us to see if the company's strategy is being delivered

The other useful element of KPIs is to see how management is performing against the peer group. This means that an understanding of the relevant benchmarks is essential to make KPIs useful, as they put the level of current performance into the 'best in class' peer group. To the extent this then provides a measure of how competitive the business is, it can be an effective performance indicator that the company can use to evaluate its performance and its performance-related-pay triggers.

Therefore a selection of the key KPIs can provide a much more holistic and balanced approach to evaluating the company's performance. This means that the market does not necessarily have to focus on just one variable (e.g. consensus earnings, see below). Therefore decisions that will improve certain KPIs and thus improve the competitiveness of the business but at the short-term cost to another KPI (e.g. EPS) can be put in context. This more long-term approach helps decisions to be understood in that context rather than simply focusing on short-term earnings targets.

The list of examples below is not comprehensive and each sector or industry will have its own set of appropriate KPIs. There may also be several relevant KPIs that are non-financial but which reveal commitment to employee, environmental and social responsibility, which are just as important and could be a vital source of competitive advantage.

Examples – KPIs

- Sales per customer
- Profit per customer/customer visit
- Average revenue per customer/subscriber
- Sales per square foot
- Profit per square foot
- Gross margin per product or profit unit
- Return on capital employed
- Percentage of sales from new products
- Sales per employee
- Profit per employee
- Current market share
- Cost per unit of output
- Overhead per unit of output

While some of the indicators can be quite specific and detailed, ultimately they must flow though to some higher-level ratios that really matter – especially return on capital and cash generation.

One KPI, if poorly selected, may provide too narrow a view of performance. A more comprehensive view might need to be taken. For retailers an excellent like-for-like (LFL) sales growth may combine with higher cost per square foot, higher volumes of lower margin product and falling profits. Conversely, weaker LFL could be accompanied by sales of higher margin products.

Jim Collins in *Good to Great* talks about how great companies engage in the discipline of determining what is the single most important KPI that drives success. He refers to this as the key economic denominator that 'drives your economic engine'.[1]

In the case of Walgreen it shifted the KPI from profit per store to profit per customer visit. Its strategy was predicated on convenient locations which in many neighbourhoods can be expensive. Increasing profit per store could be achieved by reducing the number of stores or opening them in less expensive and therefore less convenient locations. It is crucial to note here the link between the company's strategy and the choice of the economic denominator. On a similar tack, Gillette shifted from profit per division to profit per customer to reflect the power of the brand – selling high-value products with repeat purchases of razor blades.

These examples reflect a crucial element of KPIs and that is their link with strategy – management knows what it is doing and knows what to monitor to ensure sustained success. Getting to the right 'economic engine' driver requires real insight and understanding of the business, which of course management is paid to have. Furthermore the right KPI will also translate into a high return on capital employed.

> the right KPI will also translate into a high return on capital employed

To the extent that the KPI analysis provides sensitivities it may make the management of consensus earnings a lot easier. The market will understand far more about what drives the numbers and the sensitivities involved. Similarly it can be used to provide a much more holistic and balanced approach so that the market does not necessarily just focus on one variable (e.g. consensus earnings). Therefore decisions that will improve certain KPIs at the short-term cost to another KPI can be put in context – and a guide to the future provided. This more comprehensive view of corporate performance allows for an appreciation of the factors that affect the company's competitive position and what will deliver shareholder value in

---

[1] Collins, J. (2001) *Good to Great*, New York: HarperCollins, p. 180. Copyright © 2001 by Jim Collins. Reprinted with permission from Jim Collins.

the long run. Management's focus should be on this rather than on short-term earnings targets.

Earnings guidance

One area where the outlook is 'offered' by the company is where it provides 'earnings guidance' to the market. That is to say it will give an indication that earnings per share (EPS) will be up in low double digits or in a band of 5–7 per cent. This can be for the next 12 months and in the US it is often provided on a quarterly basis.

This then provides the market with a 'consensus' and given that it does not like surprises the numbers need to be in line. Clearly a 'game' can then ensue with the management guiding investors to numbers that are low or 'conservative' and then positively 'surprising' the market by beating the guidance. If management has a track record of doing this then investors may 'second guess' the guidance and assume the numbers will be higher! Of course a lot of trading can occur around results time with investors – especially hedge funds – taking 'bets' as to whether the earnings will be above or below guidance levels. A lot of 'shorting' by hedge funds is prior to results that they expect to be disappointing.

The current economic environment and the considerable uncertainty that it faces has seen many companies withdraw from providing this guidance. Companies such as General Electric, PepsiCo, GSK and Unilever have withdrawn from giving guidance while Google has never provided guidance since coming to the stock market. That companies with relatively stable business such as food and beverages or pharmaceuticals have responded this way is interesting as those that are far more dependent on the economic cycle will have very little credibility when offering guidance. It is extremely difficult knowing what the next three months have in store – let alone the next 12 months. Therefore we are in an economic environment where the degree of earnings visibility is low. However, sometimes it may be that guidance is given not because of low visibility but because management does not like what it sees.

There is a stock market adage that 'downgrades come in threes'. That is to say if earnings are downgraded following a profit warning, trading statement or on the back of a set of results then that will be the first of at least three downgrades. This may reflect the fact that management genuinely expects things to pick up or that it will cut costs to offset other pressures. However, experience tells us that the impact of the difficult trading conditions tends to persist longer than expected. In particular what can happen is that the full impact of the operational gearing is not fully appreciated. Therefore it is an important issue if you are holding a share where a profit warning or a change in guidance occurs. Ernst & Young suggest that share prices fell on average around 18 per cent on a downgrade in Q1 of 2009.[2] Some of this may well be in anticipation of further bad news.

If indeed there are two more downgrades after the initial one (and there have been cases where there are five or six downgrades) then management credibility will be severely brought into question. The hope then is that the management team does all it can in the first downgrade to be realistic and 'bottom out' the numbers rather than there be a continuous flow of negative news. This can then at least provide a base from which the shares can recover.

If there are three or more downgrades there may well be a call for a change of management team. If there is high operational gearing then the Ryanair approach of highlighting all the key sensitivities is an excellent way of providing guidance.

One of the key drivers behind dropping earning guidance is that the short-term preoccupation with hitting a target shifts the focus from creating shareholder value and sustaining the competitive position of the business. In effect the company manages the share price not the business.

This emphasis on hitting a target, therefore, distorts decision making. Management may take decisions that disadvantage the business in the long term. Examples of this might include cutting R&D or marketing budgets to ensure earnings meet expectations. Investors will not react favourably to these actions so what precisely is the advantage of these short-term decisions? The disappointing trading issues come into sharper relief while management's judgement is called into question.

More important and far more damaging is where accounting policies are deliberately manipulated to ensure earnings do not disappoint. This is particularly likely to occur where companies have aggressive growth targets or where remuneration policies are linked with earnings. This is at the heart of corporate governance debates: decision making is distorted in favour of policies that generate growth (or the illusion thereof) but destroy shareholder value. This favours management through status and salary rather than shareholders. Linking salary to a short-term and arguably irrelevant performance metric engenders cynicism. Crucially, it also distracts atten-

---

[2] Ernst & Young (Q1, 2009) 'Analysis of Profit Warnings Issued by UK Quoted Companies'.

tion from the key longer-term strategic issues that drive the company's performance and creation of value.

The classic example of this is perhaps Enron who reportedly had a philosophy of 'earnings before scruples' and a 'pump and dump' approach – that is, they would massage the earnings to beat the target to increase the share price so they could sell their shares and options.[3]

If shareholders subsequently find out that management has been manipulating its accounts or taking decisions detrimental to the company's long-term interests, then management's reputation will suffer irreparable harm. This may have far more damaging consequences than failing to hit a target – a target which may or may not be relevant in the first place.

Example – key sensitivities driving future profits

> 'The European airline sector is presently facing one of these cyclical downturns, with the possibility of a "perfect storm" of higher oil prices, poor consumer demand, weaker sterling and higher costs at unchecked monopoly airports such as Dublin and Stansted which account for a significant proportion of Ryanair's traffic. While it is impossible to accurately forecast full year fuel prices and yields this far in advance, there is now a significant chance that profits may decline next year. At our most optimistic, a combination of flat yields and $75 per barrell of oil would see profits grow by 6 per cent to approximately €500 million, but at our most conservative, if forward oil prices remain at $85 per barrel, and consumer sentiment and/or sterling's weakness leads to a 5 per cent reduction in yields, then profits in the coming year could fall by as much as 50 per cent to as low as €235 million (excluding profits from aircraft disposals). We would hope to be in a position to provide a more informed update on guidance with the release of our full year results on June 3rd, 2008.'[4]

The Ryanair guidance is really useful as it provides the key sensitivities and KPIs of the business and helps to bring investors closer to the way management thinks about the business. For such a volatile business as an airline this is very helpful. We are not going to be surprised that there will be a big impact on profits if oil prices go above $85 per barrel.

Therefore if a company does abandon guidance and is genuinely committed to a longer-term focus on shareholder value it may not be a bad thing. However, it must be through an open and transparent narrative reporting that investors really understand the dynamics of the business and what the key drivers are. This is far more tied into long-term value creation. The

---

[3] See the 'Smartest Guys in the room' documentary (Director Alex Gibney, 2005).
[4] Ryanair Company Announcement, Q2, 2008.

Operational gearing

This describes the extent to which profits move on changes in turnover and very much depends on the cost structure of the business. The higher the fixed costs of a business as a percentage of turnover, the bigger the rise or fall in profit for any given change in turnover.

Therefore when companies revise down their sales expectations by an apparently modest amount, profits and earnings expectations can fall alarmingly. For highly operationally geared businesses, a 5 per cent reduction in revenues can translate into anywhere between 30 per cent and 80+ per cent. The effect is greater if the revenue reductions are driven by price rather than volume falls as these come straight off profits – there is little that can be done about it.

To illustrate this, let us take a company with high fixed costs and one with high variable costs and see what happens when volumes and price fall by 10 per cent. As Table 6.1 demonstrates, a business where 70 per cent of costs are fixed with an operating margin of 10 per cent will see an 80 per cent fall in operating profit for a 10 per cent fall in turnover caused by falling volumes. Variable costs of 20 per cent will fall by 2 per cent (i.e. 10 per cent), reflecting the drop in volumes. As a result of the fixed costs

Table 6.1 A company with high fixed costs

		−10% V	−10% P
Volume	50	45	50
Price	2	2	1.8
Revenue	100	90	90
Fixed costs	70	70	70
Variable costs	20	18	20
Operating profit	10	2	0
Operating margin	10%	2.2%	0

remaining at 70 per cent, operating profit falls from £10 million to £2 million – a fall of 80 per cent. Therefore a 10 per cent fall in volumes leads to an 80 per cent reduction in profit. This means that the operational gearing is very high. Each 1 per cent move in volumes has an 8 per cent impact on profit. This works on the upside as well. A 10 per cent uplift in volumes would lead to an 80 per cent uplift in profit.

The gearing effect is greater if the falling turnover is driven by price decreases. As Table 6.2 shows, a 10 per cent reduction in prices leads to a 100 per cent reduction in profits in this case. The variable costs are tied to volumes and thus they will not reduce with falling prices. So a 10 per cent reduction in price eradicates profits.

Table 6.2 A company with high variable costs

		–10% V	–10% P
Volume	50	45	50
Price	2	2	1.8
Revenue	100	90	90
Fixed costs	20	20	20
Variable costs	70	63	70
Operating profit	10	7	0
Operating margin	10%	7%	0

Conversely, where variable costs are high, the operational gearing effect as a result of falling volumes is more limited. With variable costs at 70 per cent of revenues, a fall of 10 per cent in volumes leads to a 30 per cent fall. Variable costs fall 10 per cent in line with the drop in volumes. Therefore operational gearing is much lower with each 1 percentage point drop in volume, leading to a 0.3 per cent fall in profit.

Importantly, with falling prices the effect is the same as with high fixed costs, as nothing can be done about costs. The 10 per cent drop in price again leads to profits being eliminated.

This geared way in which profits respond to changes in turnover explains why profits can be downgraded so severely if turnover falls short of expectations. The effect is greater if the fall in turnover is driven by falling prices. This can cause major share price weakness.

You can get a quick gauge to the operational gearing by always looking at the relationship between turnover and operating profits when looking at results announcements, press reports or through reports and accounts. Of course this is slightly simplistic as there may be other factors affecting the numbers, such as one-off costs or currency movements. However, it is a useful way of getting used to the relationships involved.

This will help in your assessment of future profits and how they might be affected by future volumes and prices. It may also put you in a stronger position to sell quickly if you become worried about pricing and hence the direction of future profits. (For companies with a number of divisions you may want to get a feel for each of the divisions if the company provides a detailed divisional breakdown.)

Therefore a major difficulty in forecasting and where things invariably go wrong is in the understanding of the relationship between falling volumes and prices. When trading volumes and prices start to fall it is often the case that the initial downgrade does not fully reflect the full impact on profits – the impact is often severely underestimated. This partly reflects overoptimism and partly perhaps a reluctance to face up to the full and dramatic extent of the profit downgrade required. Accordingly, there is a familiar pattern of profit downgrades occurring in a series, with three or more downgrades often being required. Hence the stock market adage of selling on the first downgrade.

> hence the stock market adage of selling on the first downgrade

Forecasting operating margins

A good check on your forecasts for volumes, prices and costs is to make sure that the implicit resultant margin makes sense. Operating margins are an important way of both evaluating the performance of the company and valuing the shares.

The boom years saw a peak in operating margins in some sectors which we are never likely to see again. A combination of strong volumes and pricing enabled margins to expand to very attractive levels. We are also still digesting the extent to which margins were inflated by creative accounting policies.

If prices have fallen dramatically, with no convincing reason why they should recover, it is extremely unlikely that margins will get back to anywhere near their peak level. In the case of sectors exposed to the trends driving deflation, margin forecasts need to be very cautious.

In addition to the factors driving volumes, prices and costs that determine margins, it is worth examining the following:

- What margins are appropriate to reflect the capital intensity of the business?
- When and where was the last peak?
- What has happened to prices since the peak?
- What has happened to costs since the peak?
- Why should they ever get back to peak margins?
- What are margins among competitors?
- Is there new competition?
- Will cost cutting offset poor pricing trends?

Forecasting – common mistakes

Since 2008 there has been a phase of massive downgrades to earnings expectations which has obviously made it difficult for the overall stock market to progress. This reflects the market's experience that the first downgrade for a company is seldom the last – they tend to come in threes (see p. 310). Why is this and why does it take three or more goes to get earnings expectations back to a reasonable level? Partly this is due to the 'hope springs eternal' school of forecasting, based more on hope than on cold-headed analysis. This can be the responsibility of an overoptimistic management team or analysts not following the logic of pricing and volume trends and perhaps listening to management's overoptimism.

This overoptimism is often reflected in the difference between the top-down forecasts for company profits provided by market strategists compared with the bottom-up forecasts of analysts. These can often diverge quite dramatically. The top-down view, which reflects the economic conditions that companies find themselves in, tends to be a far more reliable guide to profit and earnings trends than the bottom-up projections of analysts. These tend to lag rather than predict. Companies will often say that current trading is in line with expectations only for there to be a sharp downturn two weeks before their period end (their six month or full year trading period) or just after it. In effect they are commenting on what has happened, or what is happening, rather than what will happen. A strategist is trying to predict how things will play out in the next 12 months and will be far more interested in lead indicators not lagging or current indicators.

In late 2008 analysts' expectations were actually positive for the first quarter of 2009. Earnings actually fell by more than 25 per cent. Given the uncertainty over economic activity, concerns over deflation and pricing pressure in many sectors of the market, this appears sensible.

The implication for your decision is very important. If you can find top-down projections from the financial pages of the press or brokers' research, it is worth having this figure in mind when assessing the future profits of any individual share. If profits for the economy are going to rise only 7 per cent, should you believe forecasts of, say, 15 per cent for a company you are looking at? If downgrades do happen then the share price will almost inevitably fall.

Analysts always tend to offer important reasons why the company can outperform the top-down view. The reality may be significant downgrades during the course of the year. This will be because volumes and prices will have been weaker than hoped for and this has a big impact through operational gearing on profits and earnings. In the current environment, with concerns over **gross national product (GNP)**, the impact of deflation, increasingly global (and hence competitive) markets and overcapacity in many areas, caution is needed.

Some of the factors that determine why forecasts tend to prove all too fallible include:

- over-optimism on volumes, prices and costs
- falling volumes and prices picked up with a lag or not spotted
- impact of falling volumes and prices underestimated
- impact of rising volumes and prices underestimated
- cost reductions all feed through to the bottom line – but not if prices and volumes continue to fall (operational gearing)
- not realising just how bad things are within the company, e.g. losing more market share than realised or finances (especially cash flow) much weaker than appreciated
- previous results achieved through one-off benefits or use of provisions that run out. In this case the past performance has been distorted and overstated and is therefore an inappropriate benchmark for forecasting.

Sanity checks

Given how many downgrades tend to feature in market conditions at the time of writing it is worth imposing the discipline of a series of 'sanity checks'. You need to ensure you have considered the key issues so you are happy with the forecasts for the company. This will be a crucial determinant of the performance of the shares and so is well worth spending some time on.

You may be using consensus forecasts available from some websites so think about whether the percentage profit uplift makes sense in the context of the following:

- What is the top-down forecast compared with the bottom-up?
- What are the broader trends in the economy and how does this affect the company?
- Where are we in the cycle?
- Are there structural factors that will exacerbate the cycle (e.g. too much capacity and customers in a weakened financial state)?
- What sort of volume growth is realistic given trends in the overall product market?
- Is the volume growth based on market share gains and how will competitors react?
- What is the outlook for pricing and what is the company's pricing power?
- Are there new entrants or competition from other areas?
- What are the trends in overseas markets?
- Beware of straight line forecasting!
- Beware of phrases such as 'this time it's different'.
- Longer-term assumptions: beware of extrapolating too far into the future.

Summary

When valuing any asset it is the future cash flows that determine its worth. Share prices are always looking ahead as they anticipate or 'discount' the future. Typically they will be 'discounting' what might happen in the next 18 months to two years. We need to look even longer term when doing a DCF analysis.

The outlook for the company's profits and cash flows will be determined by the economic and sector environment as well as its own competitive position. These factors will drive the volume, price and cost outlook for the business. In the current economic environment the degree of earnings visibility is very low and the timing and extent of any recovery highly uncertain. It is extremely difficult knowing what the next three months have in store – let alone the next 12 months.

As well as these 'top down' factors (at the economic and sector level) driving the outlook there will be 'bottom up' factors specific to the company that will determine its prospects – can it manage to take market share off a low cost base, introduce new products and invest in growth and expansion? It is always worth making sure that there is an appreciation of the 'top down' context to assess how well the company is placed to meet its objectives. Often 'bottom up' projections from management teams and analysts are far more optimistic than the predictions of 'top down' strategists.

When results are below expectations it is important to be aware of the stock market adage that downgrades come in threes. Therefore there may be more bad news to come if the company you are interested in has disappointed the market. One of the reasons for this is that the impact of operational gearing is not fully appreciated the first time round. So understanding the cost structure, and pricing and volume outlook, is crucial.

While we cannot predict the future we can stack the odds in our favour by selecting companies with a quality franchise that confers a high degree of pricing power, that are cash generative and that have management teams committed to improving and sustaining the company's long-term competitive position and generate value for shareholders.

OUTLOOK CHECKLIST

Outlook

- Share prices typically look two years ahead and all the factors that affect the outlook for earnings and cash flows – prices, volumes and costs especially – need to be considered.

Some of the factors that determine why forecasts tend to prove all too fallible include:

- overoptimism on volumes, prices and costs
- the impact of revenue shortfalls being underestimated as the full extent of the operational gearing is not allowed for.

Sanity checks

Think about whether the forecasts make sense in the context of the following:

- What is the top-down forecast compared with the bottom-up one?
- What are the broader trends in the economy and how does this affect the company?
- Will commodity and raw material price rises have a big impact on costs?
- Where are we in the cycle?
- Are there structural factors that will exacerbate the cycle (e.g. too much capacity and customers in a weakened financial state)?
- What sort of volume growth is realistic given trends in the overall product market?
- Is the volume growth based on market share gains and how will competitors react?
- What are the trends in overseas markets?
- Beware of straight line forecasting!
- Beware of phrases such as 'this time it's different'.
- Longer-term assumptions: beware of extrapolating too far into the future.

Pricing

Given the importance of pricing in determining the outlook for cash flows (especially if fixed costs are high) it is well worth getting to grips with the industry structure and pricing power of the company.

- What is the industry structure and is it changing?
- What are the barriers to entry?
- Are there new forms of competition?
- Will globalisation affect pricing?
- Is there industry overcapacity and if so how much?
- Are there fierce struggles for market share?
- How differentiated is the product or service?
- Are there changes in product mix affecting prices?
- If announced, why will price increases stick?
- What will the customer reaction be to those increases?
- What will competitor reactions be and what are their objectives?

7

Absolute valuation – discounted cash flow (DCF)

What topics are covered in this chapter?

- Why is DCF useful?
- DCF valuation
- DCF advantages
- DCF disadvantages
- Summary
- Checklist

Why is DCF useful?

The valuation generated by the discounted cash flow (DCF) is sometimes referred to as the company's 'intrinsic value'. This is useful as it can provide us with a reference point as to what the fundamental valuation of the business is – which is why Warren Buffett tends to prefer this technique:

> The critical investment factor is determining the intrinsic value of a business and paying a fair or bargain price.[1]

Of course the current share price can deviate significantly in either direction from the 'intrinsic value'. The short-term share price will reflect

---

[1] Miller, B., Hagstrom, R. G. and Fisher, K. (2005) *The Warren Buffett Way*, 2nd edn. New York: Wiley, pp. 122–6.

'sentiment', recent news flow and the impact of **'momentum'** investors. Accordingly the share price may be at some variance with the fundamental value of the business. Having a sense of where the intrinsic value lies can provide a useful discipline when share prices are volatile. The fundamental valuation in these circumstances provides us with a useful guide and reference point indicating whether the shares are very cheap or very expensive.

Cash flow is the ultimate driver of value. Discounted cash flow valuation is used to establish what the future cash flows of a company are worth in today's money. The objective is to find the value of an asset, given its cash flow, growth and risk characteristics. Sometimes the answer is also referred to as the **net present value**. This means we can see whether all those future cash flows, when converted into today's money, means that shares are cheap or dear as of this moment.

The ability to generate cash is critical for any business to be successful. While this has always been true it is especially true in the current environment when access to external sources of cash is not as straightforward as it once was. Accounting policies can often be used to flatter the profits and earnings of a business, but it is much more difficult to mislead investors on the cash flow of the company. There may well be year-end window dressing to flatter the debt position, but on a long-term basis the debt position will deteriorate rapidly if the company is not generating real cash.

The discipline of forecasting the company's cash flow – and the price volume and cost assumptions behind it – is a very useful way of seeing what the key variables and sensitivities are when valuing the business. Importantly, we must examine in detail the key assumptions underpinning the forecasts and really scrutinise whether those assumptions are valid – do the price, volume and cost projections really make sense? How credible are they? What about the growth assumptions? We can then play around with other assumptions to see how this impacts upon the results.

By using a 'discount' rate that reflects the risks of a business, a key reason for using a DCF is that it explicitly (albeit imperfectly) takes risk into account in the valuation process. We saw in Chapter 1 when looking at risk that while the cost of capital is a very useful number it does not necessarily capture all the risks involved. However, we can always play around with discount rates and see which ones we feel comfortable with in light of the business risks. This does of course highlight the subjectivity involved in much of the DCF process – the assumptions and the discount rate can be very subjective and as a result yield wildly different answers.

DCF is often greeted with scepticism by some investors (and with some justification). In many industries it is a challenge to forecast the next six months let alone the next 20–30 years, which is

DCF is often greeted with scepticism by some investors

especially true in the current uncertain economic conditions. Another factor is that often DCF is used to arrive at a pre-ordained valuation – so it is calculated with the assumptions necessary to 'prove' a company is worth £1 billion or whatever result is wanted. This was certainly a feature of IPOs during the dot-com boom.

Shares that have been promoted on the basis of looking attractive on a DCF basis have frequently been a disaster. Eurotunnel, Telewest (and other cable companies) and a number of the high-growth stocks of the boom years were all sold on the basis of DCF forecasts. In fairness there were few other ways of doing it – the profits and returns were a long way off and significant amounts of capital were needed to get the projects finished. Nonetheless, being aware of the dangers implicit in this method will help you have the correct degree of circumspection when looking at stocks that are deemed attractive on this basis. In particular, focusing on the assumptions being made around the price and volume outlook and the risks and dangers to the forecasts is crucial.

However, in many situations such as new product developments or new projects, IPOs and when companies engage in acquisitions, using DCF is an important tool. Indeed, if we are looking at a project with a 30-year life there is no other way of assessing whether or not to go ahead with it. It is also worth noting that when companies do 'impairment reviews' of assets or companies they acquired that turn out to be disappointing (i.e. too much was paid for them in the light of subsequent trading conditions), the accountants will use a DCF with new assumptions of pricing, volume and costs that reflect the more challenging trading environment. The new value will then be carried in the books and the 'loss' on the original price purchased will be written down – or 'impaired' – through the P&L.

Therefore being familiar and comfortable with DCF is an important element of understanding valuation. In particular, having an appreciation of its strengths and weaknesses and how to play around with the key assumptions to generate sensible ranges for the 'intrinsic value' is a very useful way of getting a feel for the valuation of the business and what is driving it.

DCF valuation

Understanding the key concepts behind DCF is important and straightforward although the maths may appear far from straightforward initially.

Essentially there are five steps to the process:

1 defining operating free cash flow
2 forecasting the company's operating free cash flows over the initial growth period
3 establishing at the end of this forecast period the 'terminal value'
4 determining the 'discount rate' by calculating the weighted average cost of capital
5 the calculation.

Step 1 Defining operating free cash flow

So what is operating free cash flow? This is normally defined as:

> Net operating profit after tax (NOPAT) + depreciation + amortisation
> − (maintenance) capital expenditure − working capital requirements
> = operating free cash flow

Depreciation and amortisation are added back as they are what are called 'non-cash costs'. This means that while the amounts are deducted to arrive at a profit number, they do not involve an outflow of cash.

Capital expenditure explicitly recognises that this is a critical component of the company achieving the forecast growth targets. Maintenance capital expenditure is often used in more slowly growing environments or phases of a company's development. This ensures that the fabric of the business is protected, recognising that maintenance expenditure is a real cost of doing business (a weakness discussed when considering EBITDA as a valuation number).

Similarly, working capital is required as the higher sales over the growth period will require cash to fund the expansion of working capital.

Things to watch out for include:

- *Is cash coming from the underlying business and is it sustainable?* While this seems an obvious point, it is always worth ensuring that the cash is coming from the business and is sustainable. A one-off movement in working capital that improves the cash flow profile may unwind in another year.

- *How much is from one-offs (e.g. asset disposals)?* There may be one-offs coming from asset or business disposals which again need to be excluded or considered separately.
- *Associate income.* As we discussed when exploring earnings quality and cash flows, it is important that associate income is excluded. In cash flow terms this generates a dividend. Often it is best to exclude this contribution and deduct a value for the associate from the enterprise value (treating it as a 'peripheral asset', see p. 275).
- *Minorities.* Again as discussed under earnings, if a part of the business is owned by outside shareholders this also needs to be considered.

Step 2 Forecasting cash flow

The initial period of forecasting is typically between five and ten years. The key variables driving operating cash flow, prices and volumes (which drive revenues) and costs need to be forecast and the relationship between these variables really need to be understood – so, for example, how does a fall in price affect operating profit?

As the section on the difficulties of forecasting made clear (p. 222), this is a hazardous process fraught with difficulties even in the short term, let alone the long term.

The frequency and extent of profits downgrades that have afflicted the stock market clearly demonstrate the risks and difficulties in forecasting. Interestingly, during the dot-com boom many of the downgrades have been in perceived growth stocks (e.g. telecommunications or technology) where DCF may well have been used to justify their share price/value. In the current environment the lack of visibility for many highly cyclical business makes for a real challenge using DCF.

Therefore, when forecasting this initial period, care needs to be taken with the following.

- *Forecasting volumes, prices and costs.* As these are the key drivers of cash, great care must be taken arriving at the forecasts. The section on the difficulties of forecasting volumes, prices and costs (p. 222) explores the issues and problems at the heart of this element of a DCF valuation. The impact of operational gearing and the sensitivity of profits and cash flow to changes in price are especially crucial. Also really appreciating the company's competitive position and 'moat' are crucial to have confidence in the sustainability of the projections and ability to prevent or withstand new entrants.

- *'Sanity checks' – do the forecasts make sense?* The level of volumes, prices and costs should be subject to a 'sanity check' so that any overoptimistic assumptions are reined in. Are the volume forecasts predicated on taking a degree of market share that will inevitably cause a price war? Are volume assumptions extrapolated on the back of high and unsustainable current levels? Are prices likely to come under pressure from new entrants or customers with strong bargaining power? Are the operating margins realistic in the context of the economics of the industry? Again, it is important to be sceptical of any forecasts used.
- *How long is the growth period?* Over the initial forecast period the company is often in a high-growth phase. This period of high growth and high returns will tend to decay as the company becomes more established. At some stage demand growth slows and increasingly competitive conditions arise affecting growth and returns. The length of this initial period of strong growth and returns is of course subject to considerable uncertainty. In many new industries the growth periods may be a lot shorter than hoped for as maturity quickly follows a period of exceptional growth. Clearly if the industry matures in Year 5 and the forecasts of exceptional growth go out to Year 8, the valuation will fall sharply.

In theory, at the end of the initial growth period returns will fall until the cost of capital is covered. When the company has arrived at this phase of its development, at the end of the initial forecast period, the valuation process turns to the terminal value phase.

Step 3 Terminal value

The terminal value is often 50–60 per cent of the total value of the company. Making appropriate assumptions at this stage of the company's development is therefore crucial. Indeed, flexing the assumptions at this stage can be used to generate a very different result (see p. 172).

There are two ways of determining the terminal value. First, a multiple of the operating profits or operating free cash flow can be used. Alternatively a 'steady state growth' approach can be used.

- *A multiple approach.* With a multiple approach you would take (say) the operating profits at this stage and apply a multiple. Let's say the company is forecast to be generating operating profits of £50 million. Having looked at similar companies with these characteristics and growth profile, you find they are trading on 7× operating profit. You simply multiply the £50 million by 7 to generate the terminal value of

£350 million. This then has to be discounted back to the current value. If the terminal value occurs in, say, Year 7, you would discount back from Year 7.

- The danger, arguably, of using the multiple method is that the absolute nature of using the DCF approach is compromised by using the relative valuation implied by the multiple. It raises questions as to what multiple should be used given the low-growth scenario at this stage of the company's development.
- *Steady state growth.* The 'steady state' refers to the maturity of the business and implicitly relatively low-growth assumptions should be used. When projecting growth at the terminal phase in a steady state approach, it may be sensible to tie the assumptions to the long-term trend in GDP growth.
- There is a formula that can be used to determine the terminal value based on something called the 'Gordon growth model'. We will not go into the basis for this here but the formula is really useful.

    Terminal value = operating cash flow/WACC – growth rate

- In this case the drivers of value are the cost of capital and the assumed growth rates. The higher the growth rate, the greater the value as you are dividing the operating profit by a much lower figure.
- The sum generated by this formula is then discounted back from the last forecast period. So again if you have forecast out to Year 7, the terminal value will be discounted back from Year 7.

We now need to assess the cost of capital and how to derive the weighted average cost of capital.

Step 4 The weighted average cost of capital (WACC)

Having decided upon the forecasts for the initial growth phase and the assumptions used for the terminal value phase, the cash flows need to be 'discounted'. This means that the future value of the cash is brought back to a current value, what the cash flows are worth in today's money. This is why the calculation is often referred to as a 'net present value' calculation. The further away the cash is and the greater the risk attaching to it the less it is worth in today's money.

In essence the discount rate will reflect how much risk attaches to the future cash flows – how predictable are the price, volume and cost elements of the equation and how volatile are profits? So the higher the perceived risk the greater the WACC. A biotech company, for example, may have a 25 per cent discount rate while with a utility with a predictable cash flow stream we may use a rate of 6 per cent.

The discount rate used is the WACC and how it is calculated was discussed in Chapter 1 (p. 27). The key element determining the WACC is the proportion of equity and debt used to fund the business. Here we use the market values (if possible) of the equity (market cap) and debt. Equity – as it is higher risk – has a much higher cost than debt (which is also tax deductible).

Step 5 The calculation

To illustrate the way in which the discounted cash flow process works we return to our two fictional companies, pharmaceutical stock Pink Tablet and manufacturing Tin Can. We shall explore the mechanics of the DCF valuation and assess how this valuation method compares with the others.

The operating forecasts are detailed in Tables 7.1 and 7.2.

Table 7.1 Pink Tablet operating forecasts

	Year 1	Year 2	Year 3	Year 4	Steady state
Operating profit	105	130	160	180	200
Tax	30%	30%	30%	30%	30%
Nopat	73.5	91	112	126	140
Depreciation	21	25	28	31	34
Capex	(40)	(45)	(50)	(50)	(55)
Working capital	(15)	(18)	(20)	(20)	(20)
Operating free cash flow	39.5	53	70	87	99
WACC	8.9%				
NPV calculation	39.5/1.089	53/1.19	70/1.29	87/1.41	2912/1.41
NPV	36.3	44.5	54.3	61.7	2065.2
Total: £2262m					

The process involves:

- defining operating free cash flow
- looking at the initial growth period
- assessing terminal value
- WACC
- the calculation.

Defining operating free cash flow

Table 7.1 lays out the components of operating free cash flow for Pink Tablet. The operating profit is taxed at 30 per cent. Depreciation as a non-cash cost is added back on. We then have to deduct the amount spent on capital expenditure. In this case it is relatively modest as, for pharmaceutical companies, it is the R&D budget that is the major area of investment and this is charged to costs as a revenue item. Then working capital requirements are deducted. This leaves us with the operational free cash flow.

Initial growth period

We have forecast operating profits out for the first four years. The growth rate is very high in the first two years in particular, with operating profit growing at 23 per cent per annun. This reflects the success of drugs that have reached the market in year 1 and built up sales in their first two years. This slows down in year 4. For the sake of illustration we have restricted this initial growth period to the first four years. It will often be the case that the initial period will be for the first seven to ten years. Obviously the risks attaching to the numbers when forecasting out so far increase dramatically.

Terminal value – steady state growth phase

At the end of Year 4 it is assumed that the steady state growth rate slows considerably. The steady state represents an 11 per cent uplift on Year 4. Thereafter it is assumed that the growth rate at this stage falls to 5.5 per cent. This is considerably above the growth rate of the economy (which for the sake of argument grows at a long-term rate of 2.5 per cent).

We will use the formula:

Terminal value = steady state cash flow/(WACC – growth rate)

We then need to establish the WACC.

Weighted average cost of capital

Cost of debt: we already know that Pink Tablet is very low geared and highly cash generative. As a result it can borrow money very cheaply. We will assume that it pays 6.5 per cent on its debt. Given that interest payments are tax deductible, the net cost of debt is 70 per cent of 6.5 per cent – or 4.6 per cent.

Cost of equity: we know that for a pharmaceutical company the impact of the economy on operating results is relatively low, the operational gearing is relatively low and the company is very low geared (it has little debt). The impact of the economy on operating results is relatively low. As a result the beta of the shares is going to be low. We will use 0.7 – consistent with pharmaceutical shares in the market.

If we take the risk-free rate on a long-term government bond as being 5.5 per cent and a relatively high equity risk premium of 5 per cent given the uncertainty of the current environment then:

> Cost of equity = risk-free rate + (equity risk premium × beta)
> = 5.5 per cent + (5 × 0.7) = 9 per cent

The mix of equity and debt is very much skewed towards equity. The market capitalisation is £2415 million, while there is debt of £50 million. This gives a business 98 per cent funded by equity and 2 per cent by debt.

Therefore the WACC is:

> 0.98 × 9 + 0.02 × 4.6 = 8.9 per cent

The calculation

We are now in a position to calculate the DCF of Pink Tablet. The discounting process works as we have seen by dividing the operating free cash flow by 1 plus the WACC with this is factored by the relevant number. The formula is normally expressed as:

> $OPFCF/(1+WACC) + OPFCF2/(1+WACC)^2 + OPFCF3/(1+WACC)^3$ .... $OPFCFN/(i + WACCC)^n$

Table 7.1 demonstrates how the numbers are put together. The series for the initial growth period runs:

> $39.5/1.089 + 53/(1.089)^2 + 70/(1.089)^3 + 87/(1.089)^4$

Using the formula, the terminal value is 99/(8.9 per cent – 5.5 per cent) = 2912. As this is the value at the end of Year 4 we then have to discount this back to obtain a net present value. Discounting this back from the end of Year 4, i.e. £2912 million/(1.089)4, gives us £2065.2 million.

The total sum is then £2262 million.

This value is the value of the whole business, the enterprise value. To arrive at the value of the shares we have to take the debt off this amount to generate the equity value. Therefore on this basis the equity value is £2262 million − £50 million = £2212 million.

From the market capitalisation, we know that the stock market values the shares at £2415 million. Therefore we can say that the DCF is producing a value 8.5 per cent below that of the company's stock market value. On this basis, if we believe all our numbers and projections, we would conclude that the shares are overvalued. Alternatively, we can argue that the stock market is making more optimistic assumptions than our central case.

To illustrate the sensitivities involved, if we flex the terminal growth assumption to 6 per cent (feasible given the growth profile of a drug company), the terminal value becomes £3414 million; discounted back this is £2421.2 million: a £356 million uplift on the original valuation. This gives an equity value of £2568 million, 6 per cent more than the price of the shares.

Flexing the steady state growth assumption by 0.5 per cent equates to the shares going from being 8.5 per cent dear to 6 per cent cheap.

Table 7.2 Tin Can operating forecasts

	Year 1	Year 2	Year 3	Year 4	Steady state*
Operating profit	25	23	25	22	22
Tax	30%	30%	30%	30%	30%
NOPAT	17.5	16.1	17.5	15.4	15.4
Depreciation	20	22	23	24	24
Capex	(20)	(15)	(20)	(15)	(15)
Working capital	(12)	(12)	(15)	(12)	(12)
Free cash flow	5.5	11.1	5.5	12.4	12.4
WACC	10%				
NPV calculation	5.5/1.10	11.1/1.21	5.5/1.33	12.4/1.46	155/1.46
NPV	5	9.2	4.1	8.5	106.2
Total: £133m					

Once again the process is as follows:

- defining operating free cash flow
- looking at the initial growth period
- assessing terminal value
- WACC
- the calculation.

Defining operating free cash flow

Table 7.2 lays out the components of operating free cash flow for Tin Can. The operating profit is taxed at 30 per cent. Depreciation as a non-cash cost is added back on. We then have to deduct the amount spent on capital expenditure. In this case we have assumed that maintenance capital expenditure is £15 million, £5 million below depreciation.

Initial growth period

We have forecast operating profits out for the first four years. For the sake of illustration, we have restricted this initial growth period to the first four years. It will often be the case that the initial period will be for the first seven to ten years. Obviously the risks attaching to the numbers when forecasting out so far increase dramatically.

The forecasts reflect the cyclicality of the markets and the non-existent growth prospects.

Terminal value – steady state growth phase

At the end of Year 4 it is assumed that the steady state growth rate slows considerably. The steady state is unchanged in Year 4. Thereafter it is assumed that the growth rate falls to 2 per cent. This is in line with the growth rate of the economy (which for the sake of argument grows at a long-term rate of 2.5 per cent). This could be a little optimistic given the characteristics of the business.

To generate the terminal value we will use the formula:

Terminal value = steady state cash flow/(WACC – growth rate)

We then need to establish the WACC.

Weighted average cost of capital

Cost of debt: we already know that Tin Can is highly geared and there are question marks over its cash generation. However, it has locked in long-term loan rates at an attractive 7.5 per cent.

The cost of debt is then 7.5 × 70 per cent = 5.3 per cent.

Cost of equity: we know that Tin Can is very sensitive to changes in volumes and pricing (which is highly competitive and subject to import competition) and so operational gearing is high. With 50 per cent gearing the company is also highly financially geared. As a result the beta of the shares is going to be high. We will use 1.3 (which is reasonably consistent with engineering shares in the market).

If we take the risk-free rate on a long-term government bond as being 5.5 per cent and a relatively high equity risk premium of 5 per cent given the uncertainty of the current environment then the cost of equity is:

Risk-free rate + (equity risk premium × beta) =
5.5 per cent + (5 × 1.3) = 12 per cent

The market capitalisation is £138 million, while there is debt of £60 million. This gives a business funded 70 per cent by equity and 30 per cent by debt.

Therefore the WACC is:

0.7 × 12 + 0.3 × 5.3 = 9.9 per cent (rounded to 10 for the calculations)

The calculation

We are now in a position to calculate the DCF of Tin Can. The series for the initial growth period runs:

$$5.5/1.1 + 11.1/(1.1)^2 + 5.5/(1.1)^3 + 12.4/(1.1)^4$$

The terminal value is 12.4/(10 per cent – 2 per cent) = £155 million. As this is the value at the end of Year 4 we then have to discount this back to obtain a net present value. Discounting this back from the end of Year 4, i.e. £155 million/(1.1)4, gives us £106.2 million.

The total sum is then £133 million.

This value is the value of the whole business, the enterprise value. To arrive at the value of the shares we have to take the debt off this amount to generate the equity value. Therefore on this basis the equity value is £133 million – £60 million = £73 million.

From the market capitalisation information we know that the stock market values the shares at £138 million. Therefore we can say that the DCF is producing a value almost 50 per cent below that of the company's stock market value. On this basis, if we believe all our numbers and projections we would conclude that the shares are considerably overvalued. The stock market may be taking into account a more dramatic recovery in its earnings or a much higher growth at the terminal value phase. The characteristics of the business make this an unlikely expectation. However, there is often an overoptimistic view of the scale of earnings recovery. Furthermore, it may be that the price is assuming that the company may be subject to a bid approach – the characteristics of the industry certainly suggest this is needed. Whether it actually happens or not is another issue.

> there is often an overoptimistic view of the scale of earnings recovery

To illustrate the sensitivities involved, if we flex the terminal growth assumption to 4 per cent, the terminal value becomes £200 million, which discounted back is £136 million. This is a £33.1 million uplift on the original valuation to give an equity value of £102.8 million. Flexing the steady state growth assumption by 2 per cent equates to the shares going from being 48 per cent dear to a more modest 25 per cent expensive.

DCF advantages

- *Cash – key driver of value.* In theory the value of any asset is the discounted value of the cash it will generate. Therefore cash is the key driver of value. We have identified the manipulation that can occur in the profit and loss account to produce an earnings number that gives the impression of good performance. We have also seen that one of the weaknesses of earnings is that it may not bear any relation to the amount of cash being generated. However, it is much more difficult to distort the cash coming into (or going out of) the business.
- *Absolute measure.* One of the advantages of using a DCF is that it measures the absolute measure of a business – it does not rely on getting a value through comparisons with other 'similar' companies.
- *No accounting issues?* DCF valuation avoids all the accounting issues that have recently plagued markets. The methodology also means that different accounting policies for depreciation or amortisation can be ignored.
- *Takes capital expenditure into account.* Unlike the use of EBITDA, the requirement of either growth or maintenance capital expenditure is

explicitly taken into account. This spending is crucial to generate the growth on which the forecast cash generation is based or to maintain the competitive position of the business which also directly affects the company's cash flow profile.

- *Long term.* Another virtue (and possibly a vice) is that a DCF valuation relies on long-term forecasts of cash flows to determine value. It should not, therefore, be affected by one unsustainable good year or one exceptional bad year. It is the long-term value that matters. As we have seen, around 60 per cent of the value is determined by the 'terminal value'. This arguably overcomes the short-termist criticism often levelled at other valuation measures.

- *Takes early year losses into account.* An advantage of DCF is that it can be used for long-term growth companies that may be incurring heavy start-up losses. This method allows an equity value to be arrived at where other valuation techniques are clearly inappropriate.

- *Explicitly brings cost of capital into account.* The cost of capital is a crucial cost to the company that is often overlooked. Discounting the cash flows by the company's cost of capital explicitly recognises its importance in generating value. In turn this reflects the risks attaching to the company and its funding structure. In particular, the operational and financial gearing and the company's stage of development are brought into the equation. The higher the risks, the lower the value created by the cash flow when it is discounted back.

- *Sensitivity analysis ... playing with assumptions.* One of the key advantages with using a DCF approach is the way you can play around with various assumptions to see what impact these have on the valuation. Playing around with growth numbers enables you to work out what might happen to the share price if the market's view on growth changes. Similarly, if you feel the risks are higher than the market (or you have a lower tolerance for risk than the market), you can apply a higher discount rate and see whether the shares are still attractive.

- *What is the market valuation assuming?* An important way in which many analysts use this approach is to look at the EV (the company's market capitalisation plus debt and other liabilities) and then see what assumptions the stock market is implicitly making about the growth rate of the company. If, for example, the EV is assuming a 2 per cent growth rate and you feel this is the very least the company can achieve, the shares are potentially cheap. You might then want to explore the company's prospects further and consider other valuation methods. You need to be aware of the cost of capital and growth assumptions being used.

DCF disadvantages

There have been a number of spectacular disasters for investors where DCF has been the major valuation methodology used to support the share price or bring a company onto the stock market. Eurotunnel, the cable companies, internet and many technology stocks have to some extent relied on DCF valuations to support their investment case. The example of an initial public offering (IPO) on p. 229 highlights the range of values that can be generated by flexing the assumptions in favour of the company.

In many instances this poor record reflects the risks involved in forecasting for companies or projects that are start-ups or at an early stage of development where there are no sales, profits or earnings to value. Another issue has been the fact that the growth potential has attracted a lot of competitors hoping to profit from that growth. Unfortunately that high level of competition depresses returns – there is overinvestment in the sector or industry which leads to a price war to try to win market share. This inevitably depresses returns.

Overoptimism about the growth potential is also a major factor that leads to disappointment. The hoped-for demand often fails to materialise. In addition, the costs of many projects escalate, especially if they involve long-term construction expenditure.

Therefore great care should be taken when using this technique for valuing a share. Some of the key concerns are as follows:

- *Validity of short- and long-term assumptions?* As discussed under 'The risks in forecasting' section (p. 222), significant risks attach to all the key variables that drive cash flow. This can affect both the short term and the long term with equal force, though longer-term forecasting is notoriously difficult. The problem with changes to the short-term forecast is that these tend to drive down forecasts over the entire forecast period. In addition, short-term numbers are far more valuable in that they are discounted less heavily. Therefore getting the early periods wrong can see a very severe revision to the DCF valuation.
- Similarly, with the terminal value driving around 60 per cent of the result, assumptions made here are crucial. But this is the key problem: they are just assumptions – they are being applied to a point in the future beyond which forecasting is impossible. Given the volatility and difficulty in getting the near-term forecast right, why should assumptions of a company's growth rate in ten years' time have any validity?

- *Subjectivity and sensitivity – assumptions changed to get the 'right' result?* Assumptions made both for the initial growth phase and for the growth at the terminal value phase are highly subjective. This can lead to assumptions being changed to generate the 'right' result. This may be done to make an IPO attractive or an out-of-favour stock look more interesting on valuation grounds.
- The sensitivity of the value to assumptions made can be easily demonstrated. Let's take a company being prepared for a float on the stock market. The sponsoring broker has provided the forecasts and a DCF model as detailed in Table 7.3. The steady state growth is assumed to be 5 per cent occurring after Year 3.

Table 7.3 Discounted cash flow for IPO Plc

	Year 1	Year 2	Year 3	Steady state
Depreciation	20	25	28	30
Amortisation	7	7	7	7
EBIT	100	110	122	135
Tax	–30	–33	–36.6	–40.5
Capex	–30	–35	–40	–40
Working capital	–5	–5	–5	
Free cash flow	62	69	75.4	86.5
DCF with WACC at 11%	55.9	56.1	55.2	1054.6
NPV	1221.7			
Steady state OPFCF	86.5/6%			
WACC – growth rate	1441.7			
Discounted from Y3 to Y0	1054.6			

The DCF approach yields a net present value of £1221.7 million. The company will have debt of £300 million. This implies an equity value of:

£1221.7m – £300m = £921.7m.

However, if we feel that the broker is being too optimistic about:

- the steady state growth assumption of 5 per cent
- the level of risks involved

we can input our own assumptions. Let's see what happens if the cost of capital rises to 13 per cent and the steady state growth rate falls to 3 per cent (Table 7.4).

Table 7.4 A rise in the cost of capital

DCF at 13 per cent	54.9	54.0	52.3	599.4
NPV	760.6			
Steady state OPFCF/	86.5/10%			
WACC – growth rate	865			
Discounted from Y3 to Y0	599.4			

The 2 percentage point increase in the cost of capital and the 2 percentage point reduction in the steady state growth rate leads to an almost 40 per cent fall in the DCF to £760.6 million.

With debt fixed at £300 million the equity value would be:

$$£760.6m - £300m = £460.6m.$$

This represents a fall in the equity value of 50 per cent. So a 'tweaking' of assumptions leads to a 50 per cent reduction in the value of the shares. The big impact is on the terminal value calculation, with the reduction in the growth rate and the higher cost of capital reducing the terminal value from £1054.6 million to £599.4 million. Instead of dividing the operating free cash flow by 6 per cent (11 per cent – 5 per cent) we are dividing by 10 per cent (13 per cent – 3 per cent). Therefore it can be seen how incredibly sensitive the company's value is to relatively minor adjustments to changes in the assumptions. (It should be noted that this example is illustrative only, as in most DCF projections the initial growth phase would stretch out to Years 7–10.)

With this approach we can examine what has happened to the valuation of the high-tech growth stocks. Having disappointed expectations, growth forecasts have been reduced dramatically as it has become clear that they were susceptible to trends in the broader economy and in particular falling capital expenditure. Whether these areas of the market offer real growth is now increasingly questioned.

Effectively both the period and the extent of super-normal growth have been reduced, with devastating consequences for the DCF. Similarly, the extent of the growth at the terminal value stage has been revised down substantially. The development of operating profits and hence cash flow has therefore been downgraded dramatically.

The rising cost of capital as well as the downgrading of cash flow forecasts has also exerted pressure on valuations. The greater risks and higher volatility that have become increasingly apparent translate into a much higher cost of capital. The whole market has seen the equity risk premium rise, increasing that component of the cost of capital.

The substantial downgrades, as the impact of operational gearing became apparent, highlighted the volatility and risks at the individual stock level. In addition, the companies' financial position deteriorated dramatically, with higher debt levels resulting from:

- debt taken on to fund deals that did not deliver hoped-for returns
- debt taken on for massive investment programmes
- the reduced profit forecasts and lower margins producing weaker cash flow and higher debt.

This combination of higher operational volatility and higher debt has led to the company's beta increasing significantly.

A combination of these can see the discount rate required rise rapidly. An increase of 2 percentage points in the equity risk premium (ERP) and the move of, say, 1.5 to 2 in the beta can see the cost of capital rise considerably. With the risk-free rate at 5.5 per cent, if the ERP was 4 per cent and rose to 6 per cent, the cost of equity would rise from 11.5 per cent to 16.5 per cent. This would seriously damage the DCF valuation, as the examples illustrate.

- *Forecast period of super-normal growth and returns?* As discussed earlier, one of the key components in the DCF calculation is forecasting out to the terminal growth phase. This early period tends to be the period of 'super-normal' or higher growth. Again, the difficulty is forecasting both the level of this growth and how long this phase will last. With a growth industry a lot of capital may be attracted which depresses pricing below forecast levels. In addition, maturity can happen very quickly and the industry settles down into a more mature phase much earlier than anticipated. Mobile telephony is an industry which has seen explosive growth but has arguably become mature sooner than anticipated. With massive investment in new technology (3G), the low growth level damages the DCF model considerably. Much debate is

taking place over what will be the key driver that will enable superior growth rates to be re-established.
- *Complexity of calculation.* For private investors in particular, the complexity of both doing the forecasts of operating cash flow and arriving at the cost of capital makes this approach to valuation rather esoteric. Finding the beta and the cost of debt can be awkward. Even if you do not intend to use this rather complex method, it is nonetheless important to be aware of its strengths and weaknesses to enable you to spot flaws in research that might be championing a share because of its attractiveness on DCF grounds and to help you approach it with a healthy dose of scepticism.

Summary

Given that cash is the ultimate driver of value, any asset is in effect worth the discounted value of its future cash flow. The value is derived from making long-term forecasts of a company's cash flow and then 'discounting' these cash flows back into what that cash is worth today. Discounted cash flow is an 'absolute' measure of a company's valuation and is sometimes referred to as net present value or intrinsic value. The discount rate used is the cost of capital which in theory reflects the risks attached to the company. That this risk is explicitly used in arriving at a valuation is clearly welcome.

To do a DCF effectively we need to forecast the price, volume and costs for the company long term and make assumptions about the capital expenditures and working capital requirements of the business. However, in an environment where forecasting the next quarter is challenging enough, using a method which relies on forecasting the next 10 to 20 years has many potential problems.

Having said that, while clearly challenging, having a sense of what the DCF generates as the value of the business is a useful exercise. We can feed in a variety of scenarios of prices and volumes (as well as other variables) to establish a feasible range for the valuation of the business. Alternatively, we can look at the stock market value of the business and then see what assumptions are being made about future operating profits and capital expenditures to arrive at that valuation. If you think these are too cautious you can see whether your assumptions led to a higher intrinsic value and buy the shares.

DCF is often viewed sceptically by some fund managers and analysts as the forecasts are so subjective and prone to revision. In addition, very ambitious/overoptimistic assumptions may be fed into the model to make the shares look attractive. This is often done during IPOs and was very much a feature of the floatations (and valuation of other businesses) during the dot-com boom. The valuations would be manipulated considerably by raising long-term growth forecasts or reducing the cost of capital – as we have seen, by making some very modest adjustments to our assumptions the equity value can be quickly halved or doubled.

Value investors will often look at out-of-favour and undervalued stocks and by doing a conservative DCF (or using a range of feasible assumptions) will see where the intrinsic value may lie. They can then assess whether the shares are worth buying on fundamentals despite the negative sentiment.

DCF CHECKLIST

Definition of cash flow

- The calculation of DCF includes the following components:
  Net operating profit after tax (NOPAT)
  + depreciation
  + amortisation
  − (maintenance) capital expenditure
  − working capital requirements
  = operating free cash flow

The discount rate

- This will reflect the risks involved in the enterprise – the higher the risk the higher the discount rate.
- The discount rate will also depend on the financing of the business. Debt is cheaper than equity and has tax advantages. Therefore the more debt funding the lower the cost of capital (up to a point!)
- The blend of debt and equity funding is taken into account to calculate the weighted average cost of capital. This is then used to discount the future cash flows.

The advantages of using DCF

- It is an absolute measure of value and can be used for all assets.
- It focuses on cash, the key driver of value.
- In theory, given the emphasis on cash there should not be the accounting issues that can distort measures such as P/Es.
- It explicitly factors in the risk of an investment through the cost of capital/discount rate.

- It takes into account the long term and any early losses that may occur for an investment.
- For certain projects, new product developments and M&As, it may be the only rigorous methodology available.
- By having different assumptions for prices and volumes, etc. we can build a range of values for the business and do sensitivity analysis depending on the environment we anticipate.

Disadvantages of DCF valuation

- The validity of short- and long-term assumptions is highly questionable.
- The subjectivity and sensitivity of the forecasts and wide range in valuations that results may not always be helpful.
- It is a real challenge to forecast the period of super-normal growth and the long-term growth rate.
- The cost of capital is only an approximation to risk and in the real world there may be lots of other factors to take on board that will make the use of the discount rate highly subjective.
- For many people the complexity of the calculation is off putting (though the use of spreadsheets has helped make this much more feasible).

8

Relative valuation

What topics are covered in this chapter?

- Why use relative valuations?
- Price/earnings (P/E) ratio
- P/E relative
- Peg ratio
- Yield – investing for income
- Enterprise value (EV)
- EV/EBITDA
- EV/operating free cash flow
- EV/sales
- Price to book
- Summary
- Checklist

Why use relative valuations?

We have seen the process in arriving at an absolute valuation for a company. By forecasting its long-term cash flows, assessing the risk profile to generate an appropriate discount rate and assuming a growth rate in the future we arrive at the 'intrinsic' value of the shares.

Clearly this can be quite a complex procedure. Furthermore, we are giving most of the weight of the valuation to the distant future when our confidence around trends and numbers can at best only be indicative. This is especially true at present when the next six months is very difficult to forecast and shape, and the timing of the recovery is so uncertain. So assumptions about growth rates in ten years' time are inevitably pretty arbitrary.

Reflecting this, most analysts and fund managers tend to use 'relative valuations' and as a result they are widely reported in the press and media. Here in effect we are comparing a company with other similar companies and/or against the stock market overall. So we may want to compare GSK with Pfizer, or Diageo with Pernod-Ricard, for example. Clearly in some instances it may be a challenge to find companies that really are 'similar'.

We need to work out which performance number (or 'metric') to value – sales, EBITDA, earnings – we are going to use to make the comparisons. As we are looking at one metric over the next couple of years (rather than a 30-year projection) it is easier and simpler, as well as less time consuming, to reach a view on the relative case for buying or selling the shares.

Of course this runs the risk that being relative, if the whole stock market or the selected peer group are all systematically over- (or under-) valued by the market then we could buy something that is relatively cheap but absolutely expensive. It is a bit like buying a house at the top of the housing market because its price per square foot was much lower than other houses on the same street. Relatively it may be a bargain, but we will still lose money as house prices fall.

What this example also highlights is that the house may well have been in very different condition to the other houses with different features and amenities. The same is true with companies so we need to be careful about concluding that just because the P/E of company A is a lot lower than company B that necessarily means it is 'cheaper'. This is where the Valuation Villa is so useful – because we need to examine at the very least the growth, risk and quality profile of the two companies as well as the returns they are generating before reaching any conclusion. These characteristics will inevitably shape the performance of the 'metric' we are valuing and accordingly the valuation we are prepared to pay. We will pay a lot more for high-quality earnings combined with growth at lower risk and so pay a higher **'rating'** or **'multiple'** for that company.

Importantly, it is always a good discipline to make sure you are clear whether you are doing a valuation that is for shareholders or for all providers of capital. If you are doing an equity measure you need to ensure that the performance metric 'belongs' to the shareholder. So, for example, using a share price to earnings per share is an obvious equity measure – EPS is, by definition, what is left for shareholders. Doing a market capitalisation to sales figure is sometimes used. However, this is using an equity-based number (market cap) and comparing it to sales which will have been generated by all providers of capital – the enterprise value as opposed to the equity value. A company with a lot of debt and a low market cap (think about General Motors) may have a superficially attractive market cap to sales ratio but the enterprise value (EV) to sales ratio – that takes into account the debt – is far more comprehensive and appropriate.

The most useful way of thinking about EV is that it is the sum of the liabilities required to purchase 100 per cent of a company's cash flow. Its great advantage is that it takes debt and other debt-like liabilities into account with respect to valuation. This is obviously crucial in an investment context and also highlights one of the major deficiencies of using equity-based valuations such as P/E – they do not take the company's funding structure or liabilities into account. In an environment where debt was the funding option of choice and share buy-backs and deals funded by debt were the norm, then using EV is far more sensible when comparing companies.

Given the widespread use of relative valuation techniques and the advantage of the ease of calculating and using them, it is very important to be familiar with how they are used and the strengths and weaknesses of this approach.

The valuation of a company is driven by the elements in the Valuation Villa matrix (see Figure 1.1). These factors can be used to assess why one company's valuation differs from another. It may be that one company is perceived to have a much better management team with a compelling strategy and, as a result, is valued more highly even though all the other factors are similar. Alternatively, the performance and returns may be much weaker, with no real probability of a sustainable recovery – as a result the valuation will be much lower. This matrix provides a useful way of diagnosing the factors affecting the relative valuation.

When performing relative valuations one of the key questions is: what is the most important 'performance metric' that drives the share price in the long term? Many people focus on earnings but, as we will see, this is not necessarily the most useful indicator of corporate performance and can be prone to manipulation. Enron, for example, with its 'earnings before scru-

as we saw with absolute valuation, however, cash is the key driver of value ples' philosophy generated earnings but not cash! As we saw with absolute valuation, however, cash is the key driver of value. So how much cash the company generates is at the heart of long-term value creation. It allows the company to invest in maintaining its competitive advantage, invest in value-added growth opportunities and pay a rising stream of dividends to shareholders.

In the current environment this is especially true as it means that the company will find it easier to fund its strategy and have far more flexibility than if it were very reliant on external providers of capital. Recent developments have put risk at centre stage and again all performance and valuation criteria need to be appreciated in the context of the risks you face as an investor.

There are a number of ways to assess the value of a company. This in turn should give an indication of whether the shares are priced correctly. In practice, analysts use a number of measures and then take a 'blended' view.

We will explore the following valuation methods:

- price/earnings ratio
- price/earnings relative
- peg ratio
- yield
- EV
- EBITDA
- EV to operating free cash flow and **free cash flow yield**
- EV/sales
- price to book.

Price/earnings (P/E) ratio

This is one of the simplest and often a very effective way of establishing the value of a share. The P/E ratio is simply the share price divided by the earnings per share of the company. This tells you how many years the company would take, with profits at current levels, to make enough money to cover the cost of all the shares in issue. The P/E (and indeed other valuation measures) is often referred to as the stock's 'multiple' or 'rating'.

Be aware that there are some companies for which P/E is completely inappropriate (see 'When not to use P/Es', p. 265).

Earnings per share is calculated by dividing post-tax profit by the number of shares in issue.

Example – P/E calculation

> Let us return to fictional brake-unit manufacturer Full Stop. This company has operating profits of £7.5 million. Let us assume that interest costs are £2.5 million, so deducting that from the operating profits gives a pre-tax profit of £5 million. If the standard tax rate of 30 per cent is applied, post-tax profits are £3.5 million. Assume there are 30.5 million shares in issue. This gives earnings per share of 11.5 pence (3.5 million divided by 30.5 million). If the share price is currently 115 pence, you divide that by the earnings per share to give a P/E of 10× (ten times).

So far this measure is based on historic information: the earnings per share from the last set of figures. However, P/E becomes much more useful to investors if a forecast of EPS is used. This, if you like, is shorthand for all the factors analysts believe are relevant to the profit outlook – demand, prices and costs. The analysts should have factored all these into their EPS forecast.

If analysts predict earnings per share rising gently over the next three or four years it tells us they think things are going well. A falling forecast for earnings per share (especially a rapidly falling EPS) tells us that a great deal is going wrong.

P/Es – anticipating the future and reflecting the risks

Share prices, driven by the future outlook, are always looking at what might happen in the next 18 months to two years. Therefore share prices contain a mix of the market's hopes and fears for the next two years, and the balance of sentiment between buyers and sellers. If a company announces record profits for the year just gone but is cautious about the next 12 months, the share price will fall. What can often happen is that the company's current trading is absolutely fine and in line with expectations. The share price, however, is falling and creating a very low P/E. This reflects the fact that the market is looking beyond the next 12 months. So in 2007, for example, housebuilders' and banks' shares were on very low P/Es. Trading was still very good leading some managers to think that the shares were cheap. However, the key here is that the shares were anticipating a sharp slowdown in the economy, especially in the housing market, and reflecting the high risks in that sector especially for those with a lot of debt. On this occasion the share prices were accurately predicting the looming problems – they were not cheap. The market is not always correct as it may become excessively optimistic or pessimistic. Nonetheless it is always worth reflecting whether a low P/E means something is cheap – or anticipating poor trading and reflecting high risk.

This anticipating the future and reflecting the risks is often referred to as 'discounting' or examining what is already 'in the price'. The prospects may indeed be very poor but the share price may be at a level that discounts the problems. As a result it might be that the shares are cheap.

In essence the P/E (and the **P/E relative**) is driven by the elements of the Valuation Villa. The higher-level factors influencing valuation therefore are

- growth (of earnings)
- quality (of earnings)
- risks.

It is wrong to focus on one of these in isolation when assessing whether the shares are attractive. As we discussed on pp. 131–3 when exploring the quality of earnings, not all earnings growth is going to be valued equally. It depends on where the growth has come from and whether it is sustainable or due to one-off factors. These one-off factors may be property disposals or a reduction in discretionary spending, such as marketing or R&D, that has delivered the growth. Growth needs to be generated by a good performance of the underlying business (strong volumes and prices and a close attention to cost control) if it is to command a high valuation. On the face of it a low P/E is going to be more attractive than a high P/E. But this may not always be the case. There are a number of situations that commonly produce low P/Es but may not mean the shares are cheap. The main factors will revolve around the Valuation Villa matrix we identified above.

> the P/E is driven by the elements of the Valuation Villa

Why a low P/E may not mean a share is attractive (or 'cheap') may reflect a combination of:

- uncertainty over a company's prospects for earnings
- the market anticipating earnings coming under pressure over the next 18 months or so
- a highly cyclical sector – again giving a high level of uncertainty

- a company serving volatile markets
- a sector with overcapacity and weak pricing power
- a sector or company with consistently low returns (operating profit margins and/or ROIC) and not adding economic value
- a mature sector, with little prospect of growth
- a company which is ex-growth
- poor management
- a management with no convincing strategy for growth
- poor cash generation
- a weak balance sheet.

The first four factors mean it is difficult to forecast earnings with any accuracy; they have low quality of earnings. This volatility suggests a low P/E. If the earnings are revised down, the shares become a lot more expensive. Indeed, the low P/E may be 'discounting' or anticipating just such a downgrade.

Importantly, the factors in the Valuation Villa matrix are clearly interrelated. Furthermore, they tend to reinforce one another. So, for example, a poor profits outlook due to weak pricing as a result of overcapacity would lead to weak returns – low margins and returns on capital employed. This in turn leads to weak cash generation (the higher the margin, the greater the cash generation) and a poor financial position. This puts pressure on the company's plans for investing in the business to generate higher returns and growth. This 'vicious circle' obviously makes it extremely difficult for the company, and hence the shares, to make money.

There may be instances where the company is actually doing reasonably well but where there is little prospect of further growth, perhaps due to the company dominating its market and/or having good margins, but with no clear strategy for generating growth. The company is effectively ex-growth. Again this would lead to a low P/E. If there is no convincing strategy for value-generating growth, there will be pressure on management to distribute the cash it generates (or indeed any surplus cash on the balance sheet) to shareholders. The shares would then be attractive on yield grounds but the lack of growth leads to a low P/E.

Conversely, there are a number of situations that commonly produce a high P/E but which may not mean the shares are expensive. These tend to be the mirror image of those driving low valuations and include:

- companies with an excellent growth record and prospects for growth
- a high-growth sector
- high confidence in the company's forecasts
- predictable/stable revenues
- strong market share
- high barriers to entry
- companies that have strong pricing power
- companies that have high margins and produce excellent ROCE and add value
- strong cash generation
- strong balance sheet
- excellent growth strategy.

The first two factors mean the company is seen as a **growth investment**. As a result of the strong earnings growth, the P/E is likely to be high. The confidence in forecasts and the predictability of revenues suggest that the quality of earnings is high – again a characteristic that will command a higher rating.

The economic characteristics such as high market share, strong barriers to entry and strong pricing power are all likely to translate into high returns on both sales and capital. A good management track record would also suggest that the cost base is being managed well and that the company is focused on the market and takes customer care very seriously. Again these characteristics will lead to a higher valuation.

As mentioned with the 'vicious circle' earlier, the factors here are also closely interrelated. A 'virtuous circle' of growth and high returns will lead to strong cash generation. This will enable the company to fund its own growth strategy without recourse to shareholders. Invested properly, this cash flow will generate even higher growth in the long term. This is dependent on the management having in place an effective and credible strategy for growth.

a 'virtuous circle' of growth and high returns will lead to strong cash generation

Re-ratings and de-ratings

When looking at the company you may conclude that the P/E is too low, with respect to both the outlook for earnings and the quality of those earnings. The company is a better business with better prospects than the rating is allowing for. If this is the case, the shares will benefit from what is referred to as a re-rating. This can make for very profitable investing. If the P/E stands at a modest 8× earnings but actually the business deserves a 10× rating, this represents a considerable 25 per cent increase. You need to be confident of the assessment you have made to buy the shares on this basis and you should have a sense of what will act as the catalyst to prompt the re-rating.

Some of the factors that might trigger a reassessment of the company's valuation might include:

- results that comfortably beat market expectations
- the market the company operates in performs more strongly than anticipated
- the company continues to gain market share
- a disposal of a business that has been holding back the main business
- a disposal or deal which transforms the balance sheet
- the cash flow profile is far more attractive than originally thought
- a new CEO or management team
- takeover and consolidation activity among similar companies
- improved industry pricing as a result of consolidation.

While there may well be a good case for a re-rating, it often happens that without a catalyst, the shares continue to languish at low valuations. Therefore care needs to be taken.

Conversely, shares that disappoint expectations can undergo a severe de-rating. If the growth expectations that justify the high rating are not fulfilled, the P/E will fall dramatically. As well as the growth being disappointing, the downgrade is likely to flag up risks and issues that were previously thought to be unimportant.

A de-rating might result from factors that cause the earnings to disappoint and lead the growth assumptions to be questioned, such as:

- a new entrant has taken market share
- extra competition from a new product or service
- pricing disappoints
- demand proves to be susceptible to economic slowdowns when it was previously thought to be recession proof
- costs go out of control
- a poor acquisition or strategic decision is made.

The last factor is more a case of management disappointing rather than the growth of the business falling below expectations. Nonetheless, it can be an important trigger for reassessing the company's rating.

The issues of re-ratings and de-ratings tend to affect value stocks and growth stocks respectively. We will explore these investment styles in more detail on p. 301.

The advantages and disadvantages of using P/Es

The case for using P/Es is very much linked to the analysis of earnings as a performance number. We saw that accounting issues, the manipulation of earnings and the relationship between earnings and cash were real concerns. However, by focusing on the quality of earnings, we can try to sidestep some of these problems.

Given the widespread use of the P/E, it is vital to get to grips with the pros and cons of this valuation measure.

As a performance metric, earnings are an effective shorthand for the issues driving price, volume and costs. The performance of these variables is what will determine the success of the company and the share price. This is corroborated by the attention that is given to consensus earning numbers and when results are announced the relationship between earnings and market expectations. Therefore it is a key number to understand and follow.

The *advantages* of using the P/E are that:

- it is easy to compute
- it is conventionally and widely used
- it takes forecasts into account
- earnings provide a measure of what is generated for shareholders.

The widespread use of the P/E makes it a valuation measure that needs to be understood. For many private investors it also has the advantage of being simple to understand and to calculate. In addition, a lot of information on earnings forecasts is available on the web. Earnings have the advantage of being what is left to shareholders after all other claims on the company's income have been satisfied.

However, even with these genuine attractions, when using a P/E it is important to be aware of the potential pitfalls that attach to it as a valuation measure. This is not an attempt to undermine its effectiveness, but to ensure that great care is taken.

The *disadvantages* or problems with using the P/E include the following:

- it does not take debt/financial structure into account
- gearing up/share buy-backs increase earnings – but this may be a one-off effect and achieved at the cost of increased risk
- comparisons are undermined by different accounting policies across companies and countries (depreciation, amortisation, tax, etc.)
- earnings are particularly prone to manipulation
- targeting earnings may lead to decisions that disadvantage the business
- it cannot be used to value loss-making, early-stage growth or cyclical businesses
- it does not take cash generation into account
- it does not take investment returns into account
- growth of earnings may take place at the expense of ROIC
- growth of earnings may take place at the expense of net asset value (exceptional provisions or provisions set up on acquisition are written off shareholders' funds but allow earnings to grow)
- it presents difficulties in assessing the quality of earnings.

One of the difficulties with earnings is when valuing cyclical businesses. Here the logic is often inverted – you buy on a high P/E and sell on a low P/E. This is because earnings are depressed or non-existent at the bottom of the cycle. If earnings are low, the P/E will be very high. If we are indeed at the bottom of the cycle, things can be expected to improve. Investors may want to buy for the recovery and so will take the very high P/E as indicating that we are at, or approaching, the bottom. Conversely, when we come to the top of the cycle, earnings will have recovered substantially, reducing the P/E. Concerns that the cycle will turn down do not make the low P/E attractive.

We have covered the growth of earnings at the expense of returns or assets in the earnings section and when looking at M&A activity. However, it is crucial to ensure that earnings growth is not being achieved by deals or exceptional charges that flatter earnings while returns and assets fall. Similarly, earnings growth that is achieved through increasing the risk profile also needs to be treated with caution.

We explored the benefit of using debt rather than equity and its impact on earnings when looking at acquisition activity. Here we saw that the tax advantages of using the all-debt option resulted in a massive boost to earnings of the deal. However, the subsequent fall in interest cover illustrated the greater degree of risk involved in this option.

It is interesting to note here the difficulty in valuing the earnings generated by this gearing-up given the higher risk attaching to this strategy. A company that used a combination of debt and equity would have a lower boost to earnings but a much lower risk profile. The problem of considering the whole capital structure and valuation is corrected by looking at a company's enterprise value, which we shall discuss on p. 273. As we have seen, the use of discounted cash flow analysis also takes the whole funding structure into account.

P/E relative

Once you have established a company's P/E there is a slightly more sophisticated equation that helps to tell whether its shares are cheap or expensive. This compares the P/E of the company to the P/E of the stock market as a whole. The P/E of the stock market and of individual sectors is listed, among other places, in the *Financial Times* on the back page of the Companies section in a table entitled 'FTSE Actuaries Share Indices'. For industrial companies the figure to use is the P/E for 'non financials' (see 'When not to use P/Es', p. 265).

If, for example, the stock market trades on a P/E of 20×, a company that trades on 15× is said to have a P/E relative of 75 per cent (15 being 75 per cent of 20). Conversely a stock trading on 30× compared to a market trading at 20 is said to be on a relative of 150 per cent.

The great advantage of using the P/E relative is that it takes into account how the company is valued compared with the stock market overall. In particular, it factors in the performance of the company relative to the market in terms of earnings growth. There is an obvious difficulty here if the whole stock market is overvalued – you may be in a company in a better relative position than the market overall, but the absolute level may not be correct. The same analysis can be carried out for the appropriate sector to see whether the company is cheaper or dearer than its sector peers.

As with the P/E, the P/E relative is driven by a combination of:

- growth of earnings relative to the market
- risk and
- quality of earnings.

Clearly companies that have a P/E relative above 100 per cent are those that are perceived to have better growth prospects and better-quality earnings than the market average.

The pros and cons for the P/E apply equally to the P/E relative. The danger of accounting differences between companies creates a particular problem given that the valuation is conducted relative to the market or relevant sector.

What determines the extent of the premium?

The extent of the premium will depend on how long the earnings growth is expected to continue at a high rate and the visibility (quality) of that growth. If we take an example of a company growing at 20 per cent over the next five years while the stock market overall is expected to grow at 8 per cent, then you would expect the premium to be:

$$(1.20/1.08)^5 = 69 \text{ per cent}$$

So a stock delivering this sort of growth would stand on a premium of 69 per cent. In relative terms the stock would be on a P/E relative of 169.

P/E and P/E relative in practice

We will now look at examples of both the P/E and P/E relative working in practice.

Example

Pink Tablet

We return to our fictitious pharmaceutical company Pink Tablet. It has a reliable income stream from a range of drugs including a popular and well-established anti-asthma drug. It also has excellent growth potential from three new drugs which have begun to sell well and from some exciting drug development work which is expected to bring new products to market in the near future. Pink Tablet, therefore, combines a reliable profit stream (quality earnings) with excellent growth prospects. These two factors are reflected in the profits forecasts which, as can be seen in the table below, grow rapidly. Note that today's share price is used for the calculations. The example also assumes that overall the market is forecast to grow at 10 per cent per annun.

The table tells us a number of things.

- The P/E at 34.5× in Year 1, on first viewing, suggests that the shares are quite expensive. It would take 34.5 years for the company to make enough money to buy back all its shares at today's price. However, as we know that Pink Tablet has a high-quality earnings stream and good growth prospects, this is not a surprise.

- Looking at the P/E for Year 2 and Year 3 shows us that once the rapid growth in earnings is factored in at today's price, the shares are beginning to look cheaper.
- The P/E relative at 173 per cent in Year 1 tells us that these shares are much more expensive than the average for the market. With earnings growth at 25 per cent compared with a market growing at 10 per cent, the extent of the premium would be determined by the length of time this differential growth was expected to continue. If it was for, say, four years, you might say that as $(1.25/1.1)^4$ suggests a P/E premium of 67 per cent this is not far from its actual rating.
- Similarly, the falling P/E relative for Year 2 and Year 3 tells us that the shares begin to look cheaper relative to the market when the higher earnings growth is factored in.
- The key problem is determining the extent to which the earnings growth and quality are already reflected in the share price. To the extent that the share price is factoring in the 25 per cent growth relative to a market growing at 10 per cent over the next four years, if this is how it turns out, you will not necessarily make money. For the share price to perform it may need growth to be even higher or a new drug to do even better than hoped.

Share price today 875p

	Year 1 forecast	Year 2 forecast	Year 3 forecast
Pre-tax profit	**£100m**	**£125m**	**£155m**
Tax	30%	30%	30%
Earnings (after tax)	£70m	£87.5m	£108.5m
Number of shares	276m	276m	276m
EPS	**25.4p**	**31.7p**	**39.3p**
P/E calculation	875/25.4	875/31.7	875/39.3
P/E	**34.5×**	**27.6×**	**22.3×**
Market P/E	20×	18×	16×
P/E relative calculation	34.5/20 × 100	27.6/18 ×100	22.3/16 × 100
P/E relative	**173%**	**153%**	**139%**

Tin Can

A rather different example is the fictitious company Tin Can. It manufactures tin cans, which are steadily going out of fashion. A high proportion of its costs are determined by the price of raw materials, which have been volatile over the past few years. There is intense competition, and Tin Can is dependent on a few large contracts with food producers which can easily change suppliers. This is therefore a commodity business (it is very easy to make these cans), costs are difficult to forecast, it is operating in a mature market and there is a high risk that revenues could be affected by the loss of an important contract. It has low-quality earnings (they are unpredictable) and no growth prospects. Both these factors will be reflected in today's share price.

Share price today 100p	Year 1 forecast	Year 2 forecast	Year 3 forecast
Pre-tax profit	**£20m**	**£18m**	**£20m**
Tax	30%	30%	30%
Earnings (after tax)	£14.0m	£12.6m	£14.0m
Number of shares	138m	138m	138m
EPS	**10.1p**	**9.1p**	**10.1p**
P/E calculation	100/10.1	100/9.1	100/10.1
P/E	**9.9×**	**11×**	**9.9×**
Market P/E	20×	18×	16×
P/E relative calculation	9.9/20 × 100	11/18 × 100	9.9/16 × 100
P/E relative	**50%**	**61%**	**62%**

The table tells us a number of things.

- The P/E at 9.9× in Year 1, on first viewing, suggests that the shares are quite cheap. It would take only ten years for the company to make enough money to buy back all its shares at today's price. However, as we know that Tin Can has a low-quality earnings stream (i.e. the forecasts are not likely to be accurate) and no growth prospects, this is not a surprise.
- Looking at the P/E for Year 2 and Year 3 illustrates that as there is no earnings growth the P/E remains pretty much the same.
- The P/E relative at 50 per cent in Year 1 tells us that these shares are much cheaper than the average for the market.
- The rising P/E relative for Year 2 and Year 3 tells us that the shares are becoming more expensive relative to the market as other companies in the market grow their earnings more rapidly than Tin Can.

This example shows how useful the P/E relative is when assessing how cheap or expensive a share might be compared with the stock market overall.

If Tin Can were to lose a key contract, which reduced profits by £5 million in Year 3, the picture would be very different.

	Year 1 forecast	Year 2 forecast	Year 3 forecast
Pre-tax profit	**£20m**	**£18m**	**£15m**
Tax	30%	30%	30%
Earnings (after tax)	£14m	£12.6m	£10.5m
Number of shares	138m	138m	138m
EPS	**10.1p**	**9.1p**	**7.6p**
P/E calculation	100/10.1	100/9.1	100/7.6
P/E	**9.9×**	**11×**	**13.2×**
Market P/E	20×	18×	16×
P/E relative calculation	9.9/20 × 100	11/18 × 100	13.2/16 × 100
P/E relative	**50%**	**61%**	**83%**

Here we see that the risks to forecasts can quickly convert an apparently cheap share into looking horribly expensive. This company, despite all its problems, is trading at only 17 per cent discount to the market as a whole. For such low-quality earnings and no growth prospects, this discount needs to be much greater to represent good value.

Given the background market characteristics that Tin Can faces, we can also see what happens to the P/E if prices fall 5 per cent. Let's say prices fall 5 per cent at the end of Year 1. Revenues are £250 million. Therefore, a 5 per cent reduction in prices takes 5 per cent off revenue, i.e. £12.5 million. With costs unchanged, operating profits are reduced by £12.5 million: from £25 million to £12.5 million. This illustrates the impact of operational gearing. With interest costs fixed at £5 million, the pre-tax profit falls to £7.5 million. The table below demonstrates the effect on earnings.

This fall in profits also leads to a weaker cash flow. We have effectively lost £12.5 million of operating profit. While this will also reduce the tax charge by 30 per cent, let's assume that with tax of 30 per cent, the net loss is £8.75 million. With interest costing, say, 7.5 per cent, this reduces profits by £0.65 million.

So if we assume that the lower prices prevail for Year 3 and all other things remain equal (highly unlikely but it illustrates the point), Year 3 forecasts are reduced due to the higher interest costs.

	Year 1 forecast	Year 2 forecast	Year 3 forecast
Pre-tax profit	£20m	£7.5m	£6.8m
Tax	30%	30%	30%
Earnings (after tax)	£14m	£5.3m	£4.8m
Number of shares	138m	138m	138m
EPS	10.1p	3.8p	3.5p
P/E calculation	100/10.1	100/3.8	100/3.5
P/E	9.9×	26.3×	28.6×
Market P/E	20×	18×	16×
P/E relative calculation	9.9/20 × 100	26.3/18 × 100	28.6/16 × 100
P/E relative	50%	146%	178%

Therefore, these modest changes to pricing assumptions have dramatically changed the valuation. The P/E relative of 61 in Year 2 is transformed to a P/E of 26.3× and a relative of 146 per cent. Given the low quality of earnings and the fact that earnings are falling while the market is growing, the shares become progressively more expensive against the market.

Clearly the share price looks unsustainable on this basis. The question is then, how far might the share price fall?

If the shares fall back to a P/E relative of, say, 70 for Year 3, the P/E will fall to 16 × 0.7, which is a P/E of 11.2. Multiplying this by 3.5p of earnings suggests a price of around 40p. This represents a fall of 60 per cent. It is contentious whether 70 would be an appropriate P/E relative in these circumstances. The previous relative of 50 or 60 might be more appropriate. However, there might be some sense that the earnings have been hit so hard that they are due to bounce. This may well be the triumph of hope over experience. To a certain extent this is academic – the shares will lose at least 60 per cent of their value.

When not to use P/Es

The use of P/Es may not be appropriate in certain circumstances (e.g. there may be no earnings) or for certain sectors/industries (e.g. financial companies such as those in insurance, banking or property).

No earnings

This may reflect a highly cyclical company where operating profits have fallen into losses. This obviously makes a P/E inappropriate. If profits have fallen to very low levels (but remain positive) the P/E will be so high that it is not meaningful. Alternatively, the absence of earnings may reflect a company that is in a 'start-up' phase. The costs associated with developing the business mean that earnings are negative.

In these instances EV/sales or EV/EBITDA measures may be used. We will come on to explore the advantages and disadvantages of these valuation methods.

Financial companies

These are valued on asset values rather than earnings. For example, an insurance company is commonly assessed on how much money is left in its pot of investments after it has paid out all projected liabilities. The equivalent of earnings per share in this case is the money left in the pot divided by how many shares are in existence. Similarly, a property company is commonly assessed on the value of its bricks and mortar, with the equivalent of earnings per share being that value divided by the number of shares in existence. This is called net asset value (NAV).

Peg ratio

This is a measure of value that combines a company's P/E and its rate of earnings growth. It is calculated by dividing the P/E by the growth rate. So, for example, a stock on a P/E of 20× growing at 10 per cent would be on a peg ratio of 2×. The P/E is in theory what investors are prepared to pay for growth and so it should be correlated with growth.

A lower peg value indicates that investors are paying a low price for future earnings growth. Conversely, a high peg value tells us that investors are paying a relatively high price for future growth.

> shares are attractive when the peg ratio is somewhere between 0.6 and 0.8

This method of valuation is most commonly used for valuing companies that are good growth prospects with good earnings quality. The peg ratio approach to valuing shares has been publicised by investment guru Jim Slater. He suggests that shares are attractive when the peg ratio is somewhere between 0.6 and 0.8. It is often associated with an investment style called 'growth at a reasonable price'.

So let us see what this method would do to our pharmaceutical company Pink Tablet. Its earnings are forecast to grow 25 per cent a year over the three-year period considered above. Let's take year 1, where the P/E is 35×.

$$35/25 = 1.4$$

Some analysts would suggest that a peg ratio of 1.4 was much too high, indicating that the share was already overvalued; others, however, would take the view that the strong and consistent earnings growth and high-quality earnings were worth paying for. Again it depends whether you take earnings growth over one year or whether you take a longer-term view.

Interestingly, the engineering company has falling earnings in Year 1 but rising earnings of 11 per cent in Year 2. This makes the first year peg ratio meaningless while in Year 2 it is 0.9×.

This raises a central problem for the peg ratio – it works far less well for cyclical or volatile earnings patterns. If earnings have collapsed, the next year may show a sharp bounce but from such a depressed level as to make the degree of growth meaningless. The growth over one year is high, but the earnings may just be catching up on where they were two or three years previously. After this recovery they may well fall back again, suggesting that medium-term growth is very low. However, you have to be careful about what the peg ratio is telling you.

As with low PEs, a low peg ratio may be telling you a number of things that may mean the shares are not necessarily cheap:

- High risk and high beta – does this mean volatile finances and operating gearing?
- There is high risk attaching to earnings forecasts which argues for a lower peg.
- Profits will not hit growth targets.
- The quality of earnings is low.
- The projects driving the growth are expected to produce a low return on invested capital.

The peg may also transmit the wrong message if growth is being depressed by revenue investments in marketing, R&D or other longer-term projects, all of which are improving the longer-term growth capability. In this case the peg is not taking a sufficiently long-term view of things.

The message as ever is that: you need to look at other aspects of the business performance apart from earnings growth, and in particular returns on invested capital; whether value is being added; and whether cash is being generated.

Yield – investing for income

Another way to assess the value of a share is to look at the income the investor receives from holding the shares. This is calculated by dividing the full year's dividend by the share price. The advantage of this method is that it is very simple and can be very effective.

$$\text{Dividend yield} = \frac{\text{dividends per share}}{\text{share price}} \times 100\%$$

So assuming a share price of 100p and a dividend of 5p, the yield is 5 per cent. The stock market average yield in 2009 was around 4.5 per cent so such a stock may be attractive if you are looking for income.

Dividends normally consist of two payments: an interim and a final. The **interim dividend** tends to be around 25–40 per cent of the full year total, while the final typically represents between 60 per cent and 75 per cent. This is because the interim dividend declared at the halfway stage is based on unaudited numbers with only half the year gone and carries more risk. The declaration of the full year dividend will be on audited figures, with not only the full year performance under the belt but also a good sense of how the current financial year has started.

Income can be an important requirement for many investors and is of course a key component of total shareholder return (TSR). A high yield may be attractive on income grounds. However, as with companies on a low P/E, it may reflect poor-quality earnings and low growth. This will mean the shares will find it difficult to increase in capital value. Therefore you may be sacrificing capital growth for income.

Importantly, as we discussed with earnings, it is the future direction of dividends, not their historic level, that is important. Growth of income, as well as initial income, can be an extremely important aspect of the income equation. For example, if you take the last full year dividend of Tin Can, which we will assume was 5p, and divide this by the share price of 100p, it gives a yield of 5 per cent. This compares with a market yield of 3.3 per cent, making it an attractive income stock. The yield relative to the market is therefore 5 per cent/3.3 or 152 per cent.

But bearing in mind some of the problems of Tin Can's business and its limited growth potential, the share price may well fall, wiping out the advantage of the dividend income. Moreover, it is worth noting in this case that as the earnings cover the dividend only two times (i.e. an EPS of 10p and a dividend of 5p), and earnings are forecast to be flat, there is no realistic prospect of that dividend being increased.

Another factor to be aware of with high-yield stocks is that they are paying out to shareholders a large proportion of their profits. This means that there is relatively little left to be reinvested in the business. This, in turn, may mean that the management is not maintaining the quality of the assets, which may affect its competitive position. In businesses which are relatively asset intensive and where keeping the quality of assets up to scratch is crucial for the competitive position of the company, this could be very damaging. As well as a weakening of competitive position, the lack of investment will limit potential growth. Share price weakness of Pizza Express during 2000 was attributed to a lack of investment in the core restaurant chain leading to its premises and service offering being less attractive in a competitive restaurant sector. If the restaurants need a huge investment to be refurbished to an appropriate standard, this could put pressure on the dividend.

Alternatively, the high payout ratio may reflect the fact that there are few opportunities open to management for profitable, value added investment – in this context returning funds to shareholders makes eminent sense. The issue then is to what extent the lack of profitable investment opportunities means, with the company effectively ex-growth, that the share price will show little capital growth. Remembering that 'total return' is what drives investors (i.e. income and capital growth), this can make for a very poor investment.

Dividend cover and dividend policy

Dividend cover is a measure of the affordability of a company's dividend. It is defined as the company's earnings per share divided by its dividend per share and is normally expressed as a multiple. The higher the cover, the easier it is for the company to pay the dividend and also the greater the scope for growth in that dividend.

Factors affecting security and growth of dividend include:

- level of dividend cover
- financial position – cash flow and gearing
- prospects for the business – the outlook for earnings growth
- investment needed in the business
- returns that can be generated by investment.

A higher level of dividend cover also allows for the dividend to grow in the future. The growth in the dividend will normally be determined by the performance of the company and how this translates into earnings growth. Clearly other criteria will come into play. The need for capital for investment, for example, will affect dividend policy, as will the indebtedness of the company (gearing). This highlights that the level of the dividend is effectively a capital allocation decision.

Another key issue determining the dividend decision will be the outlook for the company and the confidence the management team has in those prospects. Often a big increase in the dividend is regarded as a bullish signal by investors as it conveys a high degree of confidence by a management team in its future. Conversely, a good set of results that is accompanied by a very small dividend increase may be a cautious message from the management team as to how it sees the future.

> often a big increase in the dividend is regarded as a bullish signal

While the dividend cover is expressed as earnings/dividends, it has to be paid out of hard cash. Accordingly the cash flow profile of the business needs to be watched when assessing a company's ability to service/grow the dividend.

The stability of the company's earnings and cash flow profile is clearly important in this regard. A low level of cover may be of less concern for a utility that has predictable revenue and earnings streams than for, say, a bulk chemical company where earnings are hugely sensitive to relatively modest movements in demand and pricing (see operational gearing on p. 219).

Example – factors influencing the attractiveness of income

> To illustrate the issues involved let's consider two very different companies that might appear attractive on yield grounds. Company A is a utility with visible revenue streams. It has a dividend covered 1.5×, gearing of 65 per cent and stands on a yield relative of 160 (i.e. the yield is 60 per cent greater than the yield of the overall market). Our bulk chemical company, Company B, is in an internationally competitive

market that is both cyclical and prone to overcapacity and severe price competition. Gearing is 50 per cent, the dividend is covered 2× and the yield relative is 225.

On the face of it Company B would be more attractive on dividend grounds. The yield is much higher and gearing is lower. However, the utility would be more attractive on the grounds that the revenues and cash flows are highly visible when compared with those of the engineering company. This means its debt/equity profile and its dividend payments are far more manageable. So although the yield relative is lower, the income is far more secure.

Conversely, the level of dividend cover given the business risks facing Company B raises serious issues as to how sustainable this dividend is. A sharp fall in prices would see operating profits drop dramatically. This would see the dividend cover (and interest cover) fall to unsustainable levels and hence the very high possibility of a cut in the dividend.

Cuts in dividend

In the UK the dividend being cut was normally seen as an extreme measure – often in response to a company being in a crisis situation. However, the plight of the financial sector has seen dividends cut at most of the banks while we have also seen companies as diverse as BT, Marks and Spencer and Wolseley cut their payouts. This also serves to highlight that the size of a company is no defence when it comes to the security of the dividend. The 'credit crunch' has arguably seen a shift in attitude from investors: if the dividend cut can help pay down debt and help fund investment in the business to ensure long-term survival then the cut is, if not supported, at least clearly understood.

In the UK just seven stocks – BP, Shell, AstraZeneca, GlaxoSmithKline, Vodafone, HSBC and BAT – account for half the dividend payout of the market. Interestingly, the two oil majors being so dominant means that a lot of the dividend security arguably depends on the trend in the oil price. The pharmaceutical sector and tobacco then offer a relatively defensive source of income. The same would also be true of other areas not affected by the economy – utilities and food stocks for example.

Obviously the cut can be damaging in income terms, but also in capital terms. Having said that, the share price may have been falling for some time in anticipation of the cut and it may not fall further on the announcement. Indeed, if it means that management is now facing up to the relevant challenges the cut may signal an important turning point.

High yields and dividend cuts

When a stock is yielding (on its historic dividend) substantially above the market yield, say over 8 per cent, the market is anticipating that the dividend will be cut. As a rule of thumb yields that are more than 1.5× the risk-free rate are anticipating a dividend cut. More than 2× the risk-free rate and the share price is likely to be signalling a company in trouble with lots of risk rather than a cheap source of income. The share price is being based on what the market believes is a sustainable dividend and hence income level. The dividend is therefore likely to be cut the next time the company reports its results. If you believe the dividend is sustainable, however, and can convincingly argue that case then the shares may be cheap.

Given that the share price may well have already fallen quite sharply and be in a 'crisis' situation, it is a difficult call as to what you should do with the shares. They may be a 'buy for recovery' as the cutting of the dividend conveys to the market that the company has fully grasped the seriousness of the situation and this will presage a turnaround. Clearly in this situation a whole range of initiatives will be required (not just the dividend cut) to convince investors that there is a strong chance of the company's fortunes being restored. But if the actions enable dividend growth to be resumed in the relatively near future then staying for the recovery may make sense.

High yields and low growth

High yields can also be an indication that there is little prospect for capital growth. This may signal a mature phase in a company's development or that the company operates in a low-growth part of the economy (e.g. a utility).

If investors are expecting little capital growth they need a high income to compensate. Also, with a mature business, the management may be faced with the dilemma of whether to invest in new product or geographic areas for growth. If the management has a good record in generating high returns from its investments, investors may well be prepared to allow this. If, however, investors are wary of the returns that any investment may generate (perhaps feeling that the track record is far from encouraging or that funds are being used outside the management's area of competence), the best thing to do is to distribute funds to shareholders through higher dividends. Investors can then choose for themselves where to invest for higher returns. The past ten years or so have seen an increasing emphasis on companies remaining focused, with diversification being achieved by fund managers/investors.

Low yields and high growth

Conversely, a high-growth company will require all available resources to invest in the business. A low yield in this situation is not deemed a problem, as investors will be rewarded with capital growth. If the money invested in the business is capable of generating a much higher return than is generally available to shareholders, it is clearly beneficial for cash to be retained within the business. Again it is worth scrutinising the management's track record as well as examining the prospects for the markets within which the business is operating. Does the investment make sense? Are the anticipated returns realistic? How will competitors react?

Special dividends and buy-backs

Companies occasionally pay what is called a 'special dividend'. This is, as the name implies, a one-off dividend to shareholders. It is normally done when the company is sitting on a lot of cash for which there is no immediate requirement. The cash on the balance sheet may be the result of the company having disposed of non-core operations. The alternative to a special dividend would be to mount a share buy-back. There may be tax reasons for share buy-backs being preferred. Where there is a 'double taxation' of dividends, i.e. the company pays tax and then shareholders are also taxed on their dividends, buy-backs may be more efficient. The buy-back may also favour investors if it triggers capital gains tax rather than perhaps higher rates of income tax that a dividend might attract. Where this double taxation exists there may be a tendency to minimise dividends and keep the cash within the business. This is not a problem provided it is used effectively. With debt attracting tax relief, this may also lead a company to have a preference for debt rather than equity.

As discussed above, it may also be that the market is sceptical as to the management's ability to use the funds effectively in a strategic move such as an acquisition. It may be felt that the return on the money invested, taking into account the risks involved, would be lower than investors could generate in other companies. Accordingly the cash will be distributed to shareholders.

This payment is normally a one-off and it is important to note whether the trend in dividends includes this one-off payment. This is because it might appear that the dividend has been cut when in fact the comparative dividend includes the one-off payment.

Yields back in favour

The fall in capital values since the end of 2007 and the uncertainty attaching to future profit levels (and hence where share prices are going) have seen the importance of dividends increase dramatically. Consensus expectations of total returns (capital growth and income) have fallen back to a level of around 7 per cent. With yields in the UK of 4.5 per cent this accounts for two-thirds of the expected total return from equities. However, in an environment where companies are faced with challenging trading conditions, constrained of cash and where accessing bank or debt finance is very difficult, and cash flow is being diverted to meet other liabilities such as pension fund deficits, ensuring the security of the dividend is crucial.

> ensuring the security of the dividend is crucial

More than ever, high yields may signal a company in trouble and not an attractive source of income – especially if the company has high gearing and weak cash flows. Related to this, studies suggest that it is companies that grow the dividend that prove the better long-term investment. Therefore an attractive yield, with a secure and growing dividend backed by strong cash flow, is likely to offer a better total return.

Enterprise value (EV)

The recent debate over pension deficits, the importance of health care liabilities and the use of off-balance sheet vehicles has focused attention on the liability side of the equation in any valuation. (This has been reinforced by the IFRS accounting standards.) Establishing the total cost of buying a business is reflected in its enterprise value (EV). While this is a term often used, its calculation is often not as comprehensive or detailed as it should be.

The most useful way of thinking about EV is that it is the sum of the liabilities required to purchase 100 per cent of a company's cash flow. Its great advantage is that it takes debt and other debt-like liabilities into account with respect to valuation. This is obviously crucial in an investment context and also highlights one of the major deficiencies of using equity-based valuations such as a P/E – they do not take the company's funding structure or liabilities into account. In an environment where debt was the funding option of choice and share buy-backs and deals funded with debt were the norm, then using EV is far more sensible when comparing companies.

Many users of EV and definitions of EV simply add on debt. This is easy to compute and certainly has its advantages. It must be borne in mind, though, that there are other liabilities a company may have (pension fund liabilities in particular are topical and extremely important). These liabilities are potentially very significant. Critically, these liabilities have an impact on earnings, cash or both. A company having to invest in an underfunded pension scheme is using money that could have been invested in the business or returned to shareholders. This obviously reduces cash available to the company and its shareholders, damaging the value of the shares. Therefore if you invest in a company without being aware of these liabilities it could prove costly.

In recovery-type situations, for example, many investors assume that as the share price has fallen from 100p to 25p it is potentially very attractive. If, however, there has been a significant cash outflow or the emergence of previously unknown liabilities (off-balance sheet debt, pension fund shortfalls), the valuation on an EV basis might be identical to that before the share price decline. So a market capitalisation fall of £1 billion may be offset by debt and other liabilities rising by a similar amount.

EV is especially useful when comparing companies that may have different corporate structures, accounting or tax regimes. This is critical in an increasingly cross-border/global investment environment. It evolved as a valuation technique to enable pan-European comparisons. Many European countries have a history of cross-shareholdings and significant minority holdings. Accordingly the company will not enjoy 100 per cent of the cash flows of its related companies, investments or majority owned holdings.

The other important aspect of EV is its focus on valuing the 'core' business. Stripping away the effect of cross-shareholdings, associates and minorities enables the core business to be valued on a 'clean' basis. Critically, this allows comparisons with peer groups to be conducted on an appropriate 'like for like' basis. Were peripheral assets such as investments or related companies to be excluded, for example, it would distort comparisons of exit multiples for the core business.

Reflecting these considerations, the formula used for calculating EV is:

> Market cap + average debt + buy-out of minorities
> + provisions − peripheral assets

Average debt

The average is used to give a much fairer view of the company's indebtedness. Debt may swing markedly during the course of the year for seasonal trading reasons. In addition, a company will often make sure it manages assets, especially working capital, quite aggressively towards its year end to minimise year-end debt. Indeed, year ends may be selected to fit in with a seasonal low in debt levels.

Another important thing to bear in mind is any outstanding preference or convertible bonds; make sure these are reflected in the debt number. Companies may not include these in their definition of debt and gearing, so care is needed. These can be converted into equity if preferred. Similarly, as Chapter 5 makes clear, pension fund deficits, off-balance sheet debt and finance leases also need to be taken into account to get a comprehensive view of the company's indebtedness.

Buy-out of minorities

Where a company has, say, 80 per cent of another company, while it consolidates 100 per cent of the profit the owners of the other 20 per cent have a right to the income on their share of the investment. Therefore you would need to buy out the minority shareholders if you were to enjoy the benefit of controlling 100 per cent of the cash flows. They might or might not wish this to happen and again it can be difficult saying what this might cost. The value of the parent company can be used as an approximate guide.

Provisions

These may relate to the liability that would be assumed by a new owner in connection with making good any environmental damage the company may have caused in the course of its operations. These can be very substantial amounts and need to be considered carefully. In a takeover situation, another form of liability may be the costs of closing operations and the associated costs of redundancy payments. As an investor these provisions will see a cash expense even if there is no impact on earnings.

Peripheral assets

With the EV you are trying to value the 'core' business. Accordingly, the value of non-core assets is subtracted. These may be property assets or investments in other companies or assets. Investments in other companies are called 'related' companies. Normally a company will book its 'share' of the profits of that investment (e.g. it may 'book' 20 per cent of the profit of a company where it has a 20 per cent holding). If associates are treated as a non-core asset, care must be taken to strip out their contribution to profits and earnings. That is why ratios using EV tend to refer to 'operating' income or assets precisely to exclude the non-operating income from associates or investments. In addition, it is worth pointing out that while 20 per cent of profit may be 'booked', the income/cash flow effect is determined by the amount of dividends distributed by the related company.

Enterprise and equity valuation

The computing of all the liabilities of a company may appear complex. It is a good discipline to try to establish potential drains on the company's earnings and cash flow. You may well find it much easier to use market capitalisation plus debt as your proxy for EV. This is going to be useful as it takes into account a company's funding structure. However, being aware of other potential liabilities may help you walk away from investing in companies which are high risk because of those potential liabilities.

Having established the EV of the company and got a full sense of the company's funding and liability structure, we can now use that to perform some valuation techniques.

Importantly, it is always a good discipline to make sure you are clear whether you are doing a valuation that is for shareholders or for all providers of capital. The performance metric we choose influences whether we need to do an equity or enterprise valuation. If you are doing an equity measure you need to ensure that the performance metric 'belongs' to the shareholder. So, for example, using a share price to earnings per share is an obvious equity measure – EPS is what is left for shareholders. On the other hand, a market capitalisation to sales figure is often used. However, this is using an equity-based number (market cap) and comparing it to sales which will have been generated by all providers of capital – the *enterprise* value as opposed to the *equity* value. A company with a lot of debt and a low market cap (think about General Motors) may have a superficially attractive market cap to sales ratio but the EV to sales ratio – that takes into account the debt and in GM's case its other extensive liabilities – is far more comprehensive and will reveal a very different picture.

As Figure 8.1 makes clear, it is very straightforward to establish which are equity or enterprise value performance numbers – anything above the interest line (i.e. before debt charges have been serviced) has been generated by all providers of capital, so we use EV. Anything below the interest line (and after tax) belongs to shareholders.

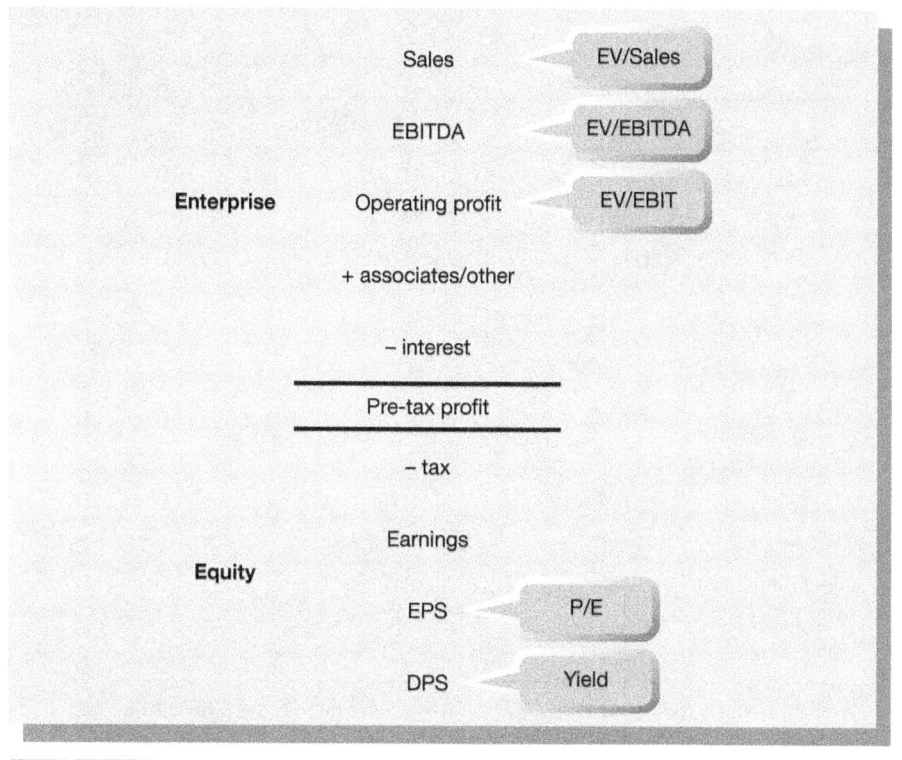

Enterprise
- Sales → EV/Sales
- EBITDA → EV/EBITDA
- Operating profit → EV/EBIT
- + associates/other
- − interest
- Pre-tax profit
- − tax
- Earnings

Equity
- EPS → P/E
- DPS → Yield

Figure 8.1 Establishing equity or enterprise value performance numbers

EV/EBITDA

The EBITDA can be worked out by taking the operating profit (from the profit and loss account) and adding back the non-cash costs of the business, depreciation and amortisation (see the advantages and disadvantages of EBITDA, p. 279).

EBITDA on its own is of limited use because it tells you only what the cash stream is, not what you are paying for it. Therefore analysts compare the EBITDA to the EV, which is the total cost of the company (market capitalisation plus all its liabilities). As the EBITDA is generated by all the assets at the company's disposal, you need to take the whole funding structure into account to value it.

Example – EBITDA calculation and multiples

In the case of Tin Can we are assuming it has debt of £30 million and environmental liability to clean up some contaminated land which is expected to cost £10 million.

	Year 1
Pre-tax profit	£20m
Interest	£2.5m
Forecast operating profit	£22.5m
Depreciation	£20m
Amortisation	£2m
EBITDA calculation (in millions)	22.5 + 20 + 2
EBITDA	£44.5m
Market capitalisation	£138m
(138m shares × 100p)	
Liabilities:	
Debt	£30m
Environmental liabilities	£10m
EV calculation (in millions)	138 + 30 + 10
EV	£178m

The next step is to divide the EV by the EBITDA (similar to a P/E, this gives a measure of how many years it would take to generate the cash to pay the full value of the company). This is normally expressed, again like a P/E, as a multiple. The average EV/EBITDA for companies in the stock market is normally between 8× and 10×. The lower it is, the cheaper the share is looking, although bear in mind earlier warnings about the quality of the company. In addition, all the issues surrounding the quality of earnings apply with equal force to EBITDA. Of course, again one must remember that it may be worth paying for an 'expensive' share if the company has both steady income and good growth prospects.

So for Tin Can the EV/EBITDA calculation is:

178/44.5, which gives a multiple of 4×.

As we would expect, this makes the share look very cheap. However, we have noted all the risks attaching to the forecasts and the quality of earnings. Therefore, as with P/Es, EV/EBITDA depends on the growth and quality of the number. In addition, it also depends on the capital intensity of the business – the more capital you need in the business, the lower the multiple. Obviously, it is more attractive to have growth that does not require a lot of capital investment.

The other danger with using this valuation, as we discussed when looking at it as a performance number, is the fact that it does not take into account the need for capital expenditure. Depreciation is a real cost of doing business and maintaining the fabric of the business is crucial. This is why the operating free cash flow measure is preferred as it explicitly takes into account the need for capital to generate the company's sales performance and growth. (It also takes into account the taxation impact on returns.)

As with P/Es, the issue of growth and the impact on returns needs to be considered. Many of the companies that promoted the use of EBITDA and focused on its growth have been consistent destroyers of shareholder value. The deals or investment undertaken, while having delivered growth in EBITDA, have failed to cover their cost of capital.

The *advantages* of EBITDA are that:

- it takes the whole funding into account (unlike P/Es)
- it allows comparisons between companies with different accounting policies towards depreciation and amortisation
- it ignores exceptional charges, again allowing comparison
- it is a cash flow-based measure
- it can be used for growth companies incurring start-up losses.

The *disadvantages* of EBITDA as a valuation number are as follows:

- it may be used when all other measures are disappointing
- depreciation is a very real cost of doing business
- the need for maintenance capex within a business and the need to fund working capital suggest that it is not a true measure of cash flow
- ratio will vary with differing capital intensity
- it measures neither cash nor profitability
- earnings can still be manipulated
- we could miss the crucial story of what is happening further down the P&L.
- investment can grow EBITDA (EBIT, depreciation and amortisation), but you need to find the rate of return on that investment compared with the cost of capital
- you need to find out what is happening to interest costs
- and the impact on gearing and risk

- it is used in capital-intensive, high-growth industries where no profits and/or EPS are generated but you need to consider overinvestment and low returns
- variations in tax charges may mean a different outcome for shareholders.

EV/operating free cash flow

Recognising the concern over EBITDA, given that depreciation is a real cost of doing business and crucial for maintaining the competitive advantage of the business, we can also use another cash flow-based measure by using EV/free cash flow as a multiple. Here we are using the free cash flow as defined in Chapter 7 (see p. 230). However, we are using the figure in one particular year rather than forecasting out for 30 or so years. Therefore if you are confident that the cash flows are of high quality – which is reasonably easy to predict – then this will provide you with a very worthwhile valuation metric offsetting as it does the disadvantages of EBITDA and DCFs. Allowing for the fact that maintenance capex is crucial to maintain the competitiveness of the business, this is especially appropriate.

Care has to be taken to decide whether the total or maintenance capex figures are being used. If using the total figure we need to consider whether this expenditure will add value and what cash it will generate in addition to the existing cash flow from assets currently employed. A company with a record of adding value but investing aggressively may be disadvantaged compared to one with no growth opportunities.

We also need to be wary as EV is made up of market capitalisation and debt and other liabilities. Have we allowed for all the other liabilities in the calculation? In addition, the risks are obviously a lot higher if most of the EV is made up of debt (think about GM in this context where the market cap was very small in relation to the massive debt and liabilities).

Because we are using operating profit and that is subject to taxation (NOPAT) the 'free cash' flow may not be representative – if there is a lot of debt then the cash flow will be servicing that debt and certainly not 'free' for ordinary shareholders and possibly not available for reinvestment. (We could alternatively use the cash flows from the R&A which deducts interest payments and calculate free cash flow per share.)

Nonetheless, this is a very useful valuation technique. A useful way of thinking about it is that if the EV/free cash flow is say 10× – then, without any growth, in ten years' time the company will have earned the free cash to redeem all its liabilities. As an investor you are thereafter on a 'free ride'. Another way of thinking about it is that free cash flow can fund the business's growth and/or dividends to shareholders. And here we need to be very confident that management will use the cash to good effect.

> we need to be very confident that management will use the cash to good effect

Free cash flow yield: operating free cash flow/EV

Many investors will perform screens on the inverse of the EV/operating free cash flow number. This is known as the *free cash flow yield*. Here an EV/OPFCF of 10 therefore becomes a free cash flow yield of 10 per cent. Similarly an EV/OPFCF of 8× is equivalent to a free cash flow yield of 12.5 per cent. This suggests an EV/OPFCF ratio of less than 10× is potentially attractive on a cash flow yield basis subject to the debt weighting in the EV and the growth profile of the cash.

We then compare this with the returns on other competing investments – say a government or corporate bond. If we are getting more than the yields there and have potential for growth in that cash flow then it is potentially very attractive. (Many private equity players would think this way as if they could borrow the money post-tax at 5 per cent and get 10 per cent post-tax from buying a business then it would represent a good investment.)

Similarly, if we can calculate the WACC we can see what the free cash flow yield is compared to the cost of capital which allows for the risks of the investment.

The key issue then is how the cash flow is used to the benefit of shareholders.

EV/sales

Another way to measure the value of shares is to consider the sales of a company compared with its enterprise value. This measures how cheap or expensive it is to buy the company's sales – so are we paying £1 for 50p of sales (an EV/sales ratio of 2× or 200 per cent), or are we paying 50p for a £1 of sales (an EV/sales ratio of 50 per cent or 0.5×)?

The sales figure can be found in the P&L. The EV is calculated by adding the market capitalisation of the company to the debts and liabilities as outlined above. Some commentators use market capitalisation to sales ratios as a valuation technique. EV/sales is more comprehensive and takes into account the fact that sales are generated by the whole capital structure, not just equity (which drives the market capitalisation).

So assuming sales are £60 million and the EV is £120 million, the calculation is 120/60 which gives EV/sales equalling 2× or 200 per cent. This effectively means that you are paying £2 for each £1 of the company's sales.

EV/sales should not be used when comparing companies with very different profit margins. The EV/sales ratio will be much higher for companies that have a high profit margin – these sales are inevitably more valuable as each pound of sales makes more money. In theory, higher capital intensity should lead to higher margins (see returns, p. 285).

These higher margins are often found in companies that employ a lot of capital, for example a cement works or complex manufacturing process where the plant is expensive. Of course, these higher operating margins are required to ensure that an appropriate return on capital is generated. Conversely, where relatively little capital is needed, e.g. in a distribution business, margins will tend to be lower and the EV/sales will therefore also be lower. Comparing the EV/sales of two diverse activities, with differing capital intensity, would tell you little of value.

The valuation of sales is critically dependent on the profitability of those sales. As we discussed when looking at sales as a performance number, a company that goes for market share might drive down the profitability (operating margins) of those sales dramatically. These low-margin sales are clearly worth less than very profitable sales.

The EV/sales ratio therefore is related to:

- the operating margins the company generates
- the confidence in those margins being sustained
- the growth rate of the company's sales
- the quality or visibility of those sales.

> As a rule of thumb, a company with operation margins of around 10 per cent, generating sales growth of around 5 per cent, would trade on around 100 per cent or 1× sales.

With respect to our manufacturing company, Tin Can, there are a number of threats to prices and therefore the confidence in margins is correspondingly low. Accordingly one might expect to see a lower EV/sales ratio, perhaps in the range of 70–80 per cent of sales.

We have seen that a 5 per cent reduction in prices, an all-too-feasible possibility, would halve operating margins and see margins fall to 5 per cent. This would suggest that the EV/sales ratio would fall to 40–50 per cent or 0.4–0.5×. Interestingly, looking at the EV/sales ratio for Corus (previously British Steel), by getting its market capitalisation data, debt and sales figure from its R&A, this revealed a value of around 0.3×. This suggests the market has a cautious assessment of its sales growth and likely margins.

Conversely, the high margin, predictable sales and potential from the research pipeline at Pink Tablet suggest that it should command a very high EV/sales ratio. The margins at 25 per cent would immediately imply a ratio of 250 per cent. The high sales growth would expand the premium significantly while the R&D potential would also need to be taken into account. (This research will generate sales in the future.) In our example the ratio emerges at 4.5× sales. This compares with an EV/sales ratio for the sector of around 3.5× at the time of writing.

The risk in this case is if a major drug comes off patent and is subject to generic competition. This would see margins for this product fall dramatically. Clearly, while average margins for a drug company are high this will inevitably conceal a wide variation, with ex-patent parts of the portfolio generating low margins and best-selling, well-protected products very high margins. So the drug going off patent is likely to be achieving margins much higher than the average.

The sharp contrast between Pink Tablets and Tin Can's margins and corresponding sales valuations is important. You can also get a sense of an industry's margins by looking at the EV/sales ratio. If it is low you will have a reasonable expectation of margins and sales growth being low or uncertain to predict.

The food retailing sector has a ratio of around 0.5× and margins for the individual companies do indeed tend to be in the region of 4–6 per cent. These companies have relatively little capital employed as the working capital tends to be financed by suppliers. As a result this low ratio is not a problem as the companies generate very good returns on invested capital. Automobiles and parts are trading around 0.4×. Margins due to competitive pressures and the purchasing power of the big car manufacturers also tend to be very low. Unfortunately, unlike the food retailers, these companies tend to employ significant amounts of capital. As a result returns on invested capital tend to be low and not cover their cost of capital. This is why care is needed when comparing EV/sales ratios across sectors – capital intensity and the type of capital needed may vary enormously.

care is needed when comparing EV/sales ratios across sectors

Historically it has been felt that sales were one of the few numbers not subject to widespread accounting manipulation. As a number tends to become popular as a valuation measure, however, there is an incentive to manipulate that number. This tends to boost profits as there is a 'mismatch' – the costs related to those sales are invariably not recognised until they are incurred at a much later date.

Therefore, when looking at the EV/sales ratio, things to bear in mind include:

- do not compare ratios of industries with different capital intensity
- be careful of sales manipulation, especially in long-term contract-type businesses
- ratio will be driven by margins and sales growth
- falling prices will dramatically reduce margins.

Returning to Tin Can and Pink Tablet we can see how the interplay of a company's prospects, operating returns and financial position impact on the valuation of its sales. We also consider some of the risks to those prospects and returns and the dangers to the valuation of the shares.

Financial position

Gearing at 60 per cent (Table 8.1) is moderate to high, but not necessarily a major problem if the performance remains at current levels (a big if). The cash generation and the need for capital within the business do need to be watched closely, however.

Similarly a 5× interest cover is reasonable, though subject to the same caveats (see below).

Returns

Operating margins at 10 per cent are reasonable. However, bear in mind that if a contract is lost, raw material costs rise or prices fall (all distinctly possible given the nature of the industry/business), so these operating margins are very vulnerable.

Return on invested capital at 12.5 per cent before tax translates to 8.75 per cent after tax and is unlikely to be covering the cost of the capital (which in this instance would be around 10 per cent). Even before bearing in mind the risks shareholders are running, the return is not attractive.

Table 8.1 Tin Can – financial position and returns

Debt	£60m
Shareholders' funds	£100m
Gearing calculation	
Debt/shareholder's funds	60/100
Gearing	60%
Total sales	£250m
Operating profit	£25m
Depreciation and amortisation	£20m
EBITDA	£45m
Operating profit margin	10%
Invested capital	£200m
Return on invested capital calculation	25/200
Return on invested capital	12.5%
Interest cover (operating profit/interest)	25/5
	5×
Share price	100p
Market capitalisation	£138m (100p × 138m)
Enterprise value	£198m
Enterprise value/sales ratio	0.8× or 80%
Enterprise value/EBITDA	4.4×

How would you value these sales? Remember that both the sales and the return on those sales are difficult to predict, and that the sales are static (no growth in the medium or long term).

The stock market is giving a low valuation of the sales of Tin Can – each £ of sales is being valued at 80p. The (relatively) low margins, static/declining sales outlook and the vulnerability of those margins all suggest that the market is right to do this.

Risks to returns – key sensitivities

- Any fall in margins would of course reduce operating profit and the return on invested capital. In the example of the lost contract (see the example on p. 263), this falls to 10 per cent.
- Falling prices would be even more devastating. A 5 per cent drop in prices would take 50 per cent off profits (5 per cent of the company's turnover of £250 million is £12.5 million). This is called operational gearing – price reductions come straight off the bottom line.
- The pre-tax return on invested capital also halves to 6.25 per cent.

Why is this important?

- Covering cost of capital – is it worth the risk? A 5 per cent reduction in prices (very feasible given the nature of the industry and competitive structure) automatically means that the company is destroying more value. The fact that it is failing to cover the cost of capital means that investors would be better off with their money in the bank (which would be risk free).
- The interest cover would also fall to 4× in the lost contract scenario. This is not too problematic, but getting scary.
- However, on a 5 per cent price reduction, interest cover falls to 2.5×. This is potentially a very serious state, with banking covenants possibly being breached.

Conclusion

This example neatly demonstrates the interplay between performance and prospects on the one hand and the financial position of a company on the other. Deterioration in the trading environment, weaker volumes and/or prices could cause a serious decline in performance. This in turn would lead to question marks being raised over the company's financial position.

Pink Tablet's financial position

With gearing of 12.5 per cent the Pink Tablet balance sheet is very strong (see Table 8.2). The excellent interest cover of 21× reinforces this. Therefore there is little financial risk in Pink Tablet.

Table 8.2 Pink Tablet – financial position and returns

Debt	£50m
Shareholders' funds	£400m
Gearing calculation	
Debt/shareholders' funds	50/400
Gearing	12.5%
Total sales	£420m
Operating profit	£105m
Depreciation and amortisation	£21m
EBITDA	£126m
Operating profit margin	25%
Invested capital	£450m
Return on invested capital calculation – Operating profit/Invested capital	105/450
Return on invested capital	23.3%
Interest cover (operating profit/interest)	105/5
	21×
Share price	875p
Market capitalisation	£2415m (875p × 276m)
Enterprise value	£2465m
Sales	£425m
Enterprise value/sales ratio	5.82 or 580%
Enterprise value/EBITDA	19.6×

Returns

The operating margins at 25 per cent are at a very attractive level. The success of new drugs should help sustain or possibly increase these margins.

The pre-tax return on invested capital of 23.3 per cent translates to a post-tax return of just over 16 per cent, which is well above the cost of capital and rewards shareholders amply for the risks involved.

How would you value these sales?

- Remember not only the high returns but also the fact that these sales are growing rapidly driven by the new drugs coming through the sales pipeline.
- The stock market is putting a high value on these sales – each £ of sales is being valued at £5.80. The high margins *and* the rapid growth in sales are being factored into this valuation.
- The EV/sales is also, in effect, putting a value on the pipeline of sales. If you assume that a certain portion of the drug pipeline converts into future sales and the value of these is discounted back, the ratio would be lower.
- These high margins translate into a very high post-tax return on capital employed of 16 per cent. This is well above the cost of capital.
- The risks would revolve around patent expiry, a withdrawal of a drug due to adverse side effects, government pricing pressure and a rival developing a more effective drug. While important, these are less likely to affect the company in the short term than the issues affecting Tin Can.

Risks to returns are as follows:

- If a drug with £200 million of sales goes off patent (or is affected by a new, more effective competitor drug), operating margins on that product may fall from, say, 30 per cent to 10 per cent. This would take £40 million off profits – or 40 per cent off Year 1 forecasts. The share price would fall 40 per cent if the P/E was to remain constant.
- However, the stock market may also question the basis for that high P/E, i.e. that the previous earnings growth is no longer attainable and therefore the P/E falls from, say, 35× to 25×. In this latter scenario the share price falls to 380p from 875p – a fall of 57 per cent (25× (25.4p × 60 per cent) = 25 × 15.2p).
- Clearly this is an unrealistic example, as these issues are unlikely to happen so suddenly. Nonetheless, they highlight the potential downside and valuation risks for high-multiple/high-return growth stocks that lose that tag.

Conclusion

The returns and growth potential of Pink Tablet are clearly very attractive. In addition the financial position is robust. The difficulty is trying to work out when these strengths are fully discounted in the share price.

Price to book

Finally, another way to measure the value of a company is to see how the share price relates to the book value of the company's assets. As a result it is often known as the price/book ratio. This is very popular among value investors and they will often screen for companies on a discount to book value.

Measuring value on an asset basis is particularly useful for property companies and financial organisations such as insurance companies and banks. Investment trusts are also valued this way. These companies are measured according to their net asset value, also sometimes known as shareholders' funds. This is simply the value of the company's assets. So in the case of a property company it would consist largely of the collection of properties in which it has invested (minus any debt). For an insurance company the assets are largely the group's investment portfolio, those things in which the company is putting its income and from which, in the future, it expects to pay any claims. Of course this is after liabilities have been deducted.

Increasingly, with many companies having few assets (e.g. service-related companies) or intangible assets or goodwill that has been written off, price to book-type considerations are irrelevant for many sectors or companies.

Net asset value (NAV) can be expressed either as an overall figure or, if it is divided by the number of shares in issue, referred to as NAV per share. One key thing to remember with NAV is that companies often trade below their asset value. For example, a property company with net assets of £100 million may trade at a market capitalisation (price of shares multiplied by the number of shares in issue) of £80 million. This would be expressed as trading at a 20 per cent discount to assets. There may be good reasons for this.

Shares may be on a discount due to the following factors:

- the assets may not easily be sold (illiquid)
- the assets may be difficult to value
- the assets may be overvalued

- there may be concerns that the assets are falling in value
- they are generating a very poor rate of return, with little prospect of that changing
- selling the asset would create a tax liability.

Banks are often valued on a price to book basis. In the current situation the concern with 'toxic assets' makes valuing banks extremely difficult on an asset basis (or indeed any other). There is great uncertainty over the loans to certain groups of borrowers and/or against certain assets such as housing and commercial property which in some areas are still falling in value. Investments in asset-backed securities or derivatives on these assets are very complex and liquidity can be very low for some of these investments. Another factor complicating the situation is if they have off-balance sheet exposures to these areas. In addition, assets may be vulnerable where there are loans to heavily indebted companies or companies operating in sectors where asset prices are falling. If insolvency rates continue to increase, which is certainly possible, then further asset write-downs are inevitable. So given all those uncertainties the price to book is arguably very academic.

given the uncertainty over asset values, the price to book is arguably very academic

In other circumstances shares on a discount to asset value may indeed be attractive. The question to ask is what will trigger the shares moving back towards their asset value. This may be a realisation that the assets are correctly valued, are generating good returns and are likely to grow in value. Often cyclical stocks may be looked at in relation to their asset value at the bottom of the cycle as there are no earnings to use.

Of course it is possible for companies to trade above their asset value, known as at a premium to assets. This could be because investors are expecting an improved valuation of the assets shortly or the assets are generating excellent returns.

Another factor, which can cause a reassessment of asset values, is takeover speculation. The assets may be valued low by the stock market but might be worth a lot more to a competitor or another industrial company. Buying a share because you believe the company may be taken over is a high-risk strategy. For one thing it may not happen; more commonly you may have to wait a lot longer than you think and you would have been better off invested elsewhere.

Sum of the parts

A variation of looking at NAV is to do a 'sum of the parts' calculation. For a company with very different businesses with a wide variation in growth, risk and quality characteristics, it may be more appropriate to value each of the businesses separately, commonly by reference to similar companies quoted on the stock market. This is often done if one of the businesses is a 'jewel in the crown' and the overall valuation fails to take into account the quality of this division. It may be that there is pressure for the value to be unlocked by demerging the quality business, which would create value for shareholders.

Summary

As the valuation section shows, there are strengths and weaknesses with all commonly used valuation measures. Alas there is no holy grail, no one ratio that compellingly provides all you need to know. It is critical to use a combination of valuation measures when assessing a share to get a comprehensive view of the factors influencing valuation.

While P/Es are often a very useful valuation technique and widely used, they suffer from the weaknesses of not taking debt into account and not reflecting the returns the business generates. They can also suffer because of accounting practices or management decisions that may be taken to boost the earnings number. Shares on a low P/E may be cheap or the 'low' valuation may simply reflect the fact that it is a company facing significant risks (business and/or financial), generating low returns and with low-quality earnings.

The advantage of using the triumvirate of 'growth, risk and quality', combined with the returns being generated, is that it creates an effective way of seeing the bigger picture and taking into account all the forces impacting on valuation. It helps to differentiate winners and losers. This will help avoid looking at earnings growth in isolation and therefore seeing value destroyed by management as everyone applauds the 'ability' to grow earnings. Again it is important to consider earnings quality as well as quantity. Vitally, it also ensures you examine the risk profile of the company to ensure it is a degree of risk you are prepared to take on – after all, there is nothing wrong with risk provided you get a return to reward you for taking it.

Enterprise value compensates for the weaknesses in P/Es by taking debt and other liabilities into account to establish how much is required to secure 100 per cent of a company's' cash flow (the key driver of value).

This ensures you have a comprehensive view of the company's assets and liabilities and you can see the financial profile of the business in terms of how much of the funding is debt (including pension fund deficits and off-balance sheet liabilities) and how much is equity.

In an environment where returns on cash are so derisory, attention will focus on how extra income can be generated effectively and securely through investing in shares. Dividend yield is an increasingly crucial part of total shareholder return (capital growth plus income) – especially if the market makes little headway in overall terms. A high yield may be very attractive or alternatively a sign that the market expects the dividend to be cut. The evidence suggests that it is not just finding high yields that matters, but finding those companies with strong yields who are in a position to grow the dividend. A good and growing yield is a strong predictor of long-term share price performance, so examining the outlook for dividend growth is very important.

The other key factor is to consider which performance metrics have the most predictive power in terms of subsequent long-term share price performance. The emphasis here is on measures that capture the returns the company generates and the consistency of those returns. High returns on capital are a sign of a company with a strong competitive position and a management team using your money to good effect. To the extent that the return on capital exceeds the cost of capital then shareholder value is being created – that is, investors are being compensated for the risks involved. Looking at value creation can help eliminate potential disasters (where value is consistently destroyed) or investments that are unsuitable because they do not meet your appetite for risk. High and consistent returns on capital are an excellent predictor of future share price growth.

As we have seen, cash is the ultimate driver of value. Many investors will use 'cash flow return on capital' as their preferred measure for company performance and therefore use this to value the business. Cash generation is a much more comprehensive and effective measure of the company's performance and future potential. Cash, after all, services debt and allows for investing in the business to maintain competitiveness and growth, as well as funding the dividend. In the current environment it also reduces dependence on external funding or makes that funding much easier to obtain.

Taken together, all these techniques will allow you to take a much better-informed view of the company's ability to make money for you.

RELATIVE VALUATION CHECKLIST

Price earnings ratios

The advantages of using the P/E are that:

- it is easy to compute
- it is conventionally and widely used
- it takes forecasts into account
- earnings is a measure of what is generated for shareholders.

Some problems with the P/E ratio:

- it does not take debt/financial structure into account
- earnings are particularly prone to manipulation
- it does not take cash generation into account
- it does not take investment returns into account.

Income

A high yield may well be a very attractive component of total shareholder return. However, growth of dividend may be as important as the initial yield.

Dividends

- What are the economic characteristics of the business? Does it operate in a defensive sector?
- How certain are volumes and prices? Price falls will see profits fall dramatically and hence dividend cover and, in turn, the dividend.
- What is the financial profile of the company in terms of debt (gearing) and cash flow? Does the cash need to service interest costs and debt repayments?
- What is the cash conversion ratio – i.e. do earnings correspond with cash?
- How many times is the dividend covered?
- If EPS is manipulated through flexible accounting policies, the cover will be distorted – it will not be a true measure of ability to pay.
- Cash, not earnings, pays the dividend.
- Is the company under-spending on maintaining the fabric of the business (capex) to sustain a dividend?
- Has there been an erosion of competitive position due to under-spending?
- If the money is needed in the business, what return would it generate?
- If the dividend is uncovered, the dividend is effectively being paid out of reserves, thus reducing shareholder assets – are you any better off?
- What are the prospects for dividend growth?

Enterprise Value (EV)

EV is a far more comprehensive valuation technique as it takes all the company's assets and liabilities into account – the equity valuation (market capitalisation) plus debt, pension fund deficits, provisions, etc.

The EV/sales ratio sees how much each pound of sales is valued ... which is influenced by:

- the operating margins the company generates
- the confidence in those margins being sustained
- the growth rate of the company's sales.

EV/EBITDA is a widely used valuation measure using EBITDA as a proxy for cash flow.

The advantages of EBITDA are:

- It takes the whole funding into account (unlike P/Es).
- It allows comparisons between companies with different accounting policies towards depreciation and amortisation.
- It ignores exceptional charges, again allowing comparison.
- It is a cash flow-based measure.
- It can be used for growth companies incurring start-up losses.

The disadvantages of EBITDA as a valuation number are:

- Is it being used because all other measures are disappointing?
- Depreciation is a very real cost of doing business.
- The need for maintenance capex within a business and the need to fund working capital suggest that EBITDA is not a true measure of cash flow.
- The ratio will vary with differing capital intensity.
- What does it measure, neither cash nor profitability?

EV/cash flow

Given the limitations of EBITDA, looking at free cash flow is a more useful and comprehensive measure.

- Enterprise value to operating free cash flow is a very useful valuation technique.
- Inverting this ratio to look at operating free cash flow divided by the enterprise value gives us a free cash flow yield.

9

The investment decision – buy or sell?

What topics are covered in this chapter?

- Why fundamentals are important ... but not the whole story
- The decision process
- Step 1 Putting together prospects and valuation
- Step 2 Ascertaining the investment style
- Step 3 Looking at the risk/reward profile
- Step 4 Considering timescale – trading v investment
- Weighing up your decision
- Key issues in the current market
- Summary
- Checklist

Why fundamentals are important ... but not the whole story

One of the interesting aspects about valuation is that it may not bear any relation to the share price. The share price will be affected by a whole host of short-term factors and influences. This is often referred to as 'the sentiment' affecting a share as distinct from the 'fundamentals' driving it. And clearly the sentiment can persist for a long time. Benjamin Graham, mentor to Warren Buffett, summarised this very effectively by commenting: 'In the short run the market is a voting machine and in the long run it is a weighing machine.'[1]

This is a useful investment discipline when taking a decision – are you 'voting' about a short-term issue and taking a view on how long the sentiment is going to prevail or have you done a careful analysis to 'weigh' up the qualities and prospects of a business and what you are prepared to pay for them? Of course what you are 'weighing' from a fundamental perspective is the competitiveness of the company's position and how that translates into returns on capital and cash flow.

Sentiment on the other hand can be influenced by the twin axes of 'fear and greed' and the psychology of the crowd. Of course the discipline here is to be brave enough to buy when fear is at its height and sell when greed is the dominant currency. This is easier said than done. But if everyone is openly talking about how wonderful something is the share price is already going to reflect this – making it very hard to make money. You are then riding the sentiment wave. There is nothing wrong with this necessarily, provided you know how to get off in time. Importantly, at a time of greed such as the dot-com boom very little attention is paid to traditional valuation techniques and the virtues of cash flow.

Sentiment may also be driven by the news flow from the company or the sector it operates in. Another aspect that often drives sentiment is how the management team is perceived – the current focus on corporate governance can really influence the performance of the shares. Here, however, we need to be careful as governance issues can be a really fundamental driver of the company's performance.

Share prices, driven by the future outlook, are always looking ahead. Typically, as we have seen, they will be anticipating or 'discounting' what might happen in the next 18 months to two years. Therefore share prices contain a mix of the market's hopes and fears for the next two years and the balance of sentiment and how that influences buyers and sellers. If a company announces record profits for the year just gone but is cautious about the next 12 months, the share price will fall. What can often happen is that the company's current trading is absolutely fine and 'in line with expectations'. The share price, however, is falling and creating a very

---

[1] Graham, B. (2003) *The Intelligent Investor*, London: Harper Business Essentials.

low valuation. This reflects the fact that the market is looking beyond the next 12 months.

In 2007, for example, housebuilding and banking shares were on very low valuations including a low P/E. Trading was still very good, leading managements to think that the shares were cheap. However, the key here is that the shares were anticipating a sharp slowdown in the economy, and especially the housing market, and reflecting the high risks in the sector, especially for those with a lot of debt. The banks had seen loan books for long-term assets increase dramatically, funded by short-term wholesale money market deposits. Often the lending criteria and multiples of income were not as disciplined as was historically the case. House prices were at unprecedented levels and affordability correspondingly really stretched. Banks were also lending aggressively to many segments of the population who may have had no history of servicing their debts and paying off the loan. This seems to have been one of the many perverse aspects of incentives as they were purely based on volumes and not on the underlying risk or long-term profitability of the loan. This clearly highlights a critical failure of management.

On this occasion therefore share prices were accurately anticipating the looming problems – valuations were not cheap, they merely reflected that these sectors were either ex-growth and/or at the top of an incredible boom. In addition, the risks of so much debt in the system and poor management decision making also conspired to suggest that the companies were heading for a very difficult time.

When taking a decision then to buy a share that is lowly valued you are in effect saying that the market is wrong – it is being too pessimistic about the prospects and pricing in too much risk. This is perfectly possible – as is the possibility that collectively the market has reached a sensible conclusion as it did with banking and housebuilding shares. It is vital therefore to respect the views of the market – though you do not have to agree with them. However, having clarity and precision about which elements of the Valuation Villa you are confident about and why the market is wrong will introduce rigour to the stock selection process.

A key discipline therefore is to ask yourself why you are right and the person selling to you (who may well know a lot more than you do) is wrong. George Soros says he is fundamentally extremely critical of his own decisions and tries to identify where he might be wrong. This avoids what in behavioural finance is called 'confirmation bias' – where we only see the evidence that supports our view and ignore any evidence that challenges our thesis. Soros is looking for evidence to prove himself wrong and if he finds it he will reverse his position immediately.

Not getting caught up in the sentiment of the market is a natural strength of Warren Buffett, who really does live his commitment to investing in companies with sustainable competitive advantage. He missed out on the early phases of the dot-com boom but was ultimately proved to be absolutely right to be wary of these stocks. Indeed, one might argue that living in the American Mid-West gives him a very useful distance from the cosy 'consensus' thinking that can develop on Wall Street or the centre of any financial market. That distance and perspective combined with a very fundamental approach to companies appears very useful to the most successful investor in the world.

The decision process

When you have assessed the prospects for your target company and its sector and valued your company in two or three different ways you must decide whether to buy, sell or hold the shares. All the information gleaned must be pulled together. Having decided whether the share is good or poor value you need to reassess the risks and rewards. Then, in the case of buying a share, it is necessary to think about how long you plan to hold it. Finally there is the problem of deciding at which exact point to buy or sell the shares.

Reflecting these issues there are four key steps:

1 pulling together prospects and valuation
2 ascertaining the investment style
3 looking at the risk/reward profile
4 considering timescale – trading v investment.

This framework will help you reach your conclusion – whether you should buy or sell.

Step 1 Putting together prospects and valuation

Deciding whether to buy or sell a share rests on the interplay of the company's prospects and how those prospects are valued (or rated). The prospects for the company may be excellent, but you may not make any money if the shares are very expensive (whether that be on a multiple of sales, earnings or other valuation basis). This is sometimes referred to as the excellent prospects already being 'in the price'. Another phrase that means the same thing is that we may say the prospects are 'fully valued' or 'discounted'. In effect we like the company but we do not like the valuation. Similarly, a company that faces a difficult future may be priced very cheaply and all the difficulties correctly incorporated in the share price.

you may not make any money if the shares are very expensive

When a company's prospects deteriorate the share price will fall in line with the less rosy prospects – the valuation may remain the same as the share price falls in line with the lower earnings. However, the valuation (rating) may also fall as the market becomes concerned about the risks involved and less confident about the outlook. This is referred to as the stock being 'de-rated'. Conversely, if the prospects improve and the market becomes more confident about the outlook, the shares may be re-rated (the valuation improves).

Do your homework, have respect for the market and remember:

Prospects + valuation = recommendation.

Given the importance of the investment decision, it is well worth getting to grips with the issues highlighted, especially the prospects for the company and the sector in which it operates, the valuation of the company and the risk/reward ratio. This will help produce a much better-informed decision.

When looking at the valuation it is important to remember that it contains the collective wisdom of the entire market – the balance of views of all buyers and sellers. This is not to say that the market has valued the share correctly. There is an academic theory called the efficient market hypothesis which suggests that shares are, on the whole, valued correctly and it is very difficult through active management to beat the market. However, the stock market bubble of the late 1990s, which burst so dramatically, cast strong doubt on the notion of market rationality and further nails in the coffin have been driven in by the bubble of the boom years 2004–07 fuelled by debt and the subsequent collapse.

More attention now focuses on behavioural factors that determine share prices. This is summed up by the twin emotional factors of fear and greed that are always invoked to explain market movements. In particular the behaviour of crowds – and the collective wisdom or otherwise of crowds – has been a key area to consider. Here it seems that investors tend to follow other investors with risk being defined as being left behind, rather than assessing the risks of the business and its financial structure. In the financial sector it was arguably true of management too: they could not risk getting left behind as their peers made massive gains in areas such as securitisation (even if they had relatively little expertise in such areas).

Nevertheless, it is always worth asking and respecting what the market's valuation is. Why it is attributing such a low (or high) valuation to a share? If, following your assessment, you believe the shares are cheap (expensive), ask yourself why you are right and the market is wrong. In effect, why do you know more than the market? This again underlines the need to do your homework and, using the essential building blocks of the Valuation Villa, be clear on why you have arrived at your conclusion.

What's in the price? What is the valuation saying?

As discussed earlier, the market's valuation of a company may be telling you that a downgrade may be imminent, that the financial position is poor and deteriorating, that returns are low and will remain low, or that management will continue to fail to add value (either due to its inability to do so or the economic constraints of the sector).

The share price is, in effect, conveying the market's view of the key valuation drivers of the Valuation Villa – look back at Figure 1.1.

Therefore the share price is conveying important information on each of these aspects of the company's situation. A low valuation may be telling us that one or all of these factors is problematic. It is worth exploring therefore what you think of the market's view of these issues before you arrive at your conclusion. You can then take a view as to whether you think the market is being too negative (or positive). It also helps you identify what might need to change and how likely that change is before the market reconsiders its valuation.

You can of course weight these components to suit your own risk/reward preferences. In the current market environment you may want to give greater weighting to a company's financial position and the returns it is generating. Given the difficulty in reading the outlook and the related uncertainty over profits and earnings forecasts, you may wish to downplay this element (though it will always remain an important part of the equation).

There can of course be a wide variety of recommendations on the same company. The matrix of valuation drivers can be useful here. It is always worth road testing your conclusion by seeing what those with a contrary view are saying. If available, it can be worthwhile exploring where the disagreement lies:

- Is it on the prospects for the company or the valuation?
- Is it the assessment of the management and strategy?

Step 2 Ascertaining the investment style

As well as considering the prospects and valuation, it is worth knowing what 'type' of share it is. This will help you form a view of what drives the shares and how the stock market perceives the shares. To a certain extent the distinctions between value and growth can be arbitrary and you may want to focus for example on whether a share meets your return on capital criteria or cash flow profile. Nonetheless, being aware of the differing styles can be useful and provide a framework for understanding the issues the market is looking at. It can also be useful to establish your own style and system for establishing whether shares are attractive or not.

> to a certain extent the distinctions between value and growth can be arbitrary

The pros and cons of each investment style will be considered, which will provide a sense of the potential risks and pitfalls. They are in essence:

- Value investing
- Value investing – income stocks
- Value investing – cyclicals
- Investing in growth
- Momentum investing

Value investing

This investment style has returned to favour as the demise of the growth-oriented sectors has caused such damage to the market. The fall from grace of many growth stocks – and the risks, especially financial, incurred in pursuing that growth – has highlighted the dangers inherent in this type of investment style. The share price of growth stocks that do not hit their projected growth rate suffer the double whammy of an earnings downgrade and a collapse in the multiple as the P/E adjusts to lower projected growth rates, giving a lower quality of earnings (i.e. the downgrade will normally mean a reappraisal of the visibility of earnings) and of course higher risk. This has led to some spectacular share price collapses.

By contrast, standing on lower multiples, value stocks may well offer a more stable/lower-risk investment.

Value stocks tend to have a combination of the following characteristics:

- a significant P/E discount to the market
- a big discount to net asset value (price to book)
- a higher yield than the market
- a very low EV (market cap plus debt) to sales ratio (i.e. it is very cheap to acquire the company's sales).

It may well be that the prospects for these companies are far from inspiring. A value investor might retort that the share price already tells us that and so we should not be put off.

Some investors adjust the P/E by looking at the earnings growth rate. This gives the peg ratio and is used by many investors as a means of valuing growth. Therefore, standing on lower multiples and having the protection of higher yield and asset backing, 'value' shares have tended to be relatively attractive in the current market. Those shares expected to benefit from the economic recovery/lower interest rates may be especially interesting.

One of the great difficulties with value stocks is that the P/E may be low for a good reason: the stock is not cheap. There may be no prospect for growth, quality of earnings is very low and the business and financial risk excessive. In addition:

- The earnings forecast may be highly speculative and awaiting a major downgrade.
- The quality of earnings is very low.
- The company may be ex-growth.
- The company may be in terminal/structural decline.
- Company/industry returns may be very low.
- Management is deemed to be poor.
- The financial position is very poor.
- The real economic value of the assets is considerably less than their stated value (a low ROCE may tell you that the assets are overstated in value).

Many cyclical stocks may emerge as value players (see 'Value investing – cyclicals', p. 306).

What is the catalyst?

Another issue with respect to value investing is what will be the catalyst for a change in the shares' valuation? If the shares have been standing on a low P/E relative for some time, it may be the case that the shares are a 'value-trap', i.e. they look cheap but those parts of the Valuation Villa 'trapping' it in a low valuation are expected to persist for some time yet. So if the risk profile is very high or the company is definitely ex-growth then there is no reason for the valuation to change.

So what circumstances will lead to a change in this valuation? In effect one or more elements of the Valuation Villa need to change to see the shares respond. This is often referred to by investors as the 'catalyst' and is an event that will lead to a re-rating of the shares (see p. 256). The catalyst could be any of the following:

- Results that comfortably beat market expectations highlighting that the quantity and quality of earnings are far better than perceived by the market.
- The sector that the company operates in performs more strongly than anticipated.
- The company reduces costs and has success with new product introductions (competitive position improves and there is higher growth potential) and demonstrates increased market share.
- The company disposes of a division that has been holding back the main business and improves the risk profile and quality of earnings.
- The company makes a disposal or a deal which transforms the balance sheet improving financial position and reducing risk, and sees a focus on a core business with improved growth potential.
- The company's cash flow profile is far more attractive than originally thought.
- There is takeover and consolidation activity among similar companies.
- Sector pricing improves as a result of industry consolidation, which also allows costs to be reduced.
- A new CEO or management team is appointed with better corporate governance (lower risk) and a greater commitment to shareholder value.

Any of these will create a 'momentum' that will appeal to both value and momentum investors: as the improved performance and good news starts to improve then this will attract momentum investors, which will see the share price responding strongly on a sustained basis.

Obviously breaking out of the 'value trap' requires a catalyst – and if management fails to create it then there will inevitably be pressure from investors – especially activist investors and hedge funds, and increasingly institutional funds that are taking their responsibilities more seriously. This may well lead to a change in management.

While it is often the case that activist investors, especially hedge funds, are seen as being aggressive in this situation, it needs to be borne in mind that if the shares have been languishing for some time then management should have been alive to the issues and responded much earlier (rather than watching over the poor share price performance without doing anything to credibly reverse it). It is normally quite easy to spot where the activist investor will apply pressure – it reflects the list above of the catalysts likely to create momentum, for example a change in management, a disposal of a business, merging with a competitor, share buy-back (though far less common now), increased dividends, etc.

This is not to say the active investors' views are necessarily correct – but management should be anticipating their views and creating a momentum story of its own buy taking decisions that add value for all shareholders. One of the concerns about activist investors' pressure is that decisions are taken in favour of one particular group of shareholders with one specific agenda, which may nor create value for all shareholders in the long run.

Value investing – income stocks

With interest rates on cash very low many investors may be looking both to participate in any recovery in the equity markets this might lead to and to find an alternative source of income. This suggests that stocks yielding significantly more than the market may remain in favour. This is a subset of the value style of investing and has been very successful over time, especially if dividends are growing and dividends are reinvested.

If looking for income, investors should consider whether the level of income is sustainable and how likely it is to grow (as this is a crucial driver of performance longer term). Assessing the following aspects of a company's financials may help in deciding both the attractiveness and the outlook for income:

- Dividend cover – a low level of cover suggests that any deterioration in trading will inevitably lead to the dividend being cut.
- If there is little or no cover, are dividends being distributed from reserves? Does this make sense? It may be appropriate if the poor year is a 'one off', but not if there is likely to be a prolonged period of poor

volumes and prices. Otherwise declining net assets are paying for your income – as a shareholder you may not be any better off.
- If there is little or no cover, are the dividends being paid out of asset sales?
- Financial position (gearing and interest cover): this provides information on whether the balance sheet or cash flow can support the dividend.
- Earnings and cash flow: is the earnings figure coming from wholly owned business and effectively coming through in cash? Any accounting manipulation that improves earnings but does not alter the underlying cash flow undermines the dividend cover ratio. Cash pays dividends not earnings (see quality of earnings, pp. 131–3).
- How much capital does the company need to invest? A need to replace a large amount of depreciated assets, for example, will restrict what the company can distribute to shareholders. Receiving a dividend while the competitive position is undermined through lack of investment is likely to prove at best a very short-term gain.
- Earnings forecasts: dividends are very much linked with earnings trends. So how confident you are in the forecast is an important factor in the sustainability and growth of the dividend.
- Dividend forecasts: will the dividend grow?

Dividend forecasts can be important as a high and growing yield is often a better predictor of good performance than just a very high initial yield.

As with the potential pitfalls expressed on value stocks, investing for income has the same list of reservations. It can be argued that if the company is paying out a lot of shareholders' money, precious little is left for growing the business; not necessarily an encouraging sign for the long term or for the company's competitive position. Importantly, it may be the case that the management does not have either the opportunities or the skills to generate higher returns.

In this sort of situation, shareholders may insist on the funds being distributed to them, as they believe that they can do a better job of reinvesting them. This questions shareholders' 'trust' in the management – if you are sceptical about its ability to invest your money effectively, why should you trust it to manage the existing assets well? And if it cannot manage the existing assets well, maybe investing in the company is not going to make you money.

Value investing – cyclicals

The performance of cyclical stocks depends on the trend in the cycle and the trend in interest rates. While cuts in interest rates should benefit a cyclical stock it may be that demand does not revive or industry overcapacity threatens pricing.

However, there is a 'Catch 22' situation for cyclicals with respect to falling interest rates. Interest rates being cut is good for cyclicals as profits are very sensitive to GDP and falling rates should stimulate economic growth in time. Often these companies are highly geared financially, so their interest burden is likely to be reduced. This accounts for them having a high beta. However, the reason interest rates are coming down may also be important. If interest rates are cut because the economy is slowing rapidly and inflation is well under control, this may well see volumes and pricing come under pressure. The current concerns over the impact of deflation are important here. Deflation, to date, has been a particular concern to the manufactured sector for some time. Globalisation and the transparency created by the internet have been deflationary forces for internationally traded goods.

This concern is particularly acute in the current environment given the nature of this cycle – a downturn triggered by a crisis with the banks/financial sector that fund economic activity. In the current 'credit crunch' environment, the availability of funds, not their price (interest rate), is the key issue. With no access to capital – either the banks have no capital to lend or are not prepared to risk doing do – it could be some while before activity picks up and confidence is restored to enable the purchasing of 'big ticket' items by corporates as well as consumers.

Any fall in volumes or prices has a massive impact on earnings forecasts, so there is a significant degree of risk attaching to earnings. Normally these stocks have high fixed costs and so small reductions in volumes have a big impact on profits (called 'operational gearing'). The effect of falling prices can be even more devastating. Any reduction in prices tends to come straight off profits, and with a vengeance. To illustrate this simply, take a company making £10 million on £100 million of turnover (a margin of 10 per cent). If prices fall 5 per cent, turnover falls to £95 million and profits are £5 million (all other things remaining equal). As can be seen, a 5 per cent reduction in price leads to profit halving in this instance.

Pricing will be affected if there is overcapacity in an industry; this overcapacity is exacerbated by a volume downturn. Companies may look to maintain their volumes or defend their market share, which will inevitably lead to lower prices as their competitors follow suit. The extent of any price reductions will depend on the degree of market concentration that exists.

As well as market structure, pricing will be much more sensitive if the industry is subject to international competition. Structurally, pricing levels for manufactured goods have been subject to the twin forces of globalisation and the deflationary impact of the internet for some time.

The effect of these two forces is to drive prices lower and lower, and this depresses earnings. It also reduces returns on capital to levels that do not cover the cost of that capital, let alone compensate for the risks involved in such competitive markets. This has seen these internationally traded goods sectors underperform for some time. As a result a process of national and international rationalisation has been initiated to try to reduce capacity levels and improve pricing and returns on investment.

Therefore, while an expected reduction in interest rates may provide a background that favours investing in cyclical stocks, the situation is far more complex. Some of these sectors rarely cover their cost of capital and struggle perennially in the face of swings in volumes and weak pricing power. Accordingly, earnings disappointments are virtually inevitable if there is a long economic slowdown, especially a global one. Critically, there is a direct link between high rates of returns and outperforming the major indices.

> earnings disappointments are virtually inevitable if there is a long economic slowdown

So, while there may be value in cyclical stocks, great care is needed to establish that they have:

- good control of costs/start with a low cost base
- a degree of pricing power conferred by market share and/or product superiority
- financial robustness
- cash generation and are well managed with a proven track record of dealing with difficult trading environments
- relatively high returns.

It is important that these issues are considered thoroughly before making a long-term investment in this area of the market – though there may well be short-term trading opportunities to consider.

Investing in growth

In assessing a growth stock you may wish to check that it can deliver a combination of the following:

- sales growth well ahead of the market
- earnings growth well ahead of the market
- high rates of return on capital – growth adds value
- high capex to depreciation ratio
- strong financial position and/or cash flow to fund growth.

Falling interest rates are positive for growth stocks as they reduce the rate at which future earnings are discounted. Historically growth stocks (and especially cyclical growth stocks such as software) have performed well coming out of a bear market. This suggests that good-quality, lower-risk growth stocks generating good returns on capital with some GDP sensitivity might be an interesting way of playing the economic and market recovery. This is, of course, subject to the caveat that this economic cycle is very different and overcapacity exists in many cyclical growth areas that may weaken the earnings recovery this time round.

Looked at generally, growth can be delivered in a number of ways or from a number of sources:

- being in a growth market
- developing a new product or technology
- taking market share
- taking products and/or services into new regional markets
- investing in new facilities
- acquiring competitors.

It is important to fully understand what kind of growth a company is delivering. This is because the market will tend to favour, and therefore value more highly:

- organic growth over acquisition-led growth
- growth that is driven by sales rather than cost reductions.

The market takes different approaches to these growth generators largely because there may be more risks involved in, say, a new acquisition compared with an existing product that is taking market share in a growing market. Accordingly, the market will value more sustainable and lower-risk growth more highly than 'one-off' growth.

Frequently acquisitions may enlarge a business but not improve its longer-term growth potential. The problem with cost reductions is that they again tend to be a one-off. They will boost earnings in the following year but not necessarily thereafter. Also, as we have seen, there may be diseconomies of scale as managements fail to manage the enlarged entity effectively.

While growth is obviously an attractive feature for making money in the long run, it needs to be borne in mind that:

- growth attracts a lot of capital, which depresses returns
- growth may need a lot of capital in the early phases and not generate cash
- growth may not add value
- you do not know how long the growth will last (e.g. mobile telephony)
- valuing growth can be difficult
- the growth can be very attractive – and therefore the share price may already reflect the potential (it is 'discounted' or 'in the price', making it very difficult to make money)
- the share price will tumble dramatically if growth falls short of expectations.

Value v growth: performance over time

It would appear that over time value tends to outperform growth. It might be argued that the preference many value investors have for the certainty of income as the main component of total shareholder return, combined with the benefits of reinvesting that income, leads to long-term outperformance. A consistent and preferably rising dividend – signalling as it does management's confidence in the sustainability of the payout – tends to mark out winners. This, it could be argued, is especially true in the current uncertain market conditions – especially if the yield stock in question has a strong balance sheet and strong cash flow (which in turn will come from high returns on capital, another indicator of quality).

Conversely, the uncertainty of capital growth over time may often disappoint. This may be because share prices are bid up very high initially, discounting the high growth rate. By definition, all the anticipated growth is already 'in the price' which limits the scope for any upside. However, any disappointment if the growth fails to materialise will be heavily punished. That disappointment may come because the market for the company's products is slower to take off than we think, more investment is needed, competitors crowd the marketplace – all of which depress and delay returns and defer cash flow for a considerable period of time (as we have seen in our DCF examples, the later the cash flow the less it is worth in today's money). This highlights the importance of finding businesses that are cash generative or become cash generative very quickly. Historically, many growth stocks have needed a significant amount of capex for a lot longer than originally anticipated (and therefore been cash negative for quite some time).

In the current environment it may well be that a blend of value and growth from the same company is what will deliver outperformance. Having high returns due to a strong competitive position and strong cash flows allows for companies both to invest in developing the organic growth of the business and to increase dividend payouts.

Momentum investing

Momentum investing is based on the 'trend is your friend' philosophy. Run with your winners and cut (or sell) your losses is another way of putting it. This is important because momentum investing places as much emphasis on selling as it does on buying. Given that selling well often poses a real problem, this can be a useful and disciplined aid to the decision-making process.

As a style it is far more focused on 'earnings surprises' or share price trends (as well as the assumption these trends will continue) than any of the fundamental techniques of valuation covered here.

The two key trends that are monitored by momentum investors are

- earnings surprises (positive and negative) and
- relative share price performance.

Earnings surprises

Momentum investors will favour shares which have started to beat – or are anticipated to beat – consensus expectations (as defined by analysts' forecasts). These expectations are displayed on a variety of websites. Results coming in above or below these figures are referred to as 'earnings surprises'.

If the earnings have beaten, or are thought likely to beat, consensus expectations this is taken as a sign that a process of improvement has started. Money can be made, the argument goes, as the improvement is expected to continue and will attract extra investor interest, fuelling share buying and hence share price rises. The improvement may reflect a pick-up in the trading conditions the company is facing (better volumes and pricing) or internally generated improvements such as a cost reduction or investment programme yielding positive results.

As a proxy for **earnings momentum** we can look at the relative change in consensus estimates over various periods (any changes over one month or three months are obvious ones to monitor). At any one time this can give us a fairly clear picture as to how optimistic or pessimistic analysts are becoming.

A momentum investor will not be too concerned about what is causing the surprises, what the recent trading record has been, what sector the company is in, what the long-term growth outlook is or how good the management team is thought to be (all of which a growth investor would focus on). If a company disappoints – or is anticipated to disappoint – consensus expectations, a momentum investor will sell straight away. This is likely to herald a profits downgrade or other bad news and trigger an extended period of poor performance – so sell on the first downgrade, as invariably more will follow. Falling volumes and prices tend to damage earnings numbers far more than is initially appreciated and the difficult conditions last a lot longer. In addition management often continues to have an overoptimistic view of how the business will perform.

> if a company disappoints consensus expectations, a momentum investor will sell straight away

As a result one downgrade is rarely enough and so the news flow is likely to remain negative and therefore act as an ongoing depressant on the shares.

Relative share price performance

Relative strength basically means that a share price is rising more rapidly than the market overall. This suggests continued demand for the stock. A share price hitting new highs may well be deemed a buy signal for the momentum investor. (Paradoxically, a more traditional fundamental investor would more likely take this as a sell signal!)

Most momentum investors will watch the volumes being bought as well as the price trend as an expression of the degree of support or interest. A rising share price with little volume may indicate that the period of outperformance is coming to an end. The volume provides an indication of the sustainability of the trend. However, it must always be borne in mind that supply or demand imbalances – the lifeblood of share price momentum investors – can be brought into balance by extra supply (rights issues, placings, etc.), not just higher share prices.

Importance of trends in the current market

Given the great volatility that has been an increasing feature of the market recently, and the lack of confidence in the numbers given the extremely uncertain economic outlook, the use of charts and trends has become more popular and arguably more useful.

In addition, the advantage of selling on negative earnings momentum has been very effective – downgrades remain a dominant feature and share prices react sharply to earnings disappointments. On a news flow basis, credit rating changes also appear to be a clear sell signal.

Having the discipline to sell well can be difficult. There is often a high degree of attachment to the original decision and emotional factors take over. There is a tendency to hope that things will get better or that the price fall is temporary. However, using a momentum-type approach can provide a good discipline when it comes to the effective selling of shares.

Step 3 Looking at the risk/reward profile

When investing in shares it is crucial that you consider one of the key fundamentals of investment: the balance between risk and reward. For accepting a higher degree of risk you must be compensated by a much better return on your investment. However, you need to be comfortable with the degree of risk you are taking on.

It is a good discipline to think about what the potential risks are to your target company and what the potential downside is. This will help determine whether it fits in with your overall risk tolerance. Avoiding disasters is an extremely important element in good investing!

There are three main types of risk for share buyers.

- Market risk – the market as a whole may fall for reasons outside the control of the company. Inflation fears, an economic slowdown, poor trade figures and rising interest rates will affect share prices across the board.
- Company risk – this includes external factors such as a recession or a rise in interest rates when the company is highly indebted. Falling demand, rising raw material costs and new competitors would affect

the whole sector in which the company operate. The company may also do badly due to internal factors such as weak management or a poor acquisition.

- Financial risk – the debt structure and the cash flow profile of the business. This is why you need a portfolio of shares to diversify away what is called 'stock-specific risk'.

Table 9.1 highlights just some of the risks that may affect the value of shares.

Table 9.1 Risks that may affect share value

Sector	Cyclical industry, low barriers to entry, overcapacity, low margins and the risks associated with a new or emerging industry
Company	Financial risk (high debt/weak cash flow), business risk – poor management, poor market or product positioning, and strategic errors (e.g. poor acquisitions)
Valuation	Share becomes valued too highly by the market and suffers a setback
Stock market	Possibility of a sharp fall in the stock market

Benchmarks

When considering whether your investments have been successful you need to consider a couple of benchmarks.

- *Risk-free returns* – your first benchmark should be the interest you would get per year in a savings account. This is a risk-free rate (though also a limited-reward rate) and represents the 'opportunity cost' of putting your money into shares. Therefore you need to earn progressively more than the risk-free rate the higher up the risk curve you go.

- *Index returns* – the other key benchmark is the return you earn when compared with the stock market overall. Without running the company-specific risk of buying an individual share, you can benefit from equities with no company-specific risk by buying the whole market. This can be done cost effectively through an index fund. The point of buying individual shares and constructing your own portfolio is to try to achieve a higher return than the index. This is known as 'relative performance' and something that professional money managers often focus on. This can lead to the claim that in their attempts not to under-perform the index, they become closet tracking funds.

Absolute v relative

You may be more concerned with the absolute amount of money you make rather than performance against an index. This is very much how hedge funds operate. This can make sense for a private investor. However, remember that the opportunity cost is either a risk-free rate of return or what you might get from investing in a low-charge index fund. Again, your absolute targets should also bear in mind the risks you are undertaking.

Step 4 Considering timescale – trading v investment

Long-term

If you are planning to hold the shares for several years, you should be looking in a fundamental way at both the prospects for the company and its valuation. You need to feel comfortable with both the prospects and the fact that the valuation still leaves room for future growth – i.e. all the attractions are not already 'priced-in' or 'discounted'.

Short-term trading

If you are thinking of trading on a shorter timescale, you will be taking a view that the share looks 'cheap' (or expensive). You may be indifferent to the company's prospects in this situation and more concerned about 'sentiment' in the stock market, share price or earnings momentum and anticipated news flow. It is worth stressing that this 'timing' decision is extremely difficult to get right, even for the professionals. Academic evidence suggests that making trades at the right moment is almost impossible statistically.

Buy or sell?

Having got to this stage it is worth having fairly clear criteria for your desired outcome. This will depend on the risk/reward ratio, which will be different in each instance.

Buy

To reach a 'buy' conclusion you will obviously need to be convinced that you will make more money in the share than simply putting the money on deposit. How much in excess of the risk-free rate you are looking for will depend on your individual approach to risk. You will also need to take into account dealing charges and any dividends likely to be received.

The greater the risks, the more demanding the total return target you need to set. An anticipated 12 per cent return from a well-managed, well-financed, company with a good spread of activities, say, may suit your risk tolerance a lot more than a hoped-for 30 per cent from a company that is operating in a difficult market with a poor financial position. The downside in the latter case could be considerable if something goes wrong.

Sell

A 'sell' decision may be expected to underperform the market by 20 per cent or to have an absolute downside of that amount. Being prepared to sell, and having the discipline to do so, is one of the most difficult aspects of good investment management, even for the professional. Facing up to your mistakes and drawing a line under losses is much easier said than done for most people, but it is a critical part of protecting your portfolio. This reinforces the need to continually monitor your portfolio and make sure that your investments continue to have the risk/reward profile you are comfortable with.

If a share you buy goes down, analyse why, as far as you can, and react accordingly. A natural – albeit somewhat illogical – tendency when seeing shares fall is simply to hold on and hope things will improve. Much better to ascertain why this has happened. Have prospects deteriorated since you bought? Has the general outlook changed materially? Has new information come to light? Looking at the shares today, would you still buy them? If so perhaps you should buy some more. If you think the valuation is now expensive, you should have the discipline to sell even if the price is lower than you paid.

> you should have the discipline to sell even if the price is lower than you paid

Weighing up your decision

It can be seen that all the various approaches to investing have potential strengths and weaknesses, especially in an environment that remains very difficult to read. The 1990s were characterised by a preference in a low-inflation environment to seek out real growth opportunities. Interestingly, one of the issues in the celebrated case of *Unilever* v *Merrill Lynch Asset Management* revolved around the underperformance of an investment portfolio that was dominated by value stocks when growth stocks were performing more strongly. Conversely, with the onset of the bear market, value stocks have been the better place to be.

The preference for growth in the 1990s ultimately led to the stock market bubble and the (over) allocation of capital to the perceived high-growth technology, media and telecoms (TMT) sector. Investors buying on momentum, and index funds which have to buy shares that become a larger and larger portion of the index, exaggerated the upside for these shares. With hindsight, what is crucial to appreciate is how increasingly arcane valuation methodology was becoming to justify valuations. The more complex or more arcane things become, the higher the risks involved. As many of the features traditionally used in valuation, sales, earnings and cash, were not being generated, valuations would rest, for example, on the number of people visiting a website. Obviously this has no clear correlation with revenues being generated (let alone cash) or money being made. It is worth pointing out that the further the basis of valuation moves away from core valuation numbers such as cash, earnings or sales, the greater the risk and the more money you are likely to lose.

EBITDA was promoted by many of these companies as a valuation measure as all the other performance criteria were irrelevant. Sometimes this may have been perfectly legitimate as the company was in an early stage of development. Often, however, it reflects the weaknesses and issues associated with the use of this figure (discussed on p. 279). If the company was at an early stage of development with no track record or a very short one, then in effect investors were being venture capitalists – which is fine if one realises the much greater degree of risk involved with companies at a very early stage of development. And as stressed, if the risks are that much greater, the cost of capital is much higher, so you need much higher returns to compensate.

The other element is, of course, that the timescale for growth stocks (and stocks at an early stage of development) was being pushed further and further into the future. Even if they delivered this growth (which they did not), the valuation was, at the very least, fully reflecting the prospects. This long-term perspective was reflected in a stock such as Cisco. At its peak, the shares were on a P/E of around 150. Using the definition of a P/E as the number of years it takes to pay for the shares, you would be taking a very unhealthy view of your life expectancy. In effect it is a 'hereafter' valuation.

On a value-added basis, as discussed in the growth section, high growth attracts capital which drives down returns. A lot of the investment in the boom period will never cover its cost of capital and will in all likelihood be written off.

Key issues in the current market

Macro factors

At an economic level the combination of low growth, weak corporate spending, the corporate sector's weak financial position and concerns over the indebtedness of the consumer on both sides of the Atlantic create a difficult backdrop. To the extent that price pressures continue to be exerted, earnings downgrades will remain a feature of the market landscape.

The preoccupation with growth that characterised the boom years has given way to paying attention to the other drivers of value in a more systematic way. In particular, taking risk and quality into account is now of paramount importance. As part of the risk equation attention is being increasingly focused on best practice corporate governance and the quality of management. The absence of 'checks and balances' and the lack of proper debate at board level (especially about the risks being run) caused major problems. The lessons learned will hopefully lead to a more rigorous testing of strategic and financial decision making.

Companies with high-quality cash flows (predictable and stable) and who can manage risk effectively will be at a premium, especially if the 'de-leveraging' process takes some time. Their strong cash flows mean they will not be dependent on refinancing expensively and they have the financial flexibility to take advantage of opportunities for investment or acquisition as they arise. Crucially, the cash flows will also fund a growing dividend stream. This is not to say that growth is not important – but that a balance is more appropriate. Quality companies that can deliver (value-enhancing) growth will make money.

More specifically the 'qualities' that are clearly very attractive in this environment include:

- strong balance sheets and cash flow
- high and consistent returns on capital (value added)
- a strong competitive position (as reflected by the excellent returns)
- clear and sustainable pricing power – a strong 'moat'
- a record of innovation and new product introduction
- investing in new areas of growth
- exposure to growth markets – emerging markets
- strong management and good corporate governance, which both improves performance and reduces risk.

Given that the macro backdrop remains challenging it may well be that the market makes little headway. If this is the case emphasis may well be on the yield component of TSR – getting a secure 4+ per cent income in a low return market would be an encouraging place to start. Accordingly, the above list still works as these characteristics support a good and rising dividend.

Focus on risk

The increase in volatility and the preference for defensive and low-beta shares clearly suggest that the appetite for risk among investors has fallen considerably. As well as there being a great difficulty in reading current trends and the future direction of the economy and therefore earnings, the financial position of the corporate sector is a key concern. The frequency and extent of earnings downgrades dramatically illustrate the difficulties the corporate sector faces. With this degree of uncertainty, risk minimisation is likely to remain a feature. This may lead to a very circumspect approach towards growth, especially if there is no value being added.

Defensive v growth – defensive attractions in the price?

Value stocks, especially high-yield value, and defensive stocks have been the relative winners since 2002. Tobacco, utilities, and household products have shown absolute gains. Sectors that did well in 2001 continued to do well for many years thereafter, suggesting that the momentum of following earnings and share price momentum has also been a winning strategy.

The recent outperformance of value stocks has also reflected disillusionment with growth stocks; valuations put on growth were excessive and the growth failed to materialise. The fact that so much value was destroyed by growth companies has also seen attention return to value creation, not growth. The issue now is whether the attractions of these defensive shares are fully valued.

This clearly depends on your view of the economic outlook – if you feel that a strong recovery is likely, you will want a more cyclical or growth-oriented portfolio. A higher beta portfolio will show stronger upside into a market recovery. Indeed, in the second quarter of 2009, very high beta stocks – cyclical with very high debt levels – bounced very strongly as the economic indicators appeared to hint at a stabilisation. This then petered out as the economic signs became more mixed.

Alternatively, if you are cautious about the economy you will still want the stability and security of defensives, especially if they offer a secure (and growing) yield. The shape of the recovery is crucial. In a top-down sense, how much exposure to corporate spending is sensible very much depends on when the 'credit crunch' eases and companies relax the purse strings a bit.

Expected market returns

The central expectation for the total returns (share price appreciation plus dividends) from equities has fallen to around 6–7 per cent – and even then over the past ten-year period it has not reached anywhere near that!

With the volatility of markets and relatively low level of total returns, the security of income is a compelling attraction. A yield of, say, 4.5 per cent will deliver more than half of any expected total return. The dangers of chasing very high-yield stocks (where as a rule of thumb a yield more than 1.5× the risk-free rate suggests a strong likelihood of a dividend cut while a yield more than 2× the risk-free rate flags that a company is in trouble, not an attractive source of income) should, however, be borne in mind. This is especially true when there are so many competing claims on companies' money – whether it is paying down debt, reinvesting in the business or topping up the pension fund.

A serious examination of the pros and cons of all styles and stock types is of paramount importance to improve the chances of outperformance. A blend of approaches is appropriate to give a balanced basket of stocks for long-term holders.

Summary

In the short term there will be lots of factors influencing the share price that come under the catch-all label of 'sentiment'. The old adage that markets are driven by 'fear and greed' has been substantiated by the market volatility of the past decade. As ever, the key is to buy when fear is heightened and sell when greed is at its maximum. This volatility and associated role of fear and greed does much to undermine any supposed 'rationality' or 'efficiency' of the market. (The market being efficient simply means that all the publicly available information is already 'efficiently' priced into the share so the share is correctly priced.)

It is important therefore to differentiate between the share price and the valuation of the business – the price does not necessarily correspond to the fundamental prospects of the business which drives its value. The momentum style looks to play the forces (news flow, earnings momentum and share price momentum) that drive share prices as opposed to the fundamentals. In volatile markets this can make a lot of sense and may certainly help with timing issues.

While the market may not always be rational, assuming a degree of market efficiency is sensible – that is to say that a share price will often reflect the collective knowledge of the market and many participants in the market will in many instances be better placed to know a lot more than you do. Therefore it is always a useful discipline to examine what the market is assuming and whether the market is right: what does the valuation tell us about the market's concerns? Are those concerns justified or overstated? That is why Warren Buffett always says you should only invest in those things you really know and understand as that will give you an edge (or not put you at a significant disadvantage). Also having a clear sense of your timescale and appetite for risk is vital.

Having assessed the returns you want in order to compensate for the risks, you need to know whether that return is going to come from the share price going up (capital appreciation) or from the dividends you receive (income). This combination of capital appreciation and income generates total shareholder return (TSR).

Value investors tend to prefer the certainty of income to the uncertainty of capital growth and, importantly, income reinvested has been a key determinant of superior returns in the long term.

INVESTMENT DECISION CHECKLIST

Some of the 'qualities' to consider in the current economic and market context include:

- Does the company have a strong balance sheet and cash flow?
- Does the company demonstrate high and consistent returns on capital (value added)?
- Is there a good yield and a strong dividend growth?
- Is there a strong competitive position (as reflected by the excellent returns)?
- Is there evidence of clear and sustainable pricing power – a strong 'moat'?
- Does the company have a strong record of innovation and new product introduction?
- Is the company investing in new areas of growth?
- Does the company have significant exposure to emerging markets?
- Is there evidence of strong management and good corporate governance which both improves performance and reduces risk?

Value investing

Value stocks tend to have a combination of the following characteristics:

- a significant P/E discount to the market
- a big discount to net asset value (price to book)
- a higher yield than the market
- a very low EV (market cap plus debt) to sales ratio (i.e. it is very cheap to acquire the company's sales).

Value stocks may be on low valuation for a good reason. There may be no prospect for growth, earnings are low quality and high risk.

- The earnings forecast may be awaiting a major downgrade.
- The quality of earnings is very low.
- The company may be ex-growth.
- The company may be in terminal/structural decline.
- Company/industry returns may be very low.
- Management has a poor record of generating value.
- The financial position is very weak.
- The real economic value of the assets is considerably less than their stated value.

Growth

Companies that can deliver strong sustainable organic growth will make money over time. Growth may come from:

- being in a growth market
- developing a new product or technology

- taking market share
- taking products/services into new regional markets
- investing in new facilities
- acquisitions.

However, growth stocks historically have not necessarily delivered sustained out-performance.

- Growth attracts a lot of capital, making the industry very competitive which depresses returns.
- Growth may need a lot of capital in the early phases and not generate cash for a long time.
- Growth may not add value.
- You do not know how long the growth will last.
- Valuing growth can be difficult.
- The growth can be very attractive – and therefore the share price may already reflect the potential (it is 'discounted' or 'in the price', making it very difficult to make money).
- The share price will tumble dramatically if growth falls short of expectations.

Glossary

adding value When a company's post-tax return on invested capital (*Nopat*/invested capital) exceeds its cost of capital. See *economic value added* and *weighted average cost of capital*.

AGM (annual general meeting) A meeting held each year by a company to which every shareholder is invited. At the meeting, some members of the board of directors submit themselves for re-election by the shareholders. The *annual report and accounts* are presented and any business requiring the approval of the shareholders is discussed, including the level of dividend to be paid.

amortisation Where intangible assets such as patents and licences are written off over their useful economic life and charged to the profit and loss account (see *depreciation*).

annual report and accounts A report made by the board of directors of a company, summarising its performance over the preceding year. Normally it will give some indication of the expectations for the year ahead and will carry detailed comments about the company's trading position. Accompanying this will be the financial statements, notably the *balance sheet*, the *profit and loss account* and the *cash flow statement*.

associate company A company in which a substantial stake (more than 20 per cent but less than 50 per cent, a level above which the company would move from being an associate to a subsidiary) is held by another company and where the owner of that stake is in a position to influence its operations. Often referred to as related company. When looking at the accounts of companies that have associates there are rules for how money earned from the investment is recorded. If 20 per cent is owned, 20 per cent of the *operating profit* will be shown together with 20 per cent of any interest paid on borrowings. This does not mean, however, that the associate company hands over 20 per cent of its profits – the only cash that changes hands is in the form of *dividends*. In the vast majority of cases, the actual dividend paid would be much less than the percentage of profit credited.

attributable profit Profits, after tax and other charges (e.g. *minorities* and preference dividends), which 'belong' to the ordinary shareholders. Used in the calculation of *EPS* (*earnings per share*) and *return on equity*.

balance sheet A statement showing the *assets* and *liabilities* that a company has at its year end – what it 'owns' and owes. It is essentially a 'snapshot' of a company's position and can and does change, reflecting seasonal factors within the business. The balance sheet is normally prepared at the company's *year end* and should always be read together with the *profit and loss account* and the *cash flow statement*.

beta A measure of the volatility of a share relative to the stock market overall. A share that moves in line with the market would have a beta of 1. A beta of 1.2 would imply that a share should rise 12 per cent for each 10 per cent rise in the market and conversely fall 12 per cent for each 10 per cent drop. A beta of less than 1 normally offers a degree of safety in a falling market as it should fall less rapidly than the stock market overall. Likewise, low beta stocks tend to underperform rising markets. Betas are not set in stone, but can – and do – change over time. Generally the beta is influenced by the degree of *operational and financial gearing* a company has as these affect the sensitivity and volatility of profits. Defensive stocks tend to have a low beta and cyclical, highly indebted stocks a high beta.

bonus issue An issue of new shares where the intention is not to raise new money for investment but to a) increase the number of shares and correspondingly b) reduce the share price. Normally the intention is to improve the *liquidity* and appeal of the shares to investors – if the share price is high (e.g. over £10), it may be a deterrent to small investors.

The value of the company does not change – if a company has 100 shares trading at £10 each and makes a 1 for 1 issue, the number of shares will double (to 200) but the price will halve (to £5). No new money is being raised so the overall value of the company should be unaltered. Also known as a scrip issue or capitalisation issue as an element of the group's reserves are transferred to the shareholders' premium account. See *share split*.

book value Normally shown on a company's *balance sheet*, the book value is calculated by subtracting a company's liabilities from its assets. Book value will frequently differ from the share price as the latter is more open to short-term influences such as market sentiment and economic outlook.

capex/depreciation ratio The relationship between how much a company spends on *capital expenditure* and the level of *depreciation*. In theory, the higher the ratio, the more the company is investing in future growth. A mature company will be investing at or below its depreciation charge. The returns generated from capex need to be monitored – there may well be different returns from replacement and growth capex and differing risk profiles attaching to them.

capital employed The total amount of funds used by a business in its day-to-day activities. The figure includes *shareholders' funds* and net debt.

capital expenditure (capex) The amount the company invests in physical assets such as plant, machinery and equipment to generate revenue. In effect it is all assets that have an economic life of greater than one year. See *capex/depreciation ratio*.

capitalisation (or market capitalisation) The total value of a company, defined by the value of its ordinary *shares* (based on the mid-market price) multiplied by the number of ordinary shares in issue.

cash return on invested capital (or CROIC) The amount of cash or *free cash flow* generated by the assets invested (*capital employed*) in the business. Many investors and brokers use this number as there is strong evidence of its strong predictive power as a performance measure and reflects the critical importance of cash flow as a driver of value.

cash flow statement A statement showing the source and destination of all monies received and spent by a company in the course of the financial year. The annual cash flow statement in the *annual report and accounts* reconciles how a company's cash balances have changed during the financial year. It contains important information on whether the company is actually generating cash.

closed period The period between a company's year end (and half year end) and the date of reporting its results. During this period, the management cannot, without a stock exchange announcement, disclose new information that would affect the share price.

convertible loan stocks In the same manner as bonds, convertible loan stocks pay a fixed rate of return and may be redeemable at a given date in the future. In addition, however, they offer the opportunity to convert the stock into *shares* at specified times in the future on set terms.

convertible shares See *convertible loan stocks*.

corporate governance Following earlier work done by committees chaired by Cadbury, Hampel and Greenbury, a Combined Code on Corporate

Governance was issued in 1998. The essence of corporate governance is to ensure that management is acting in the best interests of shareholders. Examples of issues involved include the role and composition of the board, the number of non-executive directors, a clearly defined separation between the chairman (who should be non-executive) and the chief executive, and levels of executive pay, length of contract, share options and so on. A statement made by the board of directors of a company confirming that it has complied with agreed and accepted standards of best practice in their day-to-day management activities should be contained in the group's *annual report and accounts*.

cost of capital A company will normally fund its business activities using a combination of debt and money from shareholders. The cost of capital then simply becomes the 'weighted' average of the *cost of debt* and the *cost of equity* (i.e. in proportion to the equity/debt funding of the business). See *weighted average cost of capital (WACC)*.

cost of debt Straightforward to appreciate and to calculate. If the company can borrow from the bank or in the debt markets for, say, 8 per cent, this tells you the cost of servicing the company's debt. Importantly, the interest payments are tax deductible, which makes the debt even cheaper relative to equity. So in this case the cost of debt would be 8 per cent × 0.7 or 5.6 per cent (i.e. deducting the 30 per cent tax charge).

cost of equity The equity component is somewhat more difficult but nonetheless crucial to assess. Essentially, the cost of equity must reflect what rate of return an investor requires to compensate for the risks attaching to shares in general and to a particular company (which may be more risky than the stock market overall).

Reflecting these considerations, it is calculated by reference to 1) the risk-free rate of borrowing, which is normally based on the interest on a government bond, 2) an *equity risk premium* to allow for the risks associated with investing in shares, and 3) the volatility of the individual share which is measured by its *beta*. The cost then becomes 1 + (2 × 3). If the risk-free rate is 6 per cent and the equity risk premium is 4 per cent, a stock with a beta of 1.2 would have a cost of equity of 10.8 per cent, i.e. 6 + (4 × 1.2). As this example shows, the cost of equity is significantly higher than the cost of debt – essentially reflecting the higher risks associated with shares.

credit rating An indicator of the financial strength of a company. A number of factors are taken into account when establishing a credit rating, such as overall assets and liabilities, the debt/equity ratio known as *gearing*, *interest cover* and *cash flow* profile. The rating is set by credit rating agencies such as Moody's and Standard & Poor's.

cum-dividend If a stock or share price is quoted as being cum-dividend, the purchaser will receive the most recently declared *dividend*. See *ex-dividend*.

current assets Short-term assets such as stock, short-term debtors and cash. Used to establish short-term solvency. How quickly stock can be converted into cash varies enormously from sector to sector. A food retailer will be able to 'turn' its stock into cash rapidly. For a manufacturer the process is likely to be much longer subject to the production cycle.

cyclical stocks Companies whose shares are directly linked to the business cycle. These stocks are influenced by outside factors such as the overall business climate, interest rates, commodity prices and trends in the global economy. Cyclical stocks tend to be the heavier, more traditional industries such as construction, chemicals, engineering, motor manufacturers, paper and pulp, and steel, though clearly some service-sector activities can also be cyclical (e.g. media and advertising, pubs, hotels and restaurants). Profits in these industries are very sensitive to changes in volume and price as *operational gearing* is high.

defensive A stock with a low *beta* believed to offer a safe haven in difficult economic circumstances. Food manufacturers and retailers, and utilities would tend have these characteristics.

depreciation Reduction in the value of an asset. Most commonly applied in company accounts where the initial value of an asset is reduced each year to reflect the wear and tear and/or obsolescence of the asset. The reduction is called the 'depreciation charge' – a cost incurred in running the business deducted before arriving at operating profit. However, it is not a cost that involves spending additional money – the book value of the asset is merely written down. Therefore this charge to the *profit and loss account (P&L)* is referred to as a 'non-cash cost'.

The life of an asset will vary – it may be very short and so annual depreciation charges are commensurately high where technological change is rapid (such as computers), or much longer for assets such as a cement kiln or land and buildings. The shorter the period the assets are written down, the more financially conservative the company (and the greater the short-term negative impact on profits).

derivatives Essentially, financial instruments that derive their value from the price of an underlying security (such as a *share* or a bond) or commodity.

Derivatives are used by investment professionals to manage risk, as they offer a way to limit losses on other investments and also to get greater exposure to a company than that available by going solely down the ordinary share route. The most commonly encountered types of derivative are options and futures.

dilution Refers to the impact of a transaction on ordinary shareholders. It is normally calculated as the impact on *EPS (earnings per share)* of a transaction. So if a company announces a takeover, the new earnings per share number will be calculated to see how the new earnings number compares with the situation before the deal. The deal is dilutive if earnings are below the pre-deal number. It is normally expressed as a percentage and will depend on how the deal has been financed (i.e. *shares* or debt) as well as the price paid for the deal.

It may sometimes be used to refer to the dilution of the shareholders' holding in a company. This may occur, for example, in a refinancing involving equity for bond swap. Ordinary shareholders may find they have been 'diluted' from owning all the company to holding a very small percentage.

discount rate The rate at which future cash flows are 'discounted' to a present value. This rate is normally the company's *weighted average cost of capital (WACC)*, which is a composite of the cost of debt and cost of equity.

discounted When the prospects for a company are fully known by the market and therefore reflected in the share price. Phrases such as 'in the price' or 'fair value' are also sometimes used. A company may be well run, highly regarded with excellent prospects, but the share price is on such a premium to its sector/market that it is fully 'discounting' its qualities. Therefore the shares will not make money unless the prospects turn out to be even better than first thought. Conversely, a very poor company, in a weak financial position and with a difficult outlook, may be valued very low. Again it is 'in the price'.

discounted cash flow (DCF) One of the key fundamental valuation techniques (though not the easiest for private investors to use). The *operating free cash flow* (cash generated by the business, operating profit after tax plus *depreciation* and *amortisation* less cash invested in the company and working capital needed as it expands) of the business is projected out into the future. It is then 'discounted' back using the company's *cost of capital* to generate a present value of the income stream. Lots of 'assumptions' are made which are both subjective and highly susceptible to change and significant error.

dividend A payment made by a company to its shareholders. Usually dictated by overall level of profitability. Many companies do not pay a dividend at all if trading conditions have been particularly poor or if the company is in a start-up situation and can use the cash more effectively in the development of the business. See *interim dividend* and *final dividend*.

dividend cover EPS divided by DPS. The number of times a company's *dividend* is covered by the *earnings* it generates. It is normally expressed as a multiple. The higher the level of cover, the more sustainable the payout and the better the scope for future dividend growth. Low level of cover raises the possibility that the dividend is not sustainable and may be cut (depending on other aspects of the company's financial profile and need for capital within the business).

earnings Profits attributable to ordinary shareholders. Earnings are post tax and after minority or preference dividend charges. Care needs to be taken to ensure consistency of use, i.e. prospective or historic, pre- or post-*exceptional* and *amortisation* charges.

earnings momentum The trend in both the reported and projected earnings of a company. Where a company's reported earnings beat market expectations and profit forecasts are upgraded, the earnings momentum is described as positive. This can be a critical factor in the shares outperforming the market as the improving earnings momentum reflects a better performance of, and outlook for, the company in question. Clearly, where a company reports earnings that are below expectations and profit forecasts are downgraded, the shares are likely to underperform the market. See *momentum investing*.

earnings per share (EPS) *Attributable profit*/number of *shares*. The amount of profit attributable to each ordinary share in issue. For example, if the company's attributable profit is £1m and there are 1m shares in issue, the EPS would be £1. The attributable profit is post tax and is struck after any *preference* dividends or *minorities* have been deducted. See also *price/earnings (P/E) ratio*.

earnings quality How predictable and sustainable the company's earnings are, ensuring that the earnings are coming from the core business and that they convert into cash efficiently. Also depends on conservative accounting policies by the company.

EBIT Earnings before interest and tax. Also commonly known as *operating profit*.

EBITDA Earnings before interest, tax and *depreciation*. A measure of performance used in valuation. The advantages of this measure are that it takes into account the whole funding structure of a business (equity and debt), unlike the *price/earnings (P/E) ratio*, and allows comparisons of companies with different accounting policies towards depreciation and *amortisation*. It also ignores *exceptional* charges. It has become increasingly controversial as a method of valuation because many companies have promoted it as all other performance measures have been disappointing and they have run into serious financial trouble. Similarly, there has been a focus on the growth of EBITDA at the expense of returns. Another problem is that depreciation is a real cost of doing business and needs to be taken into account.

economic value added (EVA) *Nopat – WACC* × capital invested. A critical way of assessing the performance of management is its use of assets. Value is added when the post-tax *ROCE (return on capital employed)* (normally done as net operating profit after tax divided by the amount of capital invested in the business) exceeds the *weighted average cost of capital (WACC)*. The cost of capital reflects the risks shareholders undertake – risks that need to generate an appropriate reward. A useful way of assessing the success of capital investment and mergers and acquisitions.

enterprise value (EV) The sum required to secure 100 per cent of the company's cash flows/acquire all its liabilities. It takes into account its funding structure and any cross-shareholdings that might exist. Importantly, it takes into account all provisions. In effect it is the sum of all the company's liabilities. Normally calculated by adding market capitalisation, average debt, provisions and subtracting peripheral or non-core assets.

equity risk premium The return required by investors over and above the return on risk-free investments such as government bonds to compensate for the additional risks involved in equity investment. This is normally calculated by looking at the historic return on equities compared with government bonds, with the difference being deemed the premium required for investing in shares. However, investing in shares is forward looking, which creates a problem. Generally the equity risk premium is thought to be between 3 per cent and 6 per cent. See also *cost of capital*.

exceptional items Items in a company's *profit and loss account (P&L)* that are deemed to be 'one off'. Examples may include a profit or loss on the disposal of fixed assets or business operations, large redundancy charges as a result of restructuring, costs associated with the integration of acquired companies or bid defence costs. Some definitions of exceptionals treat as exceptional only those items of a financial or capital nature (e.g. disposals) while excluding those items that relate to the core business.

EPS numbers in the UK are normally quoted before the impact of these one-off exceptional charges, as this gives a truer measure of the underlying performance of the business. However, exceptional costs that appear frequently (e.g. redundancy costs) or relate to the company's core operations should be scrutinised to ensure that they are not in fact a normal cost of doing business and therefore should not be treated as exceptional.

ex-dividend When a stock or share price is quoted as being ex-dividend, the purchaser will not receive the most recently declared *dividend*. See also *cum-dividend*.

final dividend The dividend payable by a company after its year end. Normally this dividend is higher than the *interim* and typically represents anywhere between 60 per cent and 75 per cent of the year's total. This is because the interim dividend (declared at the half-year stage and on unaudited numbers) carries more question marks.

fixed assets Tangible and intangible assets the business requires to generate turnover. The tangible assets may include land, plant and machinery. The intangible assets might consist of *goodwill* relating to brands or patents. Intangible assets are *amortised* while tangible assets are *depreciated*.

free cash flow Operating profit plus depreciation and amortisation less maintenance capex and tax and working capital requirements. Used in *DCF*. More useful than EBITDA in many cases as it allows for the need for maintenance capex to protect the competitive position of the business. Free cash flow can be reinvested in the business or service higher dividend payments.

free cash flow yield A valuation measure used by many investors reflecting the importance of the amount of cash generated by the company. The *free cash flow* generated by the company is divided by the *EV*. We then compare this with the returns on other competing investments – say a government or corporate bond. If we are getting more than the yields there and have potential for growth in that cash flow then it is potentially very attractive.

fundamentals The most basic aspects of a company that need to be examined before making an investment decision – essentially what a company does, how well it does it and how much money it makes doing it. Key factors in this assessment include type of company, market position, efficiency, financial position, cash-generation ability, management record, past profitability and future outlook. An examination of these issues is referred to as 'fundamental analysis'.

gearing Net debt/equity. A measure of the level of debt carried by a company related to its *shareholders' funds*, normally expressed as a percentage. See also *interest cover*.

The performance of an investment, especially warrants or options, which move in a sharp manner relative to the underlying security. See also *operational gearing*.

goodwill The premium over *net asset value* a company pays when acquiring another company. Obviously, in service- or brand-based businesses, where there are few tangible (or physical) assets, the goodwill element of the amount paid can be significant.

gross domestic product (GDP) The total value of goods and services produced by a country over a specified time period. This is normally quarterly or annually. See also *gross national product*.

gross national product (GNP) *Gross domestic product* plus the income from overseas investments less the income due to overseas investors in the domestic economy.

growth investment An investment strategy where the main objective is to identify companies with the potential for high, long-term growth in sales, earnings and *dividends*. Ideally, these companies should be growing at a rate well in excess of the stock market average and should also be able to demonstrate good growth rates even when the economy slows down.

hedge fund A collective investment that tries to make money for its investors in absolute, not relative, terms. So it will try to make money when share prices go down as well as up. It does this by *shorting* stocks and by buying put options as well as simply buying (or 'going long') stocks (the traditional investment management route sometimes referred to as 'long-only funds'). Allied to this, hedge funds usually 'gear up' (sometimes alarmingly so) to fully exploit market opportunities. For a traditionally run investment fund, it is hard to make money in bear markets; for hedge funds, bear markets are a key opportunity. With opportunity comes risk and hedge funds are not for the financially conservative. In addition, charging structures are high.

illiquidity The inability to deal quickly in a reasonable size in certain classes of security, especially in volatile markets. Where there is little or no cash available for investment, either at hand or within a portfolio.

impairment review The assets companies have acquired are now subject to annual assessments of their value. If they are worth less than was paid for them they are written down in an impairment review and will be charged to the P&L. The value of the asset is arrived at by doing a *DCF*.

interest cover operating profit divided by interest paid. This is an important measure of a company's financial strength as it reflects the company's ability to service its debt. This measure may be a more relevant indicator of financial strength than the debt/equity ratio *(gearing)* for companies such as those involved in service industries that have few assets on the *balance sheet*.

interim dividend When companies pay *dividends* twice a year, the interim dividend is declared for the first half of the company's year at the time the interim results are announced. See also *payment date*.

interim report Companies that are listed on the stock exchange are required to submit trading figures twice a year. The interim figures give the company's trading position at the end of the first half of the financial year; the final report (or preliminary report) shows the position at the close of the year as a whole.

intrinsic value Fundamental value of the business derived from doing a DCF.

investment bank As distinct from a clearing (or high street) bank, an investment bank is generally involved in larger, corporate-style banking, providing finance for takeovers, overseas expansion and so on. They also frequently act as advisers for companies seeking a listing on the stock exchange. Sometimes referred to as merchant banks, investment banks tend to be integrated in the sense that they carry out a full range of activities, including corporate finance, stockbroking, market-making and fund management. This has recently led to concerns over conflicts of interests and this integrated structure is being questioned.

liquidity The level of cash either held in a portfolio or available for investment. The ability to deal easily in a class of asset or *share*. The amount of cash and funds that are easily accessible in the economy generally.

market capitalisation see *capitalisation*.

minorities (or minority interests) The deduction of the share of profits that outside interests have in a partially owned subsidiary. For example, if an 80 per cent-owned subsidiary is consolidated, 20 per cent of its after-tax income would be due to the owners of the remaining 20 per cent of the company. Minority charges are deducted before calculating the profit attributable to ordinary shareholders – and hence determining EPS (*earnings per share*) and *retained profit*.

momentum investing The practice of buying shares that are showing an upward trend relative to the stock market overall. This may reflect positive *earnings momentum* or may simply reflect a trend/fashion towards a particular sector or share. Naturally, if a sector or share is doing well, this will generate interest from investors. See also *technical analysis*.

multiple A term used in describing the valuation of a *share*. The shares may be said to be on a multiple of 15× earnings. The term is used with any valuation measure used, e.g. sales multiple, *EBIT* multiple or *EBITDA* multiple.

net asset value (NAV) The value of a business as defined by the difference between the value of its assets and liabilities. Sometimes this is expressed on a 'per *share*' basis, that is, where the NAV is divided by the number of shares in issue. This is a useful way of assessing the relationship between a company's share price and its NAV. For example, investment trust and property shares are valued in this way by referring to the *discount*/premium to NAV the shares are trading at. In addition, *value stocks* can be assessed in this way.

Net operating profit after tax (NOPAT) A key component of *discounted cash flow (DCF)* and also used to assess the post-tax returns on capital (NOPAT/invested capital).

net present value (npv) *DCF* calculation yields the npv – the future cash flows are expressed in today's money.

operating free cash flow Net operating profit after tax (*NOPAT*) + *depreciation* + *amortisation* – maintenance *capital expenditure (capex)*. A useful definition of cash flow used in *discounted cash flow (DCF)* valuations.

operating loss Losses incurred by the core operations of a company before taking into account any interest charges/credits or the contribution from *associate companies*.

operating profit Profits made by the core trading operations of a company before taking into account any interest charges/credits, asset disposals or the contribution from *associate companies*.

operating profit margin *Operating profit*/sales. This is a useful measure of a company's profitability and management efficiency. It is perhaps most useful when comparing operating performance with companies in the same sector. Operating margins should vary directly with the capital intensity of the business (i.e. the greater the amount of capital, the higher the margin). A key driver of sales valuations.

operational gearing The impact of a percentage change in revenues on the operating profit of a business. It is determined by the relationship between fixed and variable costs – the higher the fixed costs, the greater the operational gearing. It will also be affected by whether the revenue reduction is driven by a fall in price or volumes with the greater impact coming from price movements.

overweight A position where a fund has more invested in a stock or sector than the proportion in the relevant index/benchmark. For example, if a share represents 5 per cent of the All Share index and the fund has 8 per cent of its investments in that share, the fund is said to be overweight. (In this case, 60 per cent overweight.)

payment date The date that *dividends* are sent to shareholders.

P/E ratio See *price/earnings (P/E) ratio*.

P/E relative A measure of how the company's *price/earnings (P/E) ratio* relates to that of the market overall. This is normally expressed as a percentage. For example, if a company is on a P/E of 20× and the market is trading on 25×, the P/E relative is 80 per cent.

pre-exceptional pre-amortisation profit Profits before both any *exceptional items* or any *goodwill amortisation* are taken into account.

pre-exceptional profit Profits before any *exceptional items* (credits) have been deducted (credited).

preference shares In return for receiving a fixed rate of return (even if the company prospers dramatically in the future), preference shareholders have a certain level of protection in that, if the company goes bankrupt, they will receive their money back (if there is any left to give) before the ordinary shareholders. There are a variety of preference shares which can include those that are redeemable (where the initial investment is repaid) and/or convertible into ordinary shares. For example, a 'cumulative convertible redeemable preference share' offers the following characteristics.

- It is cumulative in the sense that, if the preference *dividend* is not paid in any one year, it 'rolls up' in subsequent years (during this time, ordinary dividends cannot be paid).
- It is convertible into ordinary shares on an agreed basis.
- It may be redeemed at par at the end of the agreed period if not converted.

price/earnings (P/E) ratio The share price divided by the *EPS (earnings per share)* of the company. It provides a simple and often effective way of valuing a *share* price. In effect, this tells you the number of years that the investment takes to pay for itself. It is normally expressed as a *multiple* (e.g. the shares are on 12× earnings). This 12× ratio is also referred to as the *rating* on the shares.

The P/E may be for the company's last financial year (this is referred to as 'historic') or for future financial years (referred to as 'prospective'). Prospective P/Es are generally used by analysts. Normally, a high P/E reflects a high degree of confidence in the company's growth profile and/or the sustainability of those earnings (often referred to as the 'quality of earnings'). A low P/E will normally reflect a combination of much lower-than-average growth, high cyclicality of earnings and 'low-quality' earnings. Sometimes a high P/E can be the result of very low earnings, for example, a *cyclical stock* which suffers from the impact of falling demand and prices at the bottom of the cycle (in these circumstances the shares may be attractive despite the high *multiple* as the shares are at the bottom of the cycle).

profit and loss account An integral part of a company's *annual report and accounts*, this is a statement that outlines the company's income, costs and profitability (or lack of it) in the period to which it relates.

rating Describes the valuation put on a *share*. The shares may be said to be on a rating of, say, 15× earnings, but the term can be used to describe any of the valuation measures used (e.g. sales, *EBIT* or *EBITDA*). In investment terms the key is to determine whether the rating is fair given the quality and outlook for the business. If the shares are cheap, investors may buy them on the basis that they will be re-rated (i.e. the *multiple* increases). Conversely, a high-growth company that does not meet the expectations placed on the shares will see its rating fall, i.e. de-rated.

retained profit When a company makes a profit, some of this is normally distributed to shareholders in the form of a *dividend*. The remainder, the retained profit, is transferred to the company's reserves and may be applied to the expansion of the business.

ROCE (return on capital employed) *Operating profit/shareholders' funds* + net debt. This is a very important measure of the company's profitability and ability to use efficiently all the funds available to the management. It is important to be clear whether the number is pre or post tax. The post-tax number is used when calculating whether the company is *adding value*, i.e. whether the returns are exceeding the *cost of capital*.

return on equity *Attributable profit/shareholders' funds.* This is a key measure of how hard the share capital is being made to work and how efficient the management is being.

return on invested capital (ROIC) *Operating profit/shareholders' funds + debt + goodwill* (and other asset) write-offs. Goodwill on acquisition is often deducted from shareholders' funds and therefore reduces the amount of capital employed. The invested capital focuses on how much the company actually spent (invested), not the book value of assets employed. Accordingly, a more comprehensive and preferred way of gauging how efficiently the company allocates resources.

rights issue Where a company seeks to raise additional money from its shareholders. The shareholders will be offered the opportunity to buy new shares at a given price and in proportion to their existing holdings (e.g. one new share for every four shares held); the rights to buy them at this price then become tradable in their own right.

scrip issue See *bonus issue* and *share split*.

sector *Shares* that have common characteristics and are grouped together. The FT All-Share Classification consists of a number of clearly defined sector groupings, for example Resources, General Industrials, Cyclical Consumer Goods and Information Technology. These broad sector groupings break down further into individual sectors such as Chemicals, Health, Pharmaceuticals and Telecommunication Services.

share buy-back When a listed company buys back shares on the open market for cancellation. When the *balance sheet* is very strong (the company may have cash in hand or have very low levels of debt) and the management believes that the stock market is failing to value the company properly, the company may seek to remedy the situation by using the surplus money to purchase what it believes to be its undervalued shares. This has the effect of reducing the number of shares in issue and the cost of servicing the *dividend* and may improve the *EPS (earnings per share)* figure. Companies often do this in order to reduce the *cost of capital*.

shareholders' funds The net assets of a company belonging to ordinary shareholders, i.e. the balance of assets and liabilities.

shares Shares, also known as ordinary shares (as opposed to preference or convertible shares), represent ownership of a company. Shareholders are entitled to receive *dividends* (if the board of directors decides to pay them) and to vote at the company's *AGM*. See also *preference shares*.

share split Done for the same reasons as a *bonus/scrip issue*, i.e. to improve *liquidity* and reduce a heavy share price. It differs from a bonus issue as it involves reducing the nominal value of the company's shares. For example, a five-for-one split would see the shareholder holding five new shares for every one held but the nominal value would fall from, say, 25p to 5p. No adjustment takes place to the company's *balance sheet*.

shorting The act of selling a share you do not own in the expectation that it will fall in price. As you do not own the shares concerned it is referred to as going short of the shares.

technical analysis As opposed to *fundamental* analysis, technical analysis attempts to predict the future direction of *share* prices (or markets and other assets) by examining the trend in the share price represented in chart form (hence sometimes called chartism). Certain key patterns are held to be predictive because of historical repetition.

trading statement A review of how a company has performed over the half or full-year trading period. These statements are normally issued either immediately before or after the trading period in question. The review is normally phrased with respect to the market's expectations for the company. They are useful as they provide investors with an assessment of the company's performance before it enters its *closed period*.

value investing A fund management style that focuses on the selection of *value stocks*. Normally, a screening process will be adopted to identify those *shares* which meet the preferred criteria. For example, the shares may have to be on a certain *price/earnings (P/E) discount* to the market, *yield* premium to the market or *discount* to *net asset value (NAV)* to be considered worth adding to the portfolio. Historically a very important and successful method of investing which has returned to favour over recent years following the fall from grace of growth stocks post the TMT bubble. By contrast, *growth investments* have performed poorly.

value stock A *share* that appears cheap on a combination of the following criteria (among others): a significant *price/earnings (P/E) discount* to the market and/or its sector; a high *yield* relative to the market; a discount to its net asset value (NAV); an undervalued cash flow stream.

While a share may be cheap on one or indeed all of these criteria, there can be good reasons why this low valuation is appropriate, normally reflecting a combination of poor outlook, poor financial position, poor management.

weighted average cost of capital (WACC) The *cost of equity* multiplied by the proportion of funding that is made up by equity (the *capitalisation (or market capitalisation)*/market cap + debt) added to the *cost of debt* multiplied by the proportion of funding made up by debt (debt/market cap + debt). See *cost of capital*.

yield *Dividend/share* price expressed as a percentage. Sometimes the yield will be expressed in prospective terms, that is, the yield for the current financial year, taking into account any dividend growth that may be projected. In the case of a bond, the yield is determined by the coupon payable divided by the price paid for the stock.

Index

ABN Amro 5
absolute returns 314
accounting policies
   earnings manipulation 11, 13, 15, 139–42, 150, 217–18
   International Financial Reporting Standards 126–31
   mark-to-market accounting 127–8
   and sales 118, 140
acquisitions *see* mergers and acquisitions
activism 88–90, 304
adding value 69, 83, 97, 99, 102–4, 109–10
advertising costs 141, 208
agency problem 80
airlines 10, 11, 38–41, 49, 218
amortisation 125–6, 128, 143, 161, 230
annual general meetings (AGMs) 86
annual report and accounts 73, 211
Apple 64
assets
   disposals 92–3, 140, 192, 193, 231
   fixed assets 169
   impairment reviews 128–9, 176–7, 229
   intangible assets 169
   net asset value (NAV) 125, 289–91
   peripheral assets 275–6
   valuation 176–7
associate companies 13, 133, 231
   and economic value 276
attributable profit 120
audit committees 80, 87
automotive industry 35–8, 50

BA 173
balance sheets 130, 212
   efficient 27, 185–95
   inefficient 188–9
Balfour Beatty 173–4
banking covenants 9, 168, 182–3

bankruptcy 184
banks 205–6, 253–4, 290, 297
Barclays 196
bargaining power 50, 67
barriers to market entry 48–9, 61, 151
benchmarking 16–17, 213, 313–14
beta 7, 9, 20, 22–4, 318–19
Blankfein, Lloyd 127
bonds 17, 21
bonuses 81
   see also remuneration
book value 125, 289–91
bottom-up approach 41, 225
brand strength 10, 66
BT 78, 93, 173
Buehler, L. 7
Buffett, Warren 10, 24, 61–2, 67, 74, 79, 94, 140–1, 189, 227, 296
bullish management views 77
bureaucratic structures 78, 93
business risk xiv–xv, 7, 30, 202
buy decision 315
buy-back programmes 28, 165, 185, 186, 188–95, 272
   asset disposals 193
   capital allocation decision 189, 190–1
   corporate governance 190
   cost of capital 189, 193
   dividends 191–2
   earnings 190
   intrinsic value 189–90, 192
   investor objectives 188–9
   shareholder value 190–1
   strategy 192–3
   taxation 188, 272

calendarised earnings 122
CAP Gemini Sogetti 140
capacity position 34, 36, 47, 208

Index

capital allocation 64, 72, 172–3, 212
  buy-back programmes 189, 190–1
capital asset pricing model (CAPM) 20
capital employed 18
capital expenditure 43, 71–2, 161
  discounted cash flow (DCF) 200–1, 230, 240–1
capital requirements 6, 34, 48
capital-intensive businesses 152
Carillion 192
cash
  generation 70–1, 115, 201, 228
  return on invested capital xvi, 115, 160–2
  returning to shareholders 188–9
  as a value driver 202, 240, 292
cash flow 11, 137–8, 143, 145, 199–202, 317
  capital expenditure 200–1, 230, 240–1
  and debt 168, 179–80, 183, 188, 200
  and dividends 269, 305
  as a driver of value 202, 240, 292
  forecasting 228, 231–2, 241
  free cash flow 161, 199–200, 230–1, 235, 238, 247, 281
    EV/free cash flow 280–1, 294
  gross cash flow 199
  importance 200–1
  net cash flow 199
  relationship with EPS 133–4
  return on capital xvi, 115, 160–2
  sustainability 230
  working capital 201
  see also discounted cash flow (DCF)
catalyst for change 302–4
CEOs (chief executive officers) 73, 79, 82–3, 84–6
  internal/external appointments 93–4
  skills 94
chairman 84, 86–7
changes in management 90, 91
Chrysler xv
Cisco 317
clarity 64
Collins, D. 63
Collins, Jim 62–3, 64, 83, 109, 215
commodity-based businesses 13–14, 34, 47, 132–3
company profile 68
company risk 22, 312–13
competitive advantage 62, 63

competitive position xv, 10, 15–16, 61
  checklist 112
  cost structures 67
  debt 168
  international competition 47
  outlook 204–5
  pricing xvii, 10, 15–16, 45–8
  strategy 61
confirmation bias 297
conflicts of interest 80
consensus expectations 122, 216, 310–11
conservative management views 77
consolidation 45–6, 149
consumer stocks 43
  retailers 50, 215, 283
convertible shares 121, 175, 275
corporate governance 10, 11–12, 16, 79–90, 190, 296
  activism 88–90, 304
  best practice 84–8
  length of employment contracts 87
  principal–agent problem 80
  and strategy 82–3
cost of capital 9, 12, 16, 20, 27–8, 241, 286
  and acquisitions 99–100
  and buy-back programmes 189, 193
  economic value added 160–2
cost capitalisation 127
cost cutting 28, 91–2, 138
  and acquisitions 105–6
  marketing/advertising 141, 208
cost of debt 20–1, 184, 236, 239
  and cash flow 200
cost of equity 18, 21–2, 24–7, 236, 239
cost structures 36, 38–9, 49, 51–2, 59, 209–10
  airlines 38–9, 49
  automotive industry 36
  and competitive position 67
  discretionary costs 52
  fixed costs 51–2, 149–50, 219–20
  forecasting 231–2
  marketing/advertising 141
  outlook 209–10
  sales costs 52
  sunk costs 36
  variable costs 51, 209, 219–20
  wage costs 52
credit ratings 17, 21, 181–2, 184
cross shareholdings 274
cult of debt xiii, 181

culture 68, 74–5, 78–9, 82, 93
  marketing culture 78
  monopoly culture 78
  in privatised companies 78
currencies
  exchange controls 134, 137–8
  transaction effects 57
  translation effects 56–7, 141
current market conditions 317–19
customer service 49
customer value proposition 61
cyclical shares 23, 34, 42–4, 54–5, 259, 306–7

de-leveraging 195, 317
de-ratings 257–8, 299
debt xv, xvi, 144, 164–8
  advantages 165–6
  banking covenants 9, 168, 182–3
  and cash flow 168, 179–80, 183, 188
  and the competitive position 168
  cost of debt 20–1, 184, 200, 236, 239
  credit ratings 17, 21, 181–2, 184
  cult of debt xiii, 181
  de-leveraging 195, 317
  and demand 43
  disadvantages 166–7
  and dividends 168, 184, 305
  EBITDA cover 179–80
  and enterprise value 275
  financing acquisitions 99–104
  fixed charge cover 180
  interest cover 9, 102, 169, 177–8, 179, 182, 202
  maturity structure 171, 175–6, 212
  off-balance sheet 174–5
  and return on equity 4
  year-end window dressing 228
  see also gearing
debt/equity ratio 168–71, 202
defensive shares 23, 53–4, 318–19
deflation 55, 208–9, 306
delegation 73
Dell 67
demand
  and debt 43
  outlook 42–5, 58
depreciation 71, 141, 143, 161, 201, 230, 235, 279
derivatives 127
Diageo 173, 178
differentiation 47–8, 49, 66

discount rates 172, 228, 233–4, 245, 247
discounted cash flow (DCF) 128, 193, 227–48
  advantages 240–1, 247–8
  assumptions 229, 242
  calculation 234–40
  and capital expenditure 230, 240–1
  disadvantages 242–6, 248
  forecasting cash flow 231–2, 241
  sensitivity analysis 237, 240, 241, 243–4
  subjectivity 228, 243
  terminal value 232–3, 235, 238, 242
  WACC 233–4, 236–8, 239–40
discounting the future 205–6, 224, 253–4, 296–7
discretionary costs 52
disposals 92–3, 140, 192, 193, 231
distribution channels 48
diversification 70
dividends xvi, 9, 18, 120, 267–73, 292, 293
  buy-back programmes 191–2
  and cash flow 269, 305
  cover 268–70, 304–5
  cuts 270–1
  and debt 168, 184, 305
  growth 191–2, 267–8, 269, 271–2
  income shares 268, 271, 273, 304–5, 319
  interim dividends 267
  and management confidence 269
  pension fund deficits 171
  special dividends 190, 192, 272
divisional profit breakdown 69, 119
downgrades 210, 216–17, 221, 222, 231

earnings per share (EPS) 1, 119–42, 207–11
  amortisation 125–6, 128, 143, 161, 230
  beating expectations 310–11
  buy-back programmes 190
  calculation 120–1, 130–1, 137
  calendarised 122
  cash flow relationship 133–4
  consensus expectations 122, 216, 310–11
  exceptional items 122–5, 126, 131, 137
  growth *see* growth in earnings
  guidance 77, 206, 216–19
  headline earnings 124
  impact of acquisitions 5, 74, 80, 81, 98–105, 139, 259–60
  manipulation 11, 13, 15, 132, 139–42, 150, 217–18
  quality *see* quality of earnings
  from related companies 13, 133, 231

earnings per share (EPS) (*continued*)
   stock options 126–7, 140–1
   surprises 310–11
   targets 12–13, 14–15, 75–7, 80–1
   visibility 12, 132, 206
   see also P/E ratios; profits
EBITDA 76, 142–6, 179–80, 199, 316
   debt cover 179–80
   EV/EBITDA 277–80
economic cycle 42, 43–4
   turning points 44
economic strength 10
economic value added 160–2, 185
economies of scale 48
efficient balance sheets 27, 185–95
efficient market hypothesis 299, 320
Einhorn, David 127–8
emerging markets 70, 134
employment contracts 87
Enron 64–5, 128, 175, 218
enterprise value 241, 251, 273–89, 291–2, 293–4
   and acquisitions 100
   average debt 275
   cross shareholdings 274
   EV/EBITDA 277–80
   EV/free cash flow 280–1, 294
   EV/sales 281–9
   formula 274
   minorities 275
   operating free cash flow 280–1
   peripheral assets 275–6
   provisions 275
   related companies 276
equity finance for acquisitions 99–104, 198–9
equity risk premium 9, 18, 21–2, 24–5, 245
Eurotunnel 229, 242
exceptional items 122–5, 126, 131, 137
exchange controls 134, 137–8
expected market returns 319
Exxon 186

fear and greed psychology 296, 299, 320
finance directors 73
finance leases 130
financial companies 265, 289
   banks 205–6, 253–4, 290, 297
financial risk xiv–xv, 7, 23, 30, 164–5, 202, 313
financial scandals xiii–xiv
financing acquisitions 99–104, 198–9

five forces model 10, 45–50, 62
five-year trading record 116
fixed assets 169
fixed charge cover 180
fixed costs 51–2, 149–50, 219–20
focus 69
food retail 50, 283
forecasting
   cash flow 228, 231–2, 241
   costs 231–2
   pricing power 231–2
   profits 207, 221–3
fragmentation 45, 150
free cash flow *see* operating free cash flow
Freeman, A. 7
fundamental value 10, 189–90, 192, 227–8, 229, 295–6

gearing 4, 23, 130
   and asset valuation 176–7
   and bonuses 81
   correct level 169
   debt/equity ratio 168–71, 202
   efficient balance sheets 185–95
   operational gearing 4, 7–9, 23, 45, 52, 81, 165–7, 219–24
   risks of high gearing 183–4
   and types of businesses 187–8
   see also debt
General Electric 216
General Motors 9
geographical profit profile 69–70
Gillette 61–2, 215
GlaxoSmithKline 81, 216
global sectors 56–7, 59
globalisation 55, 208, 306
GM 173, 174
goodwill 125, 128, 157, 178
Google 216
Gordon growth model 233
government bonds 17, 21
Green, Philip 173
gross cash flow 199
gross domestic product (GDP) 44
gross national product (GNP) 223
growth in dividends 191–2, 267–8, 269, 271–2
growth in earnings xiv–xvi, 2–7, 114–15, 138–9, 162, 254
   capital requirements 6
   checklist 31
   Gordon growth model 233

initial growth periods 232, 235, 238, 244–6
like-for-like growth 117, 215
and margins 151
organic growth 6, 68, 71, 77
sources of 6
steady state growth 233, 235
see also mergers and acquisitions
growth sectors 44–5, 52–3, 55
growth shares 256, 272, 301, 308–10, 316, 321–2
compared to value investing 309–10

headline earnings 124
health care liabilities 174
hedge funds 89, 304
herd mentality 299–300
Higgs review 85
high-yield shares 268, 271, 273, 304–5, 319
highly-rated paper 104–5, 108
historic P/E ratios 121–2
hollow swaps 118
Home Depot 138
horizontal integration 97
hostile acquisitions 97
housebuilders 205–6, 253–4, 297
Hulme, R. 7

IBM 13, 132, 138, 140, 141
ICI 184
impairment reviews 128–9, 176–7, 229
implementation of strategy 72
in-fill acquisitions 97
income shares 268, 271, 273, 304–5, 319
index returns 313–14
industry consolidation 45–6, 149
inefficient balance sheets 188–9
initial growth periods 232, 235, 238, 244–6
innovation 75
insurance companies 289
intangible assets 169
integration risk 5
interest capitalisation 141, 180
interest cover 9, 102, 169, 177–8, 179, 182, 202
interest rates 54–5, 306, 308
interim dividends 267
international competition 47
International Financial Reporting Standards 126–31

intrinsic value 10, 189–90, 192, 227–8, 229, 295–6
investment decision 295–322
buy decision 315
confirmation bias 297
current market conditions 317–19
fear and greed psychology 296, 299, 320
fundamental value 10, 189–90, 192, 227–8, 229, 295–6
herd mentality 299–300
market consensus valuation 297, 299–301
prospects of the company 298–9
risk/reward profiles 16–20, 154–6, 312–14
sell decision 315
sentiment of the market 295–6, 298, 320
investment style 301–12
growth investments 256, 272, 301, 308–10, 316, 321–2
income investing 268, 271, 273, 304–5, 319
long-term investments 72, 314
momentum investing 227, 303, 310–12
short-term trading 314
timescales 314–15, 316–17
value investing 53, 192, 301–7, 316, 321

Jobs, Steve 64

key performance indicators (KPI) 75, 206, 213–16

learning curve 48
leases 130
Lehman Brothers 128
length of employment contracts 87
licences 48
like-for-like growth 117, 215
liquidity 24
long-term investments 72, 314
longevity assumptions 172
loss-making companies 265

management 61–2, 73–9
bullish views 77
changes in 90, 91
and the competitive position 61
conservative views 77
culture 68, 74–5, 78–9, 82, 93
dilution 5, 74, 110
dividend policy 269

346 Index

management (*continued*)
  earnings guidance 77, 206, 216–19
  improving returns 91–2
  long-term perspective 75
  narrative reporting 211
  poor performance 90
  remuneration 76–7, 80–2, 87–8, 89
  targets 12–13, 14–15, 75–7, 80–1
  view of the future 77, 211–19
  see also corporate governance
manipulation of earnings 132
Mannesmann 81
Marconi 73, 184
margins 146–52, 153, 282
  accounting policies 150
  and barriers to market entry 151
  capital-intensive businesses 152
  comparisons 147
  drivers 148
  EV/sales ratio 282
  forecasting 221–3
  and growth 151
  high margins 150, 151, 153
  and industry structure 149–50
  low margins 148–9, 150–1
  and pricing power 150–1
  recovery stories 148–9
  trends 147–8, 152, 163
mark-to-market accounting 127–8
market capitalisation 237, 240, 276, 277–8
market consensus valuation 297, 299–301
market position 65–71
market risk 312
market segments 68
market share 46–7, 67–8, 92
marketing culture 78
marketing/advertising costs 141, 208
Marks and Spencer 10, 89, 173
mature industries 44
maturity structure of debt 171, 175–6, 212
mergers and acquisitions xiv, 6, 68, 71, 76, 77, 95–111
  adding value 83, 97, 99, 102–4, 109–10
  agreed 97
  cost of capital 99–100
  cost cutting 105–6
  earnings impact 5, 74, 98–105, 139, 259–60
  earnings targets 80, 81
  enterprise value 100
  failure factors 109–10
  financing 99–104
    rights issues 198–9
    with highly-rated paper 104–5, 108
  hostile 97
  integration risk 5
  management dilution 5, 74, 110
  market reaction 110–11
  pension deficits 173–4
  price paid 98, 110
  and pricing power 106–7
  quality of earnings 107
  reasons for 96
  return on capital 98
  revenue benefits 107
  risks 96
  success factors 108
  synergies 100
  timing of benefits 107
  types of deals 97
  volume benefits 107
minorities 120–1, 169, 231, 275
mission 63–5
momentum investing 228, 303, 310–12
monopoly culture 78
Myners report 88

narrative reporting 211
net asset value (NAV) 141, 289–91
net cash flow 199
net present value 228, 233
new product development 229
non-executive directors 80, 84–7

objectives 63
off-balance sheet debt 174–5
operating and financial reviews (OFR) 211–13
operating free cash flow 161, 199–200, 230–1, 235, 238, 247
  and enterprise value 280–1
  free cash flow yield 281
  see also cash flow
operating leases 130
operating profit 18, 146–52
  forecasting 221–3
  volatility 178–9
  see also profits
operational gearing 4, 7–9, 23, 45, 52, 165–7, 219–24
  and bonuses 81
organic growth 6, 68, 71, 77
overcapacity 34, 36, 47, 208

P/E ratios 5–6, 114, 121–2, 252–65, 291, 293
  advantages 258
  de-ratings 257–8, 299
  disadvantages 257
  financial companies 265
  high P/E shares 255–6
  loss-making companies 265
  low P/E shares 253–5, 302
  Peg ratio 265–7, 302
  re-ratings 256–7, 299, 303
  relative to the market 260–5
  start-up companies 265
patents 48
Peg ratio 265–7, 302
pension deficits 130, 140, 171–4, 274
  and acquisitions 173–4
  asset allocations 172–3
  discount rates 172
  investment returns 172
  longevity assumptions 172
  triennial reviews 173
PepsiCo 216
performance and returns xvi, 113–63
  benchmarking 16–17, 213, 313–14
  economic value added 160–2, 185
  five-year trading record 116
  key elements 114
  key performance indicators (KPI) 75, 206, 213–16
  profits 114, 118–19, 146–52
  return on capital employed xvi, 5, 18, 90, 115, 152–60
  risk/reward profiles 16–20, 154–6, 312–14
  sales 114, 116–18, 162
  total shareholder returns 18, 267
peripheral assets 275–6
Permira 173
pharmaceutical companies 53–4, 56
Pizza Express 268
placings 196
population trends 42
Porsche 37–8
Porter, M.E. 10, 45, 61
pre-emption rights 196
preference shares 120, 121, 157, 175, 180, 275
Premier Foods 188
price to book value 125, 289–91
price wars 46, 66, 67

pricing 5, 8, 28–9, 34, 36–7, 45–51, 58–9, 208–9, 306–7
  and acquisitions 106–7
  bargaining power 50, 67
  barriers to entry 48–9, 61
  capacity position 34, 36, 47
  competitive position xv, 10, 15–16, 45–8
  forecasting 231–2
  margins 146–52, 150–1, 153, 282
  outlook 208–9, 226
  product differentiation 47–8, 49, 66
  regulatory issues 50
  smaller companies 67
  substitute products 49
principal–agent problem 80
private equity 165, 186, 191
privatised companies 78
Proctor and Gamble 65
production driven companies 77–8
products
  differentiation 47–8, 49, 66
  and market position 69
  new product development 229
profit and loss accounts 9
profits 114, 118–19, 136–7, 146–52, 207–11
  attributable profit 120
  divisional breakdown 69, 119
  downgrades 210, 216–17, 221, 222, 231
  drivers 42
  forecasting 207, 221–3
  geographical profile 69–70
  margins 146–52, 153, 282
  operating profit 18, 146–52, 178–9, 221–3
  repatriation from overseas 134, 137–8
  retained profits 157
  smoothing 140
  sustainability xvi, 4–5, 12, 137
  volatility 178–9
  see also earnings per share (EPS)
property companies 187
prospective P/E ratios 121–2
provisions 129–30, 134, 139, 141
  and economic value 275

quality of earnings xv, 2–5, 12–14, 30–1, 114, 131–8, 254
  and acquisitions 107
  checklist 31
  and emerging markets 134

RBS 5
re-ratings 256–7, 299, 303
Reckitt Benckiser 75
recovery situations 91–5, 148–9
regulatory issues 50
related companies 13, 133, 231
  and economic value 276
relative returns 311–12, 314
relative valuation 249–52
remuneration 76–7, 80–2, 87–8, 89
repatriation of profits 134, 137–8
resource allocation 64, 72, 172–3, 189, 190–1, 212
  and share buy-backs 189, 190–1
restructurings 75, 92, 125
retailers 50, 215, 283
retained profits 157
return on capital employed xvi, 5, 18, 90, 115, 152–60
  and acquisitions 98
  calculation 152–4
  capital-intensive businesses 156
  high returns 155
  low returns 155–6
  taxation 159
return on equity 4, 24–6, 159–60
return on invested capital 157, 160–2
revenue improvements 92
rights issues 102, 184, 195–9
risk xiv–xv, 2–5, 7–12
  and acquisitions 96
  beta 7, 9, 20, 22–4, 318–19
  business risk xiv–xv, 7, 30, 202
  checklist 31
  company risk 312–13
  discount rates 228, 233–4, 245, 247
  diversification 70
  financial risk xiv–xv, 7, 23, 30, 164–5, 202, 313
  high gearing 183–4
  integration risk 5
  and management ability 11
  market risk 312
  operational gearing 4, 7–9, 23, 45, 52, 165–7, 219–24
  stock specific risk 22, 312–13
risk-free rate 17, 21, 24–5, 313
risk/reward profiles 16–20, 154–6, 312–14
RMC 69–70
Rukstad, M.G. 63
Ryanair 217, 218

Sainsbury's 124
sales 114, 116–18, 162
  accounting policies 118, 140
  costs 52
  EV/sales ratio 281–9
  like-for-like growth 117, 215
  trends 114, 163
scandals xiii–xiv
scope 63
sectors 10, 33–59
  airlines 10, 11, 38–41, 49, 218
  automotive industry 35–8, 50
  bottom-up approach 41, 225
  capital requirements 34, 48
  commodity-based businesses 13–14, 34, 47, 132–3
  consolidation 45–6, 149
  consumer stocks 43, 50, 215, 283
  cost structures 36, 38–9, 49, 51–2, 59
  cyclical shares 23, 34, 42–4, 54–5, 259, 306–7
  defensive shares 23, 53–4, 318–19
  demand outlook 42–5, 58
  food retail 50, 283
  fragmentation 45, 150
  global sectors 56–7, 59
  growth industries 44–5, 52–3, 55
  interest rate effects 54–5, 306, 308
  mature industries 44
  overcapacity 34, 36, 47, 208
  pharmaceuticals 53–4, 56
  pricing power 34, 36–7, 45–51, 58–9, 208–9
  profit drivers 42
  steel industry 48
  top-down approach 41, 222–3, 225
  underperforming 34–5
  utility companies 18, 19, 50
sell decision 315
sensitivity analysis 237, 240, 241, 243–4
sentiment of the market 295–6, 298, 320
share buy-backs *see* buy-back programmes
share placings 196
share prices
  consensus expectations 122, 216, 310–11
  current market conditions 317–19
  discounting the future 205–6, 224, 253–4, 296–7
  equity risk premium 9, 18, 21–2, 24–5, 245
  market consensus valuation 297, 299–301

relative returns 311–12, 314
risk/reward profiles 16–20, 154–6, 312–14
stock specific risk 22, 312–13
shareholder value xv, xvi, 14–20, 28–30, 32, 115
   and buy-back programmes 190–1
   key drivers 28–30
   and strategy 83
shareholders' funds 92, 152–4, 157–8, 169, 176–7
Shell 10
short-term trading 314
shorting 128
skills 72–3, 94
Slater, Jim 266
smaller companies pricing power 67
Smith, Sir Robert 85–6, 87
Smiths Group 173
smoothing profits 140
Soros, George 297–8
Southwest Airlines 40
special dividends 190, 192, 272
special investment vehicles (SIVs) 130, 175
stakeholders 15–16
start-up companies 265
steady state growth 233, 235
steel industry 48
stock options 126–7, 140–1
stock specific risk 22, 312–13
strategic acquisitions 97
strategy 71–4, 92–6
   checklist 112
   and the competitive position 61
   and corporate governance 82–3
   disposals 92–3, 140, 192, 193, 231
   implementation 72
   key components 62–5
   and share buy-backs 192–3
   and shareholder value 83
   simple concept 63
   skills requirement 72–3
   strategic acquisitions 97
sub-prime lending xiv
subsidiary companies 134
substitute products 49
sum of parts calculation 291
sunk costs 36
sustainability
   of cash flow 230
   of profits xvi, 4–5, 12, 137
synergies 100

takeover speculation 94–5, 290
targets 12–13, 14–15, 75–7, 80–1
taxation 142, 159, 188
   and buy-back programmes 188, 272
technology driven companies 77–8
telecommunications 207–8, 245–6
Telewest 229
term structure of debt 171, 175–6
terminal value 232–3, 235, 238, 242
timescales 314–15, 316–17
top-down approach 41, 222–3, 225
total shareholder returns 18, 267
trading statements 88
transaction effects of currencies 57
translation effects of currencies 56–7, 141
trends
   in margins 147–8, 152, 163
   in sales 114, 163
   sustainability 311–12
triennial pension reviews 173
turnaround situations 91–5, 148–9
turning points 44

Unilever 23, 216, 316
utility companies 18, 19, 50

valuation of assets 176–7
value investing 53, 192, 301–7, 316, 321
   catalyst for change 302–4
   characteristics 302
   compared to growth investing 309–10
   income shares 268, 271, 273, 304–5, 319
   long-term value 72
values 63, 64
variable costs 51, 209, 219–20
vertical integration 97, 147
visibility of earnings 12, 132, 206
vision 63–5
Vodafone 81, 192
volatility 178–9
   beta 7, 9, 20, 22–4, 318–19
volumes 107, 207–8, 221, 306
   forecasting 231–2

WACC calculation 27–8, 99–100, 233–4, 236–8, 239–40
wage costs 52
Walker report 83
Weinstock, Lord 69
Welch, Jack 14
WH Smith 173
working capital 156, 161, 201, 230, 235

Xerox 118

year-end window dressing 228
yields 17, 267–73
   free cash flow yield 280
   income shares 268, 271, 273, 304–5, 319